OXFORD LABOUR LAW

General Editors
ALAN BOGG, KEITH EWING, MARK FREEDLAND

Living Wage

OXFORD LABOUR LAW

General Editors: Alan Bogg Professor of Labour Law at University of Bristol Law School; Keith Ewing, Professor of Public Law at King's College London; and Mark Freedland, Emeritus Research Fellow in Law at St John's College and Emeritus Professor of Employment Law in the University of Oxford.

This series has come to represent a significant contribution to the literature of British, European, and international labour law. The series recognizes the arrival not only of a renewed interest in labour law generally, but also the need for fresh approaches to the study of labour law following a period of momentous change in the UK and Europe. The series is concerned with all aspects of labour law, including traditional subjects of study such as collective labour law and individual employment law. It also includes works that concentrate on the growing role of human rights and the combating od discrimination in employment, and others that examine the law and economics of the labour market and the impact of social security law and of national and supranational employment policies upon patterns of employment and the employment contract. Two of the contributing authors to the series, Lucy Vickers and Diamond Ashiagbor, have received awards from the Society of Legal Scholars in respect of their books.

ALSO AVAILABLE IN THE SERIES

Bullying and Behavioural Conflict at Work
The Duality of Individual Rights
Lizzie Barmes

The Concept of the Employer
Jeremias Prassl

The Labour Constitution
The Enduring Idea of Labour Law
Ruth Dukes

The Legal Construction of Personal Work Relations
Mark Freedland FBA and Nicola Kountouris

A Right to Care?
Unpaid Work in European Employment Law
Nicole Busby

Regulating Flexible Work
Deirdre McCann

Welfare to Work
Conditional Rights in Social Policy
Amir Paz-Fuchs

EU Intervention in Domestic Labour Law
Phil Syrpis

Towards a Flexible Labour Market
Labour Legislation and Regulation since the 1990s
Paul Davies and Mark Freedland

The European Employment Strategy
Labour Market Regulation and New Governance
Diamond Ashiagbor

The Law of the Labour Market
Industrialization, Employment, and Legal Evolution
Simon Deakin and Frank Wilkinson

The Personal Employment Contract
Mark Freedland

International and European Protection of the Right to Strike
A Comparative Study of Standards Set by the International Labour Organization, the Council of Europe and the European Union
Tonia Novitz

Freedom of Speech and Employment
Lucy Vickers

Women and the Law
Sandra Fredman

Just Wages for Women
Aileen McColgan

Justice in Dismissal
The Law of Termination of Employment
Hugh Collins

The Right to Strike
K. D. Ewing

Living Wage
Regulatory Solutions to Informal and Precarious Work in Global Supply Chains
Shelley Marshall

Living Wage

Regulatory Solutions to Informal and Precarious Work in Global Supply Chains

SHELLEY MARSHALL

OXFORD
UNIVERSITY PRESS

OXFORD
UNIVERSITY PRESS

Great Clarendon Street, Oxford, OX2 6DP,
United Kingdom

Oxford University Press is a department of the University of Oxford.
It furthers the University's objective of excellence in research, scholarship,
and education by publishing worldwide. Oxford is a registered trade mark of
Oxford University Press in the UK and in certain other countries

First Edition published in 2019

Impression: 1

Published in the United States of America by Oxford University Press
198 Madison Avenue, New York, NY 10016, United States of America

British Library Cataloguing in Publication Data
Data available

Library of Congress Control Number: 2018952413

ISBN 978–0–19–883035–1

Printed and bound by
CPI Group (UK) Ltd, Croydon, CR0 4YY

In memory of Jane Tate and in dedication to all the individuals and organisations that struggle to achieve a living wage for the precariat.

Foreword

This brilliant book breaks new ground in the global inequality debate. Economists always had an ambivalent relationship to labour regulation to guarantee a living wage. That ambivalence has been largely broken this century as most economists shifted to the view that a larger share of the benefits of production should go into the pockets of lower- paid workers. Declining labour shares in national income increasingly are accepted as a threat to the demand necessary to sustain job creation.

Historically, strong trade unions have been the drivers of shifts from the profit share to the labour share of national income. Statistically, declining unionization and declining minimum wages in the United States account for the majority of its rise in wage inequality during the past half century. This book summarizes the empirical evidence from many countries that the informalization of economies into the hands of the expanding ranks of the precariat has weakened unions and strengthened inequality.

While Shelley Marshall promotes hybrid solutions to the challenge of a living wage, she invites the international trade union movement to position itself at the fulcrum to leverage reform. Trade unions have tended to view minimum wages through a national regulatory lens. This remains an important level of governance in the multi-level-governance approach in Shelley Marshall's work. Yet Marshall argues that unions need to reinvent themselves through a transnational regulatory imagination that is more glocal (both global and local (sub-national)). A renewed role for the International Labor Organization looms large in Marshall's regulatory imaginary.

Cynics will argue that trade unions are conservative, even clientelist, organizations. They are thin reeds on which to build a regulatory architecture. It is true that thin reeds snap. Yet the strength and sophistication of Shelley Marshall's policy analysis is that it shows pathways for weaving variegated thin reeds together to craft a resilient fabric of transformation. The general direction of struggle it plots is for trade unions to ally with sympathetic civil society groups, sympathetic economists, and commentators in the mass media, social media, and crowd sourcing to complement national labour regulation with local, regional, and industry-level regimes. Civil society engagement is critical for achieving normative acceptance of the justice of a Living Wage.

Together these constituencies can recursively strengthen national and local labour regulation and harness the International Labour Organization to become a meta-regulator of national regulators. Marshall takes up the idea of her colleague and mentor Peter Drahos, from *Global Business Regulation*, of sequencing regulatory ratchets in multi-level governance. All levels of ratchets in the policy design allow each ratchet upwards in interscalar governance to be meshed with lower- and higher-level governance ratchets. The settings make it difficult for one ratchet to ratchet down another. Conversely, some ratchets-up automatically move other ratchets upwards. This might seem awfully abstract, yet this book makes the idea practical and concrete (note, for example, Figure 6.1).

Engaging with Shelley Marshall's innovative reframing of these debates is the exciting invitation of this book. She works through the details and dilemmas of her proposals. At the most macro level, she proposes organizing the poor and organizing labour to reward national political parties with support and campaign contributions when they take their nation into an ILO regime that commits signatories to continuously improve minimum wages. Unions in rich countries would support workers in poor countries in this new labour internationalism. Signatory countries falling below the global average minimum wage would be required to increase their minimum by perhaps 2 per cent each year in real terms. These minimum wage calculations would be based on Purchasing Power Parity, meaning adjusted for local living costs. My suggestion would be that perhaps *all* signatories should be required to increase their minimum wage by at least half that amount annually (1 per cent) even if they were already above the global average minimum wage and already mandate an acceptable Living Wage. This would put an extra ratchet in the policy design as further increases in the labour share of the most egalitarian countries progressively ratcheted up the labour share of national income in the most inegalitarian countries. Structurally it would also build the legitimacy that comes from all states being required to make a contribution, and it would drive up global demand from the needs of the poorest workers in all countries.

Shelley Marshall's political strategy would build the legitimacy of the ILO to do the monitoring of compliance with the Living Wage agreement. When the number of signatory states passes a tipping point, the political strategy would shift to one of targeting parties who sabotage the regime by reducing minimum wages. This can mean boycotting global brands that invest in delinquent states, Fair Trade decertification, strikes at companies that undercut living wages, a global union campaign fund to support strikers for the minimum wage, and like measures. Transnational corporations would sign up to a pledge to preferentially do business with 'Living Wage List' suppliers and states. Note that punitive political targeting would not attack all states and firms that fail to guarantee living wages. That would be mission impossible. Ultimately the strategy targets only the most inegalitarian of political parties and firms at making minimum wages worse, but only after a long period of regime-building in which none are targeted with punishment but many are targeted with political rewards for joining the regime. Only those states and firms that are particularly corrupt and persistent in their non-enforcement of minima would be punished. If the worst few countries and firms on the planet were successfully targeted every few years, in the next few years the regime would raise the bar by targeting the next few firms and countries that were worst. By this point in the evolution of such a regime, when only the worst few are being targeted, the majority of producer organizations might even join the majority of trade unions in supporting that targeting because they have a strategic trade interest in making their production more competitive against that free riding of the few on a regime that benefits global growth. Raising the bar by rewarding many and punishing few is the way to give progressive realization of ILO labour rights more strategic edge than it currently has.

Shelley Marshall combines the pragmatism of this strategy of rewarding continuous improvement in minimum wages with a global ambition for progressively realizing an absolute vision of an ethically acceptable Living Wage. She positions the Asian Floor Wage Alliance, the Brazil National Slave Eradication Pact 'dirty list' of 300 companies benefiting from slave labour, and ILO's Joint Maritime Commission statutory determination of international minimum wages for seafaring maritime workers as existing incipient manifestations of her proposed strategy.

A huge strength of the work is the way it combines this reconfigured global strategy for equality with fine-grained ethnography of four sub-national experiments—from India, Australia, Cambodia, and Bulgaria. These are experiments in increasing minimum wages, health, and other conditions for the most marginalized of informal workers. Local initiatives are shown to be especially important for informal workers who are not meshed into global supply chains. Marshall diagnoses the successes of these experiments, which are limited but real, as dependent on a combination of local attunement of design to local employment realities and integration of the strategy with such strengths as survive in national labour standards institutions. This integration recursively allows for the local to strengthen national safety nets and the national to strengthen more local safety nets. The national case studies are also positioned as different modalities of Smart Regulation. Some experiments extend labour law, others layer it, others bypass it to alternative circuits of power. Here a distinctive medical-device model of regulatory hybridity is deployed. The Bulgarian experiment is a 'stent', widening the arteries that flow to the poor. Australia experimented with 'pacemaker' innovation to stimulate a parallel system of living wage justice. India experimented with an institutional 'by-pass', an alternate institutional path to living wages. This is a virtuoso re-imagining of the theory of Smart Regulation.

There is also innovation in enforcement strategies. This is about hybrid enforcement to help failing monopolies of national labour law enforcement. At present, national governments deliver symbolic victories to trade unions at the ILO, but concrete rewards to local businesses when they fail to enforce the symbolic agreements they sign in Geneva. Bounties in the form of a proportion of fines (*qui tam*) can be game-changers for non-state parties such as whistle-blowers, who share their bounties with law firms specializing in private litigation to enforce national agreements in national courts, or international tribunals. Trade unions can cover the salaries of lawyers they hire to mount such litigation. They can recruit new union members who want access to litigation threats to enforce their government's minimum wage undertakings.

Upstream and downstream supply chain enforcement is another key element of the multiple hybridities proposed to transform enforcement design. An international disputes mechanism integrated with national living wage tribunals that mandate supply chain enforcement is another part of Shelley Marshall's transformative enforcement policy proposal. Suspension of recognition of intellectual property rights in brands at the peaks of private and public regulatory pyramids is another innovation.

Her proposal is advanced with humility as a less than perfect regulatory strategy, and one unlikely to be enacted. This is inevitable in the face of the resilience of the very political dynamics and path dependencies documented in the book. Her humble hope is that she paints a proposal that provides the basis for discussion of the re-regulation of work on a more transnational canvas than has previously been painted. Shelley Marshall is a policy strategist of how to steer actually existing institutions buffeted by complex dynamics towards 'second best' solutions.

Shelley Marshall's brush strokes introduce her to the academy as a rare force for big picture regulatory thought who also pays careful attention to policy detail and to responsiveness to the local. At ANU's RegNet (the School of Regulation and Global Governance) not only Peter Drahos as her PhD supervisor but all of us were proud to have had her in our intellectual community. She has made something very fresh from many ideas that have been circulating in our intellectual community for a long time: hybridity; global ratchets; *qui tam*; Smart Regulation; responsiveness; upstream and downstream supply chain enforcement; multi-level governance; interscalar networked governance; hope and governance; and strategic reconfiguration of intellectual property. The character of Shelley's personality and her thought will make her a great leader of the life of the mind. This work will inspire future thinkers about global regulation for generations to come.

John Braithwaite

General Editors' Preface

When this series was first conceived, it was the ambition of the editors that it should encourage innovative legal writing on labour law. As well as fostering high quality scholarship in the classical sense, we were hoping for innovation in terms of subject-matter and methodology. This ambition has been fully realized by Shelley Marshall's fascinating book, in what is a compelling account of different responses to labour protection.

The book is constructed around four diverse case studies which are well chosen and distinctive responses to the failure of traditional labour law to deal with the problems of precarious workers in largely informal economies. In a book of impressive international and comparative legal breadth, the case studies in question are drawn from India, Australia, Bulgaria, and Cambodia, countries at different stages of development yet united by a common problem of how to deal with regulatory failure.

One of the main purposes of the study is to compare these different responses to the problems of regulation, coverage, and enforcement, and to consider the circumstances in which alternatives to the standard models are likely to succeed. But the other main purpose of the study is to argue for 'a re-conceptualization of labour regulation', to address contemporary realities related to the growth of informal and precarious employment. According to Dr Marshall:

> Labour law is failing millions of workers around the world. According to the most recent estimates, non-agricultural work in the informal economy represents 82 per cent of total employment in South Asia, 66 per cent in sub-Saharan Africa, 65 per cent in East and South-East Asia (excluding China), 51 per cent in Latin America, and 10 per cent in Eastern Europe and Central Asia.

These are chilling statistics, which are addressed in part by the conclusion to this volume in which—informed the evidence such as that produced by the case studies—the author 'canvasses a long-term vision for improving the lives of those poor and precarious workers who work in informal conditions'. What is proposed is 'a [bold], transnational, networked initiative that aims to promote a global living wage and regulate supply chains'.

In welcoming Dr Marshall's book to the Oxford Labour Law Series, we do so confident in the knowledge that it not only enhances the range and quality of the series to date, but does so in a way that fills a huge gap in our understanding of the discipline and its potential. This is imaginative legal writing of a kind that should be encouraged and actively promoted, and is all the more timely for the fact that it will be published in the year of the International Labour Organisation's centenary.

A lot remains to be done to fulfil the ambitions reflected in the ILO Constitution, and subsequently the *Declaration of Philadelphia* of 1944. Indeed, in recent years there has been a general regression of standards and their application. Yet there is much in Dr Marshall's work that ought to inform policy development in the future, and in particular the ILO's commitment to 'effective' labour law, a concept paraded in the ILO *Declaration on Social Justice for a Fair Globalisation* (2008), which this study does so much to illuminate.

ALB, KDE, MRF
December 2018

Preface

As this book goes to print in late 2018, I am in Thailand advising the Thai Ministry of Labour about how to implement laws protecting home-based workers. In interviews in various towns across Thailand with workers who sew clothes in their homes for local and international supply chains and those who make fishing nets for sale in neighbouring countries, workers have told me how hard the work is. They are desperate for change, but despondent. Though the laws have been on the books for seven years, they are yet to be implemented.

This work in Thailand, like the research I have conducted in Australia, Bulgaria, India and Cambodia documented in this book, convinces me that we need new models of labour regulation and new means of enforcement if these workers are to find their ways out of poverty or near poverty.

It is my wish that the findings of this book provide cause for hope. It shows that there are effective regulatory pathways out of poverty and informality. The book documents local and national experiments in new forms of labour regulation occurring around the globe that are successful in reducing informality and increasing pay. It concludes by canvassing a bold new international scheme to promote a global living wage and regulate work in supply chains. The more time I spend with precarious workers, the more I am convinced of the necessity of the task of envisaging a new, effective international labour law.

Acknowledgements

It is ironic, given one of the key themes of this book is poverty or near poverty, that one of the less talked about outcomes of qualitative research with precarious workers is weight gain. Every visit to a homeworker's house entails another feast. In Bulgaria I was mostly served chocolate. In Australia there were almost always cakes. The interviewee would get back to work and I would eat and ask questions. And I was being nourished in more ways than one. Sometimes it tumbled out, and sometimes it started slowly and built up, but almost everyone I interviewed was generous in sharing their life story and expressed relief in having it heard. Opinions about the future were less easy flowing from workers, in particular. In the end, I came to think that having opinions and having options is somehow interlinked. Working hard, day after day, year after year, yet not making a living wage is a form of 'stuckness'. It traps people in their workplaces, which in the case of homeworkers is their homes. It cuts people off from the wider world.

The book avoided becoming struck by hopelessness and mired in detail thanks to the guidance of Peter Drahos, Valerie Braithwaite, and John Braithwaite who, with humour and kindness, shared their own ideas and pushed me to think big about how to solve some of the biggest social problems of our time. I will be forever influenced by the way they each, in their own ways, bring big-heartedness to the act of rigorous academic scholarship. Those who know them will agree, I am confident, that this description is not an embellishment. They have shown me how kindness and hope can enlarge ambition in the scope and scale of thinking.

Various assistants and intermediaries helped with the research, without whom it would have been impossible. Praveen Rao organized interviews in Maharashtra, India. Eng Kunthea organized interviews in Cambodia and interpreted. The representatives of various workers' organizations acted as crucial links with worker interviewees. It is extremely difficult to locate, and gain the trust of, informal workers. Without the help of intermediaries, I could never have gathered the rich data discussed in this book. Ly Nguyen of the Textile, Clothing and Footwear Union of Australia organized a number of interviews in Melbourne, Australia and interpreted. Violeta Zlatera and Rozalina Ivanova organized interviews in Bulgaria and various interpreters offered their assistance during interviews. The research in Bulgaria would never have occurred without the initial invitation and urging of Jane Tate of Homenet. Sunanda Sen organized a round table of labour academics and organizers in Delhi, India, which was invaluable in providing insights into the dynamics of informality in India.

I am grateful to my colleagues and friends for comments and advice with the title, in particular. Titles are so very much harder to write than any of the other words in a book.

The travel required to research this book necessitated money and time away from teaching. For that I thank the UK Department for International Development and the Economic and Social Research Council. RMIT University allowed me time to finalize this book by awarding me the Vice Chancellor's Senior Research Fellowship.

My girls—Luciana and Madelene—were part of the writing of this book. They accompanied me on some research trips, put up with my absences when they didn't, and encouraged me with their love and endless buoyancy. Thank you Daniel, Luci, and Maddie, for being integral to this book's creation.

Table of Contents

List of Figures and Tables

1

Introduction

1.1 The Problem and a Quick Insight into a Possible Solution

Elena worked in a large state-run garment factory in the town of Petrich, Bulgaria for over twenty years before the transition to a market-based economy. It wasn't all that interesting, but the hours generally left her free to spend time with friends and family in the evenings and weekends. It was secure, it gave her life-long health benefits and a pension on which she could live when she retired, and lots of her friends worked in the same enterprise.

Now, though, she works from her home conducting 'informal' work, 70–80 hours a week, every day, with no holidays or sick leave. It took a while to put together enough work to survive on after the transition, and the labour shedding that ensued, but these days she can just make do. She takes in sewing jobs when the vastly downsized local clothing factories need work done that exceeds their human resource capacity. This normally occurs when an international contractor places an order with a tight deadline. In addition, she glues together the paper shopping bags that shoppers can be seen swinging after successful retail therapy. Most of these are for High Street stores in the UK. She also raises goats. The family have over fifty of them now, wandering over the family plot of land a little outside the town. With the milk from the goats she makes feta cheese that is famous in the town. She and her son also buy cigarettes in bulk on the black market and locals can often be seen leaving her home with cigarettes and a package of feta.

She has no savings. They were all spent during her late husband's fight with cancer. She pays for health insurance but paying the taxes she would pay if she was registered as 'self-employed' is beyond her financial capacity. When asked if she feels bad about not paying taxes she shrugs her shoulders and explains that the government is corrupt anyway. Her work sits outside legal regulation: labour inspectors certainly are not coming to check if her workplace is healthy and she is being paid enough. Elena has given up looking for a 'formal' job. She is almost sixty: past the official age of retirement for women, and anyway, no-one is hiring a woman of her age.

There are millions of women and men like Elena around the world. They include homeworkers who get work from subcontractors, contract workers who work in small workshops, or small teams working in the supply chains of formal enterprises (such as branded-clothing companies or construction companies) and those who work within formal enterprises on a contracted basis. This book is most concerned with those who work in dependent work, though the level of dependency and subordination may vary. Also, many workers hold down a mixture of work like Elena, who sometimes does independent work (the feta and cigarette sales) and sometimes works in international supply chains in dependent work (the sewing and bag-gluing work). These people—sometimes called the 'precariat'—work in what is known as the 'informal economy' where work is precarious and conditions insecure, but at least there is work to be had.

Despite continued improvements in reducing the shares of working poverty, efforts to reduce the absolute numbers of working poor at the US$1.90-a-day threshold (extreme poor) and the US$3.10-a-day level (moderate or near poor) have stalled.[1] In 2015, an estimated 327 million working people were living in extreme poverty and 967 million in moderate and near poverty. On the upside, the absolute number of the extremely poor has been falling by an annual average of 4.9 per cent over the period 2000 to 2015. On the downside, the number of moderate and near poor increased by 0.7 per cent over this period,[2] and the reduction in poverty rates has not been accompanied by a decrease in the rate of informal employment. Informal employment, as a percentage of non-agricultural employment, exceeds 50 per cent in half of the countries with comparable data. In one-third of countries, it affects over 65 per cent of workers.[3]

This book is centrally concerned with what regulatory strategies can best improve the working standards and lives of Elena and workers like her around the world. It goes without saying that employment creation policies and those that foster industrial growth are crucially important for improving Elena's well-being. This book is not aimed at addressing these types of policies, however. It is concerned with the realm of regulation—hard laws, soft initiatives and other institutions that shape behaviour and set incentives in particular directions.

What types of innovations in regulation can help Elena? Given the extent of the problem, it is clear that the deployment of maximum-strength levers is required. This book draws on regulatory theory and empirical research to develop new models of regulation of informal work, including those that can be instituted immediately to improve workers lives in the short-term (see Chapter 8). In each of the countries studied, types of co-regulation were implemented, entailing the combining of two or more regulatory systems. The Cambodian experiment involved the combining of an international trade preference and monitoring system, overseen by the International Labour Organisation, with the existing state-based labour-law system. The Australian innovation entailed the combining of private monitoring and labelling with the state-based labour-law system. The Indian regulatory development created a new state-orchestrated system, which adds to and sits aside from the existing labour law system. The Bulgarian expansion of employment law was the consequence of social dialogue processes through which private industrial relations parties negotiated an outcome before it was enacted into law. The experiments in each country provide rich examples of ways that problems and gaps in labour laws can be addressed.

However, each of these examples is only national in scope, and can be thought of perhaps, as 'stop-gaps'. The book ends, in Chapter 9, by canvassing an ambitious, longer-term vision for regulating work at international and national levels. This proposal builds on the experiments in labour regulation examined in the case studies and also draws on wider examples either realized or simply proposed and not yet implemented. There have been notable developments recently in France,[4,5]

[1] International Labor Office, *World Employment Social Outlook: Trends 2016* (2016)19.

[2] Ibid. 19. [3] Ibid. 19.

[4] The duty of a vigilance obligation for French parent and subcontracting companies, enacted in February 2017 by French Parliament: Sandra Cossart, Jerome Chaplier, and Tiphaine Beau de Lomenie, 'The French Law on Duty of Care: A Historic Step Towards Making Globalization Work for All' 2 Business and Human Rights Journal 317 320; C. Slater, 'How the French are Tackling Modern Slavery' *Human Rights First (blog)* (24 March 2017) https://www.humanrightsfirst.org/blog/how-french-are-tackling-modern-slaveryaccessed 7 January 2018.

[5] Paul Davies and Michael D. Green, 'France Adopts a New Law Requiring Companies to Diligence their Supply Chains in Relation to Human Rights, Environmental, and Health and Safety Issues' *Latham & Watkins (blog)* (21 April, 2017) https://www.lexology.com/library/detail.aspx?g=488454ab-fcba-4b0f-b5cd-d6f9e783e60d.

Switzerland,[6] the Netherlands,[7,8] the UK[9] and Australia[10] which indicate willingness within the OECD to insist that businesses have responsibility for the conditions of workers within their supply chains beyond their immediate employees. These newer initiatives can be seen a consequence of the Business and Human Rights movement which has gained considerable traction in recent years. Older laws in Australia[11] and the US[12,13] have used various techniques to enforce supply chain responsibility that are also useful models.

There have been a far larger number of experiments with 'blurring traditional legal boundaries', to use Judy Fudge's language,[14] which provide rights and protections to workers regardless of their status as employees or contractors. These are too numerous to summarize here but have been well covered in a range of important publications in the field of labour law.[15]

All of these innovations—both enacted and proposed—suggest a strong and mounting trajectory towards the re-regulation of work in a way that escapes the restrictions of the contract of employment and makes parties higher in the supply chain responsible for their impact on workers. The proposal canvassed in Chapter 9 of this book is more ambitious than previous real-life experiments and academic propositions and, it is hoped, more likely to succeed in reducing poverty, inequality and informality for a number of reasons. First, it is based on a normative principle that is difficult to

[6] A mandatory human rights due diligence law is under consideration in Switzerland, where the necessary signatures have been collected for a referendum Swiss Coalition for Corporate Justice, 'This is How the Initiative Works' [2018] http://konzern-initiative.ch/initiativtext/? lang=en accessed 4 April, 2017.

[7] Child Labour Due Diligence (Wet Zorgplicht Kinderarbeid); Gerard Oonk, *Child Labour Due Diligence Law for companies adopted by Dutch Parliament* (India Committee of the Netherlands 2017).

[8] India Committee of the Netherlands, *Child Labour Due Diligence Law for companies adopted by Dutch Parliament* (2017).

[9] Modern Slavery Act 2015 UK, http://www.legislation.gov.uk/ukpga/2015/30/contents/enacted/data.htm.

[10] The Australian government has indicated willingness to enact legislation similar to the UK's Modern Slavery Act: Commonwealth of Australia, Australian Government Response to the Joint Standing Committee on Foreign Affairs, Defence and Trade Committee report: Trading Lives: Modern Day Human Trafficking (27 October 2014), http://www.aph.gov.au/parliamentary_business/committees/house_of_representatives_committees?url=jfadt/slavery_people_trafficking/report.htm.

[11] *Road Safety Remuneration Act 2012 (Cth)*, Australia, since repealed, discussed in Chapter 9 of this book.

[12] The US 'Hot Goods' provisions which permit seizure of 'hot goods' produced without complying with labour standards: *29 USC S.215*. A suit must be bought by the federal Department of Labor. There is no private right of action: (*29 USC S. 217*).

[13] The Californian 'brother's keeper' law that makes liable for labour code violations anyone who enters 'into a contract or agreement for labor or services ... where the contract agreement does not include sufficient funds to allow the contractor to comply with all applicable local, state and federal laws or regulations governing the labor or services to be provided: *California Labor Code s.2810(a)*.

[14] Judy Fudge, 'Blurring Legal Boundaries: Regulating for Decent Work' in Judy Fudge, Shae McCrystal, and Kamala Sankaran (eds), *Challenging the Legal Boundaries of Work Regulation* (Hart 2012).

[15] A short list of examples includes Judy Fudge, Shae McCrystal, and Kamala Sankaran, *Challenging the Legal Boundaries ofWork Regulation* (Hart 2012); Guy Davidov and Brian Langille (eds), *Boundaries and Frontiers of Labour Law: Goals and Means in the Regulation of Work* (Oxford/Hart 2006); Leah F. Vosko, *Managing the margins: gender, citizenship, and the international regulation of precarious employment* (2009)[Oxford University Press]; M. Freedland, 'Burying Caesar: [] What was the Standard Employment Contract?' in Katherine Van Wezel Stone (ed.), *Rethinking Workplace Regulation: Beyond the Standard Contract of Employment* (Russell Sage Foundation 2013); Katherine Van Wezel Stone and H. W. Arthurs (eds), *Rethinking workplace regulation: beyond the standard contract of employment* (Russell Sage Foundation 2013); Tzehainesh Tekle (ed), *Labour law and worker protection in developing countries* (International Labour Office 2010).

argue with: that all people should receive a living wage for their toil. This was one of the founding principles of the International Labour Organisation,[16] but it is one that has become muddied. The entire proposed regulatory system is aimed at achieving the goal that all workers, regardless of where they live or under what legal arrangements they work, receive a living wage. The right to a living wage belongs to everyone by virtue of being human. This is the proposal's starting point, and it is based on the recognition that the biggest single problem that Elena (and the millions like her around the world) faces is that she does not earn enough per hour to piece together a living wage. She is constantly at risk of not being able to pay bills and being unable to buy sufficient food.

Second, it provides for incremental steps towards the achievement of this goal. It recognizes that development is hard and slow and allows poor countries to reach the goal over a number of years. The point is that they must work towards it. Currently, ILO Conventions do not provide for incremental advances in the achievement of decent work in this way. Ideally, it would help to address the short-termism of political cycles and focus nations' efforts towards what is arguably the most important goal all—the elimination of poverty.

Third, unlike real life experiments or academic proposals for the re-regulation of work, it is a *multi-level, transnational* regulatory system, just as the dynamics that place downwards pressure on working conditions are often transnational. Existing 'hard law' experiments are nation-based, but Elena's conditions are difficult to remedy at a national level. The buyers who strike tough deals for the production of clothes and shopping bags are based outside the country. The system canvassed in this book creates a transnational tribunal system, similar to that seen in the governance of international trade. It also gives national tribunals extra-territorial powers. Importantly, also, it proposes a system of coordination between these different levels.

Fourth, it incentivizes all parties to be more active in the system of compliance and enforcement. For many years, no workers' representative groups took an interest in Elena's situation. As with trade unions in most countries around the world, they were only concerned with workers inside factories and traditional workplaces. In the regulatory system canvassed in Chapter 9, workers representatives can gain a share of damages, thus providing a means to fund further organizing of precarious workers. States are made liable for unpaid Living Wages at the international tribunal but can recover these by pursuing wrong-doers in national tribunals. This should act as an incentive for states to be more active in conducting inspections and collecting evidence regarding the conditions of informal workers. Respondents to claims, such as direct employers, are encouraged to join other responsible parties, such as brands, incentivising them to share information about the true nature of commercial arrangements. At the apex of the enforcement pyramid is the use of novel penalties such as suspension of intellectual property. In other words, brands could be made to stop using their logos for a period of time as a response to the most egregious forms of abuse. There is unlikely to any

[16] The principle of the living wage was first stated by the ILO at the 1919 Paris Peace Conference where it was defined as an 'adequate living wage' in Part XIII of the Treaty of Versailles. The language of a 'a minimum living wage' was used in the 26th Session of the International Labour Conference in Philadelphia in April-May 1944 and, more recently, at the 97th Session of the International Labour Conference in Geneva in June 2008, where the ILO Declaration on Social Justice for a Fair Globalization was adopted to address the challenges of globalization: Emmanuel Reynaud, *The International Labour Organization and the Living Wage: A Historical Perspective* (2017)[ILO]. Further details are provided in Chapter 9 of this book.

greater incentive for brands to take a greater interest in the conditions of workers in their supply chains.

Finally, the system provides for the fair attribution of responsibility. Once we have agreed that labour rights are human rights, regardless of the legal classification of the working relationship, the next question is who is responsible for these rights. As Alan Hyde puts it, 'against which economic entities may all these workers enforce their basic human rights?'[17] Like the Californian Labour Code and the Australian experiments, the proposal canvassed in this book allows contractual parties to be joined to a claim if they have in some way impaired the provision of a living wage, legal remuneration, or related conditions to the worker. This might be an international buyer, a financer, or some other contractual party depending on the arrangements in each individual case. Perhaps the biggest problem with a labour law system based on the contract of employment is that it grants powerful players in supply chains impunity against responsibility for worker conditions. The proposal in Chapter 9 of this book not only allows for claims to be brought against such parties. It also allows tribunals to create positive duties for these parties in the form of collective agreements, industry codes and so on.

This proposal is unlikely to be the perfect regulatory strategy. Nor is it likely to be the strategy that is enacted, given the importance of political dynamics and path dependence explored in this book. However, it is the ardent wish of the author that this proposal provides the basis for discussion of the re-regulation of work on a far larger, transnational scale than has previously been the case.

1.2 Definitions

This book is concerned with regulatory pathways out of precarious and informal work. The informal economy has become a popular term to define activities that are 'unregulated by the institutions of society, in a legal and social environment in which similar activities are regulated'.[18] In diverse literature, workers who toil in unacceptable conditions are referred to variously as 'precarious', 'precariat', 'contingent', 'peripheral', 'flexible', and so on.

The term 'informality' has a relatively recent history. As Hart, one of the instigators of a revival of interest in 'informality' in the 1970s explains:[19]

> The term 'informal economy' became current in the 1970s as a label for economic activities which take place outside the framework of corporate public and private sector establishments. It arose at first in response to the proliferation of self-employment and casual labour in Third World cities; but later the expression came to be used with reference to societies like Britain, where it competed with other adjectives describing deindustrialization—the 'hidden', 'underground', 'black' economy, and so on.

In 2003, the 17th Conference of Labour Statisticians adopted guidelines for measuring informal employment. The benefit of this definition is that it has allowed for data to be collected from a range of countries measuring the extent of informal work. This

[17] Alan Hyde, 'Legal Responsibility for Labour Conditions Down the Production Chain' in Judy Fudge, Shae McCrystal, and Kamala Sankaran (eds), *Challenging the Legal Boundaries of Work Regulation* (Hart Publishing 2012) 93.

[18] Alejandro Portes, Manuel Castells, and Lauren A. Benton, *The Informal Economy: Studies in Advanced and Less Developed Countries* (Johns Hopkins University Press 1989).

[19] Keith Hart, 'Barter' in *New Palgrave Dictionary of Economic Theory and Doctrine* (eds), J. Eatwell, M. Milgate, and P. Newman (Macmillan 1987).

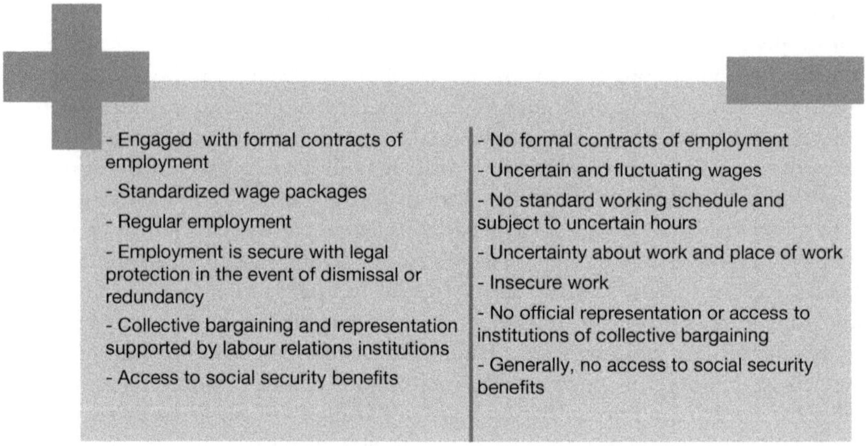

Figure 1.1 Factors that describe formal work compared with informal work

official statistical definition suffers from certain deficits. Perhaps the biggest shortfall is that it defines work of this type as an irregular phenomenon rather than a process in which the social form of labour has been reshaped and produced in a particular form.[20] When the majority of the population is engaged in work that is informal, as in India where around 97 per cent of work is 'unorganized', it is difficult to contend that it is irregular. Labour takes many forms. The fact that the law generally only recognizes and protects a narrow conception of waged labour does not mean that this is the main form in which work occurs, that the form is stable, or that it is reproduced across countries and modes of production.

A further problem with the definition, related to its dualism, is that workers themselves often move between different forms of work. In the Bulgarian case described in this book, for example, women sometimes take the same model of shoes they had been sewing in a factory under formal conditions during the day home to sew at night. They share this work with friends and family who are unemployed or suffering from underemployment as low wages are endemic across the country. The work conducted in the factory is on the books, whereas the work conducted at home counts towards the factory's productivity but stays off the employment books.[21] The same worker conducts work along a continuum of formality, enjoying more or fewer of the factors described in Figure 1.1 throughout their working lives and, often, working weeks.

The legal status of a worker who is conducting the work at home rather than in a factory is ambiguous at best. The contributing family workers and friends sit outside the category of 'wage employment', as standardized and protected by labour law. Self-employed (or 'own account') agricultural workers, homeworkers, contributing family workers, domestic workers, and unpaid care workers within the family have traditionally represented the largest part of the workforce in the developing countries. These groups typically escape the legal categories that determine the applicability of labour

[20] Portes, Castells, and Benton 11.

[21] The idioms 'under the table' and 'off the books' are typically employed to refer to the informal economy in every day speech. The term 'the grey economy' is also in frequent use, whereas the 'black economy' refers to a specific subset of the informal economy in which contraband is traded. The informal economy is generally distinguished from criminal behaviour and organized crime.

A. Labour in the informal sector

Informal self-employed (street vendors, home workers, teleworkers, garbage pickers, shoe shiners, non-self-subsistence small scale farmers, artisans), informal employees (family business workers, domestic workers, landless agricultural workers), migrant workers

B. Increasing informal labour of the formal sector: atypical labour not protected by regulatory framework.

Contracted workers (including daily workers), agency or dispatched workers, task-based casual workers, formal self-employed, disguised formal self-employed.

C. De-facto informal labour — formal workers in informalizing (or informalized) formal economy, workers who have no power to enjoy the legal and institutional regulation and standards to which they are entitled

Contracted workers, agency workers, part-timers, workers in export processing zones (EPZ), workers in developing countries with no, or few, democratic trade unions

Figure 1.2 Chang's pathways to informality[a]

[a]Ibid.

law, are explicitly excluded by labour law coverage (in whole or in part) or are subject to special regulations with lower levels of protection.[22] Most work occurs on a continuum of formality and informality (depicted in Figure 1.1).

Further, the Conference of Labour Statisticians' definition doesn't illuminate either the extent of implementation and enforcement of a law or the capacity of workers to demand access to legal entitlements or organize. Enacting new labour regulations or making workers 'formal' by expanding legal definitions, will not improve the lot of workers if they have no power of enforcement. Chang argues convincingly that the formation of the working class and any standard form of employment is based on power, not just legal form.[23] For this reason, Chang insists on a different system of classification from the ILO and others, which recognizes the importance of workers' capacity to enjoy their legal entitlements as a determinant of formality.

Workers in Chang's Category B and C are overlooked by most studies of the extent of informal labour. An example of 'increasing informal labour in the formal sector' is the growing number of contracted workers who work along-side formal workers in India's industrial sector. An example of 'de-facto informal labour' is workers in the Export Processing Zone of San Pedro de Macoris, East of Santa Domingo in the Dominican Republic. Unions complain that they are behind gates, razor wire, and armed guards and are barred from forming unions or organizing collectively so as to demand their legal entitlements.[24] In Malaysian Export Processing Zones minimum wages are explicitly not enforced for fear that investment will go elsewhere.[25] How do we categorize

[22] Tekle 35.

[23] Dae-Oup Chang, 'Informalising Labour in Asia's Global Factory' 39 Journal of Contemporary Asia 161.

[24] Jenny Holcroft, 'Export processing zones - Globalisation's great deceit' (2003) http://www.industriall-union.org/archive/imf/export-processing-zones-globalisations-great-deceit accessed 12 December 2017 [IndustriALL Global Union].

[25] Caspersz Donella, 'Globalization and Labour: A Case Study of EPZ Workers in Malaysia' [SAGE Publications Ltd] 19 Economic and Industrial Democracy 253.

these workers? They are not informal in the statistical sense. They are generally full-time employees or 'standard employees', but they lack power to enforce their formal rights. Thailand enacted a Homeworker Protection Act in 2010 to extend labour laws to dependent home-based workers but then failed to enforce that law.[26] These workers have stopped being counted amongst the informal workforce in national surveys, but their conditions of work remain unchanged from the day before the enactment of the law.[27] It might be more correct to refer the three groups of workers in the Dominican Republic, Malaysia, and Thailand as precarious workers or the 'Precariat', to use Guy Standing's term.[28] The case studies in this book confirm that two of the biggest influences on the incidence of precarious and informal work is a lack of power on behalf of the workers and a failure to enforce the law (though how the workers come to be informal in the first place is more complicated). Great laws may exist on the books, but they are no good without the empowerment of workers and enforcement by state inspectorates and other players.

Regardless of these problems with its definition, the study of informality is useful because it is the only category of precarious or vulnerable work that is measured across countries, though the data remains patchy.[29] Informal work, because it is measured, is gaining some visibility. The reader should note, however, that it is not only workers that are strictly informal, in accordance with the Conference of Labour Statisticians' definition, that are the primary concern of this book. The workers that are the subject of the case study chapters largely fall within the Conference of Labour Statisticians' definition. However, workers discussed in other chapters do not. Sometimes the term 'non-standard' worker is used, particularly if this is what has been measured in the literature. At other times the terms 'precarious' or 'precariat' are employed where this is more accurate. The aim of this book is to examine strategies that can reduce the incidence of informal, precarious, and unacceptable working conditions and ensure that all workers enjoy a living wage, not to get caught up in the minutiae of definitions.

1.3 Why Does Informality Matter? Policy Importance

Informality is widely seen as a serious problem which requires critical solutions. Informality is linked with inequality, poverty,[30] low job quality,[31] low productivity,[32]

[26] *Home Workers Protection Act*, B.E. 2553 (2010), Thailand. Since late 2017 I have been engaged by the ILO to assist the Thai Ministry of Labour implement these laws.

[27] National Statistical Office of Thailand, *The Informal Employment Survey* (2016).

[28] Guy Standing, *The Precariat: The New Dangerous Class* (Bloomsbury Academic 2011).

[29] I note the ILO's frustration, expressed in the *2016 Social Outlook* report where it notes: 'The ILO has made significant progress in collecting data on indicators such as informal employment in collaboration with governments' NSOs, but such information is often produced only on an irregular basis. There is a clear need for labour statistics to go beyond the headline indicators that are commonly collected by NSOs.': International Labour Office, *World Employment and Social Outlook: Trends 2016* (World of Work, 2016) 25.

[30] David Kucera and Theodora Xenogiani, 'Persisting Informal Employment: What Explains It?' in Johannes P. Jütting and Juan R. de Laiglesia (eds), *Is Informal Normal? Towards more and better jobs in developing countries* (OECD 2009); Johannes P. Jütting and Juan R. de Laiglesia, *Is Informal Normal? Towards More and Better Jobs in Developing Countries* (2009) 13.

[31] SEED, *Decent Employment through Small Enterprises: A Progress Report on SEED Activities* (ILO, 2003).

[32] Margaret McMillan and Dani Rodrik, *Globalization, Structural Change, and Productivity Growth* (Harvard University 2011).

and low revenue for the government; it shows no signs of disappearing in many countries around the world.[33]

1.3.1 A growing problem in many regions of the world

In many countries the informal economy has been the main source of labour force growth in recent years.[34] According to the most recent estimates, non-agricultural work in the informal economy represents 82 per cent of total employment in South Asia, 66 per cent in sub-Saharan Africa, 65 per cent in East and South-East Asia (excluding China), 51 per cent in Latin America and 10 per cent in Eastern Europe and Central Asia.[35] It was a main source of support for many affected by the Global Financial Crisis of 2008.[36]

In 2015, the ILO's *World Employment Social Outlook* revealed a marked shift away from the standard employment model, finding that fewer than 40 per cent of wage and salaried workers worldwide are employed on a full-time permanent basis—a share that appears to be declining.[37] The ILO also reported that, in emerging and developing economies, informal employment continues to be common, and very short term contracts and irregular hours are becoming more widespread at the bottom of global supply chains.[38]

The pervasive trend towards informal work is far more apparent in certain regions of the world. In the developed economies and the EU, including Central and South-Eastern Europe and the Commonwealth of Independent States,[39] around eight in ten workers are employees—whereas in South Asia and Sub-Saharan Africa, around 75 per cent of workers are either in own-account work or employed as contributing family workers.[40] The share of informal employment in most countries of Latin America has risen over the past decade. The exceptions are Mexico, Argentina, Costa Rica, Uruguay, and Chile.[41] The proportion of informal work as an overall share of work ranged from 40 per cent in Chile to 80 per cent in Paraguay.[42]

Keeping in mind that data on informal employment in African countries is very scarce, as the only source is the household labour force surveys that are carried out at irregular intervals, it is estimated that the proportion of the workforce in Africa engaged in informal work ranges between 60 to 80 per cent. The trend is towards an increase in the share of informal employment, with the exception of South Africa.[43] This increase appears to be due to a decline in formal work combined with increased sub-contracting of work in the formal sector.[44]

[33] The terms 'is linked' or 'is associated with' are used here instead of 'causes' because both informality and these other social problems may have the same causes. They may be closely associated but one may not cause the other. Still, alleviating one may help to alleviate the other.

[34] Marc Bacchetta, Ekkehard Ernst, and Juana Bustamante, *Globalisation and Informal Jobs in Developing Countries* (2009)[ILO and WTO Publications]

[35] International Labour Organization and WEIGO, *ILO: Women and Men in the Informal Economy: A Statistical Picture* (2012).

[36] Raymond Torres, *World of Work Report 2009: The Global Jobs Crisis and Beyond* (2009) [ILO].

[37] International Labour Office, *World Employment Social Outlook: The Changing Nature of Jobs* (2015) 13.

[38] Ibid. 13.

[39] CIS: Armenia, Azerbaijan, Belarus, Georgia, Kazakhstan, Kyrgyzstan, Moldova, Russian Federation, Tajikistan, Turkmenistan, Ukraine, and Uzbekistan.

[40] International Labour Office, *World Employment Social Outlook: The Changing Nature of Jobs 28.*

[41] Uma Rani, *Impact of changing work patterns on income inequality* (Discussion Paper Series, 2008) 6.

[42] Ibid. 6. [43] Ibid. 6. [44] Ibid. 6.

One of the reasons that many countries are struggling to put in place sound regulatory responses to informal work is because it is often thought of as an anomaly. For a long time, economic theories predicted that as economic development occurred, and productivity increased, the ratio of informal to formal work within a given economy would shrink. The informal economy was viewed as a temporary phenomenon delinked from modern societies and economies.

In addition to being theoretically invisible, informal workers' lives were statistically invisible as they were not counted in national labour-force surveys. This, in turn, meant that they were not analysed in labour-relations scholarship or considered in state labour policies.[45] Thanks to developments in statistical definitions and methods of collection, informality is becoming more visible. We are beginning to get a sense of its statistical dominance compared with standard work. And informal work is likely to be even more prevalent than official statistics suggest. Chen, for example, argues that women's paid work, not just their unpaid housework, continues to be overlooked by official statistics. If the magnitude of women's invisible paid work, particularly home-based remunerative work, were fully counted, both the share of women and the share of informal workers in the work force would increase.[46]

1.3.2 Impact of the 2007/8 financial crisis

As with other financial crises, the 2007/8 financial crisis has bloated informal economies around the world. The ILO estimates that the number of 'own-account workers' and unpaid family workers increased by 136 million from 2000, with 1.52 billion vulnerable workers of this type in 2011.[47] The increase in informal work was worst in Sub-Saharan Africa, accounting for nearly 70 per cent of all employment growth in the region from 2007.[48] The financial crisis and economic slowdown impacted the outlook for workers for a persistent period, beyond the initial crisis.

Evidence from previous financial crises illustrates that, once individuals move to the informal sector, it is difficult for them to return to regular work.[49] In some countries, informality returns to pre-crisis levels after two to three years, while others experience increased informality levels persisting even after five years.[50]

1.3.3 Associated with poverty

As this trend toward informal work continues, so too do the deleterious consequences of these insecure work arrangements. Unsurprisingly, informal employees earn far less than formal wage employees. In 2015, the ILO reported that the wages of informal employees are between 43 per cent (Philippines) and 64 per cent (Uruguay) lower than wages of formal employees.[51]

[45] Rita Agarwala, 'The Economic Sociology of Informal Work: The Case of India' in Nina Bandelj (ed.), *Economic Sociology of Work*, Vol 18 (2009).

[46] Martha Chen, 'Women and Informality: A Global Picture, the Global Movement' 21 SAIS Review 71 72.

[47] International Labour Office, *Global Employment Trends 2012* (Geneva, International Labour Office, 2012) 42.

[48] Ibid. 42.

[49] C. Williams and J. Windebank, *Informal Employment in the Advanced Economies: Implications for Work and Welfare* (n/a, 1998).

[50] Torres.

[51] International Labour Office, *World Employment Social Outlook: The Changing Nature of Jobs 41.*

Perhaps most importantly, many informal workers do not make a living wage. The ILO reported that poverty disproportionally affects temporary employees, the self-employed and unemployed.[52] In emerging and developing countries especially, the incidence of poverty when the household head is engaged in temporary or informal employment is especially high. In Mexico for example, the poverty rate is just under 50 per cent when the household head is not permanently employed, compared to around 25 per cent when the household head is permanently employed.[53]

Although we can say with a great deal of confidence that informal work is *most often* empirically associated with poverty and low productivity, this is not always the case. '[N]ot all informal workers are poor, unproductive workers, without access to more productive forms of employment'.[54] This has led some who study informality to argue that there are different tiers of informal work.[55]

1.3.4 Associated with low job quality

The persistence of informality is harmful to economic and social development both for individuals who toil in poor conditions, but also for countries in which there is a high incidence of informality. In particular, it hinders labour market development. Where work is informal there are insufficient quality jobs being created that are accessible to those who need them.[56] This is important because improved job quality can play a critical role in promoting and achieving better development outcomes. Higher wages can stimulate higher overall demand. Improved job skills can contribute to the development of more technologically advanced forms of work. In well-functioning labour markets, all of this, in turn, can play a positive role in the process of industrial upgrading, which is critical to development.[57]

Instability and insecurity are pervasive in the informal economy. High labour turnover in enterprises may operate as a disincentive for training and investment and thus further inhibit the economic and social development of both the enterprise and the individual worker. Indeed, those in non-standard and informal work are far less likely to receive training and skill development.[58] As all the case studies in this book testify, large informal economies hinder the shift to more profitable, higher value added and higher technology-based economic activity across economies.

1.3.5 Associated with the most egregious working conditions

Workers in the informal economy are more frequently exposed to workplace hazards and suffer more work-related injuries and illnesses than employees in larger workplaces.[59] Informal work tends to take place in small or micro enterprises

[52] Ibid. 47. [53] Ibid. 48. [54] Jütting and de Laiglesia 19.

[55] W. Maloney, 'Informality Revisited' 32 World Development 1159.

[56] Jütting and de Laiglesia: 19 Arne Kalleberg, 'Precarious, Informalizing, and Flexible Work' 57 American behavioral scientist 289.

[57] Sanjaya Lall, 'The Employment Impact of Globalization in Developing Countries' in Eddy Lee and Marco Vivarelli (eds), *Understanding Globalization, Employment and Poverty Reduction* (Palgrave Macmillan 2004).

[58] Organisation for Economic Co-operation and Development, *In It Together: Why Less Inequality Benefits All* (2015) 33.

[59] Felicity Lamm and David Walters, 'Regulating Occupational Health and Safety in Small Businesses' in Elizabeth Bluff, Neil Gunningham and Richard Johnstone (eds), *OHS Regulation for a Changing World of Work* (The Federation Press] 2004).

where compliance with occupational health and safety regulations is often very limited.[60]

Most forced labour likely occurs in informal economies.[61] Often children are engaged in forms of work that are linked to the informal economy, including in agriculture, mining, fishing, and manufacturing.[62]

Likewise, union density and collective bargaining coverage are typically very limited for informal workers.[63] Where the deliberative aspects of labour law are not available to citizens, this lowers the likelihood that existing standards will be enforced. It also reduces the 'industrial franchise' of citizens. Citizens have less say over how they conduct their work, under what conditions and hours and so forth, since the union voice and collective bargaining are generally the only strong avenues available for shaping working life. Human development is impoverished by the lack of access to industrial relations institutions. Since these institutions often act as bridges to other democratic institutions, this diminishes the overall franchise of these workers.

Social security benefits apply only to formal wage workers in most countries. Although legal provisions for informal wage workers exist in some countries, workers rarely access them. In Latin America, for example, only 20 per cent of the workers are effectively covered.[64] This leaves most informal workers without any form of social protection, including mechanisms for health, life, disability, and unemployment insurance, as well as pension schemes, childcare and maternity leave.[65] This has two consequences. First, informal workers suffer vulnerability to fluctuations in the availability of work. They need to smooth income fluctuations in other ways, including social networks, taking loans (often at very high interest rates), and so on. Second, they are more likely to become trapped in low wage, low condition work, since there is no alternative.

Informality, then, can hamper the development of what Sen and Nussbaum call human capabilities. Human capabilities are directly relevant to people's well-being and freedom, while indirectly they have the capacity to influence social change and economic production.[66] In the context of labour, 'capacity' refers to the skills, knowledge, and values of people (workers), and how, in using these skills, they can take advantage of the labour market and other 'opportunities' available to them. In this sense 'labour market opportunities' means the alternatives available to people to use their capacities (their skills, knowledge and attitudes) as a way in which to gain financial or personal reward.[67]

[60] Andrew Scott, 'Occupational Health and Safety in SMEs' 9 Small Enterprise Development 14.

[61] International Labour Office, *A global alliance against forced labour: Global Report under the Follow-up to the ILO Declaration on Fundamental Principles and Rights at Work 2005* (INTERNATIONAL LABOUR CONFERENCE, 93rd Session 2005, Report I (B), 2005).

[62] Ibid. For example, child labour and forced labour is particularly prevalent in Rajasthan's stone mines where informal work is the norm: S. Marshall, Kate Taylor, and Sam Balaton-Chrimes, *Rajasthan stone Quarries: promoting human rights due diligence and access to redress in complex supply chains* (2016) 5.

[63] Marco Biagi, 'Labour Law in Small and Medium-Sized Enterprises: Flexibility or Adjustment?' 16 Comparative Labor Law Journal 439.

[64] Torres.

[65] Simon White, *Creating an Enabling Environment for Micro and Small Enterprise Development in Thailand* (1999).

[66] Amartya Sen, *Development as Freedom* (Oxford University Press 1999) 296.

[67] R Tipples, 'The Human Capability Framework—An Important and Useful Framework for Understanding the Labour Market' 29 New Zealand Journal of Employment Relations 3.

1.3.6 Gendered work

Informal work is highly gendered. In most countries for which data disaggregated by sex are available, the share of women in informal employment in non-agricultural activities outnumbers that of men. In sub-Saharan Africa, 74 per cent of women's employment (non-agricultural) is informal, in contrast with 61 per cent for men; in Latin America and the Caribbean the figures are 54 and 48 per cent; in South Asia, 83 and 82 per cent; and in urban China, 36 and 30 per cent.[68] The informal sector is the main source of work for women in most developing countries.[69] In some countries in sub-Saharan Africa, virtually all of the female non-agricultural labour force is in the informal sector. For example, in India and in Indonesia, the informal sector accounts for nine out of every ten women working outside agriculture. In the five Latin American and four East Asian countries, for which data are available, more than half of the female non-agricultural workforce is in the informal sector. Women's share of the total informal workforce outside agriculture is also higher than men's share in nine out of twenty-one developing countries for which data are available.[70] A final, and important, dimension of the gendered nature of informal work is that women are more likely to be engaged in work from their homes (Chen estimates that over 85 per cent of home-based workers in most countries are women) and in industrial subcontracting chains as outworkers.[71] These factors exacerbate their powerlessness and their lack of visibility in statistics and to regulators.

1.3.7 Contributes to income inequality

Informality and income inequality are intertwined, with dire consequences for human development. For some time, many economists working in the development field believed that poverty mattered but inequality did not: why would it matter if the rich are getting richer as long as the poor are getting less poor? Today, there is a greater recognition that income inequality also presents a significant problem.[72] This recognition comes at a time when although the world is globally richer than ever before, more than 1.2 billion people still live in extreme poverty. The richest 1 per cent of the world population owns about 40 per cent of the world's assets, while the bottom half owns no more than 1 per cent.[73] On average—and taking into account population size—within country income inequality increased by 11 per cent in developing countries between 1990 and 2010.[74]

There is growing concern that increases in income inequality will retard the expansion of the middle class globally. Instead, growing numbers will become trapped in

[68] International Labour Organization and WIEGO, *ILO: Women and Men in the Informal Economy: A Statistical Picture* (2002) International Labour Organization and WEIGO, *ILO: Women and Men in the Informal Economy: A Statistical Picture.*

[69] Chen. [70] Ibid. [71] Ibid. 76.

[72] Organisation for Economic Co-operation and Development, *Divided We Stand: Why Inequality Keeps Rising* (Organisation for Economic Co-Operation and Development, Paris 2011); Thomas Piketty, *Capital in the twenty-first century* (Arthur Goldhammer tr., The Belknap Press of Harvard University Press 2014).

[73] United Nations Development Programme, *Humanity Divided: Confronting Inequality in Developing Countries* (United Nations Development Programme, Bureau for Development Policy, New York, 2013) 1.

[74] Ibid. 3.

poverty or near poverty, while the richest percentile becomes even richer. In 2016, the ILO projected:

> Among developing economies, the share of the middle class is expected to continue to increase, but more slowly than in recent years. This report points to renewed risks of social unrest associated with slower growth in emerging and developing economies. In these countries, slower growth and disappointing access to middle class living standards may fuel social discontent.[75]

Income inequality is driven by a number of factors. It is difficult to empirically establish the relationship between widening inequality and wage differentials between standard and non-standard work globally due to lack of reliable data. We can say with great confidence, however, that informality and inequality are intimately associated. Plotting changes in non-standard work against changes in income inequality over the past decade, Rani finds that in a majority of the countries (60 per cent) there is a rise in non-standard work *and* a rise in inequality, though in 10 per cent of the countries the reverse is true.[76] In OECD countries, people are more likely to be poor or in the struggling bottom 40 per cent of society if they have non-standard work, especially if they live in a household with other non-standard or non-employed workers.[77] In those countries that are the exception to the informality-inequality relationship, government policy is vitally important. In Brazil, for example, despite increasing wage differentials between formal and informal workers and an increase in the share of informal employment, income inequality declined over the past decade.[78] This may reflect changes in government policy which have provided for state support such as cash transfers, public works, and wage subsidies targeting the poor.

In addition to increased informality and the spread of non-standard working relations, contemporary factors contributing to rising inequality include the decline of organized labour, the fall in the real value of the minimum wage, the growth of finance capitalism, the reduction of trade barriers and skills-based technological change. Recent research from the US shows how important the decline of labour institutions has been compared to other factors. Kristal and Cohen find that the decline of unionization and the real minimum wage explains about 50–60 per cent of rising wage inequality in US private industries between 1969 and 2012.[79] Other studies reported by the OECD also show that across the OECD and emerging economies, high union density and bargaining coverage, combined with centralization or coordination of wage bargaining, is associated with higher overall wage equality.[80]

These equality promoting institutions do not cover informal workers. Their absence is one of the motivations for this book. How can we extend labour institutions to non-standard informal workers? If we fail to find a way to ensure that more workers enjoy the equality producing benefits of these institutions, inequality will continue to grow, with calamitous social consequences that we are increasingly witnessing around the world.

[75] International Labour Office, *World Employment and Social Outlook: Trends 2016 4.*

[76] Uma Rani, *Impact of Changing Work Patterns on Income Inequality* (Discussion Paper Series, 2008) 7.

[77] Organisation for Economic Co-operation and Development, *In It Together: Why Less Inequality Benefits All* (2015) *33.*

[78] Rani 12.

[79] Tali Kristal and Yinon Cohen, 'The causes of rising wage inequality: the race between institutions and technology' 15 Socio-Economic Review 187.

[80] Organisation for Economic Co-operation and Development, *In It Together: Why Less Inequality Benefits All 44.* There is some disagreement in the literature about the size of these effects and whether they hold for women.

Income inequality reduces economic growth beyond certain levels.[81] Economic modelling conducted by Sen and others indicates that whilst income inequality at very low levels may accelerate growth, income inequality at a high level—at the level it is currently sitting in most countries—diminishes growth.[82]

Inequality also diminishes the *quality* of institutions.[83] Institutions (including labour market regulation) assist in overcoming collective action problems. We trust institutions and use them when we know they work. We have a reasonable expectation that repeat use of the same institution will result in the same or similar outcomes. On the other hand, institutions are distrusted by the majority of the population when they are believed only to operate in the interests of elite groups in society. When this is the case, people tend to avoid formal institutions and instead rely upon informal networks. In Indonesia, perceptions that courts are biased stops the poor from trying to access justice through legal means. Independent unions, for instance, are reluctant to attempt to enforce labour laws through courts because of perceived bias.[84] A high degree of economic and political inequality enables elites to resist efforts to reform inefficient institutions and to capture rents from existing institutions, contributing to a vicious circle of institutional underdevelopment.

When institutions are performing poorly, informality is more likely. In the field of labour regulation, this vicious cycle of institutional underdevelopment is readily apparent. When inequality is high, and the wages of the majority of workers are low, wealthy businesses can more easily pay off labour inspectors. The cost may be low relative to net profit. Such is the case in Cambodia, discussed in Chapter 7, where labour inspectors frequently do not make it past the administrative office of factories, and companies even pay the fuel costs for the labour inspector's visit. This regulatory failure in turn contributes to inequality, with breaches of core labour standards remaining unchecked in larger companies and labour inspectors unable to visit smaller enterprises due to fuel costs and the lack of bribes to augment low wages.

Inequality undermines other institutions that are vital to democracy and justice: our parliaments, our courts, our bureaucracies, our police forces. It is vital that we find ways to stop our societies becoming more unequal, and fast.

1.4 Global Search for Policy Responses

To answer the question posed in the heading to this section, informality matters because it is linked with poverty, inequality, low job quality, harmful health and safety conditions, and systemic forms of discrimination and exploitation. It also matters because it shows no signs of disappearing in many countries around the world. On the contrary, informal economies have expanded in many countries in response to structural economic change and the financial crises that have rocked the economic South repeatedly over the last few decades and have more recently shaken the economic North. We need to know why this is the case in order to do something about it. Flowing from this, we need better regulatory responses so as

[81] Ibid. 26.

[82] Amartya Sen, *Inequality Reexamined* (Harvard University Press 1992).

[83] Alberto Chong and Mark Gradstein, *Inequality and Institutions* (Inter-American Development Bank Banco Interamericano de Desarrollo (BID) 2004).

[84] Sarah Rennie and others, 'Orchestration from Below?: Trade Unions in the Global South, Transnational Business and Efforts to Orchestrate Continuous Improvement in Non-State Regulatory Initiatives' 40 University of New South Wales Law Journal 1275.

to improve the working and living standards of those who work under informal conditions, improve tax revenue for countries in which informal work is high, and increase productivity.

1.4.1 What causes informality? The dynamics of informalization

Theories of development informed by modernism expected that informal economies would shrink as economies around the world developed. Instead though, in the latter part of the twentieth century, informal economies expanded in many advanced and less developed economies. Our understanding of these workers' social and political lives and their work conditions is thin, because relevant disciplines including labour law, industrial relations, economic sociology, and economics have allowed studies of informal work to remain in the margins. Despite burgeoning interest in the topic, for example, labour law scholars have focused nearly exclusively on formal work. As Agarwala observes:[85]

> As a result, insights have been lost as to why the informal labour force continues to expand despite urban and industrial modernization; how the informal economy is connected to other market structures and to the state; and how these connections affect informal workers' unique collective action strategies, networks, and class identities.

Without these insights about the nature of informal work and its determinants, it is difficult to design effective regulatory strategies. This study is concerned with closing this gap and developing a regulatory response that increases citizens' democratic franchise and contribute to enhanced well-being and human development.

There are numerous, sometimes contradictory and contested, reasons given for the persistence of informality in the disparate literature, which are rarely brought together. The traditional economic understanding of the cause of informality is provided by the dualist model of the economy which understands a 'modern' and a 'traditional' sector to sit side by side. As the modern, capitalist sector develops, it is expected that rural workers will be drawn to the city in search of higher paying work. Until the capitalist sector grows sufficiently to absorb the traditional sector, a large pool of workers exists in urban areas who generate income as self-employed workers providing low-skilled services.[86] Various theories have been offered for why absorption has not occurred to the extent expected, including premature exposure to global markets due to ill-timed or badly managed liberalization leading to labour shedding into low productivity areas of the economy.[87]

Globalization is blamed as the culprit in other ways, also. In the search for flexibility and lowered costs so as to increase competitiveness, large capitalist firms rely on informal labour as a cheap source of labour. Contrary to the dualist conception, informal labour is not only to be found in 'traditional' low skilled, low productivity agricultural and service segments of the labour force. Skilled, high-productivity workers linked with international supply chains are also working in unregulated conditions.[88]

[85] Rita Agarwala, 'The Economic Sociology of Informal Work: The Case of India' in Nina Bandelj (ed.), *Economic Sociology of Work*, vol 18 (2009).

[86] W. Arthur Lewis, *The Theory of Economic Growth* (Allen and Unwin 1955).

[87] McMillan and Rodrik.

[88] Portes, Castells, and Benton.

The finger is also pointed at regulatory and institutional causes for the persistence of informal work. For neo-classical economists, the problem is overly restrictive and burdensome laws which micro-entrepreneurs evade so as to increase their profitability. For other institutionalists, such as de Soto[89] and North,[90] the problem is not rigidity, but the lack of enforceability of rights including contractual and property rights. Sometimes this is because good institutions do not exist. At other times, it is because the institutions are ill-suited to their environments or untrustworthy. People need to have clear and shared understandings of what is required of an entity if that entity is to be considered trustworthy.[91] When institutions are rife with corruption or bias, or rules are applied unevenly, people have no reason to trust them. Lack of trust in institutions undercuts collective action and collective coordination. A less frequently examined consequence of this institutional failure is the corrosive impact on hope. Coordination and hope are closely related.[92]

Others focus on governance failures of a different nature. The limited scope of the employment relationship eschews the regulation of 'non-standard' or 'atypical workers'[93] and the standards regulating work are sometimes inappropriate. Governance deficits borne from global reach and power of business outstripping the reach and power of states leading to an inability to enforce existing laws[94] are also a concern.

1.5 Approach to Studying Informality Adopted in This Book

Those engaged in debates regarding the causes of informality tend to champion one generalized cause over others. De Soto, for example, focused on legal and institutional barriers to starting up formal business. There is no reason, however, why barriers to establishing formal businesses operate on their own as the basis of informality. In the case of Elena described at the beginning of this introduction, for instance, labour shedding during the transition to capitalism in Bulgaria first pushed her into informal work. The high costs of registering a business then stopped her from establishing herself as a formal micro-entrepreneur. In any case, she is mainly conducting dependent work in global supply chains. Further, her identification as a worker, after spending most of her working life as an employee of a state-owned enterprise, hinders her from imagining herself as a self-employed entrepreneur. She still has the expectation that the state ought to be responsible for economic security, and is struggling to find her place in material and ideational terms in the new economic and social system.

89 Hernando de Soto, 'Dead Capital and the Poor' 21 SAIS review 13.

90 Douglass C. North, 'The New Institutional Economics and Third World Development' in John Harriss, Janet Hunter and Colin M. Lewis (eds), *The New Institutional Economics and Third World Development* (Routledge).

91 Valerie Braithwaite, 'The Hope Process and Social Inclusion' 592 Annals of the American Academy of Political and Social Science 128.

92 Ibid.

93 ILO, *The Employment Relationship, Report V(I)* (95th Sesssion, 2005); Vosko Leah F. Vosko, "Decent Work': The Shifting Role of the ILO and the Struggle for Global Social Justice' 2 Global Social Policy 19.

94 Colin Fenwick and others, *Labour and Labour Related Laws in Small and Micro Enterprises: Innovative Regulatory Responses* ([ILO2008).

To champion one cause over others tends only to operate to confirm an existing policy agenda. The approach which drives this book is based on the understanding that mapping the causes of informality should be a matter of empirical study. Although generalized causes *may* be found that are common across countries, these will likely interact with specific dynamics in individual countries and regions that lead to gaps in regulatory reach. It is this *interaction* of factors that deserves attention if we are to begin remedying the social harms associated with informality.

In sum, the approach in this book is driven by three assumptions:

1. The process of work staying or becoming hidden from the purview of formal laws is dynamic, with multiple causes at different levels—global, regional, national, local, and individual
2. We need to understand the complex dynamics and causes of informality in order to design effective and responsive regulation
3. Because the workers are especially vulnerable, and the causes are of different realms—economic, political, legal, and psychological—the regulatory techniques should also be multiple and dynamic, working at different levels.

Identifying, interacting, and compounding causes of informality is no simple task. Informal economic activity is difficult to observe, study, define, and measure. This is because it is outside formal registration processes and subject to permanent adaptation to changing circumstances. As workers desire to preserve their informal sources of income they adapt constantly to changes in regulations and degrees of enforcement and find new ways to survive. These factors imply the need to deploy particular fieldwork techniques to gain access to, and study, these workers.

The book employs a historical institutionalist approach to studying changes in the context in which labour regulation has occurred over time, reform of labour regulation, and the proliferation of forms of work. Historical institutionalism is more an approach than a method or discipline, implying that different methods should be used to study changes in institutions and their effect. The dynamic nature of informality, together with its mixed causes, indicates that different disciplines and methods will provide important, distinct insights into its causes, and possible pathways out. This book thus takes a multi-disciplinary approach to the study of the causes of informality, drawing on different literatures and employing various methodologies for empirical work. Stories of political and institutional change are assembled to examine the macro causes of informality in each case. Ethnographic methods are used to study worker's experience of regulation and informality.

The end purpose of the study is to put together a 'responsive' regulatory approach to informality. Proponents of responsive regulation argue that it is worth experimenting with different methods of standard setting and enforcement given the negative consequences of non-compliance with the law in relation to the enjoyment of human rights, well-being, and human development.

The key argument (or 'emergent theory') of this book is that when new regulatory techniques are being considered, we first need to ask what the regulation is responding to. How do we understand the social relations and dynamics that require shaping?

In broad terms, the book addresses the following questions:

1. What is the same and different about the dynamics of informalization in different countries/settings?
2. What regulatory strategies have been implemented to address informality in each case study?

3. What has worked/has not worked? How much have the regulations addressed the dynamics identified?
4. What does this tell us about regulatory strategies for formalization?
5. How can we provide local pathways out of informal work and global strategies for addressing the causes of informality?

1.5.1 Structure of the book

The subsequent two chapters of this book expand on the approach adopted in this book. Chapter 2 discusses the literature that most informs the framework of analysis, including regulatory theory and global supply chain governance. Chapter 3 develops the methodology and provides details of the field work conducted.

The main body of the book discusses four case studies of informal work and the regulatory innovations that have been developed in each country to reduce informality: Chapter 4—transport workers in Maharashtra, India; Chapter 5—home-based workers in the textile industry in Australia; Chapter 6—light industry workers in Bulgaria; and Chapter 7—garment workers in Cambodia. Each case study is addressed in two stages. The dynamic causes of informality are first explored.

The method applied is outlined further in the methodology section, but some explanation is warranted in this introductory chapter.

The first part of each case study builds a story about why and how informal economies grew in the individual case. The primary approach is political economic. Political economy might be defined as an interdisciplinary study drawing upon economics, law, and political science to explain how political institutions, the political environment, and the economic system influence each other. Economic and political narrative histories are delved into in order to explain why economies and systems of governance and regulation have evolved in particular ways.[95] What were the contextual features that were relevant to the development of informality? What causal processes—either social or economic—may have contributed to the growth of the informal economy? This approach seeks to build a *hermeneutic* understanding of informality and actors' interaction with systems of governance. Why did the economy develop in this way? Why do actors behave as they do in relation to systems of governance? It also seeks a *causal* explanation. What social, economic, and political processes contributed to informality?

Each chapter moves from describing national development to narratives of individual and community experiences of informality. Political economy approaches are useful for constructing the 'larger picture', and for *situating* individual experience, but not for telling individual stories and exploring individuals' experience of work, business, and regulation. For this, ethnographic methods are employed. Where possible, interviews and non-participant observations are drawn on here. Where such field work was not possible, empirical research from other sources is used to augment findings.

The second part of each case-study chapter describes a regulatory development that has emerged to address informality. The chapters not only describe the functional features of these developments, they also seek to understand how such developments were possible. The inquiry is driven by a desire to understand how purposeful institutional change occurs. Each chapter ends with an assessment of the regulatory innovation in

[95] Andrew Abbott, *Time Matters: On Theory and Method* (University of Chicago Press 2001).

light of the understanding of the dynamics of informalization described in the first part of the chapter. The aim here is to assess whether and to what extent the innovation is responding to and addressing these dynamics.

The final two substantive chapters draw lessons and propose short-term and long-term regulatory solutions to informality. Chapter 8 contrasts the responses in the case studies, drawing out strategies that can be deployed in the immediate term by those seeking to reduce informality. It compares the way that institutional change has been achieved in each case. Chapter 9 canvasses a longer-term vision for regulatory reform. The chapter puts forward three interrelated regulatory pathways out of informality: first, the promotion of International Living Wages through an international instrument such as an ILO Convention or Human Rights Council treaty which would also establish an International Living Wage disputes mechanism for enforcement of these minima; second, the setting up of National Supply Chain Tribunals empowered to hear disputes concerning non-payment of living wages due to supply chain dynamics, and to hold parties in the supply chain responsible for non-payment; third, the fostering of local pathways out of informality. It hoped that this study will contribute to the search for new pathways out of informality and towards high labour conditions for vulnerable workers.

2

How Can Regulation Help?

2.1 Introduction

The purpose of this chapter is to explore how regulation might help to alleviate the burden on poor workers and reduce the incidence of informal work. Informal work is understood in this study as a regulatory problem or conundrum. The end purpose of the study is to design a new regulatory approach to informality drawing on ideas from the regulatory literature and based on empirical studies of real-life regulatory initiatives. The case studies which make up the body of this study seek to understand the way that global and regional economic and governance dynamics interact with existing labour regulations to produce informality in each country studied and in relation to the specific populations of informal workers researched. These case studies then provide the building blocks for the novel approaches to regulating work canvassed at the end of the study. This chapter explores the insights and concepts from the regulatory literature in order reflect upon the reason why labour regulation is failing so many workers around the world, leaving them stranded in a state of informality. Having established the problem, it then draws on various literatures to set up the conceptual framework for examining how institutional change could occur so that a more responsive labour regulation could be generated. The labour law and industrial relations literature, where most writing about informality occurs, tends not to provide an account of how change occurs. It also tends to be nationally focused. The conceptual framework outlined in this chapter seeks to stop these gaps by drawing on other literatures.

Labour laws, labour relations institutions, and labour market regulations, are the core institutions governing labour markets. Labour market regulation is generally taken to include not only labour laws, but also pension (also known as superannuation) laws, social security laws, and other associated regulations that impact on the rights and conditions of workers.[1] Collectively, these are referred to as 'labour regulation' in this book. A myriad of other formal and informal institutions also impacts and shapes the social structure and nature of labour markets, but it is safe to say that these are the core formal institutions deployed to regulate work. It is an assumption underlying this study that state-based labour regulation is failing because it is not responsive to the problem it seeks to address and shape. The literature suggests, first, that it is not responding to the various *forms of work* that have proliferated in recent years. Labour regulation tends to assume that workers are employees working as professionals or in the traditional jobs of the proletariat. However, the explosion of different types of self-employed workers and precarious workers of various ilks has placed great strain on the definition of employee, with most forms of work sitting outside it. Second, it is not responding to advances in the *structures of production* and relations of distribution that work occurs within. Labour regulation is inclined to assume that work occurs within integrated enterprises. Today, work frequently occurs within complex supply

[1] Simon Deakin and Frank Wilkinson, *The Law of The Labour Market: Industrialization, Employment and Legal Evolution* (Oxford University Press 2005).

chains and other economic arrangements. Third, it is not employing *tools* that are appropriate to or effective in regulating new working relationships. Labour regulation has a tendency to issue fines or issue orders that assume an ongoing and stable working relationship between employees and employers. So for example, a standard remedy in employment law is either to reinstate a worker or require payment in lieu of reinstatement. Where working relations are not ongoing or are more unstable, such tools are inappropriate. Further, penalties which are standard in labour regulation, including the payment of fines, appear not always to be effective in changing behaviour. This is because, fourth, and relatedly, it is not *creating incentives* for compliance which overcome the countervailing disincentives which arise from private and informal regulation, culture, and informal institutions.

These four categories of unresponsiveness will be considered in greater detail following a brief outline of insights from the regulatory literature which will help to elucidate the concept of responsiveness. First, though, the chapter provides a brief description of regulation and why it matters.

2.2 What is Regulation?

A useful definition of regulation is 'the intentional activity of attempting to control, order or influence the behaviour of others according to defined standards or purposes'.[2] This definition recognizes that the state is not the only actor with power to achieve policy goals. It also recognizes that regulation is a *process* involving the regulator—the State or other regulatory body—and the regulated community.

There is a great deal of overlap between the literature that deals with governance and that concerned with regulation. So, what is the difference between the two? 'Governance' is understood to be a broader term than 'regulation'. Braithwaite, Coglianese, and Levi-Faur define the two terms in relation to each other as follows:[3]

> Governments and governance are about providing, distributing and regulating. Regulation can be conceived of as that large subset of governance that is about the steering of the flow of events and behavior, as opposed to providing and distributing. Of course, when regulators regulate, they often steer the providing and distributing that regulated actors undertake as well.

Governance and regulation can be local in scope, national, regional, international and global.

Why does regulation matter, and therefore, why is the study of regulation important? As Braithwaite, Coglianese, and Levi-Faur see it, put simply, regulation matters because it affects peoples' lives:[4]

> Bad regulation, after all, can do terrible damage to people. Good regulation can control problems that might otherwise lead to bankruptcy and war, and can emancipate the lives of ordinary people. Mediocre, unimaginative regulation that occupies the space between good and bad regulation leads to results that are correspondingly between the extremes of good and bad.

Using a broad concept of 'regulation' opens up the space for states and other bodies concerned with shaping the behaviour of other parties to design new regulatory strategies. They may be *hybrid* or a form of *co-regulation*: state regulation can work

[2] Julia Black, 'Critical Reflections on Regulation' 27 Australian Journal of Legal Philosophy 1.

[3] John Braithwaite, Cary Coglianese, and David Levi-Faur, 'Can Regulation and Governance Make a Difference?' 1 Regulation and Governance 1 3.

[4] Ibid. 4.

alongside—and in some cases coordinate—other forms of regulation, including some types of private and self-regulation. This form of regulation is also known in some literatures as New Governance.[5] The strategies may be *multi-faceted*, using a number of different strategies simultaneously, or *sequential*, as in the case of networked regulation; and they may be *indirect*.[6]

A broad definition of regulation also allows to us to take into account the impact of informal norms on formal rules. All economic behaviour, whether governed by formal rules or not, is regulated in some way. Informal economic activity may not be in compliance with the law, but it is still a deeply embedded phenomenon.[78] Workers are socially and political embedded in the meaning they attach to their labour, the social networks that determine their life chances and their collective action efforts.[9] Structures, networks, and political institutions intertwine informal workers with the formal economy, society, and the state.

2.3 What Does it Mean to Say that Regulation is Responsive?

Based on these insights about what regulation is, what does it mean to say that regulation is responsive? This section draws insights from the responsive regulation literature, which is often concerned with self-regulation, and applies it to state and mixed forms of regulation. Responsive regulation is a normative proposal which has different elements. In any given regulatory ecosystem, regulation may need to respond to various factors or features of the regulatory target and their environment. This section briefly describes what things the literature proposes regulation should be responsive to.

First, literature suggests that regulation should be responsive to the *conduct* of those it seeks to regulate.[10] Baldwin and Black propose that this entails being sensitive to the operating and cognitive frameworks of the target, and to their attitudinal settings.[11] 'Micro' level theories of regulatory compliance and institutional design emphasize the importance of going beyond formal legal aspects of institutional design to encompass concern for 'living institutions' and behavioural practices.[12] This involves developing an understanding of, and responding to, *informal* norms and regulations.

[5] Kenneth Abbott and Duncan Sindal, 'The Governance Triangle: Regulatory Standards Institutions and the Shadow of the State' in Walter Mattli and Ngaire Woods (eds), *The Politics of Global Regulation* (Princeton University Press 2009).

[6] Black 8–9.

[7] Mark Granovetter, 'Economic Action and Social Structure: The Problem of Embeddedness' 91 The American Journal of Sociology; Bob Jessop, *The Social Embeddedness of the Economy and its Implications for Economic Governance* [Black Rose Books] http://www2.cddc.vt.edu/digitalfordism/fordism_materials/jessop2.htm 2001).

[8] Recent work by Petra Mahy et al. on the plural regulation of work describes these varied influences particularly well: Petra Mahey and others, *The Plural Regulation of Work: A Pilot Study of Restaurant Workers in Yogyakarta, Indonesia* (University of Melbourne 2017).

[9] Rita Agarwala, 'The Economic Sociology of Informal Work: The Case of India' in Nina Bandelj (ed.), *Economic Sociology of Work*, vol 18 (2009).

[10] John Braithwaite, 'Responsive Regulation and Developing Economies' (2006) World Development 884 886.

[11] Robert Baldwin and Julia Black, 'Really Responsive Regulation' 71 Modern Law Review 59 94.

[12] Johan Olsen, 'Institutional Design in Democratic Contexts' 5 The Journal of Political Philosophy 203 N.; Reichman, 'Moving Backstage: Uncovering the Role of Compliance Practices in Shaping Regulatory Policies' in R. Baldwin, C. Scott and C. Hood (eds), *A Reader on Regulation* (Oxford University Press 1998).

Second, Selnick suggests, regulation should be sensitive to the broader *institutional environment* and to changes in the dynamics of the context.[13] Likewise, Baldwin and Black propose that:[14]

> Regulation is really responsive when it knows its regulatees and its institutional environments, when it is capable of deploying different and new regulatory logics coherently, when it is performance sensitive and when it grasps what its shifting challenges are.

This entails developing a detailed understanding of the institutional environment and performance of the regulatory regime. Regulations sit within larger institutional complexes. Institutional complexes are local, national, regional, and international in scope.

Thirdly, regulation should be sensitive to existing *power dynamics*. On this view, compliance depends not only on rules or incentives specified in formal mechanisms, but also on the powers and motivations of social actors who may follow or resist them.[15] Some scholars emphasize processes of normative diffusion (or in many cases normative contestation or co-option) as important determinants of sustained changes in regulatory target's compliance or resistance to regulatory processes.[16]

Finally, responsiveness suggests flexibility and agility in designing *enforcement approaches*. The responsive regulation approach pervades all the different tasks of regulatory activity: detecting undesirable or non-compliant behaviour; developing tools and strategies for responding to that behaviour; enforcing those tools and strategies; assessing their success or failure; and modifying them accordingly. A regulator must be prepared to use a wide range of techniques to achieve its policy goals, and also to constantly review and assess the effectiveness of its policy approach. Ayers and Braithwaite propose that regulators enforce in the first instance by compliance strategies, such as persuasion and education, but apply more punitive deterrent responses—escalating up a pyramid of such responses—when the regulated firm fails to behave as desired. This model of enforcement was depicted by Ayers and Braithwaite in their famous regulatory pyramid.[17] The pyramid idea is seen in the figure below as a ratcheting up from self-regulation to non-discretionary punishment (see Figure 2.1).

Different combinations of instruments and actors may have the greatest chance of building on the strengths of individual mechanisms, while compensating for their weaknesses. The task is to work out which are the best combinations.[18]

Based on these views from the literature, the case study chapters of this book are framed around an assessment of the specific ways that old regulatory practices failed to respond to the types of dynamics outlined here, and the ways that the regulatory innovations studied find new ways to build on the strength of existing regulatory institutions and compensate for their weaknesses by bringing in new instruments and actors.

[13] Philip Selznick, *The Moral Commonwealth: Social Theory and the Promise of Community* (University of California Press 1994) 336.

[14] Baldwin and Black 94.

[15] L. Snider, 'Accommodating Power: The `Common Sense' of Regulators' 18 Social Legal Studies 179.

[16] Randall Peerenboom, Carole J. Petersen, and Albert H.Y. Chen, *Human Rights in Asia: A Comparative Legal Study of Twelve Asian Jurisdictions, France and the USA* (Routledge 2006).

[17] I. Ayres and J. Braithwaite, *Responsive Regulation: Transcending the Deregulation Debate* (Oxford University Press 1992).

[18] G. Gunningham and P. Grabosky, *Smart Regulation* (Clarendon Press 1998) 499.

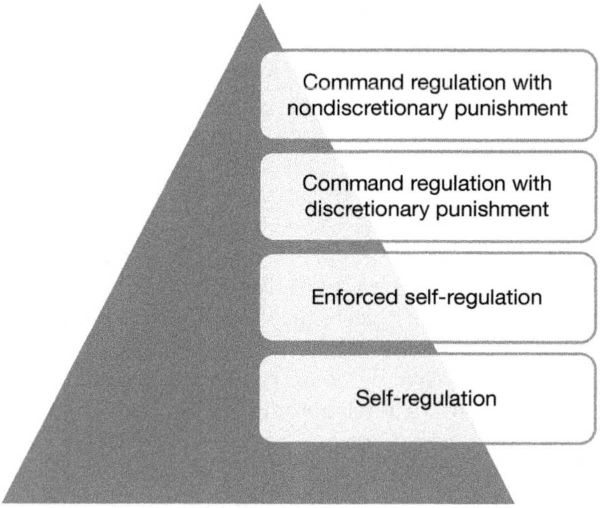

Figure 2.1 Regulatory pyramid of enforcement strategies

2.4 The Failure of State-Based Labour Regulation to Respond to Changes in the Nature of Work

Incorporating these insights from regulatory theory, we return now to the various ways that state-based regulation has failed to respond to realities and changes in the nature of work, with the result that a great deal of work occurs informally, outside legal regulation.

Capitalism (understood as a distinctive institutional system of production, exchange, and accumulation) is constantly being reinvented. Businesses respond to competitive pressures with technological advances and by reorganizing the way that production occurs, developing new patterns of accumulation and wealth generation. Nation states vie for competitive advantage by reforming the rules and institutions governing markets in various domains, including international trade and investment.[19] Such rules and institutions operate at the national, regional, and transnational level. Those with power attempt to ensure that these rules enhance their competitive advantage. Those without the power to set these rules adapt. Businesses, in turn, respond to these new arrangements by making further changes to the way that production is organized. Workers find new niches and novel ways to survive. Additional forms of work are devised. And so, the world of work is in constant flux.

While capitalism may make important contributions to the realization of social justice norms via its generation of economic growth, the inequitable tendencies that are produced through processes of accumulation and wealth generation have—throughout the history of capitalism—given rise to the demand for a range of regulatory and redistributive interventions to constrain and compensate for the more negative consequences of the system.[20] Such embedding of the capitalist market economy in both

[19] Robert Wade, 'The Invisible Hand of the American Empire' in Joel H. Rosenthal and Christian Barry (eds), *Ethics and International Affairs: A Reader* (3rd edn, Georgetown University Press 2009).

[20] Sean O'Riain, 'States and Markets in an Era of Globalization' 26 Annual Review of Sociology 187.

formal and informal regulatory norms is claimed to contribute both to stability and legitimacy within the capitalist system—both enhancing its efficiency and countering its more exploitative and commodifying tendencies.[21]

The past few decades have seen particularly swift and far reaching economic reform, resulting in massive changes in the way work occurs. Observers point to a period of 'neoliberalism', regarded as extending roughly from the early 1970s to the present—or at least until its stride was interrupted by the still unfolding 'global financial crisis' of 2008/2009.[22,23] One feature of this disembedding of markets is the failure of labour regulations to be reformulated in response to economic and social change. Although it has the potential to be an adaptive model of regulation,[24] labour regulation displays a certain resistance to change which makes the innovations examined in the case study chapters remarkable.

A common characteristic shared by labour regulations in almost all countries of the world is the link to the employment relationship.[25] Most labour rights and protections flow from being employed, which assumes a stable employer.[26] It is well established that the labour law of the twentieth century was based on the assumption that the subject of regulation was a full time, male breadwinner who worked in a Fordist, vertically integrated, enterprise.[27]

There have been some recent expansions to labour law so as to regulate 'atypical' work. For instance, labour law in Australia recognizes part-time work, and a statutory 'casual' category was added with much controversy in the 1980s. However, these categories still assume that work is paid and that there is a supervising employer. A consequence of this is that a great deal of work—probably the vast majority—sits outside the reach of labour regulation.[28] For the majority of workers around the world—especially those in the Economic South—work is not given out by a continuous employer. Feminized, domestic, caring work is perhaps furthest from the reach of labour regulation.[29] Yet, broader reform has been slow coming.

There are various reasons for this institutional inertia, which that have been explained thoroughly elsewhere.[30] Labour regulation is embedded within a larger set of

[21] Karl Polanyi, *The Great Transformation: The Political and Economic Origins of Our Time* (Beacon Press 1944).

[22] John Ruggie, 'International Regimes, Transactions and Change: Embedded Liberalism in the Postwar Economic Order' 36 International Organization; G Krippner and others, 'Polanyi Symposium: a Conversation on Embeddedness' 2 Socio-Economic Review; Robert Wade, 'Financial Regime Change?' 53 New Left Review.

[23] Some accounts, including many rooted in the French regulation school of political economy, add to this distinction a related one between 'Fordism' and 'post-Fordism': David Harvey, *The Spaces of Global Capitalism* (Verso 2006).

[24] Deakin and Wilkinson.

[25] International labour Organization, *The Employment Relationship* (2005); International Labour Organization, *The Scope of the Employment Relationship* (ILO, 2003); C Engels, 'Subordinate Employees or Self-Employed Workers?' in R. Blanpain (ed.), *Comparative Labour Law and Industrial Relations in Industrialised Market Economies* (10th edn, Wolters Kluwer, Alphen aan den Rijn 2010).

[26] P. Davies and M. Freedland, 'The Disintegration of the Employing Enterprise and its Significance for the Personal Scope of Employment Law', The Scope of Employment Law: Re-drawing the Boundaries of Protection Conference, Bellagio, 23–27 May 2005.

[27] A. C. L. Davies, *Perspectives on Labour Law* (Cambridge University Press 2004) 94.

[28] Alain Supiot, Pamela Meadows, and the European Commission, *Beyond Employment: Changes In Work and The Future of Labour Law in Europe* (Oxford University Press 2001).

[29] Jose Maria Ramirez-Machado, *Domestic Work, Conditions of Work and Employment: A Legal Perspective* (ILO 2003).

[30] Tekle Guy Davidov, 'Enforcement Problems in "Informal" Labor Markets: A View from Israel' 27 Comparative Labor Law & Policy Journal 3.

institutions. Changing one set of rules can and often does have implications for others and there is likely to be significant resistance to change on the part of those who are advantaged in the broader context.[31] Institutions can become locked in because people invest in learning the rules. Changing rules can invoke significant up-front costs and be resisted by those who do not want to bear any new costs. Labour laws' link to the employment relationship enjoys strong normative legitimacy thanks in part to the United Nation's International Labour Organization. Although, more recently, the ILO has emphasized 'work' not 'employment' rights and protections, many of the earlier conventions were based on the employment relationship. Despite the small size of their industrial sectors, many newly independent countries adopted traditional labour laws or expanded the labour laws inherited from colonial regimes, because of the seeming universality of the ILO's conventions.[32]

The defensive posture that labour unions have been forced into during the neoliberal period has often hindered them from demanding that laws reflect new working relations, despite the fact that this undercuts their membership base. In the Economic North, for instance, unions have bled members, as workers move from stable employment conditions to contract-based relations or become freelance. Yet at the same time, labour market institutions lend labour unions legitimacy as bargaining agents and representatives of labour and give them access to resources. The centrality of unions to the institution provides them with status, and this reduces their desire to act as agents of institutional change.[33] In any case, changing the rules can have long-term effects that may be difficult or impossible to predict.[34] For existing unions, continuing with the current rules—even if they are not necessarily optimal—may be safer than encouraging a wholesale reform of labour regulation in a political context which is hostile to market intervention of this type. For this, and various other reasons, labour market regulation remains largely wedded to the employment contract in most countries.

The institutional stickiness of traditional forms of labour regulation at a time of sweeping economic and social changes has left labour regulation unresponsive in a number of respects. This section outlines the broad observations in the literature. The case studies seek to build on this literature with more specific observations of the dynamics in each country researched.

2.4.1 Failure to respond to the proliferation of forms of work

Work is organized in a myriad of different ways and the structural standing of the individuals and collectives conducting the work varies greatly. There is a radical global heterogeneity in the characteristics of labour relations.[35] Some forms of work are related to particular traditions and social relations in specific localities and countries, whereas others forms of work are related to more recent trends in economic and social change, and are found across many countries. A major challenge for the design of labour regulation is regulating diverse forms of work. A related question is whether the same obligations, rights, and protections should be afforded to all workers, or whether

[31] Sven Steinmo, 'What is Historical Institutionalism' in Donatella Della Porta and Michael Keating (eds), *Approaches to the Social Sciences* (Cambridge University Press 2008).

[32] Tekle.

[33] J. M. Podolny, 'A Status-Based Model of Market Competition' 98 American Journal of Sociology 829.

[34] Steinmo.

[35] Ronaldo Munck, 'The Precariat: a View from the South' (2013) [2013] 34 Third World Quarterly 747 756.

differentiated obligations, rights, and protections should be offered depending on the nature of the work, the social relations, or the risks assumed by the worker compared with those giving them the work or supervising them.

There are various schemas for understanding or labelling different types of workers. One particularly helpful one is that offered by Guy Standing. Standing's schema is broad and does not take into account local or specific social relations. However, it helps us to think about the diverse nature of work and the differentiated vulnerabilities and risks associated with different forms of work. Labour law tends to assume that workers are employees who are either 'salariat' (as Standing refers to them), or proletariat.[36] Salariat are professionals with strong employment security who enjoy labour rights. Along-side the salariat, in terms of having similar incomes, is a growing group of self-employed consultants and entrepreneurial project-oriented types (referred to by Standing as 'proficians'), who tend to be mainly outside labour regulation. Below this is the old proletariat, who standard labour regulation is designed to protect. The great social pacts of the mid-twentieth century were developed with this class in mind. 'Proleterianization' meant being disciplined and habituated to stable labour. Instead of growing in number, as was expected with widespread industrialization, this class of workers is shrinking in most countries of the world, in inverse proportion to the new 'precariat'.[37]

The 'precariat' who are the main subject of this book, have insecure labour, being in and out of jobs, without long-term employment contracts: 'the modal situation for the precariat may be described as precariatization, habituation to a life of unstable labour and unstable living'.[38] Unlike the proletariat, the precariat do not yet have a stable occupational identity, being expected to be flexible in terms of type of labour. (Another way of conceptualizing this is as the increasing multiplicity of the proletariat.)[39] They experience both employment insecurity and job insecurity, meaning that they both do not enjoy continuing work with a single person or business giving them work, and they often have to change the types of work they do. The precariat have no control over time. They also have chronic income insecurity, experiencing volatile earnings. Because they do not attract social protections, they rely almost entirely on money income.

'Precarity' has always been the norm in the global South and it has increased in the North in recent years.[40] Standing's description of the precariat is apt for all four groups of workers examined in the case studies before the regulatory innovations had impact: immigrant home-based workers toiling in Australia's apparel industry; head-load workers in India; home-based workers in Bulgaria putting together different forms of light industry and agricultural work; and young female factory workers in Cambodia. Each of the groups of workers lived with employment and job insecurity. They did not know if they would have work the next week. Indian head-load workers, for example, travelled around the cities in search of work at ports and markets. Australian and Bulgarian home-based workers did not know if they would need to work sixteen-hour days, or whether they would be without work. They had little control over their time. They relied solely on their earnings and did not enjoy the benefits of any welfare apparatus. Their precariat status as workers meant that absolute flexibility was required

[36] Standing.

[37] The term 'précarité' was developed in the French socioeconomic literature around the changing patterns of work since the 1980s: Munck: 751.

[38] Standing 969.

[39] M. Hardt and A. Negri, *Commonwealth* (Harvard University Press, Cambridge, MA 2011) 27.

[40] Munck.

of them. They had to arrange their lives entirely around whatever work opportunities came up. However, their experience of work was deeply shaped by the workers' cultural and historic contexts, and thus, we cannot say that they experienced informality in the same way. For instance, people working informally in a context in which most work is informal—as is the case in India—might have a different experience of informality from those who are based in a country in which most work occurs in formal enterprises and is regulated by labour laws. And yet, we can see that all the workers described in the case studies in this book, across four countries, had a great deal in common.

2.4.2 Failure to respond to new patterns of production and control

A further reason that labour regulation is floundering is because it has failed to respond to new patterns of production and control, which in turn produce new social relations and forms of work. State capacity to regulate work around the world has been weakened by the increased intricacy of post-Fordist processes of capitalist development—the shift from large-scale mass-production methods pioneered by Henry Ford to the use of small flexible manufacturing units.[41] Much writing about 'disembedding' and state failure in the post-Fordist phase has focused on the challenges associated with regulating transnational business transactions and multinational corporations.[42] Yet the case studies show that the complexity of arrangements within a single jurisdiction also makes regulation difficult because of the pluralization of the actors involved in driving the relevant economic relationships and outcomes.

A new arrangement that has become increasingly common is the organization of production through supply chains (also called value chains). Supply chains take many different forms: they involve assorted and often fluctuating numbers of parties, have diverse governance structures and span distinct geographical and political spaces. The structuring of supply chains in organizationally complex and pluralized ways can make it very difficult for state-based regulators to *identify a clear locus of power and control*, and thus to determine appropriate regulatory subjects and agents.[43] Who should be held responsible for the poor conditions of workers, when so many parties are involved in passing work down the supply chain? Where production occurs in integrated supply chains (also called production networks or value chains), control is wielded in a diffuse, multipolar manner. This is a consequence of a number of the characteristics of integrated supply chains:

2.4.2.1 Spatial dispersion

Lead firms in supply chains source components from geographically dispersed locations. Sometimes this dispersion is global in reach. At other times, as in the Australian case study of garment production, the dispersion is across suburban homes.

[41] David Harvey, *The Condition of Postmodernity: An Enquiry into the Origins of Cultural Change* (Blackwell 1990).

[42] Kate Macdonald and Shelley Marshall (eds), *Fair Trade, Corporate Accountability and Beyond: Experiments in Globalising Justice* (Ashgate 2010).

[43] K. Macdonald and S. Marshall, 'Transnational Business and the Politics of Social Risk: Re-Embedding Transnational Supply Chains Through Private Governance' in Bettina Lange, Fiona Haines, and Dania Thomas (eds), *Regulatory Transformations: Rethinking Economy-Society Interactions* (Hart Publishing 2015).

2.4.2.2 *Functional specialization*

One reason for geographic dispersion is regional specialization in production. Such specialization occurs across nations and internationally. In the case of some of the triangular garment production studied in the Bulgaria case, for example, design and textile production occurs in Italy, cutting occurs in Greece, and sewing occurs in Bulgaria. In relation to the production of iPhones, for example, Germany and Taiwan supply the advanced semiconductors, Korea and Japan supply the memory, Korea and Taiwan provide the display panels and circuitry, Europe provides the chipsets, and Africa and Asia supply the rare metals.[44] Specialization is often the result of national industrial policies (or lack thereof) or as businesses refine their competitive capacities.[45] One of the consequences of functional specialization is that the supply chain relationships, pressures and incentives faced by different parties vary. High levels of specialization mean that the technical knowledge required to effectively regulate work is far greater than would otherwise be the case.

2.4.2.3 *Separation of ownership and control*

The vertical disintegration of production has also resulted in the separation of control and ownership. Labour law has generally assumed the coupling of control and ownership. Although retailers and brands may no longer own the means of production, this does not mean that they have entirely relinquished control over the governance of value chains. Rather, control is shared with other parties.

2.4.2.4 *Asymmetries in information*

A consequence of the spatial diffusion of production, functional specialization and the separation of ownership and control is that the buyer is often unaware of the choices and conduct of its supplier, or of the true costs of production. The supplier is unaware of the amount paid to competitors or the amount that can reasonably be bargained for. Isolated workers such as home-based workers rely on contractors for information about the amount other workers receive and have little information about the nature of the supply chain they work within. States have difficulty tracking or comprehending the complexity of arrangements.[46]

2.4.2.5 *Responsiveness to international and national institutional arrangements*

Supply chain structures and governance respond to international and national institutional settings. They do not operate in a vacuum or only in accordance with market principles. Those with power in supply chains seek to gain competitive advantages from existing institutional arrangements, and also seek to change institutional arrangements to their advantage. As we shall see in later chapters, vertical disintegration and

[44] Kishanti Parella, 'Outsourcing Corporate Accountability' 89 Washington Law Review 747 759.
[45] D. Eric Boyd and others, 'Corporate Social Responsibility in Global Supply Chains: A Procedural Justice Perspective' 40 Long Range Planning 341 341.
[46] Ulrich Beck, 'Politics of Risk Society' in Jane Franklin (ed.), *The Politics of Risk Society* (Polity Press 1998): 15; ibid 590.

the increased use of home-based labour in the Australian apparel industry in the 1980s and 1990s was a response to Australia opening up to import penetration by reducing tariffs and non-tariff protections. Triangular subcontracting proliferated in Bulgaria in the 1990s in response to Europe Agreements which encouraged outsourcing to Central and Eastern European Countries. These arrangements benefitted Western European brands most, encouraging de-industrialization and specialization in 'outward processing trade' (OPT) in Bulgaria.

These five factors necessitate new regulatory strategies aimed at targeting diffuse, geographically disparate and shifting loci of control. Regulations need to:

- respond to the structural standing of different parties, depending on their place and functional role in the supply chain;
- recognize the separation of control and ownership;
- bridge asymmetries in information between parties; and
- address or respond to international and national institutional complexes.

2.4.3 Failure to respond to informal regulations and norms which shape incentives and behaviour

A further reason that labour regulations are failing to regulate a great deal of work is because they are neglecting to respond to the informal norms and regulations that shape the incentives and behaviour of regulatory targets.

Labour law is a special area of the law because it seeks to regulate the exercise of 'control' and 'subjugation' by an employer over an employee.[47] In this sense, it is concerned with the exercise of 'private regulation'[48] and asymmetries in power between labour and capital. Tests of control are used to determine the scope of regulation: whether the employer exercises sufficient control or whether the worker directs his or her own work and provides the tools of the trade.[49] In contrast, the relationships that occur within supply chains are understood by the law to be 'market based relationships'. The legal consequence is that special intervention to address issues of fairness or inequality of bargaining power is not seen to be required in most jurisdictions.

That there is little regulation of the exercise of private and informal regulation outside labour law is a consequence of the influence of classical economic traditions within most jurisdictions. This tradition views the freedom to contract as a fundamental liberal principle. The role of the law is seen to be to enforce the will of the parties, but

[47] Shelley Marshall, 'An Exploration of Control in the Context of Vertical Disintegration, and Regulatory Responses' in Chris Arup and others (eds), *Labour Law and Labour Market Regulation: Essays in the Construction, Constitution, and Regulation of Labour Markets and Work Relationships* (Federation Press 2006).

[48] In this section the terms 'private regulation' and 'bureaucratic control' are used in overlapping ways. The term 'private regulation' is preferred in the regulatory literature: Colin Scott, Fabrizio Cafaggi and Linda Senden, *The challenge of transnational private regulation: conceptual and constitutional debates* (Colin Scott, Fabrizio Cafaggi and Linda Senden eds, Wiley-Blackwell 2011). Private regulation covers norms or standards that are not legal in nature but which influence the behaviour of actors. Private regulation is sometimes confused with CSR, and indeed CSR is a form of corporate self-regulation or private regulation, but it is only one example.

[49] O. Kahn-Freund, 'Servants and Independent Contractors' 14 The Modern Law Review 504; Hugh Colins, 'Independent Contractors and the Challenge of Vertical Disintegration to Employment Protection Laws' 10 Oxford Journal of Legal Studies 353; International Labour Organisation, *Employment Relationship Recommendation* (2006); B. Creighton and A. Stewart, *Labour Law* (5th edn, Federation Press, Sydney 2010).

not to determine the terms upon which the bargain was set. In order to have a well-functioning market system, parties should be free to arrange agreements between each other, which they negotiate freely. This tradition juxtaposes 'the market' where parties bargain freely, and 'the firm' where bureaucratic power is wielded.

The problem with this basis for regulation is that 'market power' and 'bureaucratic power' or 'private regulation' do not function separately. The regulatory consequence is that if business relations occur outside the firm, where a subjugating employer is not readily evident, the powerful party is free of the constraints of labour law that require them to bargain in accordance with certain principles and adhere to various rules regarding payment and so forth.

It is axiomatic that in supply chain arrangements the lead business exercises a substantial degree of market power. What is not recognized in most legal systems, however, is that *market* power brings with it the capacity in the lead business to exercise the kind of *private* regulation which may be said to typically characterize relations between employers and employees.

Various factors increase dependence by suppliers on powerful players in supply chains. Where there is high market capture by particular players—lead firms[50]—this increases their market power, and in turn their private regulatory power. Where there is a growth in the number of suppliers, also, this generates a heightened competitive pressure for the entry and maintenance of supplier relations.[51] The desire to maintain a long-term relationship with a powerful player in a supply chain acts as an effective enforcement mechanism and regulatory incentive for compliance with the norms demanded by the lead firm. The ability of a lead business to keep or discard a supplier has a significant disciplining effect on suppliers which may allow lead businesses to specify a great deal of detail about the products they wish to buy from a supplier.

There are various reasons why it is beneficial for powerful, lead businesses to wield effective private regulation. Brands, retailers and agents are particularly concerned to ensure that they receive the number of units ordered, that the products meet the required quality standards and are supplied in the time required. That is, they are particularly concerned to ensure that they have control over outcomes.[52] Empirical work on inter-firm relations by Commodity Chain theorists suggests that authority relations are used to control outcomes in business between firms in order to reduce transaction costs and risks.[53] The more risks to which lead businesses are exposed as a result of potential supplier failures, the more they will directly intervene to coordinate and monitor the supply chain. Indeed, there are vast volumes of literature in the field of supply-chain management that provide advice about how to conduct coordination.[54]

[50] This section uses the terms 'lead firms', 'lead business', 'core firms' and 'powerful players' to denote parties with particularly high capacities to wield private regulatory power within supply chains. Supply chains have differing power structures. There may be numerous lead firms within the one network of production.

[51] Gary Gereffi, 'Global Commodity Chains: New Forms of Coordination and Control Among Nations and Firms in International Industries' 1 Competition and Change.

[52] R. Coase, *The Firm, the Market and the Law* (University of Chicago Press 1988); R.H. Coase, 'The Problem of Social Cost' 3 Journal of Law and Economics 1.

[53] Raphael Kaplinsky, 'Globalisation and Unequalisation: What Can Be Learned from Value Chain Analysis?' 37 Journal of Development Studies 117.

[54] See, for example, the large number of articles in the International Journal of Logistics Management and International Journal of Physical Distribution & Logistics Management. See, also, an early example of this type of article: Graham C. Stevens, (1989) 'Integrating the Supply Chain' 19 International Journal of Physical Distribution & Logistics Management 8 3–8.

Control over outcomes may be secured through a variety of mechanisms. Quality assurance is carried out once supplies reach the lead businesses, and pieces which do not meet the standards required will be rejected and, in general, not paid for. This provides a strong incentive for getting it right the first time. In addition to the threat of discarding the supplier, elaborate performance tests and penalties for poor performance are applied. Retailers may rate suppliers based on a number of key performance indicators which form the basis of decisions for ongoing contracts. In some industries, core firms give suppliers scorecards for their performance and annual awards are presented to the best suppliers. Penalties, in the form of fines may also be applied where suppliers are late or where the products do not meet the required standards.

Control over price is another important aspect of private supply chain regulation. Price is usually treated as a variable determined in the market. However, it is frequently the case that powerful businesses (particularly those competing more on price than, for example, product quality) insist that their suppliers meet certain prices per unit in order to maintain on-going contracts.

It follows, then, that in exercising extensive private and informal regulation over non-lead businesses, the lead business in supply chain arrangements must as a matter of logic, impact upon the employees of those non-lead businesses. But in what manner and to what degree do the lead businesses control employment and work systems in those non-core enterprises?

The nature of control over the employees of suppliers by lead businesses may be direct or indirect. Where a lead business intervenes in the work processes of a supplier, control over employee work systems is direct. Other aspects of control over supplier employees by lead businesses are less direct. Most of these aspects might be characterized as outcome-based control. Where the market power of a buyer means that they are able to determine the price of units, this will have a strong controlling effect on the remuneration of workers. However, this may not be entirely determinative of their remuneration. Suppliers/employers and other intermediaries still decide how much profit to take before paying workers.

The periodic and inconsistent nature of orders from lead businesses also has an indirect influence on the employment of supplier employees. This is related to the high levels of dependency of suppliers on lead businesses. If a buyer orders a large amount of units in a short amount of time, workers will have to work over-time and work at a fast rate to produce the specified units within the time demanded by the buyer. On the other hand, at times when the lead business has placed no orders because they have no requirement for the product or because they are sourcing from another supplier, workers will have no work to carry out.

The supplier must determine how to deal with the periodic and inconsistent nature of orders from lead businesses from an employment perspective. Most commonly, the supplier deals with the problem of inconsistency in orders by extending numerical flexibility. They may employ a small core (permanent) workforce and call upon a peripheral (casual/outworker) workforce at times when orders are heavy. Some suppliers also experiment with a shorter working year and other systems in order to deal with the periodic nature of orders. In any case, whilst suppliers may ultimately determine working hours and working arrangements, the broader conditions are set by the lead business because they determine the amount of units and the time that they must be produced within. The supplier must determine how to respond to these important parameters. However, the buyer's demands are strongly determinative of hours of work and security of work for workers.

The inconsistent nature of orders from lead businesses also has an indirect influence on occupational health and safety. Suppliers may provide the premises in which workers conduct production, thus determining the occupational, health, and safety standards under which the workers labour. Where suppliers respond to infrequent or inconsistent orders by using a peripheral workforce of informal workers, they may not provide workplaces. The workers may instead be expected to provide their own workplaces. This still has a considerable effect on the OHS standards that workers experience. A study comparing the OHS experience of factory-based workers and homeworkers in the clothing industry found that homeworkers suffered three times the level of injuries experienced by factory-based workers. The two main reasons for the differences in injury rates were the use of piecework payment system and the long hours worked by homeworkers.[55]

The extent to which the private and informal regulation is exercised over suppliers by lead businesses is determinative of employment and work systems will depend upon the specific relations between the lead business and the supplier. At the very least, where lead businesses have strong market power and are therefore able to exercise bureaucratic control, they set the parameters within which suppliers must make decisions over the management of workers. In some cases, that influence goes beyond determining the parameters and is direct. The lead business has a measure of bureaucratic control for the purpose of coordination over the entire workforce or productive entities.[56]

It can be said, therefore, that powerful parties in supply chains and suppliers often at least jointly determine the conditions of workers. However, labour regulation has generally failed to recognize this broad exercise of control or private and informal regulation beyond the direct employer-employee relationship. In most labour regulation schemas around the world, the brand, for instance, does not have an affirmative duty of care towards its supplier's workers because the brand and workers lack an employer-employee relationship and the brand's involvement in the supplier's operations likely does not meet the 'control' standard for joint-employer liability.[57] This means that its regulatory reach is limited—it is not able to respond to the core causes of worker vulnerability and precariousness. It is unable to respond to significant dynamics shaping the behaviour of regulatory targets. As we saw in the section on responsive regulation, compliance depends not only on rules or incentives specified in formal mechanisms, but also on the powers and motivations of social actors who may follow or resist them.[58] If labour regulation is unable to regulate the private and informal regulation wielded throughout supply chains, it is incapable of addressing the powers and motivations of the social actors that shape working conditions.

[55] Richard Johnstone, Claire Mayhew, and Michael Quinlan, 'Outsourcing Risk? The Regulation of Occupational Health and Safety Where Subcontractors are Employed' 22 Comparative Labor Law & Policy Journal 351; C. Mayhew and M. Quinlan, *Outsourcing and Occupational Health and Safety: A Comparative Study of Factory-Based and Outworkers in the Australian TCF Industry* (1998); M. Quinlan, C. Mayhew, and P. Bohle, 'The Global Expansion of Precarious Employment, Work Disorganization, and Consequences for Occupational Health: Placing the Debate in a Comparative Historical Context' 31 Int J Health Serv 507.

[56] Hugh Collins, 'Ascriptions of Legal Responsibility to Groups in Complex Patterns of Economic Integration' 53 Modern Law Review 731.

[57] Naima Farrell, 'Accountability for Outsourced Torts: Expanding Brands' Duty of Care for Workplace Harms Committed Abroad' 44 Georgetown Journal of International Law 1491 1508.

[58] Snider.

2.4.4 Failure to deploy responsive enforcement tools

Labour relations institutions have the potential to act reflexively and deploy responsive enforcement tools. However, by failing to negotiate and enforce agreed norms against the parties who have power in production arrangements, and by deploying a restricted range of penalties and incentives, such institutions are failing to act as responsively as their potential would suggest.

Labour relations institutions, which take the form of social dialogue institutions, labour tribunals, and so on, are reflexive institutions. They are highly responsive, networked forms of governance that bring together affected individuals, collectives, and their representatives to negotiate norms and rules. Industrial relations institutions such as tribunals are generally forums in which bargaining occurs over outcomes. Where an agreement cannot be reached, tribunal members make orders or determinations which take into account the arguments and views of the parties. Such forums not only take into account the interests and wishes of affected parties, they allow for on-going revision of rules. In this sense, industrial relations institutions avoid many of the failings levelled at 'command and control' rule setting and enforcement typical of state-based systems.[59]

Where such institutions fall short of responsiveness is by engaging a limited range of parties and deploying a limited range of penalties and incentives. The parties engaged by such industrial relations are generally employer organizations and trade unions. Sometimes other interested parties, such as other industry bodies, will also be invited to negotiations. Recognized parties tend to be those directly involved in the employment relationship. This means that other powerful parties such as brands, retailers, and agents, who the previous sections of this chapter have shown to shape work conditions, are excluded from negotiations and are omitted as regulatory targets.

Industrial relations institutions and regulators, such as state inspectorates, are limited to their national jurisdictions, resulting in a mismatch in scale.[60] Additionally, the monitoring techniques favoured by labour inspectorates and unions alike have difficulty locating and extending protections to workers outside medium and large sized factories. The consequence is that precariat, informal workers, such as home-based workers, rarely benefit from labour laws, the negotiated collective agreements of labour tribunals, or inspection efforts.

The types of penalties exacted by such institutions are also limited in their responsiveness to the private regulatory pressures faced by parties that shape work conditions. The typical penalty issued by industrial relations institutions is a fine. However, for a large and powerful transnational business, a fine may not act as a strong disincentive due to the small size of the fine in relation to overall company assets and income. For medium and small-sized businesses who supply a large brand, and whose future depends on securing contracts with buyers, paying a fine may be less detrimental in economic terms than losing the work of a large buyer. There is a growing body of evidence that shows that, as rule takers, small and medium suppliers are being forced to bear

[59] S. Cooney, J. Howe, and J. Murray, 'Time and Money under Workchoices: Understanding the New Workplace Relations Act as a Scheme of Regulation' 29 University of New South Wales Law Journal 215; John Howe, '"Deregulation" of Labour Relations in Australia: Towards a More "Centered" Command and Control Model' in C. Arup et al. (ed.), *Labour Law and Labour Market Regulation: Essays in the Construction, Constitution, and Regulation of Labour Markets and Work Relationships* (Federation Press 2006).

[60] Charles Sabel, Dara O'Rourke and Archon Fung, *Ratcheting Labor Standards: Regulation for Continuous Improvement in the Global Workplace* (Columbia Law School of Public Law & Legal Theory Research 2000) 13.

the cost of ethical supply chain requirements.[61] This indicates a need to find more effective incentive setting and enforcement tools. The uneven distribution of risk and the particular interests of different parties throughout the supply chain suggests that enforcement tools should be more alive to the structural place of parties in supply chains.

One of the goals of this study is to find new, more powerful penalties and incentives. The case studies have been selected for their use of novel penalties and incentives, including market-based inducements, such as labelling and other methods of influencing the behaviour of regulatory targets. The final substantive chapter of this study (Chapter 9) brings these finding to fruition in a novel regulatory scheme.

2.5 Labour Regulation and the Dynamics of Institutional Change

Because of the problems with labour regulation identified in the previous section of this chapter, wide agreement over the need to reform the personal scope of the application of labour law has emerged at a national and supranational level.[62] In June 2006 the International Labour Organisation released a Recommendation on the Employment Relationship, R-198, and the European Commission released, in November 2006, its Green Paper called 'Modernising Labour Law to Meet the Challenges of the 21st Century'.[63] A number of important and influential volumes have come out in recent years which propose new models of labour law. These include most notably Alain Supiot's 2001 edited volume 'Beyond Employment. Changes in Work and the Future of Labour Law in Europe'[64] or what has become widely known as 'The Supiot Report' and 'Boundaries and Frontiers of Labour Law' edited by Davidov and Langille.[65] These and other intelligent and sound models for broad labour law reform to provide protection for dependent, semi-dependent, and non-waged types of work are now circulating and being debated.

Great ideas are only the beginning of any law reform process, however. A significant question driving this book is how institutional change can occur in the area of labour regulation. What drives change? Each of the case study chapters are concerned with exploring this question. This book understands change to be a *dynamic process* in which agents of social change struggle for reform within shifting political and economic conditions. Informalization (the process by which work becomes informal) and formalization (the process by which work becomes formal) are dynamic processes.

The puzzle of how institutional change occurs has absorbed regulatory and institutional theorists for some time. This book draws on various literatures to describe the way that purposeful institutional change occurs. One body of work is that generated by Kathleen Thelen to understand patterns of institutional change.[66] Thelen, with others,

[61] Jette Knudsen, 'The Growth of Private Regulation of Labor Standards in Global Supply Chains: Mission Impossible for Western Small- and Medium-Sized Firms?' (2013) [2013] 117 Journal of Business Ethics 387.

[62] Nicola Countouris, 'Book Review of 'Boundaries and Frontiers of Labour Law'' [Oxford University Press / USA] 36 Industrial Law Journal 250.

[63] European Commission, *Modernising Labour Law to Meet the Challenges of the 21st Century* (2006).

[64] Supiot, Meadows, and European Commission (Oxford University Press).

[65] Davidov and Langille Countouris (2006 Hart Publishing).

[66] Peter A. Hall and Kathleen Thelen, 'Institutional Change in Varieties of Capitalism' (2007) [Socio-Economic Review]; J. Mahoney and K. Thelen, 'A Theory of Gradual Institutional Change' in J. Mahoney and K. Thelen (eds), *Explaining Institutional Change: Ambiguity, Agency and Power* (Cambridge University Press 2010); Wolfgang Streeck and Kathleen Thelen, 'Introduction: Institutional

has identified five main methods of institutional change: layering; displacement; drift; conversion; and exhaustion. The concepts of layering and displacement, in particular, are used to describe the methods of institutional change seen in the case studies. For Mahoney and Thelen, layering occurs when new rules are attached to existing ones, thereby changing the ways in which the original rules structure behaviour.[67] The Australian and Cambodian regulatory innovations studied are examples of layering. Displacement occurs when existing rules are replaced by new ones. Often, displacement occurs when there is a revolution or regime change.[68] The Mathadi boards examined in Chapter 4, for instance, were developed in the wake of Indian independence and with the threat of communism looming. It was a time of social disruption and the end of the British colonial regime. This social turmoil allowed a group of workers to mobilise for a new system of labour regulation which displaced the existing system (though its coverage was limited to this particular population of head-load workers).

Because, in each of the case studies, institutional change—the formalization of work, entailing the reform or labour institutions and/or the creation of new institutions—has occurred following significant mobilization efforts on behalf of particular social agents, insights into the way that social mobilization and influence occurs is drawn from the social change and transnational mobilization literature. In more complex and dynamic processes of social change, actions and interactions between actors intersect, such that the actions and strategies of any given actor will shift the power resources available to other actors. This interactive quality of patterns of social action and effect, combined with the complex, path dependent and often unpredictable currents of complex social processes, can lead many forms of influence to be highly indirect, and difficult to tightly control or predict. Analysing influence thus requires that we take account of path dependent and structural patterns of causality beyond the direct intention or control of individual actors.

2.6 Conclusion

In her seminal work on the topic, Sassen wrote that the informal economy's 'expansion invites us to focus on the broader fact of a growing set of problems in the relationship between new economic trends and old regulatory frameworks'.[69] The conceptual framework set up in this chapter shows that the process of informalization is dynamic with multiple causes at different levels—global, regional, national, local, and individual. We need to understand these complex dynamics and causes of informality in order to design effective and responsive regulation. This chapter has addressed some of the broad—cross-case—causes of informality related to changes in the nature of production and the inertia surrounding the reform of labour regulation. More specific

Change in Advanced Political Economies' in Wolfgang Streeck and Kathleen Thelen (eds), *Beyond Continuity: Institutional Change in Advanced Political Economies* (Oxford University Press 2005); Kathleen Thelen, 'Historical Institutionalism in Comparative Politics' 2 Annual Review of Political Science 369; Kathleen Thelen, 'How Institutions Evolve: Insights from Comparative-Historical Analysis' in J. Mahoney and D. Rueschemeyer (eds), *Historical Analysis in the Social Sciences* (Cambridge University 2003); Kathleen Thelen, 'Institutions and Social Change' in I. Shapiro and S. Skowronek (eds), *In Crafting and Operating Institutions* (New York University Press 2006).

[67] Mahoney and Thelen 16.

[68] Ruth Collier and D Collier, *Shaping the political arena* (Princeton University Press 1991).

[69] Saskia Sassen, 'The Informal Economy: Between New Developments and Old Regulations' [1994] 103 Symposium: The Informal Economy 2289.

dynamics are explored in the case-study chapters. The aim of the case studies is to build contextually specific stories of why work became informal and why the precariat grew in number. This analysis is followed, in each case, by tracking how the reform of labour regulation occurred. Each case-study chapter follows the dynamic process by which agents of change formed networks to influence the shape of the key institutions regulating work.

3

New Approaches to the Study of the Regulation of Work

3.1 Introduction

This book attempts to implement a novel approach to the study of the regulation of work in order to generate new insights into the ways that regulation can help to improve the lives of workers.

In broad terms, the book addresses the following five questions:

1. What is the same and what is different about the dynamics of informalization in different countries/settings?
2. What regulatory strategies have been implemented to address informality in each case study?
3. What has worked/has not worked? How much have the regulations addressed the dynamics identified?
4. What does this tell us about regulatory strategies for formalization?
5. How can we provide local pathways out of informal work and global strategies for addressing the causes of precariousness and informality?

In order to answer these rather big questions, the book widens the scope of its inquiry well beyond those normally found in labour law scholarship. It uses historical institutionalism and political economy approaches to build a comprehensive picture of the varied dynamics that contributed to the growth of a precarious, informal workforce in four very different countries. It draws on rich case studies informed by often quite lengthy, semi-structured interviews in which workers, labour users, worker representatives, and policy makers described the forms and conditions under which work occurred, shared their understanding of why these forms had proliferated, and their views about the extent to which regulatory experiments were helping. Interviewees were extremely generous with their time and expertise, providing insights that the author could not have generated on her own.

The end purpose of the study is to put together a novel regulatory approach to low wages, precariousness, and informality. The framework for this responsive approach was described in Chapter 2. This restricts the scope of the book. The aim is not to design exhaustive policy approaches addressing precariousness and informality, but just to focus on regulatory responses. For instance, the book is not concerned with designing new approaches to governance that might include policies for material provision or distribution.[1] It is limited to mechanisms that steer 'the flow of events and behavior',[2] acknowledging that when regulators regulate, they often steer the providing

[1] J. Braithwaite, C. Coglianese and D. Levi-Faur, 'Can Regulation and Governance Make a Difference?' 1 Regulation and Governance 1 3.
[2] Ibid. 3.

Living Wage: Regulatory Solutions to Informal and Precarious Work in Global Supply Chains. Shelley Marshall. Published 2019 by Oxford University Press.

and distributing that regulated actors undertake as well. This is certainly a large limitation on the study, since it may be the case that providing social security to all citizens regardless of employment status may be the most effective strategy for improving the lives of workers. Despite these limitations, the study of ways that behaviour can be steered and changed by regulation remains crucially important.

This book develops new models for the regulation of work of two types. The first type is those that can be instituted to improve workers' lives in the short-term. The second type is a more ambitious, longer term vision for regulating work at international and national levels, orchestrated by the International Labour Organisation. Both are informed by case studies which examine the development of novel forms of regulation of work, aimed at re-regulating informal work. This chapter describes the methods used in conducting these case studies.

This chapter is structured as follows: the first section describes the overarching case-study methodology. The second section describes the primary approach deployed in the case studies: historical institutionalism. The third section describes additional methods and disciplines used to put together stories that span macro and micro scales.

3.2 Case-Study Methodology

Four case studies form the meat of this book. A case-study method was deployed across four countries, examining different populations of precarious and informal workers and innovative regulatory schemes. There are three attributes of case-study research that make it attractive as a method answering some of the key questions the book hopes to illuminate:[3]

1. It allows for the gathering of rich, detailed data in an authentic setting.
2. It is holistic and thus supports the idea that much of what we can know about human behaviour is best understood as lived experience in the social context.
3. Unlike experimental research, it can be done without predetermined hypotheses, and goals.

This methodology is particularly useful for conducting detailed studies of the dynamics of informalization in different countries/settings, as, used within an interpretive framework, 'researchers do not seek to find universals in their case studies. They seek, instead, a full, rich understanding (verstehen) of the context they are studying'.[4] The approach is inductive and heuristic, and involves thick descriptive data. Those employing this method commonly rely on inductive reasoning '[to] illuminate the reader's understanding of the phenomenon under study'.[5]

Stake[6] differentiates between three types of case study: the intrinsic; the instrumental; and the multiple or collective. Each of the case studies in this book might be described as instrumental because the intention is not to focus on the individuals involved, but on the insights into an issue they raise, the possibilities for generalization, and the identification of improved practice in the regulation of informal workers. The combination of the four case studies can be viewed as a multiple or collective

[3] J. W. Willis, *Foundations of Qualitative Research: Interpretive and Critical Approaches* (Sage 2007) 240.

[4] Ibid. 240. [5] Ibid. 239.

[6] Robert E. Stake, 'Qualitative Case Studies' in Norman K. Denzin and Yvonna S. Lincoln (eds), *The Sage Handbook of Qualitative Research* (3rd edn, Sage 2005).

instrumental case study because it is hoped that this will lead to 'better understanding, and perhaps better theorizing, about a still larger collection of cases'.[7]

3.2.1 Case-study selection

The cases in this study were chosen primarily because of the innovative regulatory measures developed in each country for the regulation of work. In other words, the case studies were chosen for theoretical and not statistical reasons.[8] Such a selection method can be contrasted with traditional within-experiment hypothesis-testing studies that rely on statistical sampling, in which researchers randomly select the sample from a population. In this type of study, the goal of the sampling process is to obtain accurate statistical evidence on the distributions of variables within the population. Here, instead, case studies have been chosen so as to allow for the comparison of different regulatory responses. Each regulatory scheme provides a different model for regulating informal labour, with varying levels of success providing opportunities to study what works, what doesn't work, and why. This approach accepts that there may be a certain level of incommensurability between the case studies, but the value of observing the operation of different methods of regulating work was privileged over the benefits of commensurability.

The focus of the comparative study is on the different methods that regulatory agents deployed to address the unresponsiveness of traditional methods of state-based labour regulation to the forms of informal labour found in each country. The initiatives studied have in common that they (a) expand or sidestep the employment relationship so as to encompass broader forms of work (with the exception of the Cambodian initiative); and (b) increase the strength of regulation in order to push against countervailing pressures which lower working conditions. In other words, each *added to* or *augmented* traditional labour laws. Each is a type of co-regulation, entailing the combining of two or more regulatory systems. This has been achieved in different ways and to different extents in each country, lending to a fruitful comparative study.

Each of the regulatory innovations takes place in vastly different settings. Divergences between the cases allow different causes of informality to be observed across diverse types of economies and governmental structures. Australia is an advanced liberal market economy, Bulgaria and Cambodia are transitioning from socialism to capitalism, and India is a liberalizing middle-income country with a very poor population. The countries also have differing legal traditions. India and Australia each have common law legal traditions, whereas Bulgaria and Cambodia have socialist/civil law traditions. The periods of growth in informal work also differ across the cases. Bulgaria had an active black or shadow market (or an informal economy of types) prior to the transition to capitalism in the late 1980s, but full, formal employment. In Australia, informality has grown markedly over the last thirty or so years. India and Cambodia have longer and more persistent traditions of informal work. These differences provide opportunities for understanding the dynamics of informality in contrasting settings (see Table 3.1). The inclusion of Australia, for instance, allows for the comparison of informal work in a developed economy context compared with poorer country contexts. Research on informal work is most extensive in developing regions where informal employment

[7] Ibid.

[8] Kathleen Eisenhardt, 'Building Theories from Case Study Research' in A.M. Huberman and M. B. Miles (eds), *The Qualitative Researcher's Companion* (Sage 2002) 12.

Table 3.1: Differences in case-study settings

	Bulgaria	India	Australia	Cambodia
Economic development	Transitional	Developing	Advanced	Poor and transitional
Law	Civil	Common	Common	Civil
Region	Europe	Asia	Australasia	Asia
Labour law coverage	Extended to homeworkers	Limited coverage	Extended to homeworkers in apparel industry	Limited coverage
Nature of labour law extension	Expansion	Displacement	Expansion, Complementary layering, Networked regulation.	Complementary layering, Networked regulation, Rivalry.
Development of innovative regulation	Embryonic	Advanced	Maturing	Advanced

itself is most extensive. The inclusion of Australia seeks to fill a gap in the literature on informality.

Within-case analysis is conducted in separate chapters. Each case-study chapter follows a similar structure: the first part of each chapter examines the causes of informality, employing a historical institutionalist approach described in the next section of this chapter. Possible causal mechanisms are treated as competing narratives. The second part of each case study then describes the process of mobilization and social change that lead to the enactment of institutional innovation. An assessment of the responsiveness of these advances, based on the conceptual framework provided in the previous chapter, is then carried out.

Cross-case analysis is conducted in the final chapters. Here, the emphasis is on examining the dynamics of regulatory change and comparing how innovative methods of regulating work were developed.

3.3 Primary Case-Study Approach: Historical Institutionalism

Precarious and informal work is understood by many to proliferate under conditions of regulatory or institutional failure of some type. This book, in contrast, understands precarious and informal work to be produced by particularly institutional interactions. To get to the bottom of this, the study of institutions is a vital.

This book employs a historical institutionalist approach to studying changes in the *context* in which labour regulations operate, changes to *labour regulation* itself, and changes in the *nature of work* in each case study country. Historical institutionalism was selected as the primary method for the empirical study presented in this book as it pays attention to the ways in which institutions structure and shape political behaviour and outcomes over time. It is a way of exploring the causal mechanisms behind observed empirical patterns.[9] We know, empirically speaking, that

[9] K. Thelen, 'Historical Institutionalism in Comparative Politics' (1999) 2 Annual Review of Political Science 369 372.

the incidence of informal work has increased in a number of parts of the world over the past two decades. (The data was summarized in Chapter 1.) This approach provides a way to explore what has caused this increase. Each case study examines the contextual features that were relevant to the expansion of informality. Various dynamics—either social or economic—that may have contributed to the growth of the precariat are teased out. This approach seeks to provide *hermeneutic* understanding of informality. Why do actors behave as they do in relation to systems of governance? It also seeks a causal explanation: what social, economic, and political processes contributed to informality?

The approach is particularly useful, also, for studying the implementation of regulatory experiments to improve the conditions under which work occurs and reduce informality. Why have such different initiatives been developed in different countries, despite the institutional similarities in labour laws around the world? Historical institutionalists do not accept that history necessarily develops in a straightforward, linear fashion. Instead, they examine the conditions under which a particular trajectory was followed and not others. For historical institutionalists, political events happen within a historical context, which has a direct consequence on decisions or events:[10]

> Historical institutionalists understand that behaviour, attitudes and strategic choices take place inside particular social, political, economic and even cultural contexts. Rather than treating all political action as if it is fundamentally the same irrespective of time, place or context, historical institutionalists explicitly and intentionally attempt to situate their variables in the appropriate context. Thus, by deepening and enriching their understanding of the historical moment and the actors within it, they are able to offer more accurate explanations for the specific events that they explore than had they treated their variables outside the temporal dimension.

What cascading and cumulative set of actions and decisions contributed to the particular forms of the experiments described in the case-study chapters? Acknowledging the importance of history suggests an explicit awareness that important variables can and often do shape one another. Historical institutionalists, more than political scientists in some other traditions, are explicitly interested in these interactive effects: on the interdependence of multiple causal variables.[11] It is for this reason that the case studies examine the interaction and compounding nature of various factors to explain informality and subsequent reforms to labour regulation. Regrettably, the accounts in the case studies can sometimes seem choppy, as they seek to provide narratives of the unfolding and impact of seemingly unrelated events. This choppiness is a consequence of avoiding a functionalist account of institutional change. As Kathleen Thelen, one of the foremost contemporary proponents of historical institutionalism acknowledges, 'the various pieces do not necessarily fit together into a coherent, self-reinforcing, let alone functional, whole'.[12]

The case studies do not solely provide accounts of the history of labour laws or labour policies. They provide a broad account of the factors that have put pressure on or changed the nature of the labour market. This is because 'change comes from the interactions of different institutional orders within a society'.[13] For instance, the mass labour shedding in Bulgaria explored in Chapter 6 that left workers stranded in informal work was partly a result of its economic dependence on the USSR and the specialization of production required under the rules of the Council for Mutual Economic

[10] S. Steinmo, 'What is Historical Institutionalism' in D. Della Porta and M. Keating (eds), *Approaches to the Social Sciences* (Cambridge University Press 2008).

[11] Ibid. [12] Thelen, 'Historical Institutionalism in Comparative Politics' 382.

[13] Ibid. 383.

Assistance prior to the transition to capitalism. This dependence and specialization set the country up particularly badly for integration into world markets where there was little demand for Bulgaria's products. Later, the rules of the Europe Agreements encouraged concentration in outward processing that led to further specialization in lower value-added economic activities where informal labour could flourish. The interaction of the Council for Mutual Economic Assistance and, later, the Europe Agreements with existing labour market institutions are vitally important to the story of the growth of informal work in Bulgaria. Because the case studies are primarily concerned with the interaction of institutions and factors—with their dynamic relationship—they do not attempt to place a value on the importance of each factor. The point is not to fix a single decisive factor. Change in one arena affects other ongoing processes, which is what drives institutional evolution.[14] Institutions interact in self-reinforcing feedback[15] that produce different effects.

The factors that are examined in each case occur on different *scales*. The cases track processes at the domestic level, the regional level, and the international as they unfold in relation to one another. Taking up the Bulgarian example again, domestic institutional changes such as the privatization of state-owned corporations were undertaken after they had occurred in other countries in the region. Thus, the selling off of state-owned companies to international bidders in Bulgaria occurred after the finite supply of foreign investment had already been largely absorbed by earlier privatizers, closer to Western European markets. This put in train a set of events whereby newly privatized companies lacked the capital to allow them to adapt to new circumstances, leading to the mass failure and folding of these major employers. Workers were left without any alternative except informal work. In this example, the regional scale of the transition to capitalism interacts with domestic political decisions, which in turn impact on the micro context of company-level employment relations. Each case study examines the compounding impact of institutional changes at different points and scales.

Scale and *temporality* interact in each story.[16] The accounts are not just interested in 'what' but also 'when'.[17] The mobilization of Mathadi (head-load) workers in the Indian case study (Chapter 4) provides a further example of the importance of timing. This group of workers mobilized shortly after independence when the anti-Brahmin movement had the greatest purchase. The workers hailed primarily from western Maharashtra and claimed Maratha warrior heritage. The power of their demand for specialist labour regulation was bolstered by the 'Maratha-ization' and anti-Brahminization of the ruling Congress Party in the Indian state of Maharashtra. Had their mobilization occurred earlier or later, their demands would likely not have enjoyed the same political leverage. The timing and sequence of events shape political processes.[18] It is for this reason that each case study attempts to provide a sequential story of the unfolding of events that shape informality and subsequent regulatory innovations.

[14] Ibid. 383.

[15] S. Krasner, 'Sovereignty: An Institutional Perspective' (1998) 21 Comparative Political Studies 66 83.

[16] Kathleen Thelen and Wolfgang Streeck (eds), *Beyond Continuity: Institutional Change in Advanced Political Economies* (Oxford University Press 2005).

[17] Kathleen Thelen, 'Timing and Temporality in the Analysis of Institutional Evolution and Change' 14 Studies in American Political Development 102.

[18] Orfeo Fioretos, 'Historical Institutionalism in International Relations' (2011) 65 International Organization 367 371.

Timing shapes the calculations and constraints of political actors. Fioretos offers that:[19]

> The calculations of political actors (for example, their understanding of their stakes in the current setting), and the nature of the constraints under which they operate (for example, some options may not really exist due to the sequence of prior events) may change significantly over time.

The political period in which the Mathadi mobilization occurred explains a great deal about why this group of workers did not call for the expansion of the scope of existing labour laws in the same manner as demanded by Bulgarian home-based workers or Australian industrial outworkers. The mobilization of Mathadi workers occurred some thirty years before the ILO's Homework Convention (C177), for instance, which recommended the expansion of the scope of labour law. In some ways the demand for a separate system of labour regulation is more audacious, reflecting the emboldening of Mathadi workers by the courting of political parties. Situating the choices made by the workers and their supporters examined in each case study in their broader historical context provides a richer understanding of institutional change.

Each case study throws a wide analytical net in the hope of gathering a broad range of factors causing informality. Regardless of this wide net, there is no doubt that the accounts are far from comprehensive. Putting aside this unavoidable limitation, it is hoped that the adoption of historical institutionalism has allowed for original accounts to be assembled in each case.

3.4 Other Disciplines and Methods

The historical institutionalist approach is just that, an approach rather than a method. Thus, this book draws on other methods to study the evolution of informality and the development of new initiatives for regulating work. Why is this helpful? If we accept that diverse variables shape one another, then we need a way to study or understand variables that have different forms and characters. Take economic causes for instance. Although economic factors are often treated as if they are disembedded from social causes, we know the economic is actually social. This is particularly easy to observe in the operation of labour markets, though it is equally true of the operation of any market. Labour markets are *social institutions*: social structures impact both economic outcome and efficiency of transactions.[20]

Various non-economic factors influence the behaviour of workers in labour markets, and thus the labour market as a whole. In the context of agricultural India, for example, where work is often a non-commodified aspect of family life, social structures, into which workers are integrated, affect their choices.[21] Particular castes specialize in doing certain work. Caste and other markers of social identification and categorization are especially evident in the Indian case study in this book. In this context, we can readily see that work opportunities and decisions are determined by family, caste, village, religion, outlook, and not simply those factors accounted for in the field of economics. The same is no less true of other societies, and as a consequence, we need ways to understand the interaction of different factors that shape the labour market.

[19] Ibid. 371.

[20] B. Uzzi, 'Social Structure and Competition in Interfirm Networks: The Paradox of Embeddedness' 42 Administrative Science Quarterly 35 37.

[21] S. C. Dube, *Indian Village* (Cornell University Press 1955).

So as to better understand those specific factors, the nature of work, and thus informality, this book draws on different disciplines. Various approaches, literatures and methods are mined in the course of each case study to attempt to better explain the causes of informality.

3.4.1 Political economy

One approach is drawn from political economy. Political economy is in itself multi-disciplinary. It pulls from the fields of economics, law, and political science to explain how political institutions, the political environment, and the economic system influence each other. In the course of the case studies, economic and political narrative histories are delved into to explain why economies and systems of governance and regulation have evolved in particular ways.[22]

Each case study moves from describing national development to narratives of individual and community experiences of informality. Political economy approaches are useful for constructing the 'larger picture', and for *situating* individual experience, but not for telling individual stories and exploring individual's experience of work, business and regulation. For this, ethnographic methods are employed. Interviews, observations, and the collection of data from secondary sources were all employed for the case studies in this book.[23]

3.4.2 Ethnography

The studies employ ethnographic methods to study the phenomenon of informality amongst specific populations. Ideas about what ethnography is have developed in recent years. Although sociologists once defined ethnography as the direct observation of the activity of members of a particular social group—normally by anthropologists—and the description and evaluation of such activity, this definition has evolved over time.[24] A more recent definition is:

> an umbrella term for fieldwork, interviewing and other means of gathering data in authentic (e.g. real world) environments ... [that] puts the researcher in the setting that he or she wants to study. The research is conducted in the natural environment rather than in an artificially contrived setting.[25]

Because the case studies conducted in this book were in four countries, a great deal of travel was required to conduct field work.

The type of ethnography conducted in this book is what might be called 'analytic ethnography'. An investigator: (a) attempts to provide generic propositional answers to questions about social life and organization, (b) strives to pursue such in a spirit of unfettered or naturalistic inquiry, (c) utilizes data based on familiarity with a social setting or situation that is gained by personal participation or an approximation of it, (d) strives to present data and analysis that are true, (e) seeks to provide data and analysis that are new; and (f) presents an analysis that is developed in the sense of being conceptually elaborated, descriptively detailed, and concept-data interpenetrated.[26]

[22] Andrew Abbott, *Time Matters: On Theory And Method* (University of Chicago Press 2001).

[23] Eisenhardt 13.

[24] N. Abercrombie, S. Hill, and B. S. Turner, *Penguin Dictionary of Sociology*, 4th vol (Penguin 2000).

[25] Willis 237.

[26] John Lofland, 'Analytic Ethnography: Features, Failings, and Futures' in A.M. Huberman and M. B. Miles (eds), *The Qualitative Research Companion* (Sage 2002) 137–8.

The primary method of ethnographic research utilized was the interviewing of informal workers, organizers of workers, business managers, bureaucrats, politicians, and others about their experience of informal work, their interaction with regulatory systems, and their ideas about how things could or had changed. Altogether, around 140 interviews were conducted across the cases. (A list of interviews can be accessed by request to the author.) The style of interviewing used approximated narrative interviewing. The interview questions were 'semi-structured'. The aim was to cover a certain number of standard questions across each case, but also to allow flexibility for tangents and follow up questions as personal stories unfolded. In the Australian case study, questions were particularly standardized due to the similarity in work conducted across workers. An appendix is attached to the Australian chapter which reports the standard questions.

Most interviews took between one and one and a half hours and were conducted with an individual respondent, assisted by an interpreter. Sometimes, however, interviews were with a family or conducted in groups.

Most interviews were recorded, with the permission of the respondent. In some cases, however, respondents requested that no recording be made, or it was judged that the respondent was too nervous to record or that it might hinder the interview in some way. Interview transcripts were then transcribed by professional transcribers or by the author. Notes were taken during each interview, which have been retained.

Kohler Riessman describes narrative interviewing as having the following distinctive features:[27]

> Participants engage in an evolving conversation; narrator and listener/questioner, collaboratively produce and make meaning of events that the narrator reports ... The 'facilitating' interviewer and the vessel-like 'respondent' are replaced by two active participants who jointly produce meaning. Narrative interviewing has more in common with contemporary ethnography than with mainstream political science interviewing practice that relies on discrete, open-ended and/or fixed-response questions.

Kohler recommends this method because participants will not always devolve the full story upon initial questioning. They may require further prompting and following up. They may also require time for a full story to unfold:[28]

> Some investigators, after introductions, invite participants to 'tell your story' – how an illness began, for example. But experience always exceeds its description and narrativization; events may be fleetingly summarized and given little significance. Only with further questioning can participants recall the details, turning points and other shifts in cognition, emotion and action.

In addition to interviews, I also spent time observing work and in less formal conversation with respondents. In the course of my study of Bulgarian informal workers, for instance, I spent many hours with the workers, sometimes one-on-one, sometimes in groups. The most interesting conversations occurred outside the formal interview process, often when family members or friends who were interviewed in a group were arguing about answers earlier provided or insisting that one or the other tell me more about what really happened in their life.

In all of the cases, the role of the interpreters was crucial. I sat next to the interpreter across from the interviewee. Interpreters were needed for the field work conducted in each country, including Australia. I asked a question, the interpreter translated this

[27] C. Kohler Reissman, 'Narrative Interviewing' in V. Jupp (ed.), *The Sage Dictionary of Social Research Methods* (Sage 2006) 189–90.

[28] Ibid. 190.

question for the interviewee, and would then translate after each phrase spoken by the interviewee so I had a chance to interrupt and ask for clarification as the answer to the question unfolded. As the interview progressed, a rhythm would develop with the interviewee learning to pause after short bursts of speak to allow for verbal translation.

Trust-building with interviewees depended greatly on the skills and personality of the interpreter. In Bulgaria, one interpreter began aggressively challenging the participant about their answers and their attitude and a new interpreter had to be found. Though the attitude of the interpreter harmed the relationship with the interviewee, it also provided insights into debates and points of conflict about informal work in Bulgaria. Also in Bulgaria, one of the leaders of a homeworker association became resentful about the amount I was paying the interpreter compared with the low wages she received for the piece work she conducted at home. We had long conversations about the ethics of not paying the interpreter legal wages, regardless of the pay inequity that resulted between the interpreter and the interviewees, again providing insights into the nature of inequality and the social fragmentation caused when some people are employed formally and others are not.

Often, interviews with home-based workers had to be conducted while the participants continued to work, as they could not spare time away from the order in front of them. This provided an opportunity to observe the conditions under which work was conducted and discuss the challenges entailed by sewing or constructing a particular item. It also allowed me to validate claims made by the workers and their representatives about the nature of work, size of the orders, nature of the paperwork, brands being made, and so on. Where work was conducted with family members, interviews were conducted with multiple workers at once.

In addition to these interviews, focus groups were at times arranged out with groups of workers or other categories of interviewees. In India, for example, a round table of labour academics was put brought together by an intermediary. In Bulgaria, in 2004, days were spent with the main organizers of the homeworker association in Petrich, mapping supply chains and the geography of home-based work in the region.

Non-participant observation was also a significant method used. In Bulgaria, I observed the work of Jane Tate of Homenet while she trained the Petrich group in mapping and organizing techniques. In India, I observed a two-day conference of labour and employer representatives in Mumbai as they debated the laws governing contractors and the threat entailed in the increasing prevalence of outsourcing from India to regional countries. In Australia, participant observation has been conducted over a period of twenty years entailing attending FairWear meetings, court cases, speaking at Senate Enquiries, and so on. Individual instances of participant observation are only noted when they are directly relevant. Otherwise, they provide the background to the analysis in each case.

The ethnographic methods used in each case study do not exactly mirror each other. Opportunities for interviewing key respondents depended a great deal on the connections of intermediaries who helped organize interviews in each case. Intermediaries in Bulgaria had vast political and business connections, leading to a greater number of interviews with participants of this type. The period of mobilization of Mathadi workers in India was the 1960s. Most potential respondents that had been active in that mobilization had passed away by the time I conducted my empirical research. The number of interviewees for the Indian case study who were directly involved in institutional change is therefore lower than the other case studies. Opportunities for non-participant and participant observation were far greater in Australia, where I have mainly resided over the period of research, than for other countries. In all cases, secondary sources were mined extensively to make up for gaps in primary ethnographic methods.

At some point, one has to drag oneself away from the fun and adventure of field work and undertake the hard work of analysis and thinking about what one has seen and heard. Field work for this book concluded in 2014 and thus there are likely developments which have not been noted in the case-study chapters. The dates that field work was conducted are noted at the start of the case study chapter. Analysis of other legal developments around the world which form the basis of the proposal in Chapter 9 continued until late 2017.

3.5 Conclusion

Often, legal analysis is limited to the study of black letter law with some accommodation for the influence of 'culture' or 'politics' for the form of a law or its implementation, though legal scholars struggle to find a way to analyse these 'influences'. More recently, legal scholarship has been influenced by 'regulatory studies' which has encouraged the widening of the scope of study. This book hopes to show how the regulatory turn in the study of legal institutions can become more richly historically and politically informed so as to better describe how institutions are produced, and how they in turn produce the form in which societal interactions occur. Work can be understood as the carrying out of tasks entailing the expenditure of mental and physical effort with the objective of producing goods and services. Work can also be understood as a form of social interaction undertaken within social relations, normative codes, and organizational structures or institutions that inform the behaviour, experience, and identities of people during the course of their working lives. How we understand why work is more or less precarious, more or less informal, depends on social relations, normative codes, and institutions. And these, in turn, evolve over time. This chapter is titled 'New Approaches to the Study of the Regulation of Work', but it might equally have been called 'Not Forgetting Old Approaches to the Study of the Production of Forms of Work', though this would have been a clunky title. The book draws on the rich traditions within the sociology of work[29] and 'old institutionalism'[30] to assemble methods for studying the dynamics of informalization and formalization.

The combination of methods used in the case studies allows for the assemblage of rich analyses of changes in the context in which labour regulations operate, changes to labour regulation itself, and changes in the nature of work. The cases selected afford the study of four different schemes for the regulation of work in vastly different socio-political settings. The historical institutionalist approach offers a way to examine the particular trajectories of reform pursued and the ways each scheme are a consequence of their particular contexts. The case studies track the interaction and compounding (though often in contradictory or conflicting ways) nature of factors at different scales and historical moments. By deepening and enriching our understanding of how and why informal work expanded, the case-study chapters are better able to assess the responsiveness of the labour regulation initiatives developed. The ethnographic methods used—including interviews, focus groups and participant and non-participant

[29] Stephen Edgell, Heidi Gottfried, and Edward Granter, *The Sage Handbook of Sociology of Work and Employment* (SAGE Publications Ltd 2016).

[30] John Harriss, *Institutions, Politics and Culture: A Case for 'Old' Institutionalism and the Study of Historical Change* (Working Paper Series, 2002)[Development Studies Institute].

observation—provide the basis for fertile descriptions of the nature of informal work and its causes. These accounts incorporate personal narratives and experiences. They provide new understandings of the ways attitudes to work structure labour markets and interactions with regulators. Together, these methods provide the basis for fruitful insights into ways that the regulation of work can be more responsive and redress the negative social and economic effects of informal work. This analysis informs later proposals for novel regulation, coordinated across different political and geographic scales.

4

Displacement of Traditional Labour Laws

Mathadi Boards in Maharashtra, India

4.1 Introduction

Most anyone who has spent time in India will have been struck by the incredible skill and strength of workers who balance massive loads on their heads. This chapter tracks the creation of a highly successful model for regulating the performance of load-carrying work in the Indian state of Maharashtra.[1] Such work is known locally as mathadi and hamal work. 'Matha' means 'head-load' in many Indian languages. Hamal means 'porter' from the Arabic 'hamala': to carry. Both types of workers carry out similar work. A mathadi worker is defined by the Indian National Commission on Labour (INCL) as a worker who carries a load on his head, back, neck or shoulders. The work normally consists of loading, unloading, carrying, shifting, weighing, tapping, and stacking goods. This is harsh physical labour, often undertaken in extreme heat. In 1999, Deshpande estimated that there were more than 500,000 mathadi workers across the state of Maharashtra, around 10,000 of them female.[2] Today, the number of mathadis has increased, though various factors now threaten this type of work.

Following a concerted campaign in the 1960s, a tripartite regulatory system was introduced to overcome many of the problems historically faced by the mathadi workers, such as a lack of job security and access to social security. The Mathadi, Hamal and other Manual Workers (Regulation of Employment and Welfare) Act, 1969 ('Mathadi Act') was the first regulatory method of its type in India 'to secure basic protective social security for the unorganised workers by "regularising" their intermittently available continuous work'.[3] (The term 'unorganised' is preferred to 'informal' in India.) The Act provides a comprehensive regulatory system for the mathadi workers.

In order to assess the responsiveness of the Mathadi Boards to the conditions which they aim to improve, a central regulatory question for this chapter is what specific causes and conditions of informality the boards are responding to. Why was unorganized, informal work so prominent at the time the Mathadi Boards were conceived, despite Bombay's prominence as an industrial and trading hub? What circumstances produced a large 'circulating' class of workers who had migrated from the countryside to the city in search of work? The chapter tracks the ways that the institutions of colonization and features of the independence movement converged to produce both this massive informal workforce, but also the conditions which would allow one group of workers to demand a novel regulatory system for the betterment of their working conditions.

[1] The author is indebted to Praveen Rao for his assistance with research in Maharashtra, India.

[2] Rajeshwari Deshpande, 'Organising the Unorganised: Case of Hamal Panchayat' (1999) [Economic and Political Weekly] 34 Economic and Political Weekly L19 L-29.

[3] Ramesh C. Datta, 'Public Action, Social Security and Unorganised Sector' (1998) [Economic and Political Weekly] 33 Economic and Political Weekly L2 L-2.

This study contrasts with the Australian and Bulgarian case studies for a variety of reasons. India's informal economy constitutes the overwhelming bulk of the country's workforce. In this sense, it is more similar to Cambodia. Whereas Australia is an industrialized economy, and Bulgaria a transitional economy, India remains a developing economy despite its rapid growth. According to the Indian Ministry of Labour and Employment (IMLE), informal workers comprise 94.33 per cent of the workforce and contribute about 60 per cent of GDP.[4] Out of the total workforce of 459 million (45.9 crore workers—to use Indian terminology) the unorganized sector comprises 433 million or 43.3 crore workers (1 crore = 10 million).[5] Unlike Bulgaria, where the subjects of the study had enjoyed secure, full-time employment under the state socialist regime, most workers in India have never experienced formal employment of this type.

The Indian case study is not only useful for its comparisons with the Australian, Cambodian, and Bulgarian case studies. The study is a fruitful site of regulatory learning because India's legislatures have been more active in regulating informal work, particularly in the domain of providing social security, than perhaps anywhere else in the world. The Indian state has used various mechanism to do this, the best-documented of which are the Welfare Boards of Kerala. In contrast to Kerala's Welfare Boards, there is very little written about the Mathadi Boards of Maharashtra, which have a broader regulatory reach. In addition to providing a mechanism for collecting social security for informal workers, the Mathadi Boards also provide a way of effectively regulating wages by acting as a tripartite employment agency. Labour users can only hire mathadi workers through the Boards, which are overseen by government, representatives of management and unions.[6] The Mathadi Boards therefore provide a regulatory alternative to the supply chain regulation of Australia, and the ILO Better Factories project in Cambodia. It may be that the Mathadi Boards have been more successful than the other examples because they bypass the employment relationship in favour of a triangular relationship, regulated through Mathadi Boards. The core institution of labour law was displaced by a new institution that provides largely the same functions in a different way instead of trying to modify an institution (labour law) that already has an accepted form.

This chapter describes the regulatory and social dynamics established by British colonial powers and the newly independent government in India that contributed to the creation of a landless or land-poor class who migrated to urban cities in search of work. This chapter shows that the dynamics of labour circulation from the country to the city were strongly influenced by existing and colonial social arrangements. The informalization of mathadi work was determined by complex identity-based and class relations such as caste, village affiliations, and access to land. Workers were (and continue to be) recruited through, and work within, work groups called 'tolli'. They are the mode through which workers are drawn to the city, and through which they are recruited and organized. Informal norms and social relations shape the supply of labour and influence the behaviour of workers. Thus, any new regulatory structures attempting to formalize the sector needed to take into account these informal regulatory dynamics.

[4] Sony Pellissery, 'Social Embeddedness of Informal Labour Markets: How Effective are Public Works Programmes for Social Security in India?' ('Social Security and the Labour Market: A Mismatch?' The Role of Social Security in Relation to the Labour Market and Employment Policies, 5th International Research Conference on Social Security, Warsaw, 5–7 March 2007.

[5] Government of India, *Annual Report to the People on Employment* (2010).

[6] The term 'labour user' is used in favour of 'employer' throughout this chapter where the employee-employer relationship is in question.

4.1.1 Field work described in this chapter

The field work described in this chapter was conducted over two periods. The first was in 2011 when a small handful of interviews was conducted with interviewees who had a long term involvement in the Mathadi Boards. The aim was to collect information about the period—in the 1960s—when mobilization first began, and about how they were established. A local Mumbai-based social researcher, Praveen Rao, assisted with recruitment and with the conduct of interviews. I could not have identified key players with long-term experience without his help. Due to the length of time since the Mathadi Act was first enacted, only a small number of interviewees were identified with sufficient knowledge of this period. Most of the main protagonists had passed away. In 2013, a second set of interviews was conducted in India with labour historians, sociologists and labour lawyers to gain a better understanding of the dynamics of informality in India. Through these interviews, I was introduced to the idea of 'labour circulation' and the importance of land-based factors in the creation of surplus labour in India.

This chapter is structured as follows: Section 2 charts the creation of an informal and unorganized workforce in the urban centres of Maharashtra, and describes the working conditions of the mathadi workers prior to formalization. It then explores various social causes of informality, and the legal dynamics which created this class of unregulated and unstable workers.

Section 3 tracks the dynamics of formalization, including the development of the Mathadi Act, discussing the various factors that contributed to the unusual political support enjoyed by this group of informal workers. It outlines the functioning of the Mathadi Boards, explaining how they address the various causes of informality explored in Section 2. The chapter concludes by analysing the success of the Mathadi Boards and their influence in India.

4.2 Dynamics of Informalization

4.2.1 Mathadi Workers' Conditions of Work Prior to Formalization

This section describes mathadi workers' conditions of work before the Mathadi Act. As is the case today, mathadi workers mainly toiled in ports and docks, godowns (or warehouses), market yards, transport companies, wholesale markets, retail merchants. According to one interviewee, Baburao Ramisthe, there were approximately 200,000 such workers in the city of Mumbai alone in around 1974.[7] Unloading work was dispersed throughout the more than 200 urban markets, around 3,000 public and private godowns, more than a 100 railway stations and around 400 ST stands across the state.[8]

Mathadi workers migrated from rural areas of the Maharashtra state to Mumbai and other urban centres in search of work. Upon arrival in urban areas, they either stayed with relatives in makeshift housing (slums) or at the godowns (warehouses) with the permission of those who hired them—merchants, market traders, and so on. These living conditions were rough and provided no privacy. Work was mainly undertaken

[7] Interview with Mr. Baburao Ramisthe, General Secretary, Akhil Bharatiya Mathadi Transport & General Kamgar Union, March 2011.

[8] Deshpande L-19.

outside, exposed to Maharashtra's tropical and humid climate. The heat builds before the monsoon, when it rains for two to three months. Work continued regardless of the weather.

The work consisted mainly of carrying great weights. Ramesh Data describes the nature of the work as follows:[9]

> His (sic) work is mainly of physical labour and he is expected to be strong and sturdy to withstand serious physical weights and carrying it to considerable height for stacking. His (sic) work normally consists of loading, unloading, carrying, shifting, weighing, taping, bending and stacking.

Despite the limit placed by the International Labour Organisation (ILO) of a maximum of 50 kg weight to be carried on the back, in Indian markets goods were usually packed in 100 kg gunny bags.[10] Workers suffered from back problems which were debilitating over time. They were rarely able to continue their work for more than fifteen to twenty years.[11]

In addition to the work of loading and unloading goods, other types of work were expected by labour users, including sweeping and cleaning shops and godowns, tending to cattle and even domestic work at traders' houses. These tasks were not accounted for in the wages, which were determined on a piece-rate basis depending on the number of items or gunny bags carried (Deshpande 1999: L-9).

Before Mathadi work became regulated in 1974, work was highly irregular, with no fixed hours of work, overtime payment, holidays or leave. There was no single fixed employer or fixed employment. The availability of the work was dependent on the arrival, availability, and departure of ships, trains, goods trucks, or customers. It was extremely difficult to predict the time and volume of work. As a result, work was spread over the day and across the city (Datta 1998: L-4). *Tolli* groups often worked for different labour users on a given day, travelling throughout the city in search of work. In the 2009 decision of the Supreme Court of India regarding the Mathadi Act, Justice Sirpurkar described the conditions before the enactment of the Mathadi Act in the following dismal terms (*Bhuwalka Steel Indus. Ltd v. Bombay Iron & Steel Labour Bd. & Anr* on 17 December 2009, at para 43):

> They were mostly dependent upon the toliwalas and mukdams. They were not certain that if they would be engaged to work every day. They were also not sure that they would work only for one employer in a day or many. Every day was a challenge.

As migrant workers, mathadi workers also suffered from health problems associated with the lack of availability of affordable and healthy food in urban centres, as they were removed from their families who might otherwise cook for them. They were unable to follow a fixed routine of work which would enable them to make permanent arrangements for their meals.[12] As a result, many workers lived off Indian varieties of what could be termed 'fast food', carrying limited nutritional value and the risk of contracting foodborne illnesses.

The work was also isolating—away from the familial ties of the village. Men who became mathadi workers often left the village at a young age, and did not return until their bodies were ruined. This made them bad prospects for marriage. When arranging marriages, families typically preferred to have their daughters married to agricultural labourers who remained in the village.[13]

[9] Datta L-4. [10] Deshpande L-20. [11] Ibid. L-20. [12] Ibid.

[13] Anil Awchat, 'Hamals of Poona-III: Rudiments of Organisation' 11 Economic and Political Weekly 942.

Interviewees also reported numerous instances of torture and victimization of mathadi workers prior to 1974. Such victimization was made possible by the immense power differentials between the labour users and the workers. There were also sporadic clashes between workers and labour users on issues of loading/unloading of goods and wage settlements leading to severe law and order problems. It was clear that regulation was needed, not just to improve the conditions of these workers, but also to restore industrial peace.

4.2.2 Social dynamics of informality

Patterns of social and geographic migration, circulation, and fragmentation reinforced vulnerability and contributed to the informality of work in various ways. Patterns of internal migration were shaped by colonial geography and Mumbai's place in the system of colonial extraction. Mumbai's evolution as a key seaport and business centre owed a great deal to British colonial planning.[14] Mumbai was the second biggest colonial city. Unlike Kolkata, though, where trade and industry was overwhelmingly dominated by Europeans, Indians played a much greater role as businessmen in Mumbai. Bombay was the premier *Indian* industrial city.[15] The merchant classes joined forces with Europeans with something closer to equality in the extraction of goods from India to elsewhere in the Commonwealth. Businessmen, including the mill-owners and managers, were overwhelmingly Gurati-speakers, including Parsis, Gujarati *vanis* (merchant classes), and Muslim business minority communities.[16] Educated and professional classes, in contrast, were dominated by Marathi-speakers. Brahman dominance within Mumbai was not as strong as outside the city.[17]

The creation of wealth in Mumbai was dependent on the abundance of cheap labour from the regions surrounding the city. The merchant-capitalists, who are famous for building Mumbai's thriving sea-ports, competitive textile industry, and finance sectors, relied on the constant presence of these workers in their patterns of accumulation and expansion.[18]

Migrant communities settled in Mumbai along the lines of their caste, regional, or religious affiliations. Dependent members of the household mainly stayed in the village. Though housing was sometimes provided to factory workers in India—such as the housing for mill workers in Mumbai, no such housing was provided for informal mathadi workers. Neighbourhoods were further differentiated in terms of economic status. Slum settlements were constructed close to hubs of work—next to the dock and near textile mills. In the 1970s, the share of the slum population was around half of the total population of Mumbai.[19]

As with much migration from rural to urban areas across India, labour brokers acting on behalf of labour users formed a link in the chain of circulation for migrant workers.[20] These labour brokers are most commonly referred to as 'Mukadams'. Mukadam literally means supervisor,[21] although Mukadams are described variously as 'gang leaders', 'jobbers', 'labour-brokers', 'labour-agent'. The reason for these different

[14] R. N. Sharma, 'Mega Transformation of Mumbai: Deepening Enclave Urbanism' (2010) [2010] 59 Sociological Bulletin 69 72.

[15] Gail Omvedt, 'Non-Brahmans and Communists in Bombay' (1973) [1973] 8 Economic and Political Weekly 749 729.

[16] Ibid. 730. [17] Ibid. 730. [18] Sharma 73. [19] Ibid. 77.

[20] Jan Breman, *Outcast Labor in Asia: Circulation and Informalization of the Workforce at the Bottom of the Economy* (Oxford University Press, New Delhi 2010) 4.

[21] Pellissery 12.

names is that their responsibilities extend beyond that of a supervisor. Mukadams are generally people with particular leadership skills within a village. They have a good knowledge of each household within a village.[22] Mukadams engaged labourers from their own village or from nearby villages. Their caste composition was almost exactly equivalent to that of the workers. Typically, it was the role of the Mukadam to supervise the conditions of the mathadi workers. For instance, it would be the Mukadam's responsibility to get the mathadi workers to jobs, handle, measure work output, and dispel any disputes that may arise from payment.

Owing to their considerable authority over the labour force, Mukadams often had a significant impact on the livelihoods of the workers. The structure of labour procurement and regulation has been described by Datta as follows:[23]

> All this work was performed in a 'gang' or 'tolli' system. All the workers in a tolli belonged to the same village and often, related to each other. According to their convenience some of them used to go to their native places, and some others, mostly their relatives used to come and take their place in the tolli. The tolli workers used to work under a head known as 'mukadam', who actually used to arrange for the work, was responsible to the employer, got the labour charges from the employers, and distributed the wages among the workers.

Prior to the introduction of the Mathadi Act, workers in a *tolli* were substantially controlled by a Mukadam. Mukadams made contacts for mathadi to borrow money and frequently loaned it themselves. Mukadams acted as middle people between labour users and mathadi and were implicated in their mistreatment: 'Many a time, the mukadam, by conniving with the employer, exploited tolli workers'.[24] Their position gave them tremendous social power and income derived in large part from taking a cut of the income of the workers.[25]

Rather than operating solely through the market dynamics of supply and demand, then, the conditions of informality for mathadi were socially embedded in village and caste relations (which we can think of as informal or private regulations) in which Mukadams played a key role. Links with Mukadams determined where mathadi worked, and this, in turn, impacted on the level of pay they received and the security of their work. The Mukadam's gang, or *tolli*, followed him from one job to another. Not only were the Mukadams involved in the exploitation of the workers, their role as intermediaries also explains why the mathadi workers seldom had access to other jobs. The workers' strict association with individual Mukadams reduced their labour mobility. Furthermore, the presence of intermediaries in the labour market posed a challenge for the application of labour laws, which is ordinarily conceived of as the regulation of the relationship between the employer and employee.

Mathadi workers left (and continue to leave) their villages at a young age, returning for visits and settling again in their place of origin when they were worn out. This is an enduring, widespread feature of the workforce in India. The National Commission on Rural Labour calculated in its 1991 report than about 10 million rural workers went out in search of work. This tally included 4.5 million interstate rural migrants and around 6 million intra- or inter-district rural migrant workers temporarily employed inside or outside agriculture.[26] Others believe the figures are much higher, and have continued to grow.[27] In this sense, the mathadi workers share much in common with other migrant workers across India.

[22] Ibid. 12. [23] Datta L-4. [24] Ibid. L-4. [25] Omvedt 751.

[26] Government of India, *National Commission on Rural Labour* (Archives of Indian Labour, Delhi 1991).

[27] Breman.

However, there are demographic features of these particular workers that shaped their specific patterns of migration and the subsequent dynamics of formalization and informalization. Mathadi workers migrated mainly from Western Maharasthtra.[28] In a survey of hamal panchayat (association) members in Pune conducted in 1985–86 by Vasant Deshpande it was noted that more than half of the Hamals had migrated to the city from the surrounding rural areas of western Maharashtra.[29] A large number of them were from the drought-prone districts of the Marathwada region. These families had migrated to Pune during the 1970s. More than half of the surveyed hamals were Marathas. Along with marathas, Muslims and Dalits had also entered this occupation. Though the hamals hailed from economically poor families, Marathas enjoyed a relatively high social status within the caste hierarchy and continued land tenure in the home village. The survey found that more than 75 per cent of the workers reported owning agricultural land in their native villages.[30] Their social status and traditional occupational pattern helped them retain their ties with the villages, unlike many other migrant social groups.

Though informal labour—the precariat[31]—is frequently characterized by fragmentation amongst workers, a number of additional factors allowed the mathadi workers to cultivate a sense of social cohesion. Normally, ongoing labour circulation and lack of representation reinforce each other in a vicious circle. The constant movement in and out of the workforce undermines the cohesion and mutual trust that workers require to engage in collective action. Keeping the workforce in a constant state of flux by instant hire and fire procedures stops the creation of solidarity between workers. It is often the case in such conditions that workers compete against each other in the narrow bargaining space left to them. Yet, as we shall see in the next part of this chapter, the Maratha status of workers and their relative privilege within village hierarchies, promoted a level of social cohesion which later allowed for the development of a strong labour movement.

4.2.3 Legal dynamics of informality

The dynamics of colonial and post-colonial law making played a strong role in the creation of patterns of migration in Maharashtra in the 50s and 60s; patterns which continue today. This section shows how state action contributed towards the growth of the informal workforce.[32] Legal frameworks that contour patterns of land use, labour and credit markets shape the dynamics of labour supply and demand. These close linkages between land, credit markets, and labour are one of the reasons that efforts to expand labour regulation in India to a wider group of workers has not reduced informality.[33] Labour laws are unable to address the dynamics of labour circulation necessitated by land shortages. One of the few points of common agreement among historians is the significance of agrarian relations in the structure of Indian society.[34] The land is, overwhelmingly, the single most important source of wealth and the basis of production in

[28] Deshpande L-9. [29] Ibid. L-9. [30] Ibid. L-9. [31] Standing.

[32] Prabhu P. Mohapatra, 'Regulated Informality: Legal Constructions of Labour Relations in Colonial India 1814–1926' in Jan Lucassen and Sabyasachi Bhattacharya (eds), *Workers in the Informal Sector: Studies in Labour History 1800–2000* (Macmillan India Limited, New Delhi 2005).

[33] Pellissery.

[34] D. A. Washbrook, 'Law, State and Agrarian Society in Colonial India' 15 Modern Asian Studies 649 650; Despina Iliopoulou, 'The Uncertainty of Private Property: Indigenous versus Colonial Law in the Restructuring of Social Relations in British India' (2001) 26 Dialectical Anthropology 65.

India. As a consequence, laws that shape agrarian relations shape the accumulation of wealth, production and social relations across India.

Agrarian relations continue to be shaped by patterns established by colonial law making. The imposition of colonial law had various subtle conservative implications for the development of Indian society.[35] Much of colonial law making sought to keep society in the structure of relations in which the colonial authority had found it, and enforce 'customary' and religious norms (interpreted through colonial eyes).[36] In the area of private law, courts looked to the scriptures for guidance on domestic and social norms. These interpretations reflected a Brahminical view of society. With the support of British power, Hindu law expanded its authority across large areas of society which had not known it before or which had possessed their own localized customs. This is, according to Washbrook, one of many developments which made the nineteenth century the Brahmin century in Indian history.[37] It also helps to explain why the twentieth century was to be the anti-Brahmin century—a tendency that provided the mathadi movement with the legitimacy and momentum to push for the special system of regulation described in the second part of this chapter.

Land laws

The revenue collection methods of the British administration reinforced feudal land tenure patterns. To extract revenue from its colony, the British implemented two major land tax systems and fundamentally altered the nature of existing property rights in India. In some regions, property rights and taxes were assigned to zamindars or landlords, whereas in others—including Maharashtra—they were assigned to ryotwars or cultivators.[38] The introduction of sole proprietary ownership by the British further altered the rights of property previously held by lower castes, including varying overlapping rights to occupancy and rights to shares of crops as defined by local custom and kinship.[39] Peasants were now 'free' to sell their labour and were given land to till at the discretion of the landlord.[40]

In the wake of India's independence, land reforms were carried out in keeping with promises by the national leadership in its efforts to mobilize the peasantry for the struggle against colonial rule. The architects of the post-colonial era envisaged an agricultural economy of self-cultivating owners. Though the revenue collection pattern of British India was replaced with a new bureaucratic system of land administration, land reform was halfhearted. One of the reasons for this was that land reform was undertaken at the state level, where the power of landowners was greater than at the national level. The resulting legislation was implemented by a bureaucracy which was often captured by the interests of the landowning classes. Though Maharashtra had a relatively good record with land reform in formal terms, various means were used to evade the intent of land reforms,[41] including legal appeals by chieftains and administrative confusion.[42] Those segments of the rural workforce who had little or no land

35 Washbrook 653. 36 Ibid. 653. 37 Ibid. 653.

38 Hamza Alavi, 'India: Transition from feudalism to colonial capitalism' 10 Journal of Contemporary Asia 359 372.

39 Shilpi Kapur and Sukkoo Kim, *British Colonial Institutions and Economic Development in India* (No 12613, NBER Working Papers from National Bureau of Economic Research, Cambridge, USA, 2006) 2.

40 Alavi.

41 Deepak Lal, 'Agricultural Development in Maharashtra: Some Aspects' (1969) [1969] 4 Economic and Political Weekly A207 A-209.

42 'Scuttling Land Reform' (1975) (editorial) [1975] 10 Economic and Political Weekly 656.

did not benefit greatly from the redistribution of agrarian capital. In their directives, the planners seemed to have ignored the existence across much of the country of a vast population with little or no land ownership.

Breman argues that their exclusion at this critical moment of restructuring ownership of resources explains why a large segment of the workforce remained marginal to the flurry of socio-economic development that occurred in the second half of the twentieth century.[43] Surplus land acquired by the rural poor was less than 2 per cent of the total cultivated land. Furthermore, the National Commission on Rural Labour reported that there was hardly any attempt to influence the land market in favour of the rural poor by advancing long-term loans to them for purchase of land.[44] Instead, the land poor and landless were told that a better future would come their way outside agriculture, as mill hands and workers in the city.[45] Though mathadi workers often retained rights to small plots of land, land reform left them without sufficient land to support their families. Like millions of others, land laws played a significant role in their migration to urban centres in search of work.

Labour laws

Prior to the enactment of the Mathadi Act, mathadi workers were not protected by labour laws of any type. The characteristics of their work were not captured by any of the various laws that aimed to protect workers. They fell outside the Minimum Wages Act (1948), which set the rate of pay for various industries in Greater Mumbai. Because they were neither wholly nor principally employed by any one employer, the benefits under the Bombay Shops and Establishments Act, 1948 were also not available to mathadi workers. These benefits included rights to overtime, paid weekly holiday, leave, and so on. They were also excluded from the application of the Factories Act (1948), the Employees' Provident Funds Act (1952), and the Employees' State Insurance Act (1948), as their work was not considered to be continuous or for any consecutive number of days for the same labour user.[46] With regard to compensation payments to workers for any physical injury or death, which was a frequent occurrence in the course of their loading and unloading work, their work fell outside the provisions of the Workmen's Compensation Act (1923). Labour users evaded responsibility for such payments by arguing that their dealings were only with the Mukadam.[47] According to some commentators, the traders were also careful to keep the numbers of workers below the number that would see them covered by the Factories Act (1948):[48]

> The hamals work under a large number of traders. By keeping eight to ten hamals under him, the trader evades the Shops Act and the Factories Act. Even in the railway yard there is no single boss answerable for the hamals' condition.

In summary, mathadi workers were treated as casual, unskilled workers. This meant that they were deprived of statutory protection regarding their hours of work, remuneration, and other service conditions.

The restricted coverage of labour laws flowed in part from their colonial deployment to secure a supply of labour, and partly due to the post-colonial association of labour with *industry*. According to Noronha, the earliest attempt in India to regulate

[43] Breman 11.

[44] Government of India, *Report of the National Commission on Rural Labour, Volume 1: Main Report* (New Delhi, Ministry of Labour, 1991) v–vi.

[45] Breman 11. [46] Datta L-4. [47] Ibid L-4. [48] Awchat.

employment consisted of enactments which were concerned more with providing a steady labour force, rather than with the protection of workers' interests.[49] Later revisions to labour law purposefully restricted the scope of protection. The Royal Commission on Labour, appointed in 1928 (known as the Whitley Commission) for example, determined that welfare should only be extended to a small proportion of workers, so as not to burden employers at the early stage of India's development. By depriving workers of employment security and social security, this would encourage workers to come to urban centres for periods of employment but return to villages between bouts of work and in retirement.[50]

For the architects of post-colonial India, the 'worker' worked in the modern economy. Policy makers were captured by the idea that the rural-agrarian order would soon be replaced by an urban-industrial one. The National Planning Committee, established in 1940 and chaired by Jawaharlal Nehru focused primarily on *industrial* relations. The regulations it proposed were modelled on those already implemented in the industrialized world.[51]

The barriers to thinking more broadly about the regulation of work were not just conceptual, but also political. The industrial sector had an established and influential trade union movement, and the Indian independence movement was intricately intertwined with this labour movement.[52] This labour movement grew exponentially with independence. In 1929, the number of registered trade unions in India was 29; in 1951 it was 3,987.[53] Although the unions cared for the interests of only a tiny minority of the labouring classes, that minority was its most vocal segment. The fear of the radicalization of the factory proletariat was high, and labour laws were designed to stifle unrest.

At the start of India's independence era, industrial labourers formed less than 6 per cent of the total workforce.[54] Despite its small size, the future of India's prosperity and growth was seen to hinge on this group of workers. The implicit assumption was that a social system would eventually emerge which would mirror that of the industrialized West. Breman argues that little thought was given to the way in which local and historical conditions in India had shaped the working class and the ways that India's historical conditions differed from advanced economies.[55]

In sum, the worker that labour law sought to regulate was more an 'ideal type' than a reflection of the characteristics of most workers in India. The restricted purview of labour laws, in addition to the limited scope of land reform, combined to create a mass of workers who circulated from the country-side to urban centres in search of work. The work they found was precarious and insecure.

4.3 Dynamics of Formalization

This part of the paper explores the dynamics of formalization and describes the Mathadi Act and its impact on the workers whose conditions it regulates. Though patterns of circulation and migration contributed to the informality of mathadi work, there

[49] Ernesto Noronha, 'Bombay Dock Labour Board 1948-1994: From Insecurity to Security to Insecurity?' (2001) [2001] 36 Economic and Political Weekly 4851 4851; Mohapatra.

[50] Mohapatra. [51] Breman 131. [52] Agarwala.

[53] O. A. Ornati (ed.), *Jobs and Workers in India* (Institute of International Industrial and Labour Relations, Ithica, Cornell University Press 1955) xi.

[54] Ibid. 9. [55] Breman 133.

were other factors which strengthened their power relative to other migrant workers. This part of the chapter argues that the timing of mathadi migration and their distinct identities and ties allowed mathadi workers to create 'webs of influence',[56] which chipped away in multiple, albeit marginal ways at different nodes of influence within the contested and pluralist domestic political arena of the period immediately after independence.

4.3.1 Maratha identity

The hamals in Pune were among the first migrant families coming to the city after independence.[57] This gave them comparatively easier access to the labour market. Further, the Maratha identity of the mathadis and hamals, migrating predominantly from Western Maharashtra, made them important to Congress politics in the state during the independence and post-colonial period. (Congress was the political party that led the independence movement and dominated national politics over the sixty years following independence.) The term 'Maratha' included all Marathi-speaking non-Brahman castes except untouchables.[58] In the colonial period it signalled a warrior heritage: a historical polity that resisted Mughal expansion into the Deccan in the seventeenth and eighteenth centuries.[59,60] In the independence period, it distinguished a lower-caste movement from the preponderance of Brahmans in the nationalist middle classes and the colonial order in Maharashtra.[61] Non-Brahmin movements pointed to the re-inscription of Brahman social and ritual power under the colonial order through privileged access to western education and employment in the colonial government. These groups invoked the Maratha warrior past in their protests against Brahman dominance, debunking the tacit assumption of Brahman leadership in many nationalist narratives.[62] They put forward their own versions of Maharashtra history and traditions, and in doing so created a powerful political grouping in the post-colonial period, which mathadis and hamals, hailing from Western Maharashtra, were able to network with. The assassination of Gandhi by a Chitpavan Brahman in 1948 boosted anti-Brahman feelings throughout western India. Brahman homes and estates were burned and families and individuals attacked in several places in western Maharashtra, Pune, and the Nagpur region. The 'Maratha-ization' of the Congress Party in Maharashtra contributed to burgeoning mathadi and hamal political power.

4.3.2 Unionization

The long-standing tradition of industrial conflict in Mumbai also played a significant role in the mathadi workers' quest for formalization. Labour unrest increased each year in the 1960s and early 70s, reaching a peak in 1974 before subsiding.[63] As

[56] John Braithwaite and Peter Drahos, *Global Business Regulation* (Cambridge University Press 2000); John Braithwaite and Peter Drahos, 'Ratcheting Up and Driving Down Global Regulatory Standards' 42 Development 109.

[57] Deshpande L-9. [58] Omvedt 751.

[59] Prachi Deshpande, 'Caste as Maratha: Social Categories, Colonial Policy and Identity in Early Twentieth-Century Maharashtra' (2004) [2004] 41 Indian Economic & Social History Review 7 7.

[60] The category also reflected the colonial bureaucracy's obsession with indexing patterns of behaviour which was fuelled by the colonial state's desire to predict and anticipate its subject population's actions, and was associated with theories of race and ethnology which were influential at the time: ibid. 22.

[61] Ibid. 14. [62] Ibid. 14.

[63] M. K. Singh, 'Industrial Relations in Maharashtra' (1983) [1983] 18 Indian Journal of Industrial Relations 549.

one labour historian put it, '[t]here have been more labour disputes in the Bombay cotton textile industry and they have been of greater intensity than any other place in the country'.[64] There was a tenacity in these strikes not seen elsewhere in the country. The mathadi movement was able to form ties with, and ride the influence of this existing labour movement. The existing labour movement provided the scaffolding or infrastructure for cooperative learning and sharing of norms and provided powerful leverage in negotiations.

The Indian trade union movement had its birth in Mumbai with the organizing of textile workers.[65] Mumbai was rivalled only by Kolkata as the centre of trade-union-based Marxist politics in India in the 1950s and 60s. This strong labour movement aided the development of mathadi and hamal associations. Communist ideology had taken hold of the working class,[66] and a number of influential social reformers were involved in organizing workers. Mathadis and hamals were assisted by some of the most significant public figures of the time: Anna Sahib Patil threw his efforts behind the organizing of mathadis in the late 1950s in Mumbai; Baba Adhav helped workers in Pune to form their own associations, and, in Dhule, Paranjpe helped to organize the mathadis.[67]

The hamal organization (Panchayat) was formed in 1955 in Pune. The story, as Anil Awchat[68] told it in 1976, goes that, one day as some hamals were sitting outside a restaurant drinking tea in Pune, they saw the sweeper women arrive in new clothes. The women told them that they had got the clothes from the municipal corporation in response to their demands. The hamals thought, 'these women have made gains through forming themselves into a union. We are men, we don't have any organisation to fight for our rights'. Thus, the hamals decided to form a union. The first meeting was held in a temple.

The hamals then approached Baba Adhav, a social reformer and Rashtriya Seva Dal leader (Seva Dal is the grassroots front organization of the Congress party), and a doctor with a flourishing practice. Adhav saw the category of manual labourers ('kashtakari', 'angamehanati kamgar') as a focus point for political mobilization of the lower class and castes. In addition to his efforts at mobilizing unorganised workers, Adhav led a number of social movements targeting caste, class, and gender inequalities.[69] Adhav worked hard to build up the organization. The Panchayat organized its first successful strike in 1968 with more than 3,000 hamals participating.[70] This culminated in a contract signed between the Panchayat and the 'Poona Merchant's Chamber'. The contract resulted in fifteen rules and regulations for load-carrying work and fixed rates for as many as forty-six different tasks performed by hamals. Such contracts became a regular feature of the work of the Panchayat.[71] Over the next twenty years, the Panchayat organized half a dozen strikes, transforming the lives of the hamals in Pune.[72] By 1976 the Hamal Panchayat had 3,800 members in Pune.[73] The most popular slogan amongst the hamal workers in the early years was 'I own my back'.

Annasaheb Patil, a well-known labour organizer and committed Congress party leader,[74] who came from a farmer's family in rural Maharashtra, also took up the considerable task of mobilizing and unionizing Mathadi workers in Mumbai in the early

[64] Omvedt 752 citing Morris David Morris.

[65] Anuradha Joshi and Mick Moore, 'Enabling Environments: Do Anti-Poverty Programmes Mobilise the Poor?' 37 The Journal of Development Studies 25 39; Omvedt.

[66] Omvedt 755. [67] Datta L-4. [68] Awchat 942. [69] Deshpande L-25.

[70] Ibid. L-20. [71] Ibid. L-20. [72] Awchat 942. [73] Ibid. 942.

[74] Deshpande L-25.

1950s. (Today, there is a public holiday in Maharashtra on the day of Patil's death.) Patil began collecting information about the problems of these workers. Armed with data about the Mathadi workers, together with the Mathadi Kamgar Union, and the Hamal Panchayat, he approached the Maharashtra State Government and demanded statutory protection.

In 1962, they demanded an independent inquiry into the conditions of mathadi and hamal workers. Three committee reports over a three year period were submitted to the government of Maharashtra: (a) Report of the Mathadi Labour Enquiry Committee, Greater Bombay—1965; (b) Report of the Lokhandi Jatha Kamgar Enquiry Committee, 1965; and (c) Report of the Committee for Unprotected Labour, 1967.[75] The committees suggested a separate law rather than amending the definitions of employer and employee in existing labour laws.[76] The reports were submitted by the Committee to the Maharashtra Government on 17 November 1967 (subsequently published in the 1st National Commission on Labour, 1967).[77]

We can see, then, that the interaction between the anti-Brahmin movement and the fear of industrial unrest that prevailed in Maharashtra at the time strengthened the impact of collective action for regulatory reform in a reinforcing manner, 'concatenating' into dynamic processes of influence, in the language of McAdam, Tarrow, and Tilly.[78,79] In 1969, the legislative assembly passed the Mathadi Act, which came into force in 1974.[80]

4.3.3 The Mathadi Act

This section of the paper describes in some detail the functioning of the Mathadi Act and the ways it contributed to the formalization of this group of workers. Labour law traditionally sets standards and establishes institutions for enforcing compliance, but intervenes only minimally in market interactions of supply and demand. The tripartite Mathadi Boards not only set standards, they also act as labour hire agencies. Under the Act, both workers and labour users must register with the Boards in order to operate in the industry. Payment for work takes place through the Boards, and the levies collected from labour users contribute to pensions, workers compensation insurance, hospitals, education and so on—benefits most informal, precarious workers in India never receive.

One of the factors that makes this legislation notable is its comprehensive regulatory purpose. It covers a range of benefits such as standard pay and conditions as well as provident (pension) funds, gratuities, *ex gratia* payments, bonuses, leave wages, medical benefits, and compensation for injury. It is like a labour law system in itself. The broad purposes set out in the objects of the Act are (Section 3(2) of Mathadi Act, 1969):

- to regulate the employment of unprotected workers such as mathadi workers;
- to make better provision for their terms and conditions of employment;

[75] 1967 Datta L-4. [76] Deshpande L-21.

[77] Government of India, *National Commission on Labour (1967)* (1967).

[78] Doug McAdam, Sidney Tarrow, and Charles Tilly, *Dynamics of Contention* (Cambridge University Press 2001).

[79] Mathadis continue to be courted by political parties in Maharashtra for their votes, because of their large numbers and active role in politics. See the report at http://dnasyndication.com/dna/article/DNMUM148200.

[80] Government of India, *2nd Report of the National Commission on Labour* (2002).

1.	Goods Transport Labour Board
2.	The Khokha Making & Timber Market Labour Board
3.	The Railway Goods and Forwarding Labour Board
4.	Grocery Markets & Shops Labour Board
5.	Mumbai Vegetable Market Labour Board
6.	The Cloth Markets or Shops Board
7.	The Clearing & Forwarding Unprotected Dock Labour Board
8.	Metal & Paper Market and Shop Labour Board
9.	Cotton Market Labour Board
10.	The Bombay Iron & Steel Labour Board

Figure 4.1 Tripartite Mathadi Boards operating in Mumbai

- to provide for their health, safety and welfare;
- to ensure an adequate supply and proper utilization of such workers; and
- to prevent avoidable unemployment for these workers.

The Act had two additional purposes that are not listed in the objects, but, according to interviewees, were in the minds of its drafters. The first was industrial peace. The second was a revived and expansive role for trade unions in the regulation of welfare activities.

4.3.4 The functioning of Mathadi Boards

The greatest innovation of the Mathadi Act was the establishment of the tripartite Mathadi Boards. The Boards are constituted under Section 6 of the Act. Each Board is responsible for a whole district or two adjoining districts. The tripartite Board acts as the regulator for the demand and supply of labour. The workers and labour users register with the Board, and the Board sends the worker to the labour user, who then pays the Board rather than the individual worker.[81]

The Act provides for the establishment of Boards in Mumbai and in regional centres in the state of Maharashtra, such as Raigad, Pune, Sangli, et cetera. Though the Mathadi Act was to be implemented across the entire state, it took some years to set up the infrastructure and implementation outside of Mumbai and Pune. Currently, there are thirty Boards operating across Maharashtra. Ten of these boards are located in Mumbai with estimated registration of 50,000 workers.[82]

Each of these Boards consists of equal representatives from the government, labour users and the unions. The board has separate Advisory Committees. The Labour Commissioner, a government representative, heads the Committee.

When the labour users or unprotected workers fail to nominate their representatives to the Board, or for any other reason the State Government is unable to constitute the Board, the State Government may (by Notification in Official Gazette) appoint a person to hold the Office till the Board is properly constituted.

[81] Renana Jhabvala, 'Unorganised Workers Bill: In Aid of the Informal Worker' 40 Economic and Political Weekly 2227 2230.
[82] Government of India, *2nd Report of the National Commission on Labour* (2002).

Labour users and workers must register themselves with one of the Boards when they wish to hire workers (in the case of labour users) or work as mathadi (in the case of workers). Sections 14 and 31 of the Act prohibit labour users from employing any worker directly, and specifies that labour users can employ only registered workers of the Mathadi board. Registered workers are assigned to various labour users depending on the volume of work. Wage rates are fixed by the Boards, and the labour users must deposit the workers' wages along with an additional levy of up to 41 per cent of the wages paid for social security and other benefits with the boards. The exact percentage of levy varies slightly between the Boards. An additional contribution of Rs. 600 every year is collected from each worker towards medical facilities. The levy amount varies with different boards. The boards disburse the wages to the workers periodically according to the wage periods.

Mathadi workers are employed on a piece-rate basis and they work on the principle of 'No Work No Wages'. As a consequence, the Boards do not directly address the issue of security of work. Seniority is considered only when selecting the Mukadam and wage rates are the same for all the workers in the board. According to the Joint General Secretary of the Akhil Bharatiya Mathadi Transport & General Kamgar Union, Mr. Arun Ranjane, wages range from as a little as Rs. 3,000/- to as much as Rs. 40,000 per month. The average wage is around Rs. 12,000 to Rs. 15,000 per month.[83]

The Board's staff are paid from the levy raised from the labour uses, which is negotiated every 3–4 years. The day to day work of the Boards is primarily to negotiate between labour users and the unions, to register labour users and workers, to distribute wages and implement welfare schemes.

In case of a dispute, there are mutual meetings held between the employer/management and Union representatives. If the dispute is not solved amicably it is referred to the Mathadi Board. Disputes can be appealed to the Industrial/High Court, and from there to the Supreme Court.

4.3.3.1. Board oversight

Under the Act, the Boards are overseen by the Mathadi desk at the Labour Commission. The Mathadi desk holds the Boards to account by receiving monthly returns from the Boards, receiving complaints from the workers, citizens and labour users, receiving the annual audit reports from Boards, reconstituting Boards, appointment of auditors for the Boards, monitoring the budgets of the Boards, and so on.

4.3.3.2. Social insurance

Various benefits such as a pension fund, gratuity, worker's compensation, free medical care for the worker and members of the worker's family, as well as educational assistance for the registered mathadi workers are also provided through the Boards. In this way, the Board's operation pays heed to the sentiment expressed by one interviewee, 'you can't simply make informal workers formal. You have to ameliorate the effects of informality'.[84] Social security at a basic level is a critical factor in the formalization

[83] Interview with Arun S. Ranjane, General Secretary, Akhil Bharatiya Mathadi Transport & General Kamgar Union, March 2011.

[84] Interview with Coen Kompier, International Labour Organization, Workshop at India International Centre, Delhi, December 2013.

process.[85] Although the types of benefits are the same from Board to Board, there is variation in wage rates and quantum of social security benefits. According to interviewees, this is because the type of work differs, and each Board decides the wage rates and levy contribution through its Advisory Committees.

Retirement funds are provided for by the Mathadi board system. The Provident Fund is managed by the board and not by the Employees Provident Fund Organisation (EPFO), which is the usual practice in India. Interviewees generally regarded these funds to have been satisfactorily managed, though there have been isolated instances of corruption and mismanagement.

4.3.3.3. Health care provision through the boards

Establishing accessible and high quality health care has been one of the major achievements of the mathadi workers. This is particularly important as mathadi workers are excluded from the Employees' State Insurance Scheme of India (ESIS) on the basis that they are not 'wage workers' who receive a monthly salary. In 1976, Annasaheb Patil started a dispensary under a trust on a part-time basis. By 1978 it was operating full time. As of the late 1990s there were two hospitals with an annual budget of Rs 2 crore. In addition, there were twelve pharmaceutical dispensaries.[86] The hospitals provide diagnostic services (radiology, pathology, and sonography) for around 40,000 workers and their families. Workers are given access to a number of speciality units, including dental, orthopaedics, general surgery, skin, and cardiology units. There are thirty-five medical officers, thirty-five specialists, sixty paramedics, and thirty non-medical staff in the hospitals. Everyday, around 2,500 workers receive treatment. Around five surgeries are conducted on average.[87] The hospitals also organize various educational programmes and exhibitions at workplace sites, including family planning and Aids awareness.[88]

Almost 80 to 90 per cent of workers come to the hospitals with fractures, spondylitis, hernia, and other similar problems. According to the chief medical officer, most of these workers suffer from osteoarthritis (degeneration of all joints), and prolapsed inter-vertebrate discs.[89] These diseases are primarily due to physical stress. Another major cause of death in the 1970s was tetanus. An anti-tetanus vaccination campaign was undertaken in 1976 and 1982 to prevent these deaths. Deshpande reports that not a single casualty has occurred over thirty years due to this precaution.[90] As of 2011, the two hospitals continued to be run by six Mathadi Boards across the state. During the last few years, some of the Mathadi Boards have obtained insurance against accident, injuries, and death. There is no financial contribution to these Boards nor to the hospital trust by the government.[91] They are independent and financially sustainable.

For Manohar Gajare, Retired Joint Labour Commissioner, the present health of the workers itself is evidence of the success of the Mathadi Act.[92]

[85] Ibid. [86] Datta L-5. [87] Ibid. L-5. [88] Deshpande L-20.
[89] Datta L-5. [90] Deshpande.
[91] Government of India, *Second National Commission on Labour Report* (2002).
[92] Interview with Manohar Gajare, Former Jt. Commissioner of Labour, Government of Maharashtra, March 2011.

4.3.3.4. Food

In order to address the problem of low levels of nutrition amongst hamal workers, the Hamal Panchayat set up community kitchens for hamals known as 'Kastachi Bhakar' (Earned Bread).[93] This is one of the Panchayat's most successful programmes. Initially, there were five women employees working under this scheme. By the late 1990s there were thirteen centres run under the scheme with around 150 employees among whom around 120 were women. These women are drawn mostly from families of hamal workers. These employees enjoy benefits prescribed by the government including the provident fund. Kastachi Bhakar had an annual turnover of about Rs 50 lakh during 1997–98.[94] Apart from the land offered by the government on lease, the scheme is completely self- sufficient. It is run on a no profit, no loss basis and is managed by a committee of the Panchayat appointed for these purposes. Its benefits are not restricted to hamals, but to all poor people.[95]

4.3.3.5. Reducing the exploitative role of Mukadam

One of the benefits of the Mathadi Boards is that they have overcome many of the problems cause by the *tolli* system. As described earlier in this chapter, one of the barriers to mathadi workers being considered employees under various statutory benefit schemes was the intermediation of Mukadams. Labour users had claimed that Mukadam were the employers, so as to avoid employment responsibilities. By circumventing the generalized system of employment law, the Mathadi Act avoided questions of 'control' which are a key aspect of determining who is responsible for the conditions of workers. Previously, Mukadams were implicated in the exploitation of workers by taking excessive cuts of payments. Under the operation of the Mathadi Act, the hourly rate is not negotiable and is transparent, so the space for exploitation by mukadams is greatly reduced.

Today, mathadi continue to be tightly organized through *tolli*, though some social factors are undermining the strength of this system. Each tolli consists of between 2 and 100 workers. The workers in a *tolli* still tend to belong to the same village and are often related to each other. It is common practice, when workers from a *tolli* return to their village, for other villagers or relatives to come and take their place.[96] One interviewee reported that it is tradition for registered workers to resign in order to make room in a *tolli* for their son, brother, or son-in-law.[97] Likewise, a mathadi union leader reported that, if a worker wants to retire, the normal practice is for him to be replaced by a blood relation.[98] When a new member is to be inducted into an existing *tolli*, it is generally necessary for him to obtain a recommendation from two thirds of the *tolli* members.

Interviewees provided conflicting information about whether Mukadam continue to act as wage collectors. In practice, the Boards collect a form from the labour user which specifies the quantum of daily work conducted by the worker. The Boards issue payments. Some interviewees reported that wages accumulate in the bank and workers

[93] Deshpande L-22. [94] Ibid. L-22. [95] Ibid. L-22.

[96] Government of India, *Second National Commission on Labour Report* (2002).

[97] Interview with Manohar Gajare.

[98] Interview with R.S. Dhumal, Secretary, Transport & Dock Workers Union, Mumbai, March 2011.

access their pay as they wish. Other interviews reported that the Mukadam collects the cheques of all the *tolli* members and distributes them at the workplace.

4.3.5 Assessment

This section and the conclusion to this chapter address the question of how much the Mathadi Boards redress dynamics of informalization described in Section 2 of this chapter, and further, how much they respond to the experiences of workers and the deficits in working conditions. Is this response adequate to the task of improving the conditions of informal mathadi workers in Maharashtra and/or acting as a model for addressing informality more broadly?

Official government reviews generally regard the Mathadi Boards as a great success. In 1967, the First National Commission on Labour recommended that '[w]here employment of unprotected labour is of some magnitude, legislation on the lines of the [Mathadi Act] may be considered by other State Governments for enactment'.[99] By the mid-1970s, mathadi work was much sought after in comparison to other varieties of migrant labour. In 1976 Awchat, described how unusual and valued hamal work was:[100]

> With the rate of migration from the villages to the cities having gone up, landless and poor peasant youths abound in the city and their condition is really bad. Even though the work conditions are so wretched, there is a long waiting list with the Hamal Panchayat of people seeking work as hamals ... The large-scale unemployment makes those who have found jobs, even in the most degrading conditions, more fortunate than those who have none. So the men hang on to the job for dear life. Movement from one job to another is very infrequent. Once a hamal starts working in a godown, say, at the age of fifteen, he stays in it for his life-time.

In 1998, Datta charted the improvements in mathadi conditions in the following table, adapted for this chapter (Figure 4.2).[101]

The 2002 report of the Second National Commission on Labour continued to report positively regarding the Mathadi Boards. It credited the boards with successfully decasualizing mathadi workers and also recommended the Boards as a model for the unorganized sector throughout India (see paragraph 7.376).[102] One of the most important features of the Boards is that they are self-organizing and financially self-supporting. They do not burden government finances.[103]

Yet the Mathadi Boards do suffer from some problems. They have been criticized by workers' advocates for offering different rates of payment to workers from market to market because the rates are locally decided.[104] The Boards have also been criticized for acting as wage distributing agencies and failing to make any positive intervention in the market on behalf of the workers.[105]

At times, dominant political interests operating at both state and local level have manipulated the Boards for their own purposes. The Mathadi Act provides for the appointment of state representatives on the Boards. According to Deshpande, this gave rise to a new system of political patronage. It led to politicization of the workers' organizations as workers' representatives played a crucial role in managing the Mathadi Boards.[106] The Congress Party in Maharashtra almost exclusively dominated the overall

[99] Government of India, *National Commission on Labour* (1967) *278*.
[100] Awchat.
[101] Datta.
[102] Government of India, *2nd Report of the National Commission on Labour* (2002) *129*.
[103] Jhabvala 2231.
[104] Deshpande L-21.
[105] Ibid. L-21.
[106] Ibid.

Before 1969	After the Act
Physical manual labour	
Unions present	Strong unions represent workers
Flexible work	Establishment of the tripartite board
No fixed hours of work spread over a day	Registration of employee and labour user
Workers work in "tollis" under a Mukadam with exploitation by the Mukadam	Mukadam is one of the mathadis in a *tolli*
Wages by piece rate	Bargaining minimum piece rate wages (per tonne or per piece) and levy one in three years
	Basic piece rate linked to Consumer Price Index
No fixed employer	Settlement and agreements signed over working conditions between the union and management of many large and Indian multinational companies
Multi-employers. No direct employer-employee relationship	Employer-employee relationship is mediated by the Mathadi Boards.
Volume and time of work at time when work available	
Workers in a *tolli* mostly come from the same village - often related to each other	
No regularity in or continuity of work, but permanent work	Overtime and double rate after 9.30pm
No paid weekly days off or holiday	
No retirement fund, medical benefit, accident compensation allowance, etc	A hospital has been set up for medical care and sickness.
	Social security benefits paid.
Average wages earned Rs 150–200 per month (in 1962)	Average wages earned Rs 2,000–10,000 per month (1997)
15,000 to 17,000 mathadis in Mumbai	Around 75,000 mathadis in Mumbai in 1997
Mostly illiterate	Many literate

Figure 4.2 Characteristics of Mathadi labour market

political process in the state until 1995. Deshpande reports that the Congress tried to appropriate Mathadi Boards in various ways, as it did the co-operative movement.[107]

Mathadi work is also under threat from economic liberalization and modernization. With the liberalization of the Indian economy in the 1990s, and the introduction of extensive structural adjustment programmes, medium and large enterprises in the organized sector began 'restructuring' their businesses. In the process, these enterprises shed thousands of workers under voluntary retirement schemes. When firms

[107] Ibid.

were unable to, or wished not to, pay redundancy benefits, they transferred workers to mathadi work. This led to an over-supply of workers of this type and reduced the amount of work available to existing workers. Since mathadi workers are piece-rate workers, and their social security benefits are linked to the wages they earn, it was feared this would have an overall detrimental effect on their earnings and well-being.[108]

The modernization of the loading and unloading of ships and crates also poses a threat to this type of work. The introduction of cranes and conveyor belts reduced the amount of work available to mathadi workers.[109] The semi-skilled and skilled workers that operate the machinery are not covered by the Mathadi Act, creating two categories of workers carrying out work for the same purpose.

The success of the Mathadi Act may also be affecting the demographics of migrant workers interested in undertaking mathadi work. By increasing the earnings of mathadi, and the health, education, and well-being of their families, the formalization of this work has led to a generation gap. One interviewee, Arun Ranjane, reported that the children of mathadi workers are no longer interested in doing loading and unloading work; instead they aim to find employment in more highly skilled, and paid, jobs.[110] Indeed, Ranjane reported with some pride that some of the sons and daughters of mathadi workers are medical doctors, lawyers, IT professionals, and the like.[111] A consequence is that new workers are often migrants from other states. This has led to a partial breakdown of the social cohesion of the *tolli* system.

Employer bodies and industry associations have voiced opposition to the Mathadi Act since it was passed, organizing countervailing networks against the Boards. There have been accusations from management representatives that erring workers are rarely disciplined. They complain that mathadis refuse to accept the wages as determined by the Board and demand more at the factory gates. In order to curb this, there has been a unanimous demand from industry owners to expel such workers from the operation of the Mathadi Act.[112] A further criticism is that the system is operating as a union monopoly. This point was picked up in the Second National Commission on Labour:

> ... some witnesses did point out that the system works like a closed shop. Some representatives of the management also felt that this system created a monopoly and resulted in arbitrary fixation of wages. [7.378].[113]

Numerous court challenges to the Act have been attempted by these countervailing networks. At the time the Mathadi Act was first passed, the traders of Poona went to court to apply for a 'stay'.[114] A later challenge resulted in a 2009 Supreme Court of India judgment on the Mathadi Act that reinforced the jurisdiction of the Act over labourers: *Bhuwalka Steel Indus. Ltd v. Bombay Iron & Steel Labour Bd. & Anr.*[115]

4.4 Conclusion

Overall, the Mathadi Boards are a remarkable success story. Instead of extending labour law, as in the Bulgarian example, or layering on top of labour law, as in the Australian example, the Mathadi Act sets up an alternative regulatory model. This

[108] Datta L-5. [109] Ibid. L-5. [110] Interview with Arun S. Ranjane.
[111] Ibid.
[112] 'Panel to Discuss Removal of Organised Labourers from Mathadi Act' (editorial) *The Indian Express* (Pune, 19 February 2010).
[113] Government of India, *2nd Report of the National Commission on Labour* [2002] *129*.
[114] Awchat. [115] Supreme Court of India, December 17, 2009.

model performs all the functions of a normal labour law system, as well additional features, including health and education services, which have made great differences to the social development of mathadi workers and their families.

By bypassing or displacing the normal labour law model, regulators in Maharashtra have been able to experiment with different tools and levers from those traditionally employed. The Mathadi Boards gain their power by modifying the operation of the market. Rather than using the usual command and control model of sanctioning non-complying employers seen in most employment law systems, the Boards ensure that compliance occurs by acting as an intermediary in the hire and payment of workers. They therefore play an active, rather than reactive, role in the management of mathadi working conditions. The Boards are an effective model of regulation because they have a monopoly on the supply of labour. Normally, labour relations systems impact on labour supply and demand indirectly through regulating occupational training, qualifications, and pay rates. Most labour relations systems do not impinge on the operation of labour markets beyond these means. Controlling the supply of labour is a stronger lever than the tool kit of enforcement mechanisms normally available to regulators. Indeed, it might be considered a small scale 'governance' mechanism, like tariffs, as opposed to 'regulatory' mechanism, strictly speaking.[116]

An additional benefit of displacing the normal industrial relations system is that a *localized* strategy has been made possible. Boards are organized around the target populations—on the docks, in the markets—and respond to the particular needs of those populations. Hospitals have been created in response to community demand for health services, for instance. Further, because the system is imbued with a sense of experimentation and freed of path dependency, Boards have felt at liberty to try out new strategies to achieve the improved health and human development of mathadi workers. If the system were part of the normal labour relations system, the provision of health services might not be seen a a role for the institutional complex.

The Mathadi Act quickly became a model for implementation for informal workers in other states. The opportunity to experiment has resulted in replication, though arguably with less innovation than in the original model. Delegations of workers from other states such as Gujarat, Andhra Pradesh, Tamil Nadu, West Bengal, and so on visited Maharashtra and studied the new system.

Though the boards have been praised as a model for the regulation of unorganized workers,[117] they have not yet been used as a broader model for labour market regulation by the central Indian government. Over the last decade, various government inquiries have examined ways to improve the conditions of informal workers in India.[118] The primary result has been the Unorganised Workers' Social Security Act (2008) which follows the more modified welfare board model seen in Kerala. The Act is an important starting point for improving the livelihoods of the poor in India, but falls well short of the Mathadi Board model, which provides much more than a means of extending social security to informal workers. The government of India seems hesitant to implement models that allow for the agonistic bargaining processes of traditional labour law institutions and the Mathadi Boards, preferring instead a model of universal social security provision.

[116] Braithwaite, Coglianese, and Levi-Faur.

[117] Government of India, *2nd Report of the National Commission on Labour* (2002) *278*.

[118] Fourteenth Lok Sabha Committee on Petitions, Ministry of Labour and Employment, *Nineteenth Report* (Government of India 2006); Government of India, *Report on Definitional and Statistical Issues Relating to Informal Economy* (2008).

This chapter has shown that the formalization of mathadi workers occurred under a unique set of circumstances, in the context of labour unrest and communist influence in post-Independence Mumbai. These workers were able to gain strong political purchase because they represented a category of non-Brahmin workers who the majority Congress party wished to gain the support of and be seen to represent. Their early migration to urban centres also gave them advantages that other informal workers did not enjoy. They were also predominantly male, which likely gave their role in public discourse greater legitimacy.

Despite the extension of various labour protections to informal workers in India, in many ways the conditions of these workers have worsened rather than improved compared with the situation for mathadi workers in the 1960s. In an interview, Sheila Balla, labour historian, noted that the loss of arable land is still a salient issue for smallholders, 'as speculators buy [up the land], and land prices are increasing'. Thus, much of the rural population has come to resent that they are denied access to land, and the land is being lost to agriculture.[119] Though Balla noted that there is supposed to be some legal protection providing a 'cut-off point' at which land must not be converted to industrial use, it is not implemented in practice. As most people do not have enough land to cover their subsistence needs and to generate a profit, smallholders are forced to take on multiple jobs.[120]

Competition for informal work has increased since the 1990s amongst the growing precariat. Because of poor absorption rates in the formal industrial and service sectors, the informal sector grew between 1999–2005, whereas formal sector employment declined in both absolute and percentage terms over the same period. Meanwhile, informal sector employment went up from 361.7 million to 422.6 million over this five-year period.[121]

The living conditions of workers who migrate to urban centres have also become more precarious. One of the greatest threats to informal workers in Mumbai, as with other mega-cities around the world, is the fast pace of urban development. Cases are frequently reported in the news and filed in the courts of law by occupants of chawls, old and dilapidated buildings, and slum shanties against the grabbing of their properties by unscrupulous land developers and builders.[122] Harvey calls this process 'accumulation by dispossession'.[123] The precariousness of life for informal workers today in India makes the contribution of the Mathadi Act to the betterment of mathadi workers' lives all the more precious.

[119] Interview with Sheila Balla, workshop at India International Centre, Delhi, December 2013.

[120] Ibid.

[121] Dibyendu Maiti, 'Precarious Work in India: Trends and Emerging Issues' (2013) [2013] 57 American Behavioral Scientist 507 517.

[122] Sharma 84.

[123] David Harvey, 'The Right to the City' (2003) [2003] 27 International Journal of Urban and Regional Research 939.

5

Expansion and Layering of Labour Regulation

Apparel Industry in Australia

5.1 Introduction

Workers in developed economies have not been immune to the dynamics of global trade and economic liberalization that have stranded vulnerable workers in poorer countries. This chapter tracks the informalization of apparel production in Australia through the 1980s and 1990s, and subsequent attempts to re-formalize work by the creation of innovative legislation that expanded the scope of the employment relationship as well as ethical initiatives that added levers and regulatory agents. In order to assess the responsiveness of the regulatory innovations that were layered, one on top of the other, in the 1980s, 1990s, and 2000s this study contends that it is necessary to have a sense of what it might be responding to. How did national and international factors converge to leave a migrant group stranded, without the employment conditions and protections that Australia prided itself on providing to its working population?

As with most countries around the world, beginning in the 1980s, Australia opened its economy to global competition, reducing tariffs and other protectionist measures. At that time, more and more countries were establishing themselves as sites for apparel production—a comparatively easy market to enter. One such example is Cambodia, which is examined in a later chapter. When Australia opened itself to import penetration, its manufacturers were exposed to competition from poor economies whose competitive advantage was cheap labour. At the same time, in part as an attempt to remedy the wrongs of the 'White Australia' policy and Australia's involvement in the Vietnam War, Australia opened its borders to Asian immigration. An influx of Vietnamese and Chinese immigrants followed, many of whom were refugees who had spent time in camps before being settled in Australia. These two factors together—economic liberalization and an influx of new workers—fuelled the informalization of work. These types of informal workers are referred to both as 'outworkers' or 'homeworkers', and sometimes also as 'sweatshop workers'. Not only did this influx of immigrants contribute to an over-supply of unskilled labour, the workers' particular cultural preferences, as well as their experiences of war, state socialism, fleeing their countries of origin in small and unsafe boats and then being interned for years in refugee camps, contributed to their vulnerability and predilection for working at home, within family units.

5.1.1 Field work described in this chapter

My interest in industrial outwork in Australia was piqued when I was still an undergraduate student. I attended the initial meetings in 1994 which led to the formation of FairWear in 1995 and the development of the Code of Conduct described in this chapter. The narrative of formalization described in this chapter is informed by around twenty years of participant observation. In 2013, just over thirty Vietnamese workers were interviewed in the western suburbs of Melbourne.[1] The first four of these interviews were used as pilots for the development of questions. Twenty-six of these interviews were then conducted with a group of closed questions. Further interviews were conducted with union and community campaigners, employers, and fashion designers, as well as countless conversations over the years with players in the industry which inform the views expressed in this chapter.

Conducting interviews with workers entailed visiting the homes of industrial outworkers who migrated from Vietnam in the late 1970s, 1980s, and 1990s, where I recorded their life histories and observed them work, as their homes also serve as workplaces. Often husband and wife teams or good friends worked together. Sometimes children helped. Other relatives and friends lent a hand during particularly busy periods. They had purchased sewing machines and other materials and set up a production site in their garages, sheds, and spare rooms. I witnessed the labels of a number of well-known Australian brands being sewn into jackets, blouses, and pants.

For most of these people's working lives as machinists they had never received the legal rate of pay, paid holidays or sick leave. The families I interviewed reported frequently spending sixteen hours a day in these rooms, sewing clothes. They worked long hours in order to earn enough money to support their families. Most told stories of not being paid at all for weeks of work, as the 'outworker boss' who gives them work had disappeared or simply refused to pay. Some workers interviewed had very recently begun to enjoy something close to their legal entitlements.

Regardless of the long hours and the visible strain this work had placed on their bodies (many interviewees could not bear to sit for the length of the interview, they had to stand and move around while we talked), almost all interviewees spoke of this work in positive terms. They didn't know how they would have survived in Australia without it. It had allowed them to stay close to their families, to supervise their children's homework while they worked, to take short breaks to cook and then return to making a livelihood. Staying close to family members was particularly important for those who had experienced trauma in Vietnam and in the process of fleeing. All interviewees were proud of what they had been able to provide their children because of their hard work, and most with older children reported that they had professional jobs and university degrees.

The first part of this chapter identifies a number of factors that contributed to the informalization of outworkers in Australia since the 1980s, examining the extent of the entrenchment of informalization and its effect on such workers. The second part then examines the multi-layered regulatory initiatives that were later developed to address this informality, by both state and non-state players. This chapter provides an assessment of how a market-based corporate accountability approach in the Textile, Footwear, and Clothing (TFC) industry, overseen by a multi-stakeholder industry body, is layered over the existing labour law system. The market-based initiative is coupled with 'supply chain legislation' which expands the methods available to workers for recovering unpaid wages. Despite evidence that the regulatory initiatives described in this chapter were beginning to have some success in improving the conditions of

[1] All but two of the respondents to my interviews had arrived in Australia between 1990 and 1995 from Vietnam, and all were aged between 35 and 55. Equal numbers of men and women were interviewed, which differs from the general population of outworkers who are understood to be female. All but two were married and had dependent children. The eldest children of the respondents were in their late teens or 20s. All interviewees are referred to by pseudonyms.

home-based workers, they are being stripped back and de-funded by the conservative government elected in Australia in 2013. Thus, this chapter concludes by reflecting on the susceptibility to political dynamics of initiatives of this type.

5.2 Dynamics of Informalization

There have always been outworkers working in the TCF sector in Australia. Their numbers have ebbed and flowed with waves of immigration and other economic trends such as levels of protection.[2] The period of growth of informal work in Australia—the 1980s and 1990s studied in this chapter—is only one instance of cycles of growth and retraction in informal work in the TCF industry since industrialization. Fluctuations in both the numbers of outworkers and the extent of informality can be attributed to various causes, with different disciplines emphasizing one over the other, often viewing each in isolation.

The following section identifies four important dynamics of informalization, representing an attempt to understand the ways that these dynamics intersected and compounded one another. This section then continues to explain the effects of informalization on the conditions of workers and examines the extent of its entrenchment.

5.2.1 Macro-economic restructuring and liberalization

One of the most significant triggers of informalization in Australia's apparel industry was the stripping of tariffs and import quotas in order to better integrate Australia's economy into global trade.

The TCF industry in Australia, particularly clothing manufacturers, was traditionally protected by high tariffs and/or import quotas. The early emphasis was on tariffs. The rationale for tariff protection in Australia in the early part of the twentieth century was both to provide shelter infant industries and also to foster decent work. The 1929 Brigden report stated that 'there is more to be said for protecting an industry because it employs labour at good wages than for any other reason'.[3] Tariffs supported integrated production, with most aspects of manufacturing being conducted by large enterprises who employed a large permanent workforce.

Beginning in 1974, tariffs were reduced and replaced with import quotas.[4] Further reductions in protection occurred between 1988 and 1995 under the 1987 TCF Industry Plan (or the Button Plan, as it came to be known), with the eventual effect of reducing the maximum tariff on TCF products to 25 per cent in 2000.[5] The era of protection for manufacturers was largely over. It became much cheaper for Australian

[2] Jamie Peck, 'Outwork and Restructuring Processes in the Australian Clothing Industry' 3 Labour and Industry.

[3] M. Samuelson, 'The Australian Case for Protection Re-examined' 54 Quarterly Journal of Economics 143.

[4] This section draws on the Department of Industry, Science and Resources, 'Textile, Clothing, Footwear and Leather Industries: Action Agendas: A Discussion Paper' (Commonwealth of Australia, 7–8 March 1999), available at: http://apecenergy.org.au/content/itrinternet/cmscontent.cfm?objectid=BCCB4B2B-4877-4C71-A76CB89E1A77BE3B&indexPages=/content/sitemap.cfm?objectid=48A5B076-20E0-68D8-EDDA6165C0953D2F.

[5] Department of Industry Tourism and Resources, *Review of the Textile, Clothing and Footwear Strategic Investment Program Scheme—Report* (2002).

fashion houses to source production overseas for certain segments of the market. This was facilitated by changes in the institutions governing international markets as well as the reforms within developing and emerging economies which enabled them to realize their competitive advantage in labour-intensive production.[6]

The garment manufacturing industry in Australia haemorrhaged. There were reports of factories closing on a weekly basis. Other Australian industries survived increased import penetration by improving productivity and quality. However, technological constraints placed a ceiling on the benefits to be gained by upgrading the garment industry.

5.2.2 Small-scale production makes homeworking viable

Liberalization of the apparel trade alone would not have been sufficient to create informality amongst outworkers. Indeed, the apparel industry requires specific technological and organizational conditions, the nature of which renders the industry susceptible to informality. Unlike most significant contemporary industries, much of the clothing sector remains small scale and labour intensive. The production process uses small, low-cost machinery, easily operated by an individual, and transportable raw materials with a high 'labour input to bulk' ratio.[7] There are technological limits intrinsic to clothing manufacture. Operators cannot keep up with the speed of advanced sewing machines. Handling time comprises 70–90 per cent of the sewing process, which slows the process down considerably.[8] Technological advances in pattern making, pre-programming and inventory control have given factories the ability to subcontract manufacturing processes while still ensuring that a certain level of quality is maintained.[9]

Although there are advantages of scale in conducting work in factories, the technology is basically the same in the outward processing or cut, make, and trim end of production, regardless of whether the work is carried out at home or in a factory. Homeworkers can buy their own machine(s), operate them in their home, and receive sufficient raw materials to work for a number of days.

Fashion trends in the women's and sporting sectors in the latter part of the twentieth century further opened the market for outworkers in the TFC industry in Australia. Whereas there were previously only two to four annual seasons of fashion, there was now consumer demand for constant changes in stock and greater product differentiation. This meant ever shorter lead-in times for production and smaller runs of one style of garment were required. Electronic sales and inventory systems allowed for a speedy evaluation of production requirements on individual lines. Finally, the call for swift delivery of fashion merchandise meant that Australian production had geographic advantages compared to offshore apparel producers, where retailers could be left with unsold, out-dated products if international orders were not delivered promptly.[10] This made production in urban homes a viable option for the production of certain lines of apparel in Australia. Once production was occurring at home, it was much harder to regulate, as later sections discuss.

[6] Productivity Commission, *Modelling Economy-Wide Effects of Future TCF Assistance* (Productivity Commission Research Report, Australian Government, June 2008, 2008) xv.

[7] Jamie Peck, *Work-Place: The Social Regulation of Labor Markets* (Guilford Press 1996).

[8] Bradon Ellem, *In Women's Hands? A History of Clothing Trades Unionism in Australia* (New South Wales University Press 1989).

[9] Senate Economics Reference Committee, *Outworkers in the Garment Industry* (1996) 8.

[10] Peck, 'Outwork and Restructuring Processes in the Australian Clothing Industry'.

5.2.3 Integrated firms disintegrate to pass on competitive risks

The liberalization of trade barriers, in addition to the growing propensity towards small runs, encouraged the vertical disintegration of large, integrated apparel manufacturers who had previously managed the full package of production 'in-house'. The speed of this vertical disintegration was propelled by strong downwards pressure from ever more powerful retailers and brands.

The restructuring of the TCF industry in Australia resulted in a concentration of market power amongst a small number of retailers, as many smaller retailers could not cope with import penetration and changes in the industry. The clothing retail industry in Australia is dominated by a small number of major players—Myer and David Jones at the higher end, Target and K-Mart at the lower end, and clothing chains such as those owned by the Just Group—hold the lion share of the market.[11],[12] This concentration of retailer market power, coupled with the damage to local manufacturers resulting from import penetration, gave rise to new power dynamics in the industry in the 1980s and 1990s. Retailers were able to call the shots in ways not previously possible. It is for this reason that TCF value chains in Australia have been characterized as vertical supply chains.[13]

Manufacturers responded to heightened competition from imports and local businesses by throwing off non-core aspects of their business or 'contracting in' peripheral services and functions. These forms of vertical disintegration—the breaking up of large, integrated, multi-function corporations into smaller units— led to a re-distribution of economic and social risk.[14] For lead businesses that made employees redundant, this was an important risk management and cost reduction strategy, enabling business to evade responsibility for continuing to uphold wages for workers, and to maintain occupational health and safety standards, for example—regardless of fluctuations in working capital or customer demand.

Layoffs from factories and growing unemployment and underemployment increased the supply, and decreased the bargaining strength, of peripheral, vulnerable workers.[15] The latter competed with each other for jobs, accepting the terms they were offered. The result was a further contraction in formal employment in the industry[16] and ever more complicated supply chains.

5.2.4 Social factors compound economic causes of informality

At the same time as Australia was integrating into the global economy in trade, the nation was also opening up to immigration from Asia. Following the end of the 'White Australia' policy, Australia accepted large numbers of Vietnamese immigrants, in part to remedy the perceived injustice of its involvement in the Vietnam War. These

[11] Sally Weller, *Retailing, Clothing and Textiles Production in Australia* (Working Paper No 29, Centre for Strategic Economic Studies, Victoria University, October 2007, 2007).

[12] Not all supply chains in Australia are buyer-driven. Small designers that sell from small boutiques do not wield the same level of power, and in these supply chains manufacturers may be dominant.

[13] Michael Rawling and Sarah Kaine, 'Regulating Supply Chains to Provide a Safe Rate for Road Transport Workers' 25 Australian Journal of Labour Law 237.

[14] Louise Amoore, *Globalization Contested: An International Political Economy of Work* (Manchester University Press 2002).

[15] Mayhew and Quinlan, 'Outsourcing and Occupational Health and Safety: A Comparative Study of Factory-Based and Outworkers in the Australian TCF Industry' (1999) 29(1) International Journal of Health Services 83.

[16] Peck, 'Outwork and Restructuring Processes in the Australian Clothing Industry'.

immigrants arrived in Australia with low English language levels, no savings, non-transferable skills, and suffering trauma from their experiences of social upheaval. These attributes meant that home-based work in the apparel industry was one of the only occupations available to them upon arrival. This section of the chapter explores the reasons that workers entered home-based work.

Chinese, Korean, and other Asian immigrants have also made up significant proportions of outworkers from the 1990s to today. However, this section focuses on Vietnamese immigrants, as these were the primary respondents to the qualitative interviews conducted for this study.

Vietnamese immigration into Australia charts a unique history—an understanding of which will help to elucidate how this group of immigrants became entrenched in informal outwork. The first major wave of Vietnamese migration to Australia started in the mid-1970s, with the arrival of large numbers of refugees following the end of the Vietnam War. In 1976, the first boat carrying Vietnamese refugees arrived in Australia. By 1981, the Vietnam-born population in Victoria, the state in which interviews for this chapter was carried out, was over 12,000.[17] A second wave of Vietnamese immigration occurred in 1983–84, following the 1982 agreement between the Australian and Vietnamese governments (the Orderly Departure Program) which allowed relatives of Vietnamese Australians to leave Vietnam and migrate to Australia. The third peak in the late 1980s seems to have been mainly due to the family reunion scheme. Vietnamese-born settlers accounted for 8 per cent of all settlers who arrived in 1992 and represented an outflow of 100 per million of that country's population.[18] Today Vietnam-born people represent the fifth largest migrant community in Australia, and after the United States of America, Australia is the second most common destination for Vietnamese migrants.

One reason that many Vietnamese immigrants found themselves conducting industrial outwork after arriving in Australia was because they were economically disadvantaged. Like other immigrants, Vietnamese immigrants to Australia generally do less well economically than their counterparts who have been born in the country. Even in countries such as Australia, which maintain large-scale government-funded programs to assist immigrants to settle to minimize economic disruption, economic disadvantage still takes place. Reflecting the trends in immigration literature, McAllister[19] identifies three main explanations to account for the apparently universal economic disadvantages experienced by immigrants to a new country.

The first explanation sees these economic differences as a consequence of the lower levels of human capital available to immigrants. This is reflected in the possession of fewer and sometimes inferior educational qualifications and skills, and less experience within the host society, including poor language skills and other cultural disadvantages. Once they are placed within an economically advanced labour market, competing against a skilled and experienced workforce, immigrants are immediately disadvantaged. The second explanation points to overt discrimination by employers who choose to hire those born in the country in preference to equally well-qualified and experienced immigrants. A third explanation for the economic disadvantages of immigrants put forward by McAllister is that the act of migration itself has negative consequences for a working career.

[17] Immigration Museum Victoria, *History of Immigration from Vietnam* (Victoria, Australia, 2013).

[18] Australian Bureau of Statistics, *4102.0-Australian Social Trends, 1994* (Canberra, Australia, 1994).

[19] Ian McAllister, 'Occupational Mobility among Immigrants: The Impact of Migration on Economic Success in Australia' 29 International Migration Review 441.

Each of these explanations is supported by the data collected in the interviews conducted for this study. Like Christina Cregan,[20] whose study is described in greater detail later in this chapter, I found that a major factor affecting the choice of work available to outworkers when they first arrived in Australia was low language and occupational skills. This put recently arrived immigrants at a distinct disadvantage once they arrived in Australia. Of the respondents to Cregan's study, nearly one sixth had been educated only to primary school level, over a half had attended high school level, and the remainder had attended a tertiary institution. Only about 10 per cent—those raised and educated in Australia—said they were fluent. A number of interviewees I spoke to explained that they had tried to learn English but had insufficient time due to job and family demands.

Low literacy levels are also likely to make acquisition of a second language more difficult. Vietnam has a low human development index rating compared with Australia. Most of the workers interviewed for this chapter arrived in the third wave of Vietnamese immigration—in the late 1980s or early 1990s, though some arrived in the first wave. Vietnam was a poor country at this time, with low education, health, and income. In 1990, the earliest date at which data of this type became available for Vietnam, its human development index (HDI) was 0.439.[21] Australia's ranking was 0.880 in 1990.[22] The HDI comparison shows a marked disparity between the two countries' life expectancy, education, and income levels. Even today, the mean years of attendance at school in Vietnam is 5, compared with Australia where the mean number of years is 12. Only one respondent interviewed for my research had a professional qualification. The majority had not completed high school. Very few of the women I interviewed had gone beyond year 8 at high school. Prior to migrating, most were farmers, fishermen or had worked as tailors in family businesses. There were only a few exceptions: one interviewee had finished school and been a bookkeeper in Vietnam. Her aspiration, putting all barriers to one side, was to be an accountant or bookkeeper in Australia, but she had not realized that aspiration. Apart from those who had worked as tailors, most found that their skills and life experience to that point did not help them in the Australian job market.

This low skill base of interviewees was certainly made worse by the experience of migration, in keeping with McAllister's thesis. Many of the workers came to Australia on boats or had spent a number of years in refugee camps in the very years when they would normally be laying the foundations for their future working lives. A number of respondents to my study explained to me the ways in which being in a refugee camp set them back economically. Although it provided safety and refuge, paid work is not allowed in refugee camps. Some refugees who had sought refuge in Hong Kong and gained some form of residency for a number of years before coming to Australia were allowed to work. Two worked in clothing factories in Hong Kong which provided a good background for industrial outwork. Others who were held in Malaysia were not allowed to work at all. This meant that during the years when people are normally attending university or acquiring trade skills of some type, they were excluded from skill formation.

[20] Christina Cregan, 'Vietnamese Outworkers in the Australian Garment Industry: Sweated Labour and the Social Wage' (IREC).

[21] Vietnam Country Report, Human Development Reports, United Nations Development Program, http://hdr.undp.org/en/countries/profiles/VNM, accessed 15 January 2018.

[22] Ibid.

Finding themselves without appropriate skills, but needing work quickly, they relied on friends to help them gain the skills needed to gain work in Australia. Other than those who already possessed sewing skills, most interviewees were taught how to use sewing machines by friends and family. Most respondents said that they found out about sewing work because a family member or friend told them the work was available. They relied on these social networks to find work partly because they perceived that they lacked the skills for the formal economy, and partly because they lacked the knowledge to navigate the formal job market. This is consistent with Christina Cregan's study, which was conducted in 2001[23] and which found that 70 per cent of workers found the work through friends.

Even those who were engaged as outworkers after answering ads in newspapers reported that they were encouraged to do so by friends who were doing similar work. Ads for outwork were posted in Vietnamese newspapers, and the employers or 'outworker' bosses were generally also from the Vietnamese community.

This fact of finding work through social networks is consistent with the literature on informal work.[24] Indeed, research in the field of social networks shows that the market for informal work operates differently from the market for formal work.[25] Similarly, research conducted in 1995 in South Australia found that over 50 per cent of Vietnamese respondents belonged to 'community networks', compared with fewer than a quarter of the other groups.[26] Those involved in community type networks have linked contacts, or what might be termed in the social capital literature strong horizontal 'bonding capital'.[27] Their kin, occupational, religious, and other social ties tend to intersect and overlap.

While these community networks provide a strong assurance of finding work, they also limit the *type* of occupations available. The portrayal of the nature of social networks in the Vietnamese community studied in Carson's[28] project resonates with the ways that respondents to my study described their social ties. Most interviewees could only speak very basic English and we needed an interpreter to help conduct the interviews. This limited their social interactions to those with Vietnamese language skills, and thus those within their own communities. Because interviewees lived in areas with many other Vietnamese families, they could do their shopping, attend church or Buddhist temple, and socialize within their own ethnic community. They enjoyed close relations with other community members and relatives but did not mix within broader Australian society. One respondent, who lives in St Albans, Melbourne, said that she only leaves the house to do the shopping or take the children places. As the respondent does not speak English, she 'does not know what is going on outside the house, except what her husband tells her'. She said, 'with young children and no English, I can't imagine how that would change'.

A Vietnamese couple interviewed for this study, Lan and Hung Nguyen, share a personal history which is emblematic of the factors discussed in this section. The couple described the traumatic circumstances which characterized their passage to

23 Cregan.

24 Marcelo Arbex and Dennis O'Dea, 'Informal Work Networks' 44 Canadian Journal of Economics 247.

25 Ibid.

26 Edgar Carson, *Social Networks and Job Acquisition in Ethnic Communities in South Australia* (Canberra: Australian Govt. Pub. Service 1995).

27 Michael Woolcock and Deepa Narayan, 'Social Capital: Implications for Development Theory, Research, and Policy' 15 The World Bank Research Observer 225.

28 Carson.

Australia—how they left Vietnam in 1989 with 152 others, crammed into a small boat. It was not until they were sure that they were out of Vietnamese waters and clear of Vietnamese authorities that all the passengers on the boat collectively decided which country the boat should head towards. The passengers slept propped up against a wall or leaning on someone else.

They were both from Hue, Vietnam. The husband had studied teaching at a university in Vietnam—he was the only respondent with a tertiary education. The United Nations (UN) refugee camp that they were taken to in the Philippines did not allow refugees to work. After being interviewed by the UN High Commission for Refugees (HCR), the couple were categorized as refugees and put on a waiting list until a country would accept them. Because of restrictions on working in refugee camps, the husband's teaching skills lay idle. Once again, the couple did not know where they would end up. It might have been Canada, the US, or Australia. After three years of waiting, they were sent to Australia.

When they arrived they were given the opportunity to take English classes, but the husband struggled to learn English, as he was scarcely able to find the time to attend the government-run classes. He found it difficult to fit in studying, looking for work, and doing odd jobs at the same time. By now the couple had two young children whom he needed to support. The family received unemployment benefits, but it was not enough to live on. In 1996, the husband felt despondent about the prospects for learning adequate English to become a teacher. He explained that to be a teacher you have to be highly fluent, not just proficient. He was forced, therefore, to find a new career. Many of their friends were working as homeworkers, so the husband and wife together obtained a 'licence' to sew clothes. They began their working lives as industrial outworkers, learning the skills from friends. This new job allowed the couple to remain at home for their children and also be together.

The couple placed a high value on being able to stay together. This seemed to be a consequence of the trauma they had mutually experienced. After suffering political repression in Vietnam, leaving their home country and being separated from close family, staying together was important for the pair. Working from home allowed them to work as a team in an environment that they had control over.

This finding is speculative, but consistent with the literature on refugees and trauma. Various adverse psychiatric consequences of traumatic events have been widely reported in refugee populations. Epidemiological studies have identified post-traumatic stress disorder and depression as the two most prevalent disorders in refugee populations.[29] A study of 1,161 households with Vietnamese speaking members in Australia confirms the experience of trauma by refugees in Vietnamese communities. Slightly more than half the respondents had left Vietnam by boat; about the same proportion had lived in a refugee camp for a mean period of nineteen months before arriving in Australia. Two hundred and three (17 per cent) respondents were separated from immediate family members because of their flight to Australia, and 624 (54 per cent) were separated from other close relatives. Respondents reported exposure to between two to seven different traumatic events.[30] The study found that those respondents who had been subjected to trauma were far more likely to experience mental illness of some type.[31]

The broad outline of Lan and Hung Nguyen's story was quite typical of the personal histories that other interviewees shared with me, although important personal

[29] Zachary Steel and others, 'Long-Term Effect of Psychological Trauma on the Mental Health of Vietnamese Refugees Resettled in Australia: A Population-Based Study' 360 The Lancet 1056 1057.

[30] Ibid. 1059. [31] Ibid. 1059.

details varied. Some had quite horrific stories that it is hard to imagine them ever recovering from. The husband of one of the organizers employed by the TCFUA had fled Vietnam ahead of the rest of the family, hiding in a shipping container. He was found dead weeks later when the shipping container was unpacked, thought to have starved or died from dehydration.

We can see from the personal histories of the workers how various factors combined to draw them into home-based work.

Research into outwork conducted by Peck has showed that the fact that there were so many people choosing sewing as an alternative to continuing to search for work in the broader workforce was a factor that contributed to informality.[32] The supply of labour far outstripped demand. Thousands of people were arriving in Australia with either low skills or skills which had little relevance to the Australian context. Every poor, recently arrived, immigrant that answered an advertisement in an ethnic community newspaper was effectively adding to the power of the intermediaries to demand lower and lower piece rates. As factory workers lost their jobs, they also joined the ranks of workers looking for work as homeworkers. And so, a pool of workers was created that had little incentive to push for higher wages, because they needed the work and did not want to cause ripples that might lead to them losing it.[33]

Downwards pressure on pay and conditions, created by the oversupply of labour, created the conditions for informality and mistrust of formal institutions deepened it. New immigrants had little trust in the institutions of government (and, by association, trade unions). In state socialist countries, such as Vietnam, the union and the state are not separate. They are arms of the same apparatus. Thus, workers were reticent to make a complaint or join collective action for better working conditions. The literature on refugees and mistrust is vast and will not be rehearsed here.[34] For refugees who have fled oppressive governments, there is good reason to stay clear of the institutions of the state.

Affiliations with trade unions may have helped to broaden the economic networks and established wider bases of trust for new Vietnamese outworkers. In both liberal democratic societies and state socialist ones, trade unions also provide bridging social capital[35] and the building of connections between heterogeneous groups from different walks of life. Association with a workers' organization or trade union helps to create social relations with people outside our immediate ethnic or social group. Organizations like trade unions help to broaden our 'radius of trust': the size of the circle within which people are willing to extend trust.[36] However, it seems that their experiences of political oppression in Vietnam meant they were unable to fully take advantage of these networks.

Interviewees generally spoke extremely highly of the Australian state and the bureaucracies they had contact with over their years in Australia. Yet, ingrained habits of mistrust were difficult to shake. Interviewees found it difficult to change entrenched practices of taking steps to evade state notice. This contrasted with respondents in Bulgaria, discussed in a later chapter, who mistrusted the state but still believed it was the role of the state to solve their economic problems.

[32] Peck, 'Outwork and Restructuring Processes in the Australian Clothing Industry'.

[33] Ibid.

[34] E. Valentine Daniel and John Chr. Knudsen (eds), *Mistrusting Refugees* (University of California Press 1995).

[35] Woolcock and Narayan.

[36] Francis Fukuyama, *Trust: The Social Virtues and the Creation of Prosperity* (Free Press 1995).

This distrust of the state had two effects. On the one hand, it decreased the likelihood that Vietnamese outworkers and those of other ethnic groups who fled state oppression would make a complaint to the Union or the FairWork Ombudsman (the Australian state's labour inspectorate) regarding labour conditions. Interviewees generally feared that if they made a complaint they would not receive work again, and their reputation as a worker would be marred. Outworkers I interviewed who had made a complaint to the Union reported that they had reached breaking point before going to the Union. In all cases, they only complained when they had not been paid for weeks of work, generally on more than one occasion. On the other hand, this distrust of the state encouraged further reliance on close social networks. When state repression has been your experience, it appears that staying within known and familiar social networks and harbouring a strong spirit of autonomy is a way to stay safe, even if it means working long hours for little pay. Many of workers that I interviewed expressed strong ethics of self-reliance that were both a statement of entrepreneurialism and resilience, and also a culture of keeping one's head down and trying not to draw the attention of the state and its agents.

5.2.5 Extent of informalization and conditions of workers

As a consequence of these compounding dynamics, by the mid-1990s, the number of outworkers working in the TCF industry in Australia numbered anywhere between 23,650[37] and 329,000,[38] depending on the source of the estimate. It is difficult to put forward reliable figures, due to the informal, sporadic and seasonal nature of outworker employment. The TCFUA estimated that outworkers outnumbered factory workers by 12 to 1 by 1994.[39] Unfortunately, more recent figures are not available.

Today, long-run standardized production often occurs overseas in large factories, while shorter run and overload work occurs in small factories and homes in suburban Australia. As at February 2010, textile, leather, clothing, and footwear manufacturing employed 40,600 people in formal jobs, representing 4.4 per cent of the entire manufacturing sector workforce in Australia.[40] It is important to note however, that the Australian Bureau of Statistics (ABS) data (from which those figures are drawn) accounts for the formal workforce and does not include analysis of the informal workforce, about whom it is difficult to estimate numbers. The number of outworkers is likely to have shrunk with the contraction of production in Australia, although it is broadly believed that the proportion of outworkers compared with factory workers has continued to grow. Household survey techniques would need to be employed to ascertain the current extent of home-based work and to design appropriate enforcement strategies.

Work in the TCF industry is highly feminized, likely contributing to low bargaining power. The formal textile, leather, clothing, and footwear manufacturing sector has the greatest share of female workers at 61.3 per cent.[41] Compare this with wood product manufacturing, which has the greatest ratio of male workers, at 89.4 per cent. Workers in formal TCF manufacturing earn the lowest average wages of all manufacturing

[37] Industry Commission, *The Textile, Clothing and Footwear Industries* (1997).

[38] Textile Clothing and Footwear Union of Australia, *The Hidden Cost of Fashion: Report on the National Outwork Information Campaign* (Textile Clothing and Footwear Union of Australia 1995).

[39] Ibid.

[40] Employment and Workplace Relations' Department of Education, *Employment Outlook for Manufacturing* (Canberra, 2011) 5.

[41] Ibid. 13.

sectors at $690 per week. This compares with $950 on average in all manufacturing industries. By contrast, petroleum and coal product manufacturing is the highest earning manufacturing sector with a median average of $1200.[42] Because the ABS has not collected data regarding home-based workers, figures regarding pay and conditions have to be drawn from elsewhere.

There has not been a qualitative or quantitative study of the working conditions and pay of industrial outworkers in the TCF industry for many years. The most recent and comprehensive study of these workers conditions comes from a study conducted by Christina Cregan of the University of Melbourne in 2001.[43] Cregan surveyed 119 homeworkers using a snowballing technique to recruit the interviewees. All had come to Australia from 1979 onwards. They had travelled in small boats and arrived via transit camps in South East Asia. They were ethnic Vietnamese from the South. She surveyed 116 females and 3 males whose ages ranged from 17 to 64. The average age was 39 and the mode was 50.

Cregan found that, on average, workers received around AUD $0.50 to $5.00 an hour for their work—less than half the legal minimum—once piece rates are converted to hourly rates.[44] (The legal minimum Australian wage, as of 1 July 2014, has been set at $16.87 per hour (or $640.90 per 38-hour week before tax).) Around 62 per cent of the workers worked seven days per week, and 95 per cent of respondents did not receive holiday leave, sick leave, or public holiday pay.[45] Another study comparing the occupational health and safety (OHS) experience of factory-based workers and outworkers in the clothing industry found that outworkers suffered three times the level of injuries experienced by factory-based workers. The two main reasons for the differences in injury rates were the use of a piecework payment system and the long hours worked by outworkers.[46] Working hours were particularly long. Nearly two-thirds (62 per cent) spent seven days a week sewing, with a further 26 per cent working for six days. Almost all of them worked during the school holidays and on public holidays.

The reason for the longest hours was rush jobs. When workers had to finish rush jobs they worked from very early in the morning to midnight or later. The workers expressed no choice about taking on rush jobs, since any job was needed. Another factor is that workers need to work for as many hours as possible in order to make a living wage. The excessive hours and inevitable worry lead to strains on the physical and mental health of the outworkers. Physical problems included exhaustion, dizziness, eye problems, and aches and pains. Often, after a long day, workers complained of difficulty getting to sleep. Respondents to Cregan's study reported constantly worrying about irregular work and gaps between the end of a job and the beginning of a new one. A number of homeworkers reported receiving unfair treatment. They were intimidated and controlled by their need for work and pay.

5.2.6 Entrenchment of informality

Over time, both the available data and my research suggest that a group of workers have become stuck in home-based work. Interviews with workers indicated that there are various interrelated causes.

I was struck, when conversing with these interviewees, by how hard it was to get them to talk about different working futures or aspirations for alternative careers. The respondents had limited ideas about what other work they could do after many years

[42] Ibid. [43] Cregan. [44] Christina Cregan, *Home Sweat Home* (2002).
[45] Ibid. [46] Mayhew and Quinlan.

engaged as outworkers in the TCF industry. They became animated when discussing the study and careers of their children, but their tone was flat when they responded to questions about their own working lives and the alternative occupations they could engage in. They likewise had very few opinions about what changes the government could undertake to improve their situation. They were willing to respond to closed questions but did not offer opinions or provide detailed answers to open-ended questions on these points. Responses were short or required numerous follow up questions and re-framing to elicit a response that had been answered with enthusiasm by their Bulgarian counterparts.

Lan Nguyen, described earlier in this chapter, immediately answered the question of why she kept doing this work despite the low pay and other problems with the words, 'for our children'. Homework allowed her to be home all the time. When her children were little she could work around their day sleep times and when they were occupied with other activities. When they were in bed at night, she could begin work again. Once they were at school, she could work during school hours, supervise their after-school activities, cook dinner and begin work again when the kids were resting and sleeping. All respondents rated being able to care for children extremely highly, as a reason for doing homework.

Regardless of the down-sides—the isolation, the demands of the work, the low pay—this facet of industrial outwork was greatly valued by respondents of both genders. Some women said that they would like to find work outside the house once their children were independent, so they could socialize with other people more and work regular hours. But they only saw this as an option once their children were grown.

One of the reasons that interviewees were willing to give up so much in order to stay at home was related to their cultural preferences for child-rearing. None had placed their children in childcare when they were of pre-school age. Most interviewees with children of school age took them to numerous extra-curricular activities after school, including extra tuition to boost their school marks. This is commonplace amongst certain ethnic groups, particularly Vietnamese Australians. A number of respondents said that being at home was even more important when their children were in high school than in primary school, because the children needed more supervision with homework and other activities, and because they were facing more complex social problems at school. One respondent complained that their children had faced racism at school from teachers, and had wanted to leave school, so they had needed emotional support and considerable urging to keep studying.

For interviewees whose children had finished school, they generally believed that this strategy had paid off. The children of interviewees who were past school age had, almost without fail, attended university. Many were now working in professional, well-paying and secure jobs and were able to provide financial support to their parents. This was a great source of pride for the interviewees.

The male respondents recounted slightly different reasons for remaining as homeworkers, despite the poor conditions. Their perception was that they had become trapped. For example, because Hung Nguyen was working long hours, he didn't have time to continue with English study, and because he was working from home, his English abilities stagnated and then deteriorated. His confidence in his capacity to learn English also diminished the longer he worked from home. By the time he was in his 40s, retraining seemed futile, even if he somehow managed to find the time. He didn't believe that anyone would hire a man in his 40s who was just starting out. The only option was to find work in a factory doing the same work as he was doing at home. He looked but factories were letting people go, not hiring. When I asked him what he would prefer to be doing instead of working as a homeworker he said, 'working in a factory'. Because he had already told me he didn't like doing sewing work, I pushed him, and asked, 'but would you do if things were different, and you could do anything at all?'. He answered, 'be a teacher'.

Years working as outworkers limited access to the institutions that facilitate moving into high-paid work or into other occupational fields. To use industrial relations terminology, it exacerbates 'labour market ossification' for this group of workers. There is no path of career progression within the industry for an outworker, other than becoming an intermediary and employing others to conduct the work. Projections for the future of work in the industry are gloomy. The textile, leather, clothing and, footwear manufacturing sector is expected to experience the strongest decline in employment of all manufacturing sectors with a predicted fall of around 4 per cent per year in the five years after 2014.[47] This is partially related to the further reduction in tariffs planned for this period, but it is primarily linked to the increased competition from cheaply made imports, given the consistently high value of the Australian dollar.

Most of Lan and Hung Nguyen's friends who had moved out of the industry had found work as fruit and vegetable pickers. The Nguyens said they were relieved not to be doing this kind of work, since it involves driving 2–3 hours to get to the farms that require pickers, and then home at night. They said that during picking season, those people hardly see their families. Hung said, 'It isn't work you can do at the same time as caring for children, but if someone can stay home with the kids, you can make an OK living.' It appears that for these outworkers, the acceptance of low rates of pay and poor working conditions is closely related to a lack of employment alternatives.

5.3 Dynamics of Formalization

Up until the mid-1980s, it was the policy of the relevant trade union—the TCFUA—that outwork should be illegal. The Union did not organize workers of this type and actively tried to persuade manufacturers not to use them. In the mid-1980s, the TCFUA changed its position and began to push for the extension of formal entitlements to outworkers. The response to such pressure by governmental authorities has been incremental. First, in 1987, the federal industrial tribunal adopted award provisions designed to permit regulatory agencies to supervise the contracting process and to extend minimum entitlements to outworkers. In the mid-1990s, after the TCFUA published a report titled 'The Hidden Cost of Fashion', which gained considerable community attention, the Union joined with community groups and churches to form an organization called 'FairWear'.[48] Further pressure by the Union and community groups led to the adoption of voluntary codes of practice by retailers and manufacturer employers intended to provide incentives for the core companies to ensure that outworkers were extended most of the same formal entitlements as employees. Thereafter, lobbying efforts were directed at state governments to enact specialist legislation which deemed outworkers to be employees at law and allowed workers to make claims for unpaid entitlements against parties who were not the direct contractor in the supply chain. These laws differed slightly in each state in which they were enacted. In 2011, lobbying efforts resulted in this state legislation being mirrored in national legislation.

[47] Department of Education 7.

[48] Rosaria Burchielli and others, 'The FairWear Campaign: An Ethical Network in the Australian Garment Industry' (2009) 90 Journal of Business Ethics 575.

This chapter considers each of these steps to have added a 'layer' of regulation and additional regulatory levers to the existing labour laws.

5.3.1 Expansion and layering

This section of the paper assesses reforms and layers that were added to the core regulatory instruments of labour law in order to address the informality experienced by outworkers. They include:

i. The amendment of the definition of 'employee' in the core regulatory instruments, so as to expand the scope of labour regulation for outworkers
ii. The establishment of a voluntary code, which companies may sign up to, regulated by an accrediting and promotional body called Ethical Clothing Australia, which is overseen by a multi-stakeholder body
iii. The enactment of new supply chain legislation, that allows outworkers to make claims for unpaid entitlements against another party higher up in the supply chain, even where they are not deemed employees under the award or state 'deeming' acts.

The primary aim of these interlocking regulations is that homeworkers receive the same pay, entitlements, and working conditions as workers who toil within factories. The next section describes how this layering works to bolster the core institution and alter the incentive structure.

5.3.1.1 The core institution: award regulation and labour legislation

In Australia, labour laws are constituted of legislation—the FairWork Act 2009 at the Federal level—and awards—multi-employer industrial agreements that set out the minimum conditions under which employees in a specific industry can be employed (referred to jointly as 'labour laws' in this paper). In 1987, the Federal Clothing Trades Award (now the Textile, Clothing, Footwear and Associated Industries Award 2010) was extended to cover outworkers. These provisions are reflected in state awards and provide outworkers with the same rights as other employees, including regular work, overtime pay, paid holidays, annual service leave, and long service leave, superannuation, and the right to skills assessment. In other words, the scope of labour law was expanded.

Despite this legislative advance, widespread non-compliance with labour laws continued, suggesting that expansion of the scope of labour laws was not enough. In 1996, a Senate Committee noted that with regards to outworkers '[t]he practice of non-compliance with the award wages and conditions is so widespread that it is considered to be the norm'.[49] There appear to be two major reasons for this continued non-compliance. Firstly, by requiring that outworking be regulated as a form of 'employment', the regulatory form creates incentives for evasion through creative supply chain management. Secondly, the award does not sanction those who have power within the supply chains, rendering the award an inadequate tool for shaping behaviour throughout the market.

[49] Senate Economics Reference Committee.

The legal form of the employment relationship creates perverse incentives for those organizing work to avoid compliance through choosing advantageous legal forms.[50] Employers and intermediaries often pressure outworkers to establish themselves as separate business enterprises and thus become, by definition, self-employed contractors.[51] This circumvention means that both workers who are considered employees under the relevant laws, and those who are not, may work in the same supply chain, carrying out the same work for the same intermediary. Yet because one is registered as a 'business' they are not entitled to the same conditions as those who were not.

Secondly, the expansion of the definition of employee did not address the broader power dynamics in supply chains that were contributing to non-compliance with labour laws. Private market regulation puts strong downwards pressure on supply chains and is a cause of informality. The direct employers, known as 'outworker bosses' in the TCF industry, may not have very much discretion in determining the wages (piece rates), hours (largely determined by volume of work) or other conditions under which outworkers toil. Parties above them in the supply chain, such as manufacturers, wholesalers, and retailers, often have far greater control over these factors. As has been demonstrated elsewhere[52] and discussed in Chapter 2, supply chains in the TCF industry are hierarchical markets in which 'lead businesses' (retailers, fashion houses and brand names) wield strong control over the other parties in the supply chain in order to reduce risk and increase profits.[53] They are able to do so by virtue of their high market concentration and buying power in contrast to the growing number of suppliers who compete for their work. Suppliers competing for rare contracts with retailers may be willing to risk non-compliance with the relevant labour laws in order to comply with demands for low unit costs from lead businesses—upon whom they are dependent for survival. The threat of meagre legal sanctions (the largest penalty awarded to date has been AUD $110,550 (*Textile Clothing & Footwear Union of Australia v. Southern Cross Clothing Pty Ltd* [2006] FCA 325 (28 March 2006)) is insignificant compared with the economic sanction of being dropped as a supplier by a major retailer.

5.3.1.2 The first layer: market-based incentives

In the mid-1990s the TCFUA, together with an alliance of community groups which came together under the banner of 'FairWear', developed a market-based industry-wide Code of Practice to bolster the existing legal framework governing the TCF industry. This mechanism has a number of notable features.

Firstly, the Code builds on the outworker provisions of the relevant labour laws as its base. Its aim is to *enhance* the operation of labour laws. The code therefore operates as a complementary regime.

Secondly, the Code established Ethical Clothing Australia, adding a new agent to the regulation of homeworking (see Figure 5.2). Ethical Clothing Australia oversees the operation of the code. TCFUA is responsible for receiving complaints from outworkers and monitoring compliance with the Code. If a problem is not rectified within a reasonable period of time, the non-complying company that gives work out to

[50] I. Nossar, R. Johnstone, and M. Quinlan, 'Regulating Supply-Chains to Address the Occupational Health and Safety Problems Associated with Precarious Employment: The Case of Home-Based Clothing Workers in Australia' 17 Australian Journal of Labour Law 137.

[51] Senate Economics Reference Committee 29. [52] Marshall.

[53] Gary Gereffi, John Humphrey, and Timothy Sturgeon 'The Governance of Global Value Chains' (2005) 12(1) Review of International Political Economy 78.

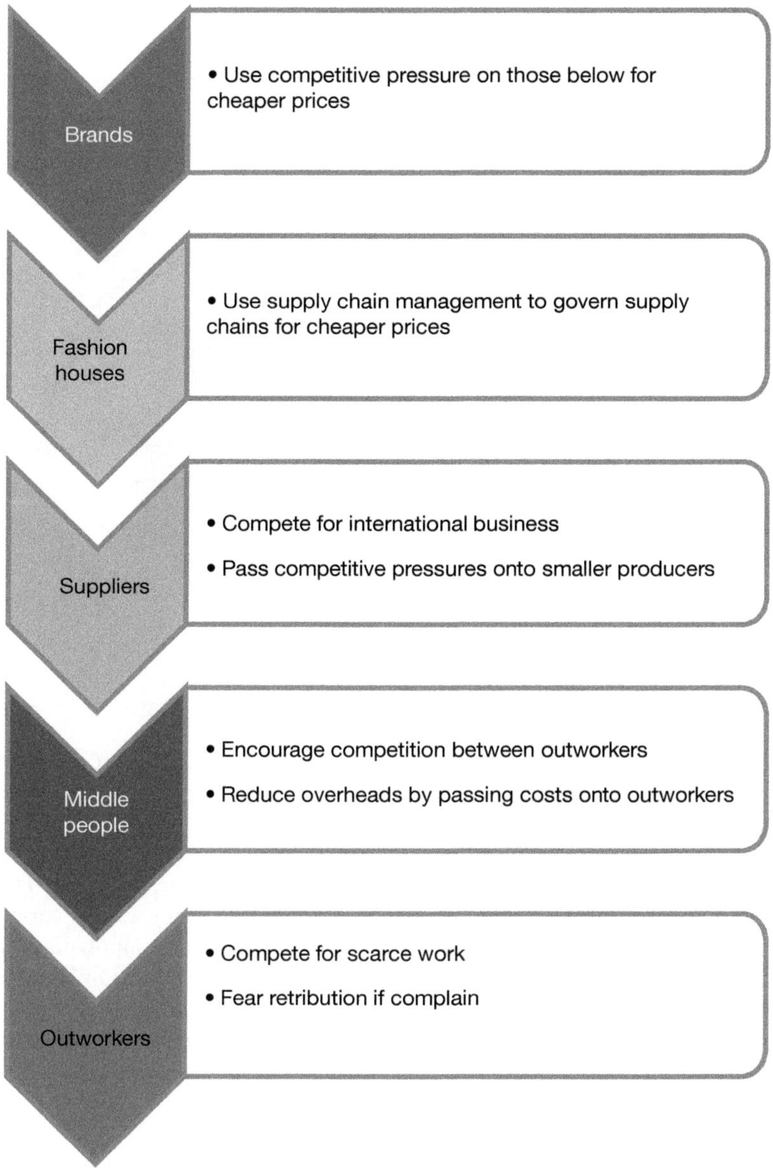

Figure 5.1 Supply-chain-based countervailing forces

homeworkers risks losing its contract to supply the retailer or accredited manufacturer after Ethical Clothing Australia's Committee considers the complaint. The Committee is also able to revoke a manufacturer's accreditation.

Thirdly, as well as creating disincentives for non-compliance, the Code also creates incentives for compliance. Manufacturers who complete the accreditation process are licensed to display the Ethical Clothing Australia label on their goods.[54] The goal is

[54] See http://www.ethicalclothingaustralia.org.au/business/how-to-apply.

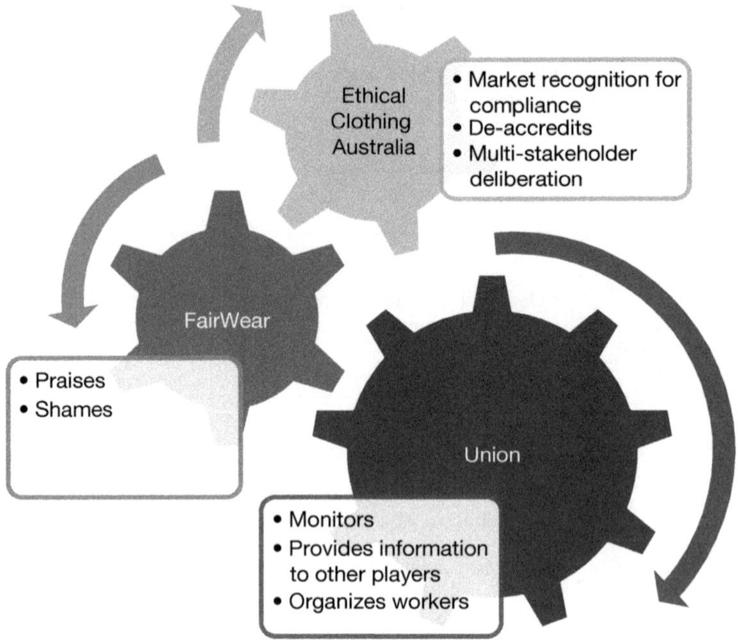

Figure 5.2 Additional agents added by layering

to attract consumer preferencing and reverse the perverse incentive that the extended definition of 'employee' had set up. It is in this sense that the market-based regulation acts like a 'pace-maker', changing the signalling in the system.

A number of aspects of this layering add market power in the service of state-based regulatory power. Because market power is so concentrated in the Australian TCF industry amongst a small number of retailers and large fashion houses, the survival of smaller manufacturers depends on receiving on-going contracts for supply to these big players. If the brands and fashion houses refuse to order from them in order to maintain their accreditation, this is the most powerful sanction available. These aspects of the Code allow market power to be captured in the service of enhancing labour standards, helping to change the signalling that the existing laws were sending to businesses to guide their behaviour.

5.3.1.3 The second layer: supply chain legislation

The second layer of the complementary regime is supply chain legislation. In the 1990s and 2000s, legislation of this type was enacted in a number of states, and in 2012 it was enacted at a Federal level (Fair Work Amendment (TCF Industries) Act 2012) following intense lobbying by the TFCUA and community organizations of the Federal Labour Government. The legislation allows for recovery of lawful entitlements against parties who may be contractually removed from the outworker (see Figure 5.3).[55] This expanded on the operation of Federal statutes such as the Fair Work Act 2009 (Cth),

[55] The right of recovery is generally for annual leave and long service leave, commission and reimbursements, or compensation for expenses incurred or loss sustained.

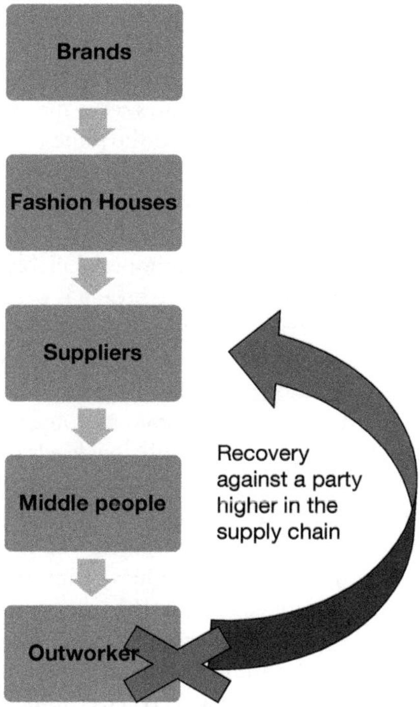

Figure 5.3 Supply chain legislation

which operate primarily by reference to the existence of a contract of employment and are therefore unable to adequately regulate supply chain dynamics.

There are a number of occasions on which this supply chain legislation can provide an avenue of redress for outworkers. For instance, when the intermediary who gave the work to the outworker wasn't paid at all by the manufacturer, or wasn't paid a sufficient amount, attempting to recover the money from the intermediary would be futile. It is simpler, in those circumstances, for the outworker to target the manufacturer directly. In other instances, if the intermediary cannot be found, a claim can be made against a party higher up the supply chain.

Perhaps the greatest innovation of this legislation is the extension of the concept of 'employer'. In a sense, the legislation recognizes that the entire supply chain acts as an employing entity.

5.3.2 Assessment

This sub-section of the chapter assesses the benefits and pitfalls of this approach to regulating home-based outwork. It queries the extent to which the amendments to the labour code are able to respond to the dynamics of informalization described in Section 5.2 of this chapter. Further, to what extend does the new multi-layered framework respond to the experiences of workers and the deficits in working conditions?

By establishing additional regulatory layers and levers, the new framework has managed to expand the scope of labour law for vulnerable outworkers without having to tackle broader institutional reform. This is perhaps the primary advantage of the complementary system described above. Thoroughgoing reform of labour law in Australia so as to expand the personal scope of its application is highly unlikely. Labour law has been under attack for meddling in the operation of the free market over the last thirty years, and thus any increase in its scope would be likely to attract fierce opposition. In this political climate, then, layering techniques seem the most politically viable way of ensuring that peripheral workers are afforded the same protections as core workers. Only transport workers in Australia have achieved similar types of 'supply chain regulation', and this was because of the high accident rates causing deaths and injuries not only to workers—truck drivers—but also to others on the road.[56]

The layers add tools to the enforcement techniques available to regulators depending on the difficulty in achieving compliance once a breach is detected.[57] By providing punitive sanctions in the event of a breach, the award supplies the formal legal mechanism through which outworkers are protected. The award also extends basic, non-negotiable labour standards to outworkers, allowing labour inspectorates or unions to ensure the enforcement of these standards in court. However, as noted above, without more supportive structures, the awards tend to attract only low levels of compliance. Therefore, they are most effective in protecting vulnerable outworkers only when combined with softer enforcement techniques, including consumer recognition of ethical behaviour.

The addition of new outworker-specific bodies to the labour law framework has been an important step in addressing the dynamics of informality. The establishment of certain regulatory entities described in this chapter has allowed weaker actors to be fortified through networks with other actors. The power of one strong actor (retailers) enrolled against another (fashion houses and manufacturers).[58] Here, actors have been added to the regulatory process who have influence at different stages of the supply chain. In this complementary networked regulatory system, the state is able to draw on the power of non-state actors who are allies in increasing compliance, including the Union and FairWear, and it builds consent from industry bodies through incorporating them into processes, such as the Ethical Clothing Australia committee which oversees the operation of the Code.

This multi-layered approach could help to overcome some of the barriers created by lack of trust discussed in this chapter, however, the evidence suggests that there is still a long way to go in this regard. Having regard to the broad sociological and psychological factors linked to the distrust of state institutions by immigrants from oppressive countries, more work is needed to fully rectify those dynamics of informality. Efforts surrounding cultural integration and community outreach should be embarked upon further. Apart from an organization that operates in one state of Australia (NSW), called Asian Women at Work, other organizations have had little success engendering the trust of homeworkers. The Victorian Branch of the Union has taken various steps to increase the trust and familiarity of Vietnamese and Chinese workers, including running English classes and social events. English classes, in particular, have been immensely popular, but one of the union organisers confided in me that it is very difficult to get workers to attend social events. The Union does not employ the same kinds of grass-roots organizing techniques as Asian Women at Work, which based its methods on the successful community organizing of the South Korean democracy movement. Asian Women at Work organizes in the geographical location of the workers—out of the homes of community representatives—with the support of the organization's

[56] Rawling and Kaine.

[57] I. Ayres and J. Braithwaite, *Responsive Regulation: Transcending the Deregulation Debate* (Oxford University Press 1995).

[58] Braithwaite 888.

coordinators.[59] Workers go walking together in the morning, hold regular social events, as well as sharing information about rights and entitlements. There is strong 'ownership' and control of the organization by workers. Unfortunately, Asian Women at Work has no formal place in the regulatory system described in this part of the chapter. Instead, the NSW branch of the TCFUA is charged with representing workers in the labour law system and Ethical Clothing Australia. It is discouraging to note that the NSW branch of the TCFUA does not even employ a Vietnamese, Chinese, or Korean speaking organizer.

Instead of viewing hard laws and market-based soft laws as alternatives, the strength of this system is that it sees different mechanisms as being best used in combination—as complements to each other.[60] The complementary layered system attempts to harness existing market dynamics in which strong private governance or bureaucratic power is wielded by parties high up in the supply chain. Because de-accreditation by Ethical Clothing Australia means that manufacturers and organizers of production cannot supply to accredited retailers, there is a strong market sanction against non-compliance. This helps to strengthen the compliance of businesses who may not have been deterred by the relatively weak formal legal sanctions.

Streeck and Thelan anticipate that new layers may gradually empower an unintended group, and thus sow the seeds of radical institutional transformation.[61] It remains to be seen what impact introducing a market-based, multi-stakeholder body into a labour market institution will have. Such bodies operate on very different principles than labour market institutions, which are founded on the idea that there is a fundamental conflict of interests between labour and capital. Multi-stakeholder bodies, on the other hand, tend to take as their starting point that all interests are legitimate and equal, and through a process of discussion amongst representatives, strive for sustainable outcomes. There is no process for mediating between distinct and incompatible interests. Within the market-based corporate accountability system, unions conduct monitoring, which is a technical act, compared with bargaining, which is an inherently adversarial act.

One weakness of the Code and Ethical Clothing labelling system is that it requires widespread voluntary participation throughout the industry for it to be a success.[62] As long as it is voluntary, the prevalence of the ethical label depends on the goodwill of brands to accredit. When only a small number of brands have accredited, the pressure on others is minimal. When a high proportion of Australian brands have accredited, those who have not accredited will stand out. There is a foreseeable tipping point for Ethical Clothing Australia: when a sufficient number of companies have become accredited it will offer a real choice for consumers, placing more pressure on those companies that have not accredited. If a mandatory code is enacted at a national level, as is provided for in the Fair Work Act, this will surely create the momentum needed. However, this seems improbable under the current federal government. For the time being, it appears that the Ethical Clothing Australia initiative will remain in its current form, as a market mechanism which depends on the moral actions of both consumers and brands. Ethical Clothing Australia enjoys low levels of legitimacy amongst

[59] Conversation with Lina Cabaero-Ponnambalam, Coordinator, Asian Women at Work, Sydney, Australia (2013).

[60] Gunningham and Grabosky 14.

[61] Streeck and Thelen.

[62] The code has been made mandatory for retailers in two states: NSW and South Australia. It was mandatory in Queensland but was repealed on the election of a conservative state government.

manufacturers, which allowed for a successful campaign by the conservative government to stop funding it.[63]

There are a number of factors which currently undermine the strength of the Code, as well as the TCF regulatory system more broadly. These include low awareness and understanding of outworker protections, combined with low levels of trust between workers, suppliers, labour rights organizations and principal companies, who do not work collaboratively and often fail to understand each other's circumstances.[64]

A further weakness is that the framework discussed in this chapter only governs clothes made in Australia, which only accounts for a small part of clothing sold in the country. One of the biggest sources of downwards pressure on labour unit costs is international competition. Most clothing sold in Australia is imported from low cost countries, and even clothing which is sewn in Australia has components that are sourced from elsewhere: the 'Cut, Make, and Trim' aspect of production may occur in Australia, but the thread and the material is sourced from elsewhere. The system of ethical regulation only governs the cut, make, and trim phase in Australia. Labels that are conducting the Cut, Make, and Trim phase of production ethically in Australia, accredited with Ethical Clothing Australia, have been found to have far less scrupulous practices elsewhere in the world.[65] The Australian model is an incomplete ethical regulatory system.

5.3.3 Conditions today

It is difficult to draw conclusions about the precise extent to which these new regulatory levers have been able to address the dynamics of informality and improve outworkers' conditions. The industry suffers from a paucity of evidence and studies which could help to inform the field. The research discussed in this chapter was conducted ten years after Cregan's study and did not involve surveying as many workers. Just over thirty workers were interviewed. Unlike the Cregan study, and previous studies of home-based workers, my research found evidence that these regulatory levers were having some impact. In contrast with Cregan's study, in which she found no evidence of workers receiving their legal entitlements, a number of workers that I interviewed were either receiving legal wages and other entitlements or close to them. These interviewees were all working in supply chains that were linked to lead companies that accredited under the Homeworkers Code of Practice through Ethical Clothing Australia. For all of the interviewees who were receiving close to their legal entitlements this was a relatively new phenomenon. Only a few months earlier, they have been receiving less favourable conditions close to those described by Cregan.

Five of the workers interviewed for my study were working as 'employees' receiving the full entitlements expected for an employee, including sick pay, holiday pay, and

[63] Nick Toscana, 'Federal Funding Cuts Hits Ethical Clothing Australia's Fight Against Fashion Sweatshops' *The Age* (Melbourne, 11 June 2014) [www.theage.com.au/politics/federal/federal-funding-cut-hits-ethical-clothing-australias-fight-against-fashion-sweatshops-20140611-zs4ay.html accessed 15 June 2014.

[64] Emer Diviney and Serena Lillywhite, *Ethical Threads: Corporate Social Responsibility in the Australian Garment Industry* (Brotherhood of St Laurence 2007); Participant Observation: Senate Hearing Inquiry into the Fair Work Amendment Bill, *Senate Hearing Inquiry by the Education, Employment and Workplace Relations Legislation Committee into the Fair Work Amendment (Textile, Clothing and Footwear Industry) Bill 2011 [2012]* (2011).

[65] Claire Cremen and Haley Wrinkle Gershon Nimbalker, *Behind the Bar Code: The Fashion Report* (Baptist World Aid Australia and Not For Sale Australia, 19 August 2013).

superannuation. They were paid a set wage on a fortnightly basis. These people were sewing labels accredited under the Ethical Clothing Australia system, and the factories or intermediaries that gave out the work had been inspected by the TCFUA. Four of these workers elected to work on a part-time basis because the pay they could receive as employees was the same as working long hours as a contractor, when the breaks between orders were taken into account.

Other workers interviewed were also working for factories operating within accredited label supply chains but were not receiving their full entitlements. They were still receiving their pay on a piece-rate basis. The piece rate had been calculated so as to ensure that they received around AUD $17 per hour. Yet these workers were not receiving holiday pay, sick pay, or superannuation. This is evidence that there is some 'creative' interpretation of the rules. When I checked with a representative of the TCFUA, she explained that the Union was working their way through the supply chain and often the process of full adoption of the legal provisions took some time, and a number of visits. Regardless of the fact that the workers were not receiving their full entitlements, the pay rate received is still well above that recorded by previous studies. Encouragingly, it suggests that the state outworker laws combined with the Homeworkers Code of Practice and operation of the Ethical Clothing Council is having an incremental improving effect within the industry.

Three of the workers interviewed were earning under AUD $10 an hour, when they translated piece-rates to hourly rates of pay. Two said they were earning AUD $7–8 an hour. The highest rate of pay was AUD $20 an hour.

All outworkers interviewed had, in the past, been given instructions by intermediaries to take steps to obfuscate the employee relationship as a condition of receiving work. Many had been told to apply for an Australian Business Number, referred to as a 'licence to work' in the industry (thus, they would be considered self-employed contractors rather than employers under law). More recently, many had been told to incorporate as proprietary limited companies and employ someone. A number of outworkers who had set up such an arrangement had employed a relative. In one case, the outworker had employed an international student who was renting a room in their house. These findings suggest that there is an effort to evade the employment relationship being made within the industry.

Twelve of the interviewees reported having a problem or dispute in relation to their work in the last year, particularly in relation to pay disputes. The most commonly reported problem was that they been told to fix problems with the sewing of garments without any pay or were refused payment for sewing on the grounds that the sewing quality was not high enough. For the latter problem, the respondents disputed that there was a genuine problem with the quality of the sewing. Research participants from the TCFUA reported that this is a common way of under-cutting the pay of outworkers. One respondent told me that she had received faulty fabric, and a dispute with the middle-person erupted over responsibility. Three respondents described not being paid at all for work they had completed. They had contacted the Union for assistance recovering these unpaid wages. One of these workers had not been paid for two months of pay, causing considerable financial hardship.

A number of interviewees who said they had not had any problems in the past twelve months explained that they had experienced frequent problems in the past, and that these had stopped once they signed agreements to become employee outworkers, rather than contractors. They attributed this partly to the paperwork that now governed any working arrangement under the award, bolstered by the Code. Intermediaries who gave them the work could no longer deny that work had been completed or dispute the volume or hours taken, because these items were set out on the paperwork. Otherwise, paperwork associated with work covers only the pattern and design, not details related to pay. For workers who are called 'contractors' (although this may not be legally correct, regardless of the registration of ABNs or companies), they generally negotiate pay rates per piece orally. This means that there is either no paper trail or a limited paper trial if a dispute erupts over pay rates of unpaid wages.

For all interviewees who were receiving either their full legal entitlements or close to their legal entitlements, this was a relatively new phenomenon. Perhaps the most significant finding was the difference that the change in conditions had made to the interviewees' lives. Interviewees who received higher pay reported a lessening in pain related to injuries thanks to the capacity to take breaks, time to spend with family and leisure time, which they had not enjoyed since arriving in Australia.

This was evidenced most clearly in the interview I conducted with Lan and Hung Nguyen. Both suffered from back pain and discomfort in their forearms. They told me that they were going on holiday this year for the first time since arriving in Australia nineteen years ago. Only three months earlier, the Union had contacted them through the Ethical Clothing Australia initiative, and because the brand they were sewing was becoming accredited under the Code, they began to receive close to their legal entitlements. The biggest impact for them was that they no longer needed to work long hours. Because they were receiving close to the hourly rates, they had decided to work part-time. They told me that they did not need a lot of money, now that they only had one child living at home, but they wanted to work less and finally have some time to themselves. Just the day before I met them, they had received large envelopes with information about their superannuation (pension plan). This was the first superannuation payment of their working lives.

5.4 Conclusion

The evidence presented in this chapter has shown that even in a developed economy, which has a strong tradition of trade unionism, informalization has occurred in industries which are particularly exposed to global trade.

This chapter has tracked the dynamics of immigration from Vietnam, in particular, drawing on interviews which collected details of the life histories of Vietnamese home-based outworkers to better understand why they began working at home in the apparel industry, and why they became stranded in this low paying work rather than finding pathways out of it. The interviews revealed that a mixture of interlocking factors had compounded each other: interviewees learned to distrust the state and its agents in repressive state socialist regimes; fleeing Vietnam was terrifying and traumatic; time spent in refugee camps robbed interviewees of the opportunity to develop new occupational skills. They arrived in Australia ill-prepared to enter the workforce and compete for work with workers who were familiar with the labour market, literate and skilled. Close community networks assisted them to find work as homeworkers. Friends and family taught them how to sew. Although this allowed them to survive their early days in Australia, it also compounded their isolation. The work had served them well in many regards: they had been able to raise children, and been able to stay close to loved ones, a quality of the work they valued greatly after the trauma of leaving Vietnam. However, their bargaining position was weak, and they had been unable to either demand their legal entitlements, voice complaints, or find work in another occupation.

In the early days of labour shedding and informalization, the relevant union viewed industrial outworkers as predators taking work from members. A policy shift in the mid-1980s made the TCFUA a pioneer in the organization of home-based outworkers. With the help of community support, the Union then campaigned for the extension of labour laws to cover these workers. Rather than campaigning for the wholesale reform of labour law, this lobby group pressured government for 'special' treatment of these workers, in view of their particular vulnerability. Market-based incentives have been layered onto traditional labour laws, with extended scope to alter the incentive structure for employers and spread responsibility for the conditions of outworkers throughout the supply chain. This is a more diffuse form of regulation to match the diffusion of control following the vertical disintegration of production.

Though the evidence presented in this chapter suggests that the strategy of deploying multiple regulatory levers was beginning to lead to formalization, the Australian approach continues to suffer from certain shortcomings. Primary amongst these is the weakness of labour market regulation strategies of this type against private market governance within global supply chains. The evidence shows that tariffs and other trade barriers were a far more robust form of labour market protection than labour laws at a domestic level. In the face of strong downward pressure on labour unit costs from cheap imports, maximum force regulation would be required to create sufficient countervailing pressure for labour standards to ratchet up. The labour laws and market-based ethical initiatives examined in this chapter are nation-bound responses to a problem which has international dynamics, and thus lacks the power or reach to address some of the strongest forces driving informalization. For example, ethical label initiatives at the domestic level have little hope of influencing consumer choice when the retail market is so heavily globalized, as those ethical choices represent only a small portion of TCF products available to consumers.

Private regulatory agents, including the relevant union, have attempted to overcome various barriers to trust experienced by Vietnamese workers who make up the majority of the home-based, informal workforce in Australia. However, their approach has had a limited effect given the broad social and psychological dynamics underlying this informalization. Indeed, many remain fearful of accessing the regulatory initiatives that have been put in place to protect them. Until stronger bridging social capital is built between these migrant workers and regulatory agents, the force of the regulation will likely remain underutilized.

6

Expansion of Labour Laws in Bulgaria

6.1 Introduction

This chapter traces the growth of the informal workforce in the light industries of Bulgaria after the collapse of the Eastern European socialist bloc in 1989. Currently, there are an estimated 500,000 home-based workers in Bulgaria, comprising both own-account outworkers (providing services such as hairdressing, tuition, translation) and industrial outworkers. The chapter will focus primarily on this latter group of industrial outworkers, working within light industries. Light industries generally comprised labour-intensive operations and end products targeted at consumers, such as clothing manufacturing and consumer electronics. In Bulgaria, home-based workers carry out work for firms or their intermediaries, usually on a piece-rate basis. The work includes hand-stitching shoes, packaging, beadwork, sewing, and gluing.[1]

The dynamics of informalization charted throughout this chapter track the country's social and political history leading up to and following the dissolution of the Eastern bloc in 1989 and its integration into the global capitalist economy. The aim is to track the way that national and international factors converged in the 1990s to create dramatic social change, leaving at least a third of the working population in Bulgaria stranded in informality by the end of the 1990s. By 2006, informal work in Bulgaria constituted somewhere around 20 per cent and 35 per cent of overall work and was an entrenched feature of the Bulgarian economy.

Bulgaria occupies a portion of the eastern Balkan peninsula, bordering five countries—Greece and Turkey to the south, Macedonia and Serbia to the west, and Romania to the north. Its location placed it on the geographical periphery of the Eastern Bloc prior to 1991. Its small population and weak political presence compounded this peripheral status. After 1991, Bulgaria became one of the favoured locations of Western European brands for Cut, Make, and Trim manufacturing in the garment sector thanks to reforms in the rules of trade which facilitated outwards processing. Work was conducted through a triangulated relationship: Western European brands would contract with Greek manufacturers, who they had established relationships with from the 1980s. These Greek manufacturers would conduct some work in Greece, and contract the rest to manufacturers in Bulgaria, where labour was cheaper.

In 2011, Bulgaria's labour law underwent a radical change, following a successful campaign for the extension of employment laws to cover home-based workers. The state's expansion of employment law was in part, a reflection of Bulgaria's desire to demonstrate adherence to European Union (EU) recommendations as part of its integration into the EU. The developments may also be viewed as a concession to the concerted domestic campaign by associations representing home-based workers. These groups succeeded in bringing to the attention of the government the significant scale

[1] Dave Spooner, 'Organising Home-Based Workers in Bulgaria' (*Global Labour Institute* 2013) http://www.globallabour.info/en/2013/08/space_and_patience_organising.html accessed 22 October 2014.

of home-based work being conducted in the country, and the failure of existing laws to provide protection to these peripheral workers.

The regulatory approach taken by Bulgaria differs from the regulatory responses examined in the other case studies examined in this book. Bulgaria's response to informal outworkers represents a universal approach to the expansion of employment law. Namely, workers conducting any type of work at home are explicitly covered by the law passed in 2011. The initiatives examined in Cambodia and India only apply to one industry. In Australia, only one state has widened the scope of its labour laws to include home-based workers across a range of industries. Thus, the Bulgarian case study provides a useful point of comparison as the only country to have implemented such wide-reaching formal legal protections to all informal home-based workers.

6.1.1 Field work described in this chapter

The first field work reported in this chapter was undertaken in 2004. It focused on the experience of small factory owners in the light industries in Bulgaria, and the workers who conducted sewing, packing, gluing, and so on either in the factories or at home. The research carried out at this time confirmed the contractual precariousness of this work. This encouraged further contracting out by Bulgarian manufacturers to home-based workers to further save on labour unit costs and pass the risks of precarious contracts onto these workers, contributing to growing informalization.

A second round of field work was then conducted in 2010. This entailed interviews with some of the same factory owners and workers, as well as union leaders, employer organizations and other policy makers grappling with the growing informal economy in Bulgaria. At this time, there was burgeoning debate in Bulgaria about how to best regulate the now well-established home-based workforce.

What was most striking about the differences in the findings of the 2004 and 2010 field work was not just that inequality had increased in the interim, worsening conditions for the poor and leaving only a minority of Bulgarians with enormous wealth. Official statistical sources had already painted a grim picture in this regard. What was most marked was the change in people's attitudes to the economic system, legal institutions, government and towards each other. Economies are embedded in normative social assumptions that can be called moral orders,[2] shaped by expectations of the state, of the collective, and of individual action. In 2004, people had lost their livelihoods, but some level of optimism prevailed. Interviewees believed that when the new market-based economy became better embedded, their livelihoods would stabilize and corruption would become less rife. In 2010, after the economy had been pummelled by the 2008/9 international financial crisis, a fog of pessimism layered perceptions. Bulgaria was particularly hard hit by this financial crisis, in part because the growth it had experienced in the mid-2000s was on the back of a property boom, as Western Europeans bought second houses. In 2010, interest rates were around 18 per cent, hurting all those who had invested in property or expanded their operations through leveraging. Adding to this pain, the rules of international trade had been further reformed in a way that had resulted in a shift of manufacturing from Eastern Europe to northern Africa and Asia. The shift in perception between these two instances of field work will be remarked upon further throughout this chapter.

[2] Claire Wallace and Rossalina Latcheva, 'Economic Transformation Outside the Law: Corruption, Trust in Public Institutions and the Informal Economy in Transition Countries of Central and Eastern Europe' (2006) [2006] 58 Europe-Asia Studies 81 83.

Section 2 of this chapter discusses the dynamics of *informalization*. It considers the growth of informal work over three periods: the late years of state socialism; the early years of the transition; and the later years as Bulgaria became a fully-fledged market-based economy. Section 2 also considers the conditions experienced by homeworkers during these periods characterised by informalisation. Section 3 tracks the dynamics of *formalization*, focussing on legal developments in 2010–11, aimed at grappling with the growth of home-based work. It then critically appraises these legal developments in light of the analyses of the dynamics of informalisation.

6.2 Dynamics of Informalization

The aim of this part of the chapter is to describe why de-industrialization and labour stripping occurred in the 1990s, stranding a large part of the population in unemployment after having been guaranteed work under state socialism. It explains how people became simultaneously disenchanted with the state, at the same time as maintaining statist values that would result in particular visions of regulatory solutions.

Rather than focusing primarily on internal policy factors that contributed to the growth of informality, consistent with most literature on the topic,[3] this chapter examines regional and international rules that made Bulgaria's transition to capitalism particularly bumpy, contributing to its high reliance on informal work. During the state socialist years, these rules were set by the Council for Mutual Economic Assistance, which was dominated by the Soviet Union. Bulgaria's close relationship with the Soviet Union left the state ill-prepared for the collapse of the Eastern bloc. Compounding the challenges of reform, adjustment, and integration into the global economy, Western Europe sought to take advantage of the new supply of cheap labour by establishing trade rules which encouraged outward processing by new members of the European community under preferential terms for Western European brands. This contributed to the specialization of Bulgarian industry in low-value added areas, where competitive advantage lies primarily with low labour unit costs. Bulgaria's diverse industrial base did not survive this period, paving the way for its later reliance on financial and property-based foreign investment.

We can say, then, that international and regional trade rules prior to and after the transition to capitalism compounded mismanagement of the transition by national governments.

Figure 6.1 shows the way that international factors and national factors aggravated each other to produce mass labour shedding and informal work. The staging of these causes of informal work from the period before the transition to capitalism to the late 2000s is mapped in the subsequent sections of this part.

6.2.1 Period one: state socialism

A number of dynamics were established during the years of state socialism which later contributed to the high dependence on informal work in Bulgaria. These dynamics included Bulgaria's dependence on the Soviet Union as a trading partner and for finance, its place on the geographic and political periphery of the Comecon, and the reliance on black market trading and 'second jobs' to attain consumer goods during this period.

[3] Will Bartlett and Rossitsa Rangelova, 'Small Firms and Economic Transformation in Bulgaria' (1997) [1997] 9 Small Business Economics 319.

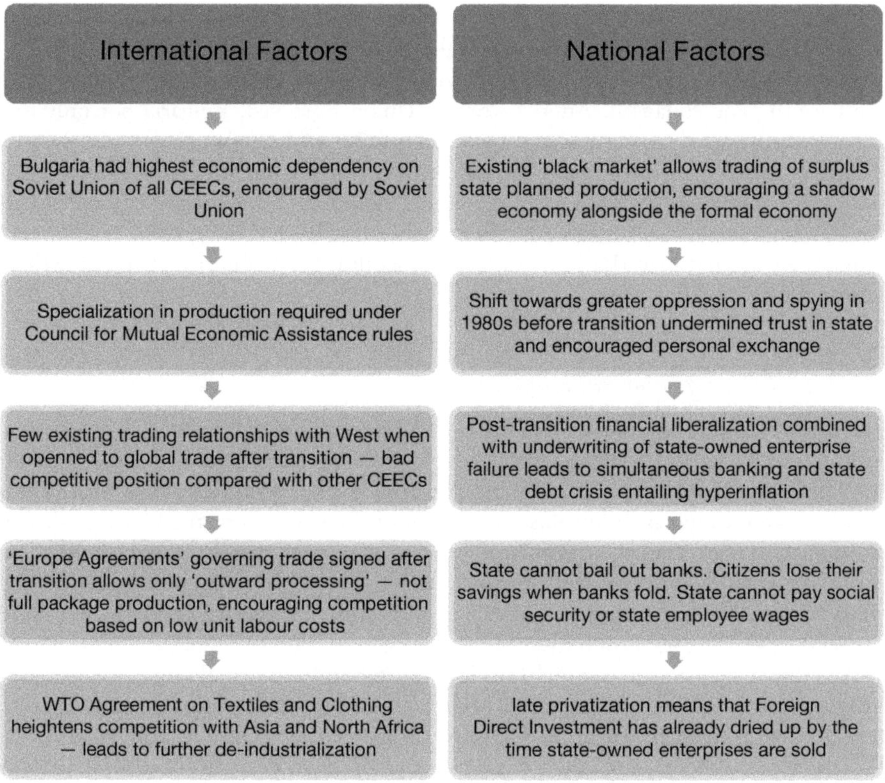

Figure 6.1 Combined international and national factors that led to mass labour shedding and informal work

Also influential was the spirit of distrust of the state which would carry over into the transition.

Bulgaria developed high levels of economic dependency on the Soviet Union under the trading rules of the Eastern bloc and diversified its trading partners less than other Eastern European countries in the later stages of state socialism. Consequently, the state was poorly positioned to integrate into the world economy after transition. Prior to 1989, the Soviet Union accounted for around 70 per cent of Bulgaria's trade.[4] Production specialization among Council for Mutual Economic Assistance members emphasized the permanent division of the development and production of commodities among countries in order to take advantage of economies of scale and to avoid duplication of research and development efforts. In line with this approach, Bulgaria was encouraged to develop its agro-industry and electronics in the 1970s,[5] and other light industries in the 1980s. Outside of the Council for Mutual Economic Assistance countries, Bulgaria fostered trading relations with some Western European and non-European countries. However, in the years leading up to the end of the Eastern Bloc,

[4] Kenneth I. Spenner and Derek C. Jones, 'Social Economic Transformation in Bulgaria: An Empirical Assessment of the Merchant Capitalism Thesis' (1998) 76 Social Forces 937.

[5] Michael Marrese, 'CMEA: Effective but Cumbersome Political Economy' (1986) [1986] 40 International Organization 287 308.

Bulgaria seemed to be opting for greater autonomy from Western trade and capital markets and orienting trade more toward the Bloc.[6]

Bulgaria's high dependence on the Soviet Union would create major problems after the Eastern Bloc collapsed. After the Soviet Union dissolved, Bulgaria not only lost access to subsidized goods and the major consumer of its products,[7] it also lost its chief financier.[8] The transition to capitalism was triggered as much by a debt crisis[9] as by disillusionment with the ideology of state socialism. As we shall see later in this chapter, high levels of sovereign debt, as well as its low level of integration in the world economy, triggered privatization and labour shedding, contributing to the growth of informal work.

6.2.1.1. Existing informal economy

The informal economy was already an entrenched feature of the Bulgarian economy prior to the transition to capitalism, although there was full formal employment. Poor state planning frequently resulted in surpluses of certain products, while other commodities were in deficit.[10] Surpluses often found their way onto the black market in Bulgaria and were traded on informal international markets. Those who wished to source consumer goods that were in deficit also had to do so on the black market. This was known as the 'second economy' which was estimated to have constituted around 35 per cent of the total economy.[11]

An ethos of self-reliance, which would later underpin informal work, was fortified by increasing distrust of the state in the later years of state socialism. Bulgaria enjoyed a more liberal form of socialism for most of the post-war period than many other Eastern bloc countries, including Russia, but in the final years of the regime became more repressive and paranoid. Ideological scrutiny and citizen-on-citizen spying was encouraged by the state in the years before the system's collapse, leading to a retreat to the family, trusted friends, and individualism. State records have now shown that around one out of every six Bulgarians was an informant for the secret service. The full social consequences of this, in terms of undermining the social fabric of a country, are difficult to comprehend.

The contempt expressed towards the socialist state was eventually its undoing. Liberal outcry at the breakup of an environmental demonstration in Sofia in October 1989 broadened into a general campaign for political reform. Despite the promise of general elections and further liberalization, demonstrations throughout the country led President Mladenov to go on national television on 11 December 1990 to announce the Communist Party had abandoned power.

[6] Laura D'Andrea Tyson, 'The Debt Crisis and Adjustment Responses in Eastern Europe: A Comparative Perspective' (1986) 40 International Organization 239 284.

[7] Ibid. 242. [8] Marrese: 311.

[9] In 1990, Bulgaria defaulted on its $10b external debt repayments held mainly with commercial banks: Bartlett and Rangelova 321.

[10] Ibid. 320.

[11] Nikolai Genov (ed), *Unemployment: Risks and Reactions* (UNESCO - MOST, Paris; Friedrich Ebert Stiftung, Bonn and Sofia 1999) Chapter 12.

6.2.2 Period two: early stages of transition to capitalism: 1989 to mid-1990s

The growth of informality in Bulgaria was exacerbated by national governance that 'was marked by a lack of vision for comprehensive structural reforms and by repeated political hesitations'[12] during this transitional period.

One aspect of this mismanagement was in the area of financial governance. The imposition of partial 'macroeconomic shock therapy'[13] was initiated early in the transition, including price liberalization, tight credit policy, and monetary reform. Large-scale restructuring of Bulgaria's pricing and financial and banking system began at the end of 1989 but was largely mishandled. Ponzi schemes flourished. The enormous losses of the enterprises owned by the state were nationalized via monetization.[14] By late 1996, internal and external debt reached alarming levels (60 per cent and 243 per cent of GDP respectively).[15] After several devaluations of the Bulgarian leva (BGN) in 1996 (altogether BGN was depreciated by 590 per cent in 1996), the exchange rate totally collapsed in February 1997.[16] The harsh devaluation of BGN was accompanied by a short period of hyperinflation. During this period, fourteen out of forty-six commercial banks folded.[17] Depositors lost more than 50 per cent of their savings in one year.[18]

By January 1997 Bulgaria was at breaking point, facing an overall political and economic crisis. People queued at bread lines for food. Hospitals were unable to afford medical supplies.[19] Tens of thousands of people were protesting daily against the government and calling for early elections, culminating in the storming of Parliament on 10 January 1997.[20] Mass strikes, nightly marches, and road blocks across the country followed a violent clamp down on the protestors, with a broad societal participation until finally, on 4 February, the government agreed to hold elections.

In July 1997, a new government implemented a new monetary policy which provided higher levels of monetary and fiscal stability.[21] It also promised to speed the process of privatization in order to rid the state of the burden of financing unviable state-owned enterprises. This increase in the pace of privatization, triggering mass labour shedding, began at a time when citizens had lost their savings, were traumatized by the economic and political turmoil of the previous years, and were struggling to find their place in the new economy. Owing to the indebtedness of the state, also, it was unable to fund the structural adjustment programmes that might have softened the impact of this process on an already fragile population.

[12] Ileana Tache and Cristina Neesham, 'The Performance of Welfare Systems in Post-Communist Europe: The Cases of Romania and Bulgaria' (2011) 2 International Journal of Economic Research 90 93.

[13] Spenner and Jones 943.

[14] Organisation for Economic Co-operation and Development, *OECD Economic Surveys: Bulgaria 1997* (OECD Publishing, Paris 1997) 74.

[15] Michael Berlemann and Nikolay Nenovsky, *Lending of First Versus Lending of Last Resort: The Bulgarian Financial Crisis of 1996/1997* (Dresden Discussion Paper In Economics, No 11/03, 2003) 21.

[16] Ibid. 20. [17] Ibid. [18] Ibid. 22.

[19] Christiane Amanpour, 'Bulgaria Suffers Winter of Economic Pain: Socialists Agree To Discuss Early Elections' *CNN Interactive* (Sofia, 13 January 1997) http://edition.cnn.com/WORLD/9701/13/bulgaria/index.html?eref=sitesearch accessed 20 October 2014.

[20] For video footage see: http://www.youtube.com/watch?v=PnvXOszEZr8, accessed 6 October 2014.

[21] Berlemann and Nenovsky.

6.2.2.1. Regional trade rules

It would not be accurate to blame the growth of informalization on internal mismanagement alone. Changes in regional trade governance also played a large part. Bulgaria didn't just enter the global economy at the same time as the rest of the Eastern bloc and much of Asia, it entered at a time when the global rules of trade were encouraging the greater integration of economies across the globe. Regional groupings and countries with the power to shape and take advantage of heightened integration manipulated these rules to their advantage. Peripheral states, such as Bulgaria, scrambled to adjust.

Regional norms governing trade in Western Europe were reformed to allow Western European brands, manufacturers, and fashion houses to profit from 'outward processing' in Central Eastern European countries (CEECs) under the 'Europe Agreements' which opened their borders to trade. Bulgaria signed a Europe Agreement in 1993.[22] Western European countries aimed to improve their competitiveness in anticipation of increasing import-penetration from Asia with the phasing out of protection under the World Trade Organisation (WTO) Agreement on Textiles and Apparel (ATC).[23]

Taking advantage of its low unit labour costs, proximity to Western Europe, and its well-trained workforce, 'outward processing trade' (OPT) from Western Europe to Bulgaria grew in the 1990s. The term 'outward processing' is used synonymously with offshore assembly production, production sharing, cut-make-trim or cut-make production (CMT/CM). EU-based manufacturers, agents or retailers contracted producers in CEECs to manufacturer apparel and footwear for re-import to the EU.[24] This primarily involved the bundled supply of most inputs and components to the producer. In hindsight, the Europe Agreements benefited EU producers and discriminated against the import of full-package products from CEECs, encouraging the least value-added forms of production in Bulgaria and de-industrialization.[25]

As a consequence of these snowballing internal and external factors, the 1990s were marked by widespread de-industrialization in Bulgaria. For example, whereas in 1988 the electronics industry accounted for 17 per cent of GDP, by 1994 that share had fallen to not more than 4 per cent.[26] By the early 2000s, light industries were the only surviving industry branch.[27] This, in turn, contributed to a negative cycle of ever greater state indebtedness, financial crisis, and eventual labour shedding, which forced people into informal work.

In sum, Bulgaria's early transition to capitalism was characterized by poorly managed state institutions, as well as large gaps in the institutional framework governing capitalism. This led to an institutional vacuum, as old state socialist institutions were dissolved. Fast structural and institutional change occurred without any existing

[22] G. Navaretti, M. Galeotti, and A. Mattozzi, 'Moving Skills from Hands to Heads: Does Importing Technology Affect Export Performance in Textiles' (2004) 33 Research Policy 879: 886

[23] Economic Commission for Europe, *Outward Processing Trade Between the European Union and the Associated Countries of Eastern Europe: The Case of Textiles and Clothing* (Economic Bulletin for Europe, Vol 47, UNECE: Geneva, 1995) 199.

[24] B. Begg, J. Pickles, A. Smith, 'Cutting It: European Integration, Trade Regimes, and the Reconfiguration of East-Central European Apparel Production' (2003) [2003] 35 Environment and Planning A 2191 2199.

[25] Economic Commission for Europe 120.

[26] Elena A. Iankova, 'Multi-Level Bargaining during Bulgaria's Return to Capitalism' (2000) [2000] 54 Industrial and Labor Relations Review 115 126.

[27] Niki Tait, 'Bulgaria: Europe's Quick Response Solution?' (*Bulgarian Association of Apparel and Textile Producers and Exporters* 2007) http://www.bgtextiles.org/?cid=78&NewsId=421 accessed 20 October.

experience of markets or attendant expectations about market behaviour. This led to the flourishing of 'an informal system of redistribution practices between different social groups',[28] leaving a large proportion of the population jobless.

6.2.3 Period three: later stages of transition to capitalism: mid-1990s to early 2010s

Following the period of great economic turmoil in the early 1990s, in the second half of the 1990s and 2000s, Bulgaria's economy began to stabilize. However, policies of privatization which sold state-owned enterprises at 'fire sale' prices, as well as a contemporaneous process of illegal privatizations at even lower prices, put in place a process that some commentators have called a 'synergistic spiralling of wealth and poverty' or the rise of a 'new feudalism'.[29] Assets worth about 100 billion BGN and enormous profits were acquired or 'privatised' under suspicious circumstances (either illegally or by 'side methods').[30][31] A small minority benefited greatly from this stage of the transition while labour shedding worsened, unemployment deepened, and informal work proliferated. The already low trust in the institutions of the state dropped further still.

Privatization was a massive task: 80 per cent of enterprises were state owned at the beginning of the transition, one of the highest percentages among the former communist countries.[32] By 2000, employment in private enterprises had risen to 70.8 per cent.[33] In the clothing industry, this process was even more acute: the percentage of employment in private enterprises increased from 55 per cent in 1996 to close to 100 per cent in 2000.[34]

The merger of two economic systems that were once largely separate produced a global oversupply of labour without a significant increase in the global stock of capital.[35] Eastern bloc countries competed for a share of existing global—and particularly Western European—investment. By the time Bulgaria began privatizing, Hungary, the Czech Republic, and Poland—countries close to Western Europe that had already developed strong trade relationships prior to transition—already had 90 per cent of the FDI to the region.[36] Bulgaria failed to attract sufficient FDI to make up for the shortfall created by the retreat of the Soviet Union as its primary bank roller and trading partner.

[28] Tache and Neesham 93.

[29] Jean Comaroff and John L. Comaroff, 'Millennial Capitalism: First Thoughts on a Second Coming' (2000) [2000] 12 Public Culture 291 291.

[30] Aristidis Bitzenis, 'What Was behind the Delay in the Bulgarian Privatization Process? Determining Incentives and Barriers of Privatization as a Way of Foreign Entry' (2003) [2003] 39 Emerging Markets Finance & Trade 58 68.

[31] This amounts to profits of around USD $64 billion according to today's exchange rate. The amount in US dollars according to exchange rates of the time is more difficult to calculate. The exchange rate slid from BGN 487 to BGN 1,588 per USD $1 in the first quarter of 1997.

[32] Bitzenis 61.

[33] Jennifer Hurley, *Garment Industry: Subcontracting and Workers Rights, Report of Women Working Worldwide. Action Research in Asia and Europe* (Working Women Worldwide, Manchester Metropolitan University, Manchester 2003).

[34] Ibid.

[35] Sandra Polaski, 'Combining Global and Local Forces: The Case of Labor Rights in Cambodia' (2006) [2006] 34 World Development 919.

[36] Barry Eichengreen and Richard Kohl, *The External Sector, The State and Development in Eastern Europe* (BRIE Working Paper 125 March 1998, prepared for the Kreisky Forum and BRIE Policy Conference: Foreign Direct Investment and Trade in Eastern Europe: The Creation of a Unified European Economy, Vienna, 5–6 June 1997) 3.

The small amount of FDI that dribbled into Bulgaria was attracted by its low labour costs. Labriandis's study of Greek small and medium-sized enterprises (SMEs) reveals that investment generally involved a relocation of 'Third Degree Subcontracting' from Greece in order to take advantage of wage differentials. The process of Third Degree Manufacturing works as follows: manufacturing had first been subcontracted from a Western European business to a Greek business. The Greek business then set up a factory in Bulgaria and subcontracted aspects of this work to that business to take advantage of the cheap labour that existed just over the border. In 1996 it was estimated that the ratio of Bulgarian and Greek wages in the apparel industry was somewhere between 1:7 to 1:15, whilst productivity was 1:1.5.[37] All components were supplied from Greece and final products were then usually exported to third countries. This is known as triangular production or triangulated supply chains.

In the 2000s, compounding the difficulties in attracting FDI, the international governance of textile and clothing was further reformed, creating even less favourable terms of trade for Bulgaria. The WTO's Agreement on Textiles and Clothing, governing the phase out of quotas, was of immense significance to nations that were highly dependent on clothing and textile exports, as Bulgaria had become following the loss of its other industries in the early 1990s. The Agreement put a stop to the preferential treatment Bulgaria had enjoyed over Asia under the 'Europe Agreements'.[38,39] After 2005, CEECs, Northern Africa, and Asia competed on equal terms.

Faced with a lack of capital *or* know-how, and now competing on equal terms with North Africa and Asia in the garment sector, firms undertook asset stripping and labour shedding. Labour shedding in Bulgaria was amongst the steepest of CEECs during the transition to capitalism. Unemployment began rising immediately after the introduction of the economic reforms at the beginning of 1991, from less than 100,000 to reach around 600,000 by the middle of 1993.[40] Of the 1.2 million jobs lost in the 1990s, 1 million were lost in manufacturing.[41] Wage-based income, which had accounted for 100 per cent of total incomes at the beginning of transition, had fallen to just 40 per cent by 2003.

The result was a quick decline in individual and household earnings. By 1997, the World Bank estimated that 36 per cent of the population was living in poverty.[42] This triggered a renaissance of the role of traditional families and 'clan factors' in economic activities.[43] Where employment became available, those already employed attempted to assure places for their relatives. Gainfully employed relatives often became financially responsible for numerous other family members. Others raised income through informal activities. By 2010, unemployment and under-employment had become entrenched in Bulgaria.[44]

[37] L. Labriadis, 'Subcontracting in the Greek Garment Industry and the Opening of the Balkan Markets' (1996) [1996] 9 Cyprus Journal of Economics.

[38] Economic Commission for Europe 121.

[39] EU membership also meant that Bulgaria had to abandon individual trade policy such as quotas and restrictions on imports of footwear and apparel, and the rules of the Common External Trade (CET) policy took effect.

[40] Bartlett and Rangelova 321.

[41] P. Garibaldi, M. Makovec, and G. Stoyanova, *From Transition to EU Accession The Bulgarian Labor Market During the 1990s* (World Bank Technical Paper No 494, WTP494 May 2001) 1.

[42] World Bank, *Growth, Poverty and Inequality: Eastern Europe and the Former Soviet Union* (World Bank 2005).

[43] Tache and Neesham 97.

[44] Eurostat, 'Euro area unemployment rate at 10.1%' (*Eurostat, STAT/11/5, 7 January 2011* 2010) <file:///C:/Users/Pc/Downloads/STAT-11-5_EN.pdf> accessed October 20.

A great deal of light industrial work shifted to the 'hidden' or informal economy. This was particularly stark in the apparel industry. According to official Department of Labour statistics, by 2004, the average number of people employed in clothing production enterprises in the country was 33.28 per cent. Research conducted by the Bulgarian Gender Research Foundation (BGRF) indicated these official figures severely underestimated the size of the industry. Industry knowledge suggested that it was common place for enterprises to operate several workshops, while registering only one. The remaining workshops operated 'in the shadow'.[45] This is consistent with broader data concerning reliance on informal income in Bulgaria at the time. By 1998, Wallace et al. found income in Bulgaria was derived 55 per cent from the formal economy, 20 per cent from the social and household-based informal, "a-legal" conomy and 25 per cent from the black or illegal economy.[46]

6.2.4 Homebased work in light industries

This section of the chapter discusses the conditions experienced by home-based workers based on interviews with workers conducted in 2004 and 2010, augmented by secondary evidence.

The retreat to informal work can be seen as an economic adjustment that provided a way to increase the competitiveness of the Bulgarian labour market and reduce unit labour costs in the face of unfavourable terms of trade. A survey of clothing workers throughout Bulgaria conducted in the early 2000s found that the majority were piece-rate workers, demonstrating the precariousness of work in the sector, and the extent of the flexibility of production. Only 31 per cent of workers were found to be permanent, while 14 per cent were on short-term contracts. 51 per cent of workers were piece-rate workers.[47]

The fieldwork conducted for this study in 2004 documented a high reliance by footwear companies on outworkers, with unregistered homeworkers sometimes outnumbering formal employees in a firm. None of the workers interviewed in 2004 had employment contracts. Likewise, a study conducted by BGRF of homeworkers in various sectors found that less than 10 per cent of homeworker respondents worked with a contract.[48] By 2009, the total number of home-based workers in the light industries of Bulgaria was estimated at around 500,000:[49] an extremely high number given that the population of Bulgaria was only 7.5 million.

In 2010, the Society for Development and Homebased Production and the Confederation of Independent Trade Unions of Bulgaria surveyed 500 homeworkers in ten Bulgarian cities. Of these workers, 82.3 per cent were women. 51.2 per cent were aged 50–65 years, and 97.1 per cent had worked for more than 15 years exclusively at home.[50] The dependent homeworkers interviewed for this study were mainly

[45] Bulgarian Gender Research Foundation, *Social Environment and Standards at the Workplace in the Garment Industry 2001[]* (results from preliminary research carried out within a Clean Clothes Campaign international project, Sofia, 2001) 19.

[46] Wallace and Latcheva 88.

[47] Women Working Worldwide, *Garment industry: Subcontracting and Workers Rights* (report of Women Working Worldwide Action research in Asia and Europe, Jennifer Hurley (ed.), Manchester Metropolitan University 2003) 211.

[48] Bulgarian Gender Research Foundation.

[49] Eurofund, 'Bulgaria; Self-employed Workers' (2009) http://www.eurofound.europa.eu/comparative/tn0801018s/bg0801019q.htm.

[50] Violeta Zlateva, 'Employment Conditions of Homeworkers' (*European Working Conditions Observatory*, 2010) http://www.eurofound.europa.eu/ewco/2011/01/BG1101021I.htm accessed 15 October.

women, but they were often joined by their husbands and other family members when the volume of work was too great to complete alone. Men also conducted dependant homework when they could not find employment elsewhere.

Interviewees for this study came from a range of occupational of backgrounds. Many workers interviewed were highly qualified and skilled workers with many years—sometimes decades—of professional experience in very technical fields. Amongst those interviewed were economists, metallurgists, doctors, and scientists, including a former professor in biochemistry, child-care workers, as well as former factory workers that might be expected to do this work.

One interviewee was Natasha,[51] a fifty-nine-year-old divorced woman who lives in Pernik, around 40km south west of Sofia. After school she worked in a number of clerical positions, working her way up to become deputy head of placement for a large factory, amongst other jobs. By 1988 she was the deputy head of the commercial department of a nearby municipality. During the transition to capitalism, these economic planning units were no longer required, and she lost her job. For ten years she worked in various shops in her local area. Although this employment paid enough to survive, it was on a casual basis and not as fulfilling as her previous high powered, highly-skilled work. In 1998 she lost this work because of her age. Her perception is that business owners sought younger people to front their shops.

Since that time she has been the victim of what is termed 'job churning'. The local employment agency placed her in short-term job after short-term job. Over a three-year period she worked as a security guard at a school and then at a library, for the Social Services department as a consultant, and for a fruit and vegetable shop, with periods of unemployment in-between.

In order to survive in periods of unemployment, in 1991, she began to do homework for a local knitwear company and also a company that sold festival souvenirs. She found this work through word of mouth. In the early 1990s, she received training, as part of an EU programme, to become a babysitter. She is now paid to babysit her grandchildren for a few hours a day. To augment this income source, she has worked for a local Greek-owned swimwear company since 1995 sewing beading onto swimsuits. This work is seasonal. Most work is conducted between March and June, to prepare for summer. The company calls her when they need work done. Sometimes, during particularly busy periods, she goes into the factory to help with packing. She calculates that she earns around 10 GBN (USD$6.96) for 8 hours work, with no benefits such as health insurance, paid sick leave or social security payments. There is no shortage of work, but the work is poorly paid and extremely demanding.

She explained that in Pernik there are many educated people, but no jobs. During the twentieth century Pernik developed as a centre for coal mining, limestone quarries, and heavy industry. (It is reported that before its industrial exploitation started, the local people dug coal up with picks and shovels and transported it with carts and wheelbarrows.) However, the larger mine in the region closed shortly after the transition to capitalism, leaving 12000 workers unemployed. She spoke of deep personal frustration, not just at being so economically vulnerable, but also at having her managerial skills wasted. She was aware that under better economic circumstances she would be at the peak of her career or beginning a fruitful retirement. Instead, she has no prospects for retirement and conducts low-paid manual work. She said, 'No-one asks us what we can do'.

[51] This is not her real name. The interview was conducted at her home in September 2010.

The work often had a detrimental effect on health in the short and long term. I observed a number of workers using toxic glue to stick the soles to shoes or to make paper shopping bags. They complained of severe headaches on a daily basis. 69.8 per cent of the respondents to a survey of 500 outworkers used hazardous materials (paint, chemicals, adhesive, dust and fertilisers) when working at home.[52] In many cases, members of their household were also in contact with these materials.

6.2.5 Remuneration

Secondary data examined for this study, along with my own research, shows that the great majority of homeworkers in Bulgaria were not receiving the income stipulated by law. Most workers interviewed described living on a subsistence level of income. A survey undertaken of clothing enterprises found that those on registered employment contracts might receive the minimum wage, but the majority of employees received their pay as 'cash in hand', and received less than the minimum wage.[53] Consistent with this finding, a large scale survey of home-based workers conducted in the mid-2000s found that 74 per cent declared that their homeworking incomes were below the national minimum wage.[54]

They had no income security. For dependent workers, this was because they did not have formal, enforceable contracts with the contractor who provided their main source of income. The nature of the relationship with contractors was a crucial determinant of income for dependent homeworkers. Most homeworkers were highly dependent on the contractor who gave them work. More than half (58.2 per cent) worked only with one contractor, 17.9 per cent with more than one contractor and 12.5 per cent were self-employed.[55] Non-payment for work done was common. Half of the respondents reported that they very often had problems in receiving the negotiated amount for their work. In most cases, the contractor often claimed that the quality of work was not sufficient or that the contract had not been observed.[56]

Non-wage factors of production were rarely paid for by contractors. Petkov's survey found that only 13.3 per cent worked in specially prepared premises for the purpose of work. The majority of homeworkers (67.4 per cent) shared their workspace with family members.[57] However, only 7.1 per cent received compensation from the contracting company for heat and light expenses and machine maintenance and equipment during the process of production.[58] Dependent and semi-dependent workers interviewed for the present study explained that the price per unit had remained the same for the last six years. However, the cost of living had increased markedly due to significant increases in food prices, power and the costs of meeting other basic needs. As such, they believed their real wages of homeworkers had decreased from 2004 to 2010.

This lowering of living conditions was part of a national trend, caused in the early days of transition by the end of subsidized oil from the Soviet Union and favourable terms of trade, and later by the 2008 global financial crisis. Other factors came into play, including rising global food and power prices, accession to the EU, et cetera. Bulgarians were growing poorer and reducing their consumption. In December 2009, each household earned just €415 per month, which was €60 less than the previous year. Around one third of the employed citizens in Bulgaria could be classified as

[52] Zlateva. [53] Bulgarian Gender Research Foundation 19–20.
[54] Plamen Petkov, *Statistical Research of Working at Home in Bulgaria* (unpublished doctoral dissertation, Tsenov Academy of Economics 2006).
[55] Ibid. [56] Ibid. [57] Ibid. [58] Ibid.

'working poor',[59] and this data does not necessarily include all informal workers who are likely poorer.

6.2.6 Fluctuations in work

Interviews with factory managers suggested that significant fluctuations in volumes of orders for factories drove the use of the large peripheral, home-based workforce. Descriptions of the factories studied are shown in Table 6.1 below. The managers interviewed in 2004 regarded orders from EU firms as precarious. The managers of all four factories studied voiced concern that the subcontractors from whom they source could easily choose to source production elsewhere. The managers of Factory B and C reported that the volume of orders of shoes from Italian companies had dropped in the past few years, as more work was sourced from Romania as well as Middle Eastern countries.[60] These managers also complained of a constant downwards pressure on prices (and therefore profit margins) from Italian companies who said that they could go elsewhere if their price demands weren't met. It was for this reason that Factory B was attempting to diversify the sources of work by establishing business relationships with Greek contractors. The manager of Factory D explained that although the contracts they had in place with major brands for supply were often for a four-year period, the volume of work is not specified. Thus, within that four-year period, the volume could become close to negligible without any breach of contract. He lamented that the last two-three years had been very hard. There were 300,000 pieces in a season from Brand X [a major Australian brand with a branch in France] two to three years ago, but now Brand X are sourcing from Morocco and Tunisia, so there is less and less work.

Factories and workshops often closed during slumps in demand, and demand for work was very much driven by seasonal fluctuations.[61] These fluctuations in orders contributed to irregularity of employment, with workers sometimes being overemployed and at others under-utilized. At peak times, work would regularly begin at 9 a.m and finish at around midnight without interruption.[62] I sat with families until late into the night, watching them sew the uppers of major brand shoes and snacking with them. Often the whole family was mobilized to fill orders during peak periods. Both in my fieldwork in 2004 and 2010, I observed the use of child labour as younger family members pitched in to complete large orders and stay on good terms with their contractors.

At other times, home-based workers received no work from contractors. Slumps in work led many workers to seek second or third jobs to augment earnings from home-based work. Most of the workers I interviewed worked in the agricultural sector growing tobacco, peaches and tomatoes to supplement their sewing income. Rozalina Ivanova, who formed a home-based workers organization called Kaloian in Petrich, described later in this chapter, had a growing herd of goats, allowing her to produce feta cheese from a building at the side of her house.

[59] Euroavtiv, 'Bulgaria: Poor not just by EU standards' (2010) http://www.euractiv.com/en/enlargement/bulgaria-poor-not-only-eu-standards-news-493653 accessed 11 November.

[60] Unit volumes were not made available to me by individual factories.

[61] Bulgarian Foreign Investment Agency, *Reasons for Investing in Bulgaria* (Government of Bulgaria 2002) 11.

[62] Zlateva.

Table 6.1 Factory Descriptions

Firm	Product	No. of workers	Working conditions (ventilation, temperature)	Export role	Subcontractor	Inputs sourced in Bulgaria	Inputs provided by subcontractor
Workshop A	Knitted wear	10–12 employees	Poor: located in basement. Dark, poor ventilation.	Third degree subcontracting	Greek owned local factory	No	Yes
Workshop B	Knitted wear	8–10 employees	Poor: located in privatized office of wood milling cooperative's office. Light, although very hot in summer.	Third degree subcontracting	Greek owned local factory	No	Yes
Factory A	Knitted wear	125 employees	Moderate: located in canteen of privatized factory. Not purpose built but airy.	Third degree subcontracting	Greek firms in Thessononiki and Athens	No. Cutting carried out in Bulgaria.	Yes
Factory B	Footwear	42 employees	Poor-moderate: factory not purpose built	Third and second/ first degree subcontracting	a. Large joint Italian and Bulgarian owned firm. b. Thessolonki based firm.	No	Yes
Factory C	Footwear	70 employees; at least 100 homeworkers at any one time	Moderate	Second degree subcontracting	Large Italian manufacturer	No	Yes

6.2.7 Homework amongst pensioners

Industrial homework and own account home-based work is carried out disproportionately by pensioners and those over 50.[63] As a consequence of Bulgaria's indebtedness, it was unable to meet its obligations to pension payments and pension levels stagnated. The pension no longer provided a liveable income for a large proportion of the elderly population by 2010, and the financial crisis of the mid-1990s had wiped out the savings of many families. This drove an unprecedented number of elderly Bulgarians into the informal workforce to supplement their pension and savings.

6.2.8 Access to social security, health insurance, and the pension

The instability of home-based work poses a significant barrier to access to social security, health insurance, and the pension. The first tier of Bulgaria's social security, health insurance, and pensions requires employer or individual contributions (depending on whether the worker is employed or self-employed) for eligibility for later payments.[64] As homeworkers were generally not formal employees or self-employed people, they described rarely having access to social insurance in times when they did not have any work because they were unable to register as 'unemployed'. This placed them in extreme hardship when work was not available. It also locked them into accepting any work they could find, instead of taking the time to search for more rewarding work which would make better use of their skills. Lack of access to social security could therefore be seen to contribute to wider labour market rigidity.

Because homeworkers were unable to contribute to pension or other retirements savings, they had little prospect of retiring later in life. Their years of service as homeworkers would not be recognized, as they were not formal employees or registered self-employed workers. Their years of service prior to the transition to capitalism may be counted, as well as any other formal jobs they have held, but these do not amount to a liveable pension. They therefore faced the prospect of either working for life or hoping that family members would support them when they were no longer able to work.

6.2.9 Social impact of homework

As we have seen, remuneration from home-based work in Bulgaria was very low at the time this study was conducted. Most women interviewed reported not being able to pay bills, or constantly feeling stress about their inability to do so. They reported this stress had a significant impact on their general satisfaction with life more broadly. This is consistent with a 2010 European-wide study which found that those with the most negative experience of life are those for whom life is more socio-economically difficult and those who have difficulties paying their bills 'most of the time'.[65]

Interviewees often complained about finding the work tiring, tedious, boring, and isolating. These complaints were most common amongst those completing 'dependent' style work, entailing repetitive work, sewing together parts of the same style of shoe over and over again, or gluing together the same shopping bag hundreds of times in one day. Beyond the tedium, women expressed frustration that their brains and skills

[63] Ibid.

[64] Editorial, 'Bulgaria: Parliament Approves Principle Pension System Reform' (*Balkans.com*, 2010) accessed 21 October.

[65] European Commission, *Mental Health, Part 1: Report, Fieldwork: February—March 2010* (Special Eurobarometer 345, European Commission, October 2010).

were not being used. They found the contrast with their former lives, before the transition to capitalism, difficult. Only the women who conducted own-account work, such as craft, reported satisfaction at being able to work creatively—although this type of work was rarely sufficient to generate a liveable income. Many women said that although they did not wish to forget those aspects of the former state-socialist system that were problematic, they at least had secure work which used a greater range of their skills and talents. The women exhibited negative social and psychological symptoms related to downward social mobility,[66] which are outside the scope of the present study but deserve greater attention.

Low piece rates meant working long hours so as to earn enough to survive. This has numerous social consequences. Interviewees were asked how much 'time they had to themselves' when they were not conducting work or family care duties. Most women reported that they had only one or two hours a week of leisure or 'time to themselves'. Instead of resting in the evenings, they carried out some form of home-based work. Not only does this result in constant tiredness, it also leads to social isolation. Many respondents said that they do not have time to catch up with friends anymore. In addition to reporting feeling lonely, they also said that they found it hard to find out about work and other opportunities. Many respondents reported feeling a breakdown of trust in their local communities, and in broader Bulgarian society. This had a significant impact on their overall sense of well-being and satisfaction with life.

6.2.10. Precariousness for a family of homeworkers in Petrich

Rumiana is a homeworker in Petrich whose experience demonstrates the nature of precariousness experienced by informal workers. When I visited, she, her son, her daughter, and her mother were sitting around a table piled with socks in the badly lit basement of her apartment building, with little ventilation. The walls were stacked with pickled vegetables, ready for winter. The family had organized themselves in a production line in order to group the socks into pairs, attach them to a cardboard backing and then fold them into packages. The sock packages were then placed in larger boxes, ready for transport to other parts of Europe.

They had been doing this job for two months for a Greek company. They showed me packaging to which they had attached socks for German and UK companies. Both teenage children were school aged and helped their mother with the work after school and on the weekends. They expected to pack fifteen boxes with these containers of socks during the two days of work over the weekend, with the four family members working long hours. They would be paid 45 GBN (USD $31.30) for the work.

They had started this work because of a recent business problem. The family owns a warehouse in which, until recently, a factory had been operating which made blouses. This provided a source of rental income for the family, in addition to the taxi driving carried out by the husband and beading homework normally done by Rumiana. One day, Rumiana visited the warehouse to discover that all machinery had been removed and the factory had disappeared. The business that rented the warehouse had left without paying two months of rent or utility bills, leaving Rumiana to pay the bills. Rumiana and her husband argued over whether it was worth trying to pursue the matter in court, to recover unpaid rent and payment of the utility bills. Even if they

[66] Kenneth Kessin, 'Social and Psychological Consequences of Intergenerational Occupational Mobility' (1971) [1971] 77 The American Journal of Sociology 1.

can find the business man who rented the warehouse, it is likely that he would claim bankruptcy. The family told me that they have little faith in the legal system.

6.2.11 Values underlying informal work

Market behaviour, including labour market behaviour, is shaped by values and norms. The period after the transition to capitalism witnessed a slow alteration of collective perceptions and values as people adapted in social terms to capitalism. Generally, trust in the institutions of the state was undermined in the period after transition. A survey conducted in 1998 of unemployed adults found that mistrust of major state institutions was considerably higher than trust. Trust in the courts was less than 10 per cent and trust in parliament was around 15 per cent.[67] Rumiana's experience of feeling unable to seek legal recourse after being wronged was typical amongst the workers I interviewed. Unless interviewees enjoyed connections with powerful people, they felt a sense of disempowerment in their public dealings. According to the survey data reported by Genov et al., civil society organizations, including political parties, trade unions and civic associations, enjoyed even less trust than the state institutions.[68]

Despite disapproval and mistrust in the formal structures governing society, various surveys in the last twenty years have shown that statist-oriented attitudes have remained strong in Bulgaria.[69] The expectation of social problem solving has continued to be directed primarily at the state. For example, survey data from 1998 showed that unemployed people agreed that the state should provide the conditions for satisfying their basic needs.[70] This statist-orientation was reflected in my conversations with home-based workers, also.

This orientation toward the state caused a sense of heightened disorientation in light of the reality that the state was no longer able to meet the needs of its citizens. This experience is known by sociologists as 'value-normative disorientation'. This is when contradictory and mutually exclusive value preferences are held by individuals and collectives. Interviewees expressed a paradoxical belief in a strong role for the state in solving societal problems *and* simultaneous distrust of it.

This sense of bewilderment and being cut adrift appeared to follow from the rapid speed of organizational and societal change, coupled with a growing discrepancy between the heady optimism of the beginning of transition and realities which appeared later in the process. Attitudes towards the transition conveyed during interviews became more pessimistic between 2004 and 2010. In the interviews I conducted, as with other surveys, Bulgarians tended to express fear for the future and dissatisfaction with their lives.[71] According to a 2010 survey, Bulgarians had the highest levels of dissatisfaction with life in general and with their standard of living in Europe. Indeed, Bulgaria was the only European country where close to half of its citizens (48 per cent) say they are dissatisfied with their life in general.[72]

Though state failure created an institutional and value-based vacuum, it also meant that people could engage in activities that were outside the law without fear of legal repercussions. None of the home-based workers interviewed feared retribution for failing to pay taxes or not registering as self-employed. Mistrust and lack of respect for the state meant that they felt little regret in acting outside the formal economy. They felt the state had left them with no other choice.

[67] Genov Chapter 10. [68] Ibid. Chapter 10.
[69] Ibid. Chapter 12. [70] Ibid. Chapter 10. [71] Ibid. Chapter 10.
[72] European Commission, *Mental Health, Part 1: Report* (fieldwork: February–March 2010) 39.

6.3 Dynamics of Formalization

Section 3 of this chapter explores the embryonic dynamics contributing towards re-formalization that were emerging as my study of Bulgarian light industries concluded, resulting in the expansion of the scope of labour laws. It then offers an assessment of the laws that have been put in place to regulate home-based work, as a response to the growth of informality in Bulgaria.

Because trade unions were key protagonists in the movement that brought down the communist government in Bulgaria, they were included in the process of transformation through social dialogue in ways that were seen in few countries transitioning from state socialism to capitalism. However, they had to reorient themselves. Podrekepa, the independent union federation which was most active in leading strikes and protests against the communist government, became less political after 1989 and focused on its role as an industrial protagonist. The traditional, state socialist unions shifted away from acting as arms of government and management. In the meantime, the growing informal economy was undermining the membership base for unions, and yet none of these unions showed an interest in organizing this growing workforce of informal workers. Instead, associations representing the interests of home-based workers emerged. The lobbying effort of these associations, coupled with Bulgaria's desire to be seen to be complying with European Union labour standards as part of its accession, resulted in new laws which regulated homework in 2010–11. This part of the paper describes the development of these laws and provides an early assessment of them.

6.3.1 A new role for labour organizations

The process of formalization which occurred in Bulgaria entailed the re-formation of the county's labour movement. Labour had held a place that was at once privileged and at the same time subordinate to the economic goals of the state under state socialism. The Labor Code of 1951 regulated a new, socialist model of collective bargaining which produced 'collective contracts' for the 'mobilization of workers' to produce more in the name of rapid industrialization.[73] These were replaced in the late 1980s with horizontal contracts between management and enterprise unions on the one side, and higher-level union personnel and state administrators on the other.[74]

Despite the strong place of unions in state socialist structures, unions were actively involved in the downfall of the socialist state in Bulgaria. Waves of strikes were instrumental in its destabilization. There were some 500 strike actions in the first few months after the November 1989 crisis, led by a new independent trade union called Podkrepa which had been formed in February 1989. The force of the strikes gave Podkrepa legitimacy and forced the government to make political concessions towards liberalization. Podkrepa became a prominent part of the Bulgarian political opposition. In December 1989, it was one of the thirteen founders of the umbrella organization of the democratic opposition, the Union of Democratic Forces. During this period, Podrekpa's goals were political: to dismantle the old political structures; create new forms of economic ownership and new attitudes toward ownership; and support its political partners and allies. Following the mass rallies of late 1989, the government agreed to roundtable negotiations on the political future of the country, which lasted from January to April 1990.[75]

[73] Iankova 118. [74] Ibid. 189. [75] Ibid. 119.

These roundtable negotiations became a key feature of the transition to capitalism. The old, official trade unions underwent a series of organizational changes to adapt to the realities of an emerging market economy, beginning with the proclamation of their independence on November 25, 1989.[76] These official unions were also invited to play a significant role in negotiations, in the spirit of inclusivity. This strong institutional role for unions in the transition was backed by strong membership: 79 per cent of workers in manufacturing enterprises self-identified as union members in 1992.[77]

Through this process, unions established for themselves a permanent institutional place in the new democratic architecture of the country. Negotiations early in the transition developed into a multi-tier bargaining system with tripartite bargaining at the national, sectoral, regional, and enterprise levels, taking different forms over the 1990s. Social dialogue and tripartite cooperation in Bulgaria occurred with the National Council for Tripartite Cooperation at its apex.[78] This was in contrast to the trend across much of the world, where bargaining was becoming decreasingly de-centralized.

Preoccupied with their role in these institutional structures and with negotiating the demise of state-owned enterprises, unions failed to organize the growing informal workforce. In an interview in 2010, a Podkrepa official explained that independent unions had decided not to attempt to organize home-based workers, as a matter of policy.[79]

6.3.2 Formation of associations organizing home-based workers

In the 2000s, local, regional, and national groups began to emerge to organize home-based workers in Bulgaria. These groups filled the gap in organization left by unions' neglect of the informal workforce. The addition of these new actors to the labour landscape played a pivotal role in helping to address the dynamics of informalization which had left informal homeworkers workers out in the cold. This occurred with the assistance of international organizations, including the Clean Clothes Campaign and Homeworkers Worldwide. These organizations have provided important material and capacity building assistance. The Clean Clothes Campaign has funded surveys of workers and conducted naming and shaming campaigns in Western Europe based on the information provided by worker associations in Bulgaria and fact-finding missions. Homeworkers Worldwide has provided advice and training in organizing home-based workers. Local groups can be said to have networked around capacity deficits in various ways.[80]

The umbrella organization representing home-based workers nationwide in Bulgaria is the Home-Based Workers' Association, comprising 35,000 members. There are 8,000 members who pay on a regular basis. Its members are drawn from twenty-two of Bulgaria's twenty-eight provinces.[81] Homeworkers are also represented by local organizations. Regional homeworker organizations, such as Kaloian, work in an alliance with the Home-Based Workers' Association, meeting a few times a year to determine

[76] Ibid. 120.
[77] Spenner and Jones 944.
[78] European Foundation for the Improvement of Living and Working Conditions, 'Capacity Building for Social Dialogue in Bulgaria' (2006).
[79] Interview with Aleksandar Zagorov, Confederate Secretary Podkrepa, Sofia, Bulgaria, 21 September 2010.
[80] Braithwaite and Drahos, 'Ratcheting Up and Driving Down Global Regulatory Standards' in Braithwaite and Drahos (eds), *Global Business Regulation* .
[81] Spooner.

strategy and share ideas. When I visited Kaloian in 2004, it had had around 3,500 members. Organizers from the group estimated that there were 7,000 home-based workers in the area it serves, out of a population of 63,000.

I observed Kaloian's organizing techniques while I was in Petrich in both 2004 and 2010. Members met in small numbers at each other's homes. They often brought food with them, sharing meals made with produce from their gardens and farming plots. I watched them conduct marathon meetings, starting early in the morning and finishing at midnight to plan their strategies. The organizers spent evenings after they had finished their own work for the day visiting other workers to keep them abreast of developments.

The Home-Based Workers' Association and its member organizations are hampered by lack of funding and other legal constraints. One legal constraint is labour law in Bulgaria, which restricts the representation of workers in social dialogue processes and collective bargaining to registered trade unions with 50,000 members. Though existing unions are in some ways important allies, they have in other respects acted as a block to lobbying and organizing efforts, which is one reason that the groups have networked with international NGOs and pursued other means of influence.

Until the mid to late 2000s, the Home-Based Workers' Association and its associated regional groups pursued diffuse lobbying objectives. Kaloian was particularly active in organizing dependent homeworkers in export chains. For example, at the time when the Olympics were held in Greece, production levels and urgency increased in Petrich and other areas in the south of Bulgaria that borders Greece. Kaloian took advantage of both the economic boom and the urgency and were able to bargain for better rates. With the help of the Mayor of Petrich, they also achieved equal pay for women in the town and villages. (This was explained to me in some detail in an interview with one of the Mayor's assistants.) Prior to the interventions of the organization, home-based workers in Petrich were generally paid more than in the villages. Later in the 2000s, the organizations turned their attention to lobbying the national government for reforms to the Labour Code to ensure that home-based workers were offered the same protections as standard workers.

6.3.3 Global norm diffusion through the Convention on Homework

This process of national lobbying coincided with the process of global and regional norm diffusion after the ILO's Convention on Homework (Convention 177) was passed. On 27 May 1998, the European Commission released recommendations for the ratification of Convention 177 on home work by all EU countries.[82] After around four years of lobbying, Convention 177 was ratified by Bulgaria in 2009.[83] Though less peripheral member states have failed to ratify the Convention (only ten countries have ratified globally), Bulgaria has been particularly keen to demonstrate adherence to EU recommendations as a way, perhaps, of insisting on its normative inclusion in the Union.

[82] European Industrial Relations Observatory On-Line, 'Social Partners Agree Regulation of Home-Based Work' (2010) http://www.eurofound.europa.eu/eiro/2010/07/articles/bg1007011i.htm accessed 14 October.

[83] Zlateva.

The government set up a special working group of the National Council for Tripartite Cooperation as part of a larger suite of anti-crisis measures.[84] The government left the social partners to decide on rules for dependent home-based work in Bulgaria and to propose legislation,[85] setting a new precedent for the operation of the National Council for Tripartite Cooperation. These negotiations included employer organizations and both trade union federations—CITUB and the Confederation of Labour Podkrepa. Throughout 2010, the National Council for Tripartite Cooperation drafted an agreement. On 16 June 2010, all groups involved signed a preliminary agreement regarding the regulation of home-based work.[86] On 24 November 2010, in the presence of the Prime Minister of Bulgaria, Boyko Borisov, and the Minister of Labour and Social Policy, Totyu Mladenov, the National Agreement on Regulation of Homebased Work was signed.[87]

6.3.4 National Agreement on Regulation of Homebased Work

The National Agreement on Regulation of Homebased Work provided for the amendment of the Labour Code to expand its scope. The amendment requires that dependent homeworkers are provided with a labour contract and enjoy the conditions, including health and safety, guaranteed by Bulgarian labour, social security legislation and collective agreements, regardless of their place of work. The agreement sets out:[88]

- definitions of what constitutes a workplace;
- necessary workplace equipment;
- procedures for joining a union;
- what is meant by homeworking;
- the elements to be included in employment contracts to protect the rights of people in atypical forms of employment.

In a press release announcing the agreement, the Minister of Labour and Social Policy, Mr Mladenov said: 'From now on the rights of the people working in atypical employment will be regulated, they will receive employment contracts, social security insurance and their working time will count towards pensions'.[89] The Labour Code was subsequently amended in line with the agreements, providing for legal regulation of employment relations and working conditions for homeworking.

6.3.5 Assessment

This section assesses to what extent the amendments to the labour code that expand its scope redress the dynamics of informalization described in Section 2 of this chapter. To what extent do they respond to the experiences of workers and the deficits in working conditions? Is this response adequate to the task of improving the conditions of home-based, informal workers in Bulgaria?

[84] Violeta Zlateva, 'National Agreements for Home-Based Workers and Telework' (Eironline, European Industrial Relations Observatory On-Line, 2011) accessed 22 October.
[85] Ibid. [86] Ibid.
[87] Zlateva, 'National Agreements for Home-Based Workers and Telework'.
[88] Ibid. [89] Ibid.

The amendment to the labour code to expand the range of workers covered marks a big step in the regulation of atypical work, putting Bulgaria at the forefront of initiatives of this type. However, the law suffers from structural and incentive-based deficiencies. The primary structural deficiency flows from restrictions in the Labour Code concerning the representation of workers. Participation in social dialogue processes, collective bargaining, and other forms of representation is limited to registered trade unions with 50,000 members. This is particularly problematic for home-based workers, who, as noted above, are primarily represented by homeworker associations not registered as unions. It diminishes the capacity of such groups to play a role in the enforcement of the laws, or in bargaining about terms and conditions. It also significantly weakens the strength of homeworkers' representation, given the lack of interest that the Light Industries Union and other representative unions have shown in homeworkers. In interviews, representatives of unions were quite open about their lack of knowledge about home-based work and their decision not to try to represent these workers. Experience from other countries, including Australia, shows that without the targeted representation of homeworkers, combined with the active enforcement of homeworker provisions in labour laws, the likelihood of the laws being enforced is low. Now that homeworkers are considered employees under the Labour Code, unions may have an incentive to be more active in representing them.

The law does not offer any additional incentives for parties to comply with the law. Yet, as we have seen in this chapter, the incentives against compliance are manifold. On the employer and contractor side, there is pressure within supply chains to lower labour unit costs in the face of global competition. Employers therefore tend to completely, or at least partially, disregard laws concerning labour contracts and contributions towards welfare benefit. As this chapter has discussed in some detail, this pressure stems from Bulgaria's industrial downgrading so that most work conducted in light industries is in outward processing where competition is based on low labour unit costs. On the worker side, because the taxation and welfare systems are regressive, there are disincentives against formalizing for those who are only receiving the minimum wage. Owing to a mistrust of the state and its institutions, Bulgarian workers tend not be uncomfortable working informally. Furthermore, because unemployment is so high, workers are wary of pushing for higher wages or formal contracts for fear of antagonizing employer/contractors and losing work. For both sides, low levels of trust in the state is likely to further erode the impetus to comply with the law, regardless of how good it appears on paper.

6.4 Conclusion

This chapter has tracked a number of dynamics which combined to first, create, and then consolidate a large informal workforce in Bulgaria. A primary dynamic was the institutional vacuum created by the dismantling of state regulatory systems and their slow or inadequate reform to new market institutions.[90] Modern capitalism is characterized not only by capitalist property relations (private ownership of the major means of production), but also by the presence of a strong bureaucratic state which shapes relations in various ways.[91] It simply took time to

[90] Patrick Hamm, Lawrence P. King and David Stuckler, 'Mass Privatization, State Capacity, and Economic Growth in Post-Communist Countries' (2012) 77 American Sociological Review 295.

[91] Max Weber, *Economy and Society; an Outline of Interpretive Sociology* (Bedminster Press 1968); Max Weber and Sam Whimster, *The Essential Weber: A Reader* (Routledge 2004).

replace the existing regulatory functions with new ones that were appropriate to the new market-based system. The retreat of the state took place faster than legislation to control and shape market activity could be passed and implemented.[92] This vacuum was related to the core tension or paradox of having a centrally-driven transition towards de-centralisation. Once the state was weakened and partially abandoned as the administrative centre, how were new agencies and regulatory functions to be created?

The institutional vacuum had a number of consequences. First, at various times in the course of the transition from the command economy, the state was not able to control aspects of economic transformation. This was witnessed in the weak oversight of financial bodies allowing the flourishing of Ponzi schemes and over lending. Second, the new economic forms existed without adequate regulation or policies. For instance, the labour force restructuring and the creation of a surplus labour force occurred without offering alternative programmes, practices, and measures for new employment, or effective institutions for the enforcement of new labour laws. A study of an unemployment office in the regional town of Pernik, for example, where some interviews were conducted for this study, found that the employees of the office were struggling to know what services to provide. There were no financial resources to meet the expectations for training courses. Further, there were no realistic prospects for alternative employment in the municipality. 'So, to train for what type of job?' the authors of the study ask.[93] The overall consequence was that individuals and households enjoyed very low income security. People suffered the loss of their existing work in an economy in which very few new jobs were being generated, and in which existing work was mainly unregulated.

Similarly, the privatization of state-owned companies occurred without the regulation and institutional knowledge that is present in mature capitalist countries with longer market traditions. Those who took over the management of newly privatized enterprises had learned their management skills in highly bureaucratized state enterprises, where the agency problems differ from those in a private enterprise. Third, the weakness of the remaining state meant that legislation was easily subverted by agents within the state who wished to 'grab' state resources in their own interests or tunnelling out state institutions from the inside.[94] Weber argued that a bureaucratic state is essential to modern capitalism because in its absence, individual capitalists might resort to political capitalism—the use of personal relationships with state officials to create extra-market opportunities for profitable activity.[95] Bulgaria witnessed a form of primitive accumulation, which resulted in the transfer of previously state-owned assets to a small group of private individuals who were in a position to grab them at enormous profit. Grabbing was associated with disobedience of the generally accepted rules of fair market competition that have evolved over years of repeat transactions in mature market economies.[96] For those who had no experience of the market system, these implicit codes of behaviour were not self-evident. Methods of capital accumulation were often ruthless.

92 Wallace and Latcheva 84.

93 Genov. 94 Wallace and Latcheva 84.

95 Max Weber, *General Economic History* (Transaction Books 1981); Max Weber, *Economy and Society; An Outline of Interpretive Sociology*.(University of California Press 1978).

96 Krastyo Petkov, *Informal Economy: Re-Conceptualisation and Policy Approaches* (CEE/NIS 2006).

Fourthly, the new legislation enacted by the state could often be characterized as what Wallace et al. refer to as 'absurd and non-viable'.[97] The welfare system—with the high rates of individual contributions expected of workers—is an example of such non-viable legislation in Bulgaria. The difficulty of complying with such laws encouraged the persistence of traditions of rule bending and corruption inherited from the days of state socialism.[98]

In additions to these dynamics, which flowed from the institutional vacuum, the economy suffered from a raft of difficulties entering the global market economy that flowed from its external relations in the Eastern bloc prior to the transition. Its close relation with the Soviet Union, which subsidized the Bulgarian economy in various ways, as well as its almost exclusive trading within the Council for Mutual Economic Assistance, meant that Bulgaria was ill-prepared to enter the global market. Its failure to attract nutritious FDI also contributed to the scale of labour shedding that occurred in the 1990s, leading to the entrenchment of unemployment and a sizable informal workforce.

Cumulatively, all of these factors contributed to the growth of a large informal workforce. To bring to life the effect of this informality, this chapter has focused on the experience of home-based workers in light industries, describing the scope of this workforce and their conditions. Prior to the introduction of new legislation addressing the informality, the picture of an informal worker in Bulgaria was often a bleak one—with few respondents expressing hope for the future or satisfaction with their present working life.

Section 3 of this chapter examined the dynamics which led to amendments to the Labour Code to ensure that home-based workers were offered the same protections as standard workers. The law was passed following lobbying by homeworker associations, norm diffusion through the EU and ILO, and a desire on behalf of the government to demonstrate responsiveness to the financial crisis. The focus on a legislative solution can be seen to flow from the 'statist-orientation' that remains strong in Bulgaria and the channelling of union activities into processes of social dialogue which lend themselves to the creation of legal responses to social problems.

Though the expansion of the scope of labour law to cover these atypical, precariat workers is an important step, its impact is likely to be limited given the dearth of additional regulatory levers to bolster its application and effectiveness. The reasons for informality explored in this chapter are manifold, and flow from both external and internal governance and economic influences. The expansion of the scope of labour law is a weak answer to these forces.

[97] Wallace and Latcheva 83. [98] Ibid. 83.

7

Complementary or Functional Rival? Labour Regulation of Garment Industry Workers in Cambodia by Better Factories Cambodia

7.1 Introduction

This chapter tracks the dynamics of the informalization and subsequent formalization of work in the garment industry in Cambodia. In particular, it explores the factors that have contributed to and hampered the effectiveness of the combination of the US-Cambodia Bilateral Textile Agreement (UCTA) and the International Labour Organisation's (ILO) Better Factories Project (Better Factories Cambodia) (which are together referred to in this paper as 'the initiative').[1] Unlike the Mathadi Boards examined in a previous chapter, about which little has been written, the Cambodian labour initiative is well-documented and frequently heralded as a model for transnational labour regulation in developing countries. BFC was put in place to make up for weaknesses in the existing enforcement system. This chapter examines whether the initiative has bolstered the state inspectorate (in the way that layering in the Australian model has achieved) or whether it has, in fact, replaced it.

In order to assess the responsiveness of this transnational labour initiative, this book contends that it is necessary to have a sense of what it might be responding to. How did the Cambodian working population come to be almost entirely working in informal conditions by the early 1990s? What international and national factors converged to produce virtually no industrial sector, high levels of poverty and governmental structures that were unable to govern and regulate the emerging garment sector?

In describing the labour regulation initiative and assessing it, the chapter makes two important interventions in the already abundant literature on the initiative. Firstly, it focuses on the role of the trade incentives, as preferential treatment in trade played a critical part in encouraging investment in formal enterprises. In this way, trade incentives were just as important as the BFC in improving the labour standards of participating enterprises. Secondly, it examines the initiative in the context of Cambodia's political economy. A great deal has been written about the programme in the industrial relations, labour law, and development literature. However, this literature almost never examines way that the initiative's operation and long-term sustainability is influenced by the interests of Cambodia's ruling elite. Although some authors have considered the initiative in light of 'corruption',[2] this offers only a thin understanding of the dynamics

[1] The research reported in this chapter was funded jointly by the UK Department for International Development and the Economic and Social Research Council. The project is headed by Professor Simon Deakin of Cambridge University and the author. The interviews referred to in this chapter were conducted by Enying Zheng, Eng Kunthea, and the author in March 2014.

[2] John A. Hall, 'The ILO's Better Factories Cambodia Program: A Viable Blueprint for Promoting International Labor Rights?' (2010) [2010] 21 Stanford Law & Policy Review 427; Kevin Kolben, 'Integrative Linkage: Combining Public and Private Regulatory Approaches in the Design of Trade and Labor Regimes' 48 Harvard International Law Journal 203; Kevin Kolben, 'Trade, Monitoring,

of power maintenance by the ruling elite. Indeed, understanding certain behaviours and sets of relations in terms of 'corruption' tends to a view that they are an aberration or somehow outside the normal order. This view inhibits an understanding of these behaviours and relationships as part of a relatively stable political economy. This chapter seeks to remedy this gap by analysing the initiative in the context of the political economy of Cambodia. This approach allows us to develop an understanding of the way that dense networks of relationships support what is understood in the West as corruption. This leads to an appreciation of the ways that the ruling elite have approached BFC and UCTA and, thus, their broader impact on Cambodia's economy and social relations.

After French colonization, decimation at the hands of Pol Pot, and years of civil war, work in Cambodia was almost entirely informal. Although a small civil service persisted, the work paid so little that workers had to supplement their wages in various ways, making it difficult to describe the work as entirely formal. Following the Paris Peace Agreement of 1991, Cambodia became crowded with international NGOs and foreign aid bodies clambering to make up for the failure to intervene during the Pol Pot regime and the subsequent years of civil war.[3] Partly because Cambodia was geographically small and poor it offered an opportunity for experiments in aid programmes and other types of assistance. The UCTA, which included a labour standards provision and heralded the creation of the ILO's BFC programme is celebrated as one of the great success stories in regulatory innovations in developing countries for its role in facilitating the formalization and the improvement of labour conditions in the garment industry of Cambodia.[4] It has since expanded to Vietnam, Jordan, Haiti, Lesotho, Nicaragua, and Indonesia under the auspices of the ILO's Better Work programme.

Today, thanks to the impact of preferential trading agreements with the US and other countries since the 1990s, the garment industry is the biggest employer in the country, employing 320,734 workers, among which 293,664 are women.[5] It is also the country's largest foreign currency earner—contributing about 80 per cent of Cambodia's annual foreign exchange earnings.[6]

However, the formalization of the garment industry is not spreading to other industries to a comparable extent. By 2003, the informal economy still accounted for 62 per cent of Gross Domestic Product (GDP) and 85 per cent of the total workforce. The remaining 15 per cent of the workforce was employed by 'formal' sectors, especially in the garment industry (230,000), the tourism sector, which employed 70,000, and public administration with 350,000 employees.[7] Although the rate of economic

and the ILO: Working to Improve Conditions in Cambodia's Garment Factories' 7 Yale Human Rights and Development Law Journal 79.

[3] From 1965 to 1975, under the administration of President Lyndon Johnson, and then during Richard Nixon's 'secret war', Cambodia was bombed as part of an effort to destabilize the Vietnamese National Liberation Frot and the rurally based communist Khmer Rouge. In hindsight, it became clear that the bombing campaign actually strengthened the Khmer Rouge movement and weakened US allies King Sihanouk and the government of Lon Nol: Katalin Medvedev, 'Picking up the Threads: Model Approach Helps Cambodia Design a New Fashion Image' (2013) [2013] 41 Women's Studies Quarterly 131.

[4] S. Polaski, 'Combining Global and Local Forces: The Case of Labor Rights in Cambodia' (2006) 34 World Development 919.

[5] Vannarith Chheang and Shintaro Hamanaka, *Impediments to Growth of the Garment and Food Industries in Cambodia: Exploring Potential Benefits of the ASEAN-PRC FTA* (ADB Working Paper Series on Regional Economic Integration No 86 2011) 3.

[6] Ibid. 3.

[7] Dennis Arnold and Toh Han Shih, 'A Fair Model of Globalisation? Labour and Global Production in Cambodia' (2010) 40 Journal of Contemporary Asia 401 402.

growth has been impressive over the last two decades—Cambodia enjoyed an average growth of 8.4 per cent from 1994 to 2008[8]—the share of wealth is concentrated in a small number of elite hands. This has diminished the capacity for growth of formal enterprises across non-garment sectors. Further, despite the perceived success of BFC, industrial relations in Cambodia's garment industry are still far from ideal. Wages are supressed through the government's minimum wage setting process. Protests and strikes have often been followed by the murder of union leaders and the injury of others, sometimes quite openly by police, and at other times in a more covert manner.

This chapter addresses these apparent contradictions in light of the Hun Sen government's skilful maintenance of neo-patrimonial interests. In particular, it brings attention to the way that the Hun Sen government has enjoyed the benefits of BFC without investing in its own labour inspectorate. Because of this, the chapter concludes by asking if BFC is encouraging the development of stronger state-based regulation (i.e. complementing and bolstering it) or continuing to make up for the failure of the Cambodian government to fund the labour inspectorate and thus acting as an institutional rival to the labour inspectorate.

7.1.1 Field work

The analysis of the operation of BFC conducted in this chapter draws extensively from interviews conducted in Cambodia in early 2014 with union leaders and other people with experience of the labour movement, personnel from BFC, representatives of factory management and representatives of employer bodies. The author has been conducting other research into neo-patrimonalism in Cambodia over the last three years. The views expressed in this paper reflect understandings developed through this research.

The chapter is structured as follows. Section 2 examines the dynamics of informalization owing to French colonization, the Pol Pot regime, and civil war. It then considers the way that the neo-patrimonial politics of the Hun Sen government hampered Cambodia's development in the post-Paris Peace Agreement period. Section 3 tracks the dynamics of the formalization of the garment industry following the signing of the UCTA and the development of the BFC project. It examines how these developments have been deployed by the Hun Sen government to maintain neo-patrimonial power, and how this, in turn, has fettered the success of the initiative.

7.2 Dynamics of Informalization

Cambodia's formalized export garment industry did not begin to develop until the 1990s when Cambodians first experienced peace after decades of social turmoil. In the decades before, there had been little industry and most enterprises operated informally or as state-owned enterprises. The informality of the Cambodian workforce is largely attributable to French colonization, mass murder under the Khmer Rouge, and years of civil war curbing the development of industry. It was hoped that Cambodia's economy would rapidly expand after democratic institutions were put in place. Though growth has been rapid, poverty reduction has been slow and, as noted, 85 per

[8] Chap Sotharith, *Industrial Readjustment in Cambodia* (Industrial Readjustment in the Mekong River Basin Countries: Toward the AEC, edited by Yasushi Ueki and Teerana Bhongmakkapat, BRC Research Report No 7, Bangkok Research Centre, IDE-JETRO (2012)).

cent of Cambodian workers continue to operate in the informal economy. One of the reasons for this is because a small elite has captured the resources of the state instead of fostering a developmental state.

7.2.1 Colonization, the Khmer Rouge, and civil war

The dynamics of colonization and civil war experienced by Cambodia in the twentieth century explain why, today, most work in Cambodia occurs in poor, small and micro enterprises that are unregulated by government. This section briefly outlines the various ways that these dynamics thwarted economic development, hampered the development of formal enterprises, and hindered rationalist bureaucratic development in the Weberian sense.

French colonization did little to contribute to economic growth in Cambodia. The French Protectorate of Cambodia was established in 1867, and Cambodia was integrated into the French Indochina union in 1887. It is often joked that France's main contribution was to develop more efficient methods for collecting taxes. The French colonial government raised agricultural taxes and imposed a head tax that had to be paid in cash. Those who could not pay the taxes conducted a 'corvée service'—a tax rival—demanding as many as ninety days a year on public works projects. Large percentages of annual rice harvests were confiscated, contributing to rural indebtedness.[9] The tax forced many peasant families to send men of working age to the cities, mines and plantations in search of waged labour, creating a supply of surplus labour. The French otherwise transformed Cambodia's village-based economy negligibly. Industry was rudimentary and was designed primarily to process raw materials, such as rubber, for local use or export.

French authorities assumed full control over Cambodian affairs in the financial, legal and commercial fields. A bureaucratic hierarchy was established, with French nationals occupying the upper echelons of the state and ethnic Vietnamese dominating the lower rungs of government. Cambodians were mostly excluded from bureaucratic roles.[10] The Cambodian people were allowed few opportunities, before the 1940s, to participate in the political process. French colonization prepared the country very poorly for independence, or for developing institutions of government. This is one of the factors which explains why it has been so hard for the Cambodian state to develop industrial relations institutions, such as effective inspectorates which could keep a check on labour conditions and encourage formality.

In 1946, Cambodia was granted self-rule within the French Union and had its protectorate status abolished in 1949. Cambodia won independence from France in 1953 and became the Kingdom of Cambodia. Just as the education system and other institutions of nation building were beginning to reap benefits under Prince Norodom Sihanouk, the Khmer Rouge occupied Phnom Penh. Up to two million people died during the four years of Khmer Rouge rule.[11] Cities were evacuated, wiping out commercial hubs. The regime put to death the majority of the nation's educated elite.[12] A lasting legacy of this period is that individuals of school age at the end of the 1970s,

[9] James A. Tyner, *The Killing of Cambodia: Geography, Genocide and the Unmaking Of Space* (Ashgate 2008) 26.

[10] Ibid. 26.

[11] Kevin McIntyre, 'Geography as Destiny: Cities, Villages and Khmer Rouge Orientalism' (1996) 38 Comparative Studies in Society and History 730 730.

[12] John A. Hall, 'Human Rights and the Garment Industry in Contemporary Cambodia' (2000) 36 Stanford Journal of International Law 119 120.

especially men, have a lower educational attainment than those in the preceding and subsequent birth cohorts.[13] This has had a long-term impact on Cambodia's rate of development. It also explains the country's high reliance on outside technical assistance, including BFC. This is the cohort who, in other countries, are today heading up government departments and leading industrial development. However, in Cambodia, this group of men were killed or largely left without secondary or University education, limiting their occupational choices and capacity to take charge of government.

In 1977, conflict erupted with Vietnam, leading to the invasion in 1978 and eventual takeover of Cambodia by Vietnam in 1979. On January 10, 1979, the Vietnamese proclaimed the People's Republic of Kampuchea (PRK) and a new regime was installed based to an extent on mid-level Khmer Rouge officials who had earlier fled to escape being purged. Together with other Cambodian communists who had spent much of the Post-World War II period in Vietnam, they formed the backbone of the new administration.[14] In 1981, the pro-Vietnamese PRK won parliamentary elections. A young former Khmer Rouge officer named Hun Sen headed the new PRK government. He had survived years of war, bloody infighting, political purges and rapidly changing alliances, and had manoeuvred himself into power.[15]

Civil war continued throughout the 1980s, with Western, Chinese and ASEAN support for the resistance groups and Soviet Bloc support for the People's Republic of Kampuchea. This not only divided the nation, it hampered economic development. Resources were diverted to fighting and more working-age men died. The industrial sector, which is usually first to formalize, accounted for only 5 per cent of Cambodia's GDP by 1985, down from 19 per cent in 1969. Industrial activity was concentrated in the processing of agricultural commodities, mostly rice, fish, wood and rubber.[16] Enterprises were small, employing an average of fewer than 200 workers.[17]

With the reduction in Cold War tensions, Cambodian politics slowly began to normalize as foreign backers of the royalists, the PRK, and the Khmer Rouge began to withdraw their financial and military support for these factions, aided by the UN-sponsored peace process.[18] After Vietnam withdrew its military forces in 1989, the PRK renamed itself the State of Cambodia, and formally abandoned socialism. The Agreements on a Comprehensive Political Settlement of the Cambodia Conflict (the Paris Peace Agreements) were signed October 23 1991. The UN Transitional Authority in Cambodia (UNTAC) followed in 1992, culminating in the 1993 elections, contested by nineteen parties.[19] These transitional processes sought to project Cambodia forward into peace and democracy.

There was a surge in civil society activity, and more vocal and diverse media emerged.[20] Yet government remained bedevilled by factional rivalry and political

[13] Damien de Walque, 'The Socio-Demographic Legacy of the Khmer Rouge Period in Cambodia' (2006) 60 Population Studies 223 233.

[14] Elizabeth Becker, *When the War Was Over: Cambodia and the Khmer Rouge Revolution* (1st edn, PublicAffairs 1998); Evan Gottesman, *Cambodia after the Khmer Rouge: Inside The Politics of Nation Building* (Yale University Press 2003); Michael Vickery, *Kampuchea: Politics, Economics, and Society* (F. Pinter; L. Rienner Publishers 1986).

[15] Hall, 'Human Rights and the Garment Industry in Contemporary Cambodia' 120.

[16] Sotharith. [17] Ibid.

[18] Andrew Robert Cock, 'External Actors and the Relative Autonomy of the Ruling Elite in Post-UNTAC Cambodia' (2010) 41 Journal of Southeast Asian Studies 241.

[19] Martin Gainsborough, 'Elites vs. Reform in Laos, Cambodia, and Vietnam' 23 Journal of Democracy 34.

[20] Ibid.

violence.[21] In 1997, after an uneasy period of sharing power with Prince Norodom Ranariddh's royalist party, Hun Sen launched a bloody coup in which his opponents were exiled, arrested, tortured, and in some cases summarily executed. Since 1997, Hun Sen has led the country and solidified his political and economic power.

7.2.2 Post Paris Peace Agreement neo-patrimonialism

Since the end of the Khmer Rouge regime, Cambodia's state has created its own relatively stable political and economic elite.[22] A relatively small number of elites hold concurrent positions within the government, legal institutions and the CPP, and remain closely associated with Hun Sen, despite the existence of a rational-legal bureaucratic system rooted in the principles of separation of power. They are largely post-Khmer Rouge-era politicos who built their influence following the economic liberalization of the late 1980s and early 1990s. The strength of ties between these elite families is fortified through intermarriage[23] as well as shared business interests. The powerful elite maintain their influence by combining political, military, economic and administrative power through an 'interlocking of pyramids of patron-client networks'.[24] This section of the chapter explores the operation of neo-patrimonialism on the growth of a formal workforce across diverse industrial sectors.

Though the concept is sometimes ambiguous,[25] in seeking to understand the structure and administrative machinery of the Cambodian political system, scholars have often turned to the Weberian concept of 'patrimonialism'.[26] Neo-patrimonialism is a highly personalized, patron focused, and often presidential system, where the benefits of resource extraction through formal state apparatus are concentrated only among a small group of elites. Neo-patrimonial systems co-opt the formal and informal mechanisms of the state to gather personal wealth, via rent seeking. The formal governance structures in the neo-patrimonial state become a machine for harvesting income and gaining resource control.

The Hun Sen government, led by the Cambodian People's Party (CPP) employs a variety of techniques to maintain power and quell dissent including violence, gifts, and foreign assistance. The predatory character of the Hun Sen regime partially explains why it needs external resources and assistance. A significant source of state revenue comes from tapping into the flows of aid provided by foreign actors to supplement what can be internally captured.[27] Much of the remaining income comes from foreign direct investment, as is the case with the garment industry which is almost 100 per

[21] Ozay Mehmet, 'Development in a Wartorn Society: What Next in Cambodia?' (1997) [1997] 18 Third World Quarterly 673.

[22] Cock 251.

[23] Bertil Litner, 'One Big Happy Family in Cambodia' *Asia Times* (20 March 2007) http://www.atimes.com/atimes/Southeast_Asia/IC20Ae03.html accessed 14 July 2014.

[24] James C. Scott, 'Patron-Client Politics and Political Change in Southeast Asia' (1972) 66 The American Political Science Review 91.

[25] Gina Zabludovsky, 'The Reception and Utility of Max Weber's Concept Of Patrimonialism in Latin America' (1989) 4 International Sociology 51; Mounira M. Charrad, 'Central and Local Patrimonialism: State-Building in Kin-Based Societies' (2011) 636 The Annals of the American Academy of Political and Social Science 49.

[26] Patrimonialism was conceptualized by Weber as an ideal type: 'an analytical construct that one compares to real-world cases, ones that correspond imperfectly to the conceptual tool at hand but that can also be illuminated by them': Mounira M. Charrad and Julia Adams, 'Introduction: Patrimonialism, Past and Present' (2011) 636 The Annals of the American Academy of Political and Social Science 6 7.

[27] Marwan Muasher, 'World Bank Confronts Cambodia Corruption' *The Wall Street Journal* (18 October 2007) http://online.wsj.com/news/articles/SB119266729725862803 accessed 14 July 2014.

cent foreign owned. These resource inflows provide Cambodian elites with a certain level of regime autonomy. As the provision of basic services is predominantly externally financed and managed, state actors have greater freedom from domestic pressures that might otherwise compel the use of their offices for public benefit.[28] These dynamics are readily evident in the area of labour relations, explored below.

7.2.3 Burgeoning garment sector

Beginning in 1994, the government of Cambodia started privatizing small and medium-sized state-owned enterprises.[29] In 1993, as part of a programme of economic and structural adjustment, the government, with the support of the World Bank and the International Monetary Fund, put in place a number of policies encouraging foreign investment. It offered significant financial packages to investors willing to begin operations in Cambodia under a new Law on Investment passed in August 1994. By 1995, this policy had attracted the establishment of twenty new garment factories, which grew rapidly to thirty-two by mid-1996, employing an estimated 20,000 workers.[30]

Due to Cambodia's slow development and the poverty spurred by colonization and the conflicts of the twentieth century, Cambodia's population represented a large pool of cheap labour. This was attractive to foreign investors and brands seeking to source garments from Cambodia for a low cost. On the other side of the coin, for families facing hunger and stark privation, the garment factories in and around Phnom Penh became a source of salvation. Young women travelled by the tens of thousands from their rural villages to work in Phnom Penh with the hope of being able to send money home to their families. According to Hall, they often offered the last chance for their families.[31]

Conditions in the Bourgeoning Garment industry

The conditions of workers in the garment industry in the mid to late 1990s were characterized by low wages, forced overtime, being locked into the factories, no paid sick leave or holidays, and the payment of pre-employment fees which placed workers in a type of indentured labour. Workers were required to work far in excess of the maximum hours permitted under law, with shifts up to fifteen hours, seven days a week, with no days off.[32] Fines were imposed on workers who refused to work on Sundays. Initially, workers were paid piece rates, rather than wages, leading to great variance in monthly incomes amongst workers in the same section of the one factory.[33] By 1998, wages were paid rather than piece rates, but wages were frequently lower than the already extremely low legal minimum. There were no provisions in the Labour Code for minimum wages until 1997, when the minimum wage was set at USD $40 per month

[28] Pip Nicholson and Sally Low, 'Local Accounts of Rule of Law Aid: Implications for Donors' (2013) 5 Hague Journal on the Rule of Law 1.

[29] Sotharith.

[30] Hall, 'Human Rights and the Garment Industry in Contemporary Cambodia' 129.

[31] Ibid. 128. [32] Ibid. 160–1.

[33] Bama Athreva, *Labor Conditions in Cambodia's Garment Industry* (International Labor Rights Forum 1996) 5.

for a 40 hour working week under a sub-decree for the garment sector.[34] In practice, this operated as a maximum rather than a minimum.

In order to gain employment in garment factories, many young women were forced to pay bribes or a 'finder's fee' to so-called 'employment brokers' (in breach of Article 7(1) of ILO Convention 181). These employment brokers were often the security guards, borrowed from the local police force, who were employed by factories both to guard factories and to recruit workers from villages. Workers were required to pay around USD $40 to USD $100 to these employment brokers to obtain work.[35] Because rural families did not have such money, family land would often be held as collateral for a loan. Interest charged on the loan was then deducted from the workers' wages.

Despite the fact that these conditions were in breach of the Labour Code, they went unchecked either by an effective state Labour Inspectorate or an active union movement. Under the 1997 Labour Code, responsibility for monitoring factories and enforcing labour law and regulations lies with labour Inspectors and Labour Controllers with the Bureau of Labour Inspection, part of the Ministry of Labour (Article 343). By 1998, the official number of labour inspectors at Cambodia's Ministry of Labour was 100, but according to a UN report, 'only about twelve in fact carry out inspections. This is not sufficient if the Ministry is to address labour disputes in a comprehensive manner.'[36] The vestiges of French colonialism and the challenges of the transition to capitalism meant that the inspectorate had limited capacity to regulate these new businesses. Corruption was widespread, and low wages necessitated the taking of 'gifts'.[37] Corruption was also fuelled by the entrenched system of political allegiances between factory owners and powerful bureaucrats and politicians. As a junior civil servant, refusing bribes and reporting serious violations of the Labour Code would result in trouble with superiors. Hall found that factories were only fined for Labour Code violations when they lost the protection of their political allies or tried to operate without such 'friends'.[38]

In the early days of the garment industry in Cambodia, collective bargaining and independent union organizing did not occur.[39] State-controlled syndicates were demobilized as part of the transition from a planned economy to a market-driven economy and most leaders of the Union Federation of Kampuchea were given important positions in state institutions.[40] In 1996, the Free Trade Union of Workers of the Kingdom of Cambodia (FTUWKC) was the first union federation to be established after democratization. It emerged as Sam Rainsy, along with other union activists such as Chea Vichea, began organizing local unions to counter those identified with the ruling party. The CPP and employers responded by fostering their own unions. The CPP formed the Cambodian Trade Union Federation in 1996, soon renamed the Independent Trade Union of Cambodian Workers, which differentiated itself from the FTUWK by rejecting militancy and encouraging direct negotiations with employers. As of July 10, 1998, a total of thirty-two garment unions were officially registered with the

[34] Parveen Shah, 'An Overview of Cambodian Women Working in the Garment Industry' (2010) 28 Asia Pacific Research Journal 1 7.

[35] Hall, 'Human Rights and the Garment Industry in Contemporary Cambodia' 153.

[36] United Nations Secretary General, *Situation of Human Rights in Cambodia, Report of the Secretary General, Fifty-third session, General Assembly, Agenda Item 110 (b), Human Rights Questions: Human Rights Questions, Including Alternative Approaches to Improving the Effective Enjoyment of Human Rights and Fundamental Freedoms* (United Nations, A/53/400 1998) 16.

[37] Hall, 'Human Rights and the Garment Industry in Contemporary Cambodia' 126.

[38] Ibid. 127. [39] Athreva Secretary General 16.

[40] Veasna Nuon and Melisa Serrano, *Building Unions in Cambodia: History, Challenges, Strategies* (Friedrich-Ebert-Stiftung Office for Regional Cooperation in Asia 2010) 24.

Ministry of Labour. Of these, only three were independent of government or management domination. Of the others, twenty-eight were either Independent Trade Union of Cambodian Workers (ITUCW) or Trade Union of Workers (TUW), 'regarded as "paper unions" established by factory management with the collusion of the Ministry of Labour'.[41]

Hall found evidence that the Ministry of Labour and high ranking CPP officials routinely colluded with employers to deny workers the right to form independent unions.[42] Employees were asked to sign membership forms for management aligned unions as a condition of employment. Various formal and informal hurdles were placed in the way of independent unions that tried to register with the government.

7.3 Dynamics of Formalization

This section of the chapter explores the dynamics that have supported the formalization of the garment industry. In the late 1990s a number of institutional changes impacted on trade relations and labour relations which encouraged the growth of the industry with close supervision by the ILO. Most of the literature on labour relations in the garment industry focuses on the labour standards aspects of the bilateral agreement between the US and Cambodia. However, other aspects of the agreement, in conjunction with a variety of additional institutional developments, had an influential role in generating large and formal enterprises and providing opportunities for the birth of a new labour movement.

7.3.1 Institutional underpinnings of the Cambodian garment industry

In the late 1990s, Cambodia's garment industry enjoyed a major boost from arrangements under the Multifibre Agreement that permitted the establishment of quotas limiting imports into countries whose domestic industries were facing serious damage from rapidly increasing imports.[43] Investors sought new locations for the manufacture of garments after their own country's quota had been filled.

In 1998, the US initiated negotiations to impose a quota on Cambodian products. The American Federation of Labour-Congress of Industrial Organizations (AFL-CIO), together with member unions including the Union of Needletrades, Industrial and Textile Employees (UNITE), the International Rights Fund and the Lawyers Committee for Human Rights, lobbied the Clinton Administration particularly hard to have a stronger Labour Code in Cambodia mandated by UCTA. While the Cambodian government and the Garment Manufacturing Association of Cambodia (GMAC) were involved, according to Kolben, 'the two primary negotiating parties were the US government and the ILO'.[44] No Cambodian trade unions or Cambodian NGOs were consulted.[45] UCTA was signed and came into effect in 1999 and was eventually extended until December 2004.

[41] Hall, 'Human Rights and the Garment Industry in Contemporary Cambodia' 145.
[42] Ibid. 136.
[43] Melanie Beresford, 'The Cambodian Clothing Industry in the post-MFA Environment: A Review Of Developments' (2009) 14 Journal of the Asia Pacific Economy 366.
[44] Kolben, 'Trade, Monitoring, and the ILO: Working to Improve Conditions in Cambodia's Garment Factories' 91.
[45] Ibid. 91.

A number of additional institutional changes were made to the landscape of labour relations during this period. In late 1998, the government liberalized procedures for trade union registration, allowing for a swift increase in the number of officially recognized labour unions.[46] This was followed in 1999 by the creation of a tripartite Labour Advisory Committee (LAC) which reviews and approves labour regulation. It also undertakes a periodic minimum wage review.

The Cambodian garment industry further benefited from the use by the US and the EU of provisions in the World Trade Organization's Agreement on Textile and Clothing to re-impose import quotas on China, in the former case until the end of 2008 and in the latter until the end of 2007. A bilateral agreement between Cambodia and the EU giving duty- and quota-free access to Cambodian garments was signed in 1999, and from 2001 Cambodia was included in the EU's Everything But Arms (EBA) initiative, which granted the same conditions.[47] Though in reality, only a small proportion of Cambodian exports benefited from duty-free access to overseas markets, these institutional factors appear to have supported the initial growth of the industry, and the emergence of a critical mass of large, privately owned formal enterprises in Cambodia.[48]

7.3.2 Structure of the garment industry

As this section of the chapter discusses, although the Cambodian economy is particularly dependent on the garment industry, the industry remains remarkably disembedded from the rest of Cambodian society, economy, and state. Embeddedness has to do with the constitutive institutions and networks of interaction that shape market activity.[49] Less embeddedness implies that markets are governed more strongly by basic forces of supply and demand, rather than being submitted to the control of various societal institutions.[50] More specifically, in a capitalist system, a less embedded market can be described as one in which powerful business actors exert market power with relatively weaker countervailing power wielded by the state. This section suggests that over time, this disembeddness presented opportunities for international civil society organizations, independent unions, and the ILO in promoting better labour conditions and continuing formalisation.

From a starting point of 1 per cent of GDP in 1993, and seven factories in 1994, the industry expanded to 14 per cent of GDP by 2011, and 72 per cent of total merchandise exports.[51] The garment industry quickly became the main income generator within the Cambodian labour force. Rather than improving with economic growth, poverty levels in the Cambodian countryside rose due to illegal logging, draughts and the granting of agricultural concessions that reduced the land available for farming.[52] The salaries of female factory workers became a vital component of the rural economy, with workers sending between 30–50 per cent of their salaries home (around $10–30 each month).[53]

46 Nuon and Serrano 17–18.

47 Beresford.

48 The reason usually cited was Cambodia's inability to meet the strict rules of origin, owing to the non-inclusion of China in the derogation list.

49 Karl Polanyi, *The Great Transformation* (Beacon Press 1957).

50 Ibid.

51 Vannarith Chheang and Shintaro Hamanaka.

52 Kheang Un, 'Cambodia in 2011: A Thin Veneer of Change' (2012) [University of California Press] 52 Asian Survey 202; Kheang Un, 'Cambodia in 2012: Towards Developmental Authoritarianism?' Southeast Asian Affairs 71.

53 Asian Development Bank, *Cambodia's Garment Industry: Meeting the Challenge of the Post-Quota Environment* 2004.

The number of apparel factories expanded at a steady rate between 1998 and 2004, but then declined slightly after the end of UCTA before recovering again without noticeably affecting employment growth.[54] This marked the first significant departure from an agrarian society organized around family farms.[55] The average size of these establishments stabilized at about 1100–1200 workers by 2008,[56],[57] large enough to support a market economy style of trade unions, with shop stewards and more than one union competing for worker membership.

The garment industry is highly disembedded from the local economy. Production is not for a domestic market: clothing mainly goes to the US, the EU, Canada, and Japan.[58] This means that nearly all inputs must be imported.[59] 93 per cent of garment enterprises are foreign-owned.[60] Though this reduces the economic nutrition of the industry for the rest of the economy, it in some ways renders the industry less beholden to patrimonial ties that bind the rest of the economy to elite networks.

The industry is further disembedded from the political forces driving the local economy by the neo-liberal logic driving the agreement with the US. In return for UCTA quotas, Cambodia agreed, among other concessions, to reduce tariffs on its apparel and textile imports, and not to exercise non-tariff restrictions, such as import licensing. Cambodia offers a generous foreign direct investment regime with 100 per cent foreign capital investment and tax holidays.[61] As a consequence, the industry's direct contributions to official government revenue have been limited almost entirely to export licences.[62]

The Ministry of Commerce holds the most powerful official domestic position in the garment industry by granting these export licenses. Because of the limit imposed on the number of garments that could be exported, the government set up a complex system for allocating export quotas to companies. The system provides opportunities for raising revenue from public quota auctions, as well as less public opportunities for officials administering the auction to obtain payoffs for granting allocations.[63] Though the Ministry of Labour is responsible for setting minimum wages, mediating disputes and monitoring compliance with the law, in practice it has less institutional sway than its formal authority would suggest. As is outlined in the next section, the acceptance of 'gifts' continues to be common place.

Other than these payments, the high proportion of foreign ownership of enterprises means that a significant part of the profits are repatriated. The Cambodian elite are relatively uninvolved in garment factories, and opportunities for predatory behaviour and opportunities for wealth extraction are limited by the neo-liberal institutional architecture of the industry. This has provided various opportunities for the burgeoning labour movement that might not otherwise have existed.

There were a number of contradictory forces at play which impacted on the willingness and capacity of employees of apparel factories to wield political and industrial

[54] Beresford.

[55] 55 per cent of the labour force were in agriculture and agricultural production accounted for 31.7 per cent of GDP in 2009: Nuon and Serrano.

[56] Beresford 371. [57] Official employment data is unreliable in Cambodia.

[58] Vannarith Chheang and Shintaro Hamanaka. [59] Arnold and Han Shih 415.

[60] Vannarith Chheang and Shintaro Hamanaka.

[61] Yoko Asuyama and others, 'Firm Dynamics in the Cambodian Garment Industry: Firm Turnover, Productivity Growth and Wage Profile Under Trade Liberalization' (2012) 18 Journal of the Asia Pacific Economy 51 64.

[62] Vannarith Chheang and Shintaro Hamanaka 4.

[63] Kolben, 'Trade, Monitoring, and the ILO: Working to Improve Conditions in Cambodia's Garment Factories' 86.

power in the early development of the garment industry. The low-skilled workers that filled the non-managerial positions were chiefly single young women, drawn from rural villages and earning low wages. Rural migrants constituted 90 per cent of all garment workers by 2010.[64] Wages were extremely low, but living in communal dorms and flats allowed these young women to live separately from their families, whereas the average income renders survival outside the family unit largely impossible for most young people.[65] As Hughes puts it, freed from scrutiny and the patrimonial ties of village life, 'garment workers represented one of a few groups who had the opportunity to respond both to a climate of greater political openness in the cities and to a widespread feeling that the regime was struggling to legitimize itself'.[66] The growth of the garment industry thus saw the development of a formal workforce that was less tied into the CPP's neo-patrimonial networks, and less dependent upon the state apparatus for employment, compared with say, state employees who constituted the largest body of formal workers prior to the expansion of the garment industry.

It is often expected (in the Western media at least) that Chinese run factories[67] will adopt repressive human resource management strategies that will generate fear about initiating labour activism. However, Chinese ownership and management may have had a converse effect in Cambodia because of historical antagonisms.[68] Workers striking against Chinese managers for improved conditions were treated with considerable sympathy by the Cambodian media with articles starting with phrases such as: 'In the garment industry the low-paid workers are ethnic Khmer; the high-paid supervisors Chinese'.[69] At a time when workers were finding their political voices, then, the numerical dominance of Chinese managers allowed workers to couch their demands in the language of national pride and the rights of Khmers to be treated respectfully in their own land.[70]

In surprising ways, then, the disembeddeness of the garment industry increased the power of garment workers relative to managers, and provided a foothold for independent union organizing. It also paved the way for the intervention of the ILO and other international actors in ways that further encouraged the formalization of garment sector work. The garment industry largely operated according to different principles from the rest of the economy: enterprises were larger, generally registered, and mainly formal.

[64] Medvedev 133.

[65] Annuska Derks, *Khmer Women on the Move: Exploring Work and Life in Urban Cambodia* (University of Hawaii Press 2008).

[66] Caroline Hughes, 'Transnational Networks, International Organizations and Political Participation in Cambodia: Human Rights, Labour Rights and Common Rights' (2007) 14 Democratization 834 842.

[67] Managers and executives were initially drawn from China. Interviewees for our study told us that recent relative wage increases in China have made it more difficult to attract skilled staff, and managerial employees are being increasingly drawn from other producing countries such as the Philippines.

[68] AthThun, President of the Coalition of Cambodian Apparel Workers Democratic Unions (CCAWDU) said, 'In the past, I acknowledge that it was fair to choose Chinese as supervisors because at the time we didn't have enough skill. But now, we have enough skill, the same as the Chinese. Today, even when they select Cambodian supervisors, they are still paid less than the Chinese. I think it is racism': Norris Lo, 'The Chinese/Khmer Divide in Factories' *The Phnom Penh Post* (16 June 2006) http://www.phnompenhpost.com/national/chinesekhmer-divide-factories accessed 14 July 2014.

[69] Ibid. [70] Hughes 842.

7.3.3 UCTA Labour conditionalities and the Better Factories Cambodia Programme

A critical feature of the US–Cambodia Textile Agreement which contributed to the formalization of the garment workforce was the provision for implementation of labour standards in Cambodian garment factories. It enabled Cambodia to earn extra quota each year if it could demonstrate that it was making progress towards improving working conditions and supporting workers' rights in the garment industry.[71] Though such clauses are not unusual for bilateral agreements—the US has been incorporating labour rights into trade agreements since 1993[72]—UCTA is one of the 'most creative experiments in linking trade privileges to the respect of labor rights in trade agreements'.[73]

The labour provision read as follows:

> Cambodia shall support the implementation of a program to improve the working conditions in the textile and apparel sector, including internationally recognized core labor standards, through the application of Cambodian labor law ... The Government of the United States will make a determination ... whether working conditions in the Cambodian textile and apparel sector substantially comply with such labor law and standards.[74]

The clause created a regulatory 'carrot' for labour improvements. In 2000, for instance, which was the first year of UCTA's implementation, the US government granted a 5 per cent increase.[75]

Both parties agreed to a regulatory compliance regime to be handled by a non-interested third party.[76] After lengthy discussions, the Cambodian and US governments agreed that the most credible and independent organization for taking on such a role would be the ILO. The ILO would run an independent monitoring programme, capacity building, and offer technical assistance by training a core group of Cambodian labour inspectors. It would also provide technical assistance in drafting regulations and labour laws.[77] On 4 May 2000, the ILO signed an agreement to run the BFC operations. It began work in 2001. From March 28 2001, the Ministry of Commerce required registration with the programme as a condition for granting an export license.[78]

[71] Though much is often made of this feature of the trade agreement between the US and Cambodia, such arrangements were not unusual. United States' Generalized System of Preferences (GSP) provided tariff preferences to some 140 countries and territories, giving them greater access to the US market that were conditional on the beneficiary country 'taking steps' to achieve internationally recognized worker rights, including freedom of association and the right to organize and bargain collectively, and prohibition of forced and child labour. See Lance Compa and Jeffrey S. Vogt, 'Labor Rights in the Generalised System of Preferences: A 20 Year Review' (2000–2001) 22 Comparative Labor Law & Policy Journal 199.

[72] Michael Hecker, 'Lesson from the East: International Labor Rights and the U.S.–Cambodia Trade Agreement of 1999' (2007–2008) 26 Buffalo Public Interest Law Journal 39.

[73] Kolben, 'Trade, Monitoring, and the ILO: Working to Improve Conditions in Cambodia's Garment Factories' 439.

[74] Agreement Relating to Trade in Cotton, Wool, Man-made Fiber, Non-Cotton Vegetable Fiber and Silk Blend Textiles and Textile Products Between the Government of the United States of America and the Royal Government of Cambodia (1999).

[75] Kolben, 'Trade, Monitoring, and the ILO: Working to Improve Conditions in Cambodia's Garment Factories' 90.

[76] Hecker.

[77] Kolben, 'Trade, Monitoring, and the ILO: Working to Improve Conditions in Cambodia's Garment Factories' 101.

[78] Hecker.

The project was funded largely by the US government from the years 1999 to 2004.[79] UCTA ended in 2004. Today, BFC earns nearly 70 per cent of its annual budget through non-donor support including contributions from: the Garment Manufacturers Association in Cambodia (GMAC), the Royal Government of Cambodia, and income from paid services such as the sale of factory assessment reports, training programmes and advisory services.[80] From 1 January 2009, BFC was placed under Cambodian supervision. The idea was that the programme would become a largely Cambodian programme rather than a purely ILO one.[81] As the next section discusses, this process of localization has been slow and dislocated.

7.3.3.1 Participation, monitoring and reporting

By 2014, the BFC monitored the working conditions of 437,181 workers and 428 factories.[82] By 2014, 362 garment factories and nine footwear factories were participating in the BFC programme.[83] Monitoring of factories occurs against a checklist which consists of 156 items, developed by the Chief Technical Advisor of the programme. These indicators are primarily based on the Cambodian Labour Code. In this sense, it strengthens the force and legitimacy of these domestic laws.[84] It also measures performance against certain standards set in ILO Conventions.

BFC releases three different types of reports based on factory visits and data provided by factories. Firstly, it publishes publicly available *synthesis reports* twice a year. These reports contain an overview of compliance, providing statistics on overall adherence to BFC indicators. They do not provide data on individual factories. Secondly, it produces *assessment reports*. These reports are provided to factories and are available to subscribing brands for a fee. Twenty-seven brands had subscribed to receive assessments reports from 299 factories by April 2014, up from eighteen brands and 213 factories in the same period in 2013.[85] Thirdly, it produces a *transparency database*. These are a form of naming and shaming, a version of which started in 2001, halted in 2006, and has resumed since 2013.[86] There are two categories of reporting for factories: 'critical issues' and 'low compliance'.

7.3.3.2. Education

The BFC offers an advisory service to factories. It also conducts worker education to enhance knowledge of labour laws using a variety of platforms.

[79] Sandra Polaski, *Harnessing Global Forces to Create Decent Work in Cambodia* (Research Series, 119, International Labour Organization, International Institute for Labour Studies, 2009).

[80] Better Factories Cambodia, 'Better Work': http://betterfactories.org/?page_id=312, accessed 4 October 2014.

[81] Hall, 'The ILO's Better Factories Cambodia Program: A Viable Blueprint for Promoting International Labor Rights?' 430.

[82] Better Factories Cambodia, *Thirty First Synthesis Report on Working Conditions in Cambodia's Garment Sector* (2013–2014) 11.

[83] Ibid. [84] Polaski.

[85] Better Factories Cambodia, *Thirty First Synthesis Report on Working Conditions in Cambodia's Garment Sector 10.*

[86] Interview with Chea Sophal, Senior Program Officer and Team Leader, Monitoring, Better Factories Program, Phnom Penh, Cambodia, 19 March 2014.

7.3.3.3. *Buyer power*

By selling factory assessments to buyers, the programme effectively calls on leverage from these powerful players. However, these reports are only available with the authorization of the factory.[87] There is some evidence that foreign buyers are placed under pressure by consumers not to source from factories with poor labour standards according to BFC indicators. This forces foreign buyers to pass on this pressure to the factories themselves, which are in turn forced to improve their performance in order to obtain contracts for work. For instance, Nike stopped sourcing in Cambodia after a BFC report showed child labour was being used in one of the factories its products were made in. It agreed to return to Cambodia only after an assurance that the factories would share monitoring reports.[88]

7.4 Assessment

BFC is respected for its thoroughness and integrity. The numerous studies that have assessed the BFC all attested to its reliability[89] as did interviewees for the present study. This chapter hopes to contribute to the literature by focusing on broader structural issues related to the political economy of Cambodia and global buyer practices. This section asks how much transnational labour regulation innovation redresses dynamics of informalization described in Section 2 of this chapter, and further, how much it responds to the experiences of workers and the deficits in working conditions. Is this response adequate to the task of improving the conditions of informal garment workers in Cambodia, or to acting as a model for addressing informality more broadly?

7.4.1 Functional rivalry with the Ministry of Labour

A number of interviewees raised concerns that BFC acts as a functional rival for the Ministry of Labour's Inspectorate, rather than acting as a complementary and capacity building institution.[90] Close coordination with the Labour Ministry might help to overcome the problem of lack of enforcement powers and the limited deployment of other potential sources of leverage (discussed below). However, such coordination has not been forthcoming, other than Labour Ministry presence on the governing body of BFC, despite many overtures to the Ministry of Labour being made over the years of BFC's operation, and a Memorandum of Understanding being signed in 2013 calling for further cooperation.

This failure to coordinate was often attributed by some interviewees to the lack of capacity held by the Inspectorate.[91] Other interviewees suggested that the reason was because joint monitoring of factories with BFC would alter patrimonial relations

[87] Ibid.

[88] Kolben, 'Trade, Monitoring, and the ILO: Working to Improve Conditions in Cambodia's Garment Factories' 105.

[89] Ibid. Don Wells, '"Best Practice" in the Regulation of International Labor Standards: Lessons of the U.S.–Cambodia Textile Agreement' (2005–2006) 27 Comparative Labor Law & Policy Journal 357 Stanford Law School International Human Rights and Conflict Resolution Clinic and Worker Rights Consortium, *Monitoring in the Dark: An Evaluation of the International Labour Organization's Better Factories Cambodia Monitoring and Reporting Program* (2013).

[90] Interview with Tola Moun, Community Legal Education Center, Cambodia, 27 March 2014

[91] Interview with *Liv Sovanna, Arbitrator, Cambodian Arbitration Council, Phomn Pehn, Cambodia, 26 March 2014*. Interview with Chea Sophal.

between the factories and patrons. Interviewees consistently reported that it is expected that when Ministry of Labour Inspectors arrive at the factory they will be provided a meal and a small payment. In return, they will not go past the administrative offices and onto the factory floor.[92] Personnel from the Labour Inspectorate corroborated that they place an emphasis on checking that factory paper work is in order.[93]

If Labour Inspectors attended the factories with BFC personnel, it is likely that they would have to step onto the factory floor more frequently, and they might be compelled to take action against companies based on shared evidence collected. The greater barrier to coordination between BFC and the Labour Inspectorate may lie with the patrons who receive far bigger payments from the factories than the Labour Inspectors.[94] After receiving these payments, the patrons promise the factories that they won't have any problems with the government. If the Labour Inspectorate begins to enforce the law in earnest, patrons won't be upholding their side of the bargain, and this could result in a breakdown of the system of patronage. Further, some interviewees who had been involved in discussions with government suggested that the government wishes to avoid funding the Labour Inspectorate, favouring, instead, the joint funding model of BFC.[95]

This places BFC and those with an interest in promoting labour rights in a difficult position. In the interests of humanitarianism, BFC cannot leave. But, in the meantime, the functional rivalry of BFC for a local regulatory system places rule-enforcing authority in the hands of the ILO, predominantly western transnational brands and western consumers.[96] The evidence collected for this study suggests that Cambodia's local institutions are not a great deal closer to being able to regulate the garment industry independently of international assistance than when the BFC was first initiated. This high dependence on international expertise and interventions reduces the long-term sustainability of the formality of the garment industry.

7.4.2 Focus on factory level standards detracts from addressing flaws in labour laws

Although the UCTA allowed Cambodia to earn extra quota each year if it could demonstrate that it was making progress towards improving working conditions and supporting workers' rights in the garment industry, the structure of BFC has meant that its focus is on factories rather than the state. Yet many of the gravest industrial relations problems stem from government policy. The grievances raised repeatedly in interviews were first, low wages, second, short term contracts, and third, oppression of unions.

Workers suffered a 16.6 per cent drop in real wages for regular work, that is, work hours excluding overtime from 2000 to 2010.[97] This decrease was projected to grow to 30 per cent by 2014 without an increase in the legal minimum.[98] The setting

[92] Interview with Morm Nhim, President, National Independent Federation Textile Union of Cambodia, Phnom Penh, Cambodia, 20 March 2014.

[93] Interview with Tor Bon Thorn, Deputy Director, Labour Inspectorate, Ministry of Labour, Phnom Penh, Cambodia, 2014.

[94] Interview with An Nan, Arbitration Council, Phnom Penh, Cambodia, March 26 2014.

[95] Interview with Basirun Nabi Khan, Office Operations Manager Cambodia and Vietnam, H&M, Phnom Penh, Cambodia, 27 Mar 2014.

[96] Tola Moun proposed that BFC should be further localized based on the Arbitration Council model: Interview with Tola Moun.

[97] International Human Rights and Conflict Resolution Clinic and Worker Rights Consortium 7.

[98] Figures differ between sources.

of minimum wages occurs through the politicized process of the Labour Advisory Committee, a government-led tripartite group. Low wages have become one of the major sources of social conflict in Cambodia. After protracted negotiations and protests, The Ministry of Labour and Vocational Training increased the industry's minimum wage to US $100 per month starting on 1 February 2014. ILO and World Bank analyses in 2014 confirm that the recent increase marked the first time that the sector's inflation-adjusted minimum wage has risen above its 2001 level.[99] Yet this level is widely accepted to be very low.

A second problem addressed by many interviewees is that of the deployment of short, fixed term contracts in order to avoid labour law obligations to workers. These short term contracts are precarious and semi-formal and are renewed every three to six months. When the contracts end, the workers lose the right to maternity leave, seniority bonuses and a range of other benefits.[100] The dismissal of union leaders without notice to the Labour Ministry and subsequent inspection is against the law.[101] To circumvent this law, interviewees reported that union leaders are placed on short term contracts, and their contracts are not renewed if they are active.[102] In a number of factories, all new employees are now being placed on short term contracts, contributing to the re-informalization of the garment sector.[103]

Despite personnel within the organization perceiving this as problematic, BFC has difficulty addressing the rising incidence of fixed term contracts because the government interprets their use to be within the law.[104] Again, this discord highlights the weakness of using the BFC programme as a means to achieve the ends enunciated in the UCTA: as BFC deals primarily with factory-level compliance, no change of governmental labour policy is advanced by the programme.

A third problem which receives considerable international news coverage and was addressed in many interviews is the continuing repression of independent union activity. Despite the well-established formal legal framework allowing for independent unions, state-backed repression of unionists has often been harsh and violent. There are continuing problems with the registration of unions, with the office responsible for registration finding small problems with the forms and stalling registration.[105] The military are sometimes deployed to break up strikes and enforce forced overtime.[106] In February and March 2014, workers were locked into factories to stop them from joining strikes.[107] The shooting and death of five protestors in January 2014 has also not resulted in prosecutions of police.[108]

The institutional preference provided to pro-CPP unions is a means of furthering neo-patrimonial power in a variety of ways. Pro-government unions deliver votes to

[99] Better Factories Cambodia, *Thirty First Synthesis Report on Working Conditions in Cambodia's Garment Sector 3*.

[100] Interview with Liv Sovanna; with Morm Nhim; with Tola Moun.

[101] Interview with Ann Vireak, Arbitration Council, Phnom Penh, Cambodia, 28 March 2014.

[102] Interview with Morm Nhim.

[103] D. Arnold and H. S. Toh, 'A Fair Model of Globalisation? Labour and Global Production in Cambodia' (2010) 40 Journal of Contemporary Asia 401.

[104] Interview with Chea Sophal.

[105] Interview with Ath Thorn, President of Cambodian Labor Confederation and President of Coalition of Cambodia Apparel Workers Democratic Union, Phnom Penh, Cambodia, March 19, 2014.

[106] Interview with Tola Moun.

[107] Ibid. Mom Kunthear and Sean Teehan, 'Workers "Locked Inside" During Overtime Strike' *The Phnom Pehn Post* (4 March 2014).

[108] Interview with Tola Moun.

the CPP at election time, receiving gifts in return.[109] The presence of these unions gives legitimacy to government industrial relations policy, and confuses the messages of independent unions, making it appear as if there is simply in-fighting between unions.[110] Morn Nihm, President of the National Independent Federation Textile Union of Cambodia (one of the only female led unions) complained that pro-government unions were the only unions consulted by the Labour Advisory Committee in the determination of the minimum wage.[111]

These three problems demonstrate the limitations of the BFC's influence. BFC personnel interviewed for this study expressed frustration that the programme does not address these serious labour breaches. This frustration is sometimes communicated in the press releases made by the programme.[112] Under the current arrangements, there is little that BFC can do to address these significant labour rights and humanitarian concerns that originate at a state level.

7.4.3 Limited scope

A further major structural limitation of the initiative is that it only addresses labour compliance in the export sector of the garment industry.[113] Because the scope of the UCTA was limited to textile trade, the Labour Code was developed with this sector in mind. BFC excludes from its monitoring those parts of the industry that do not produce for export.

There are a number of small and medium sized factories that subcontract work from the larger, export factories. In theory then, these factories should be made to abide by the same labour standards demanded of the garment industry by the initiative. However, BFC personnel interviewed for this study knew little of these small and medium sized factories. Most union representatives were largely ignorant of these peripheral factories, also, with the exception of the National Independent Federation Textile Union of Cambodia, which is attempting to organize these workers.[114] Representatives of other industries have approached BFC to request coverage. Chea Sophal proffered that because of the source of its leverage, BFC can only operate effectively in export sectors.[115] This only accounts for a small amount of economic activity outside the garment industry. The risk, when the full range of labour rights are only enforced for the core workforce, is that incentives are created for work to shift increasingly to these smaller enterprises, or to workers on short term contracts.

Because the Labour Inspectorate is also ineffectual in monitoring these enterprises, Daniel Adler summates, '[i]n practice, the current regulatory system neither protects workers' rights as individuals, nor does it extend to vulnerable workers, such as those in small and medium sized enterprises producing for local markets'.[116] In contrast to the export garment industry, work in these enterprises remains informal.

Slow progress towards unionization in other sectors is being made. Union membership among rubber and tobacco workers in 2009 was at 25 per cent of over 309,000

[109] Interview with David Welsh, Cambodia Program Director, AFL-CIO Solidarity Center, Phnom Penh, Cambodia, 20 March 2014.

[110] Ibid. [111] Interview with Morm Nhim

[112] See, for example: Better Factories Cambodia, *Statement of the Project Advisory Committee of Better Factories Cambodia* (2014).

[113] Interview with Morm Nhim. [114] Ibid. [115] Interview with Chea Sophal.

[116] Daniel Adler, 'Informalizing the Formal: Labour Relations in Cambodia', Justice for the poor briefing note volume J4P 1, issue no. 3. Washington, DC: World Bank (2007), http://documents.worldbank.org/curated/en/295501468006045754/Informalizing-the-formal-labor-relations-in-Cambodia, p. 4.

workers, around 5 per cent of over 100,000 construction workers and around 30 per cent of 10,000 Tuk tuk drivers.[117] New unions have been founded in other industries, such as the services sector, after organisers first accumulated organizing skills in the garment industry.[118] There has also been transmission of knowledge through 'informal networks of politicized individuals',[119] such as when garment workers return to their home villages.[120] This suggests that the benefits of international labour regulation may be having some spill over effects.

7.5 Conclusion

BFC was created to remedy a regulatory gap. Under the UCTA, the US government needed information about labour conditions in order to determine whether to increase quotas. The Cambodian Ministry of Labour was not a reliable source of information for these purposes. Though it was not a perfect solution to substitute the Ministry of Labour with an international body, it seemed to be a fair trade off: a growing apparel sector that created jobs and profits was part of the solution to the problem of government capacity, as it would increase the tax base and resources for essential government functions.[121] It was hoped that with this increased tax base, the government would one day be able to afford to invest in increasing the capacity of the Ministry of Labour, and to pay wages that would reduce the need for augmenting them with bribes. BFC was envisaged as a 'second best',[122] short term regulatory solution.

The garment industry owes its growth to the trade arrangements of UCTA and subsequent bilateral and multilateral agreements have made Cambodia a favourable trading partner and investment destination. The growth of the garment industry has transformed the Cambodian economy, creating employment and allowing for the growth of large, formal enterprises based on the fordist model. This has marked a swift and drastic shift, at least within the garment industry, from the underdeveloped, poor, agrarian and mostly informal economy that was a relic of French colonization, the destructive tendencies of the Khmer Rouge, and years of civil war.

However, this chapter has shown that because the garment industry is structured in accordance with the neo-liberal principles contained in the agreement between the US and Cambodia, and encouraged as part of early structural adjustment programmes by the World Bank and the IMF, the industry is almost 100 per cent foreign owned and contributes little to the tax base of the country. This has meant that the government has less capacity to collect sufficient funds to allow it to invest in a bureaucracy that would inspect and enforce compliance with labour laws. This could be seen in purely detrimental terms, were it not for the dynamics of neo-patrimonialism.

Instead, the disembeddedness of the garment industry in ownership and regulatory terms has provided opportunities for formalization that might not have otherwise been present. International labour rights influences including the ILO, international trade

[117] Nuon and Serrano 70.

[118] Interview with Mr. Sony at Cambodia Federation of Labor Service, Phom Penh, Cambodia, 21 March 2014.

[119] Steven M. Buechler, *Women's Movements in the United States: Woman Suffrage, Equal Rights, and Beyond* (Rutgers 1990).

[120] Alisa DiCaprio, 'The Demand Side of Social Protection: Lessons from Cambodia's Labor Rights Experience' (2013) 48 World Development 108.

[121] Polaski.

[122] Dani Rodrik, *Second-Best Institutions* (2008 National Bureau of Economic Research).

unions and workers' rights groups such as Solidarity and international brands have enjoyed enhanced levels of influence. Workers are freed from the scrutiny and networks of patronage that dominate village life and informal sectors. BFC has been allowed to operate relatively unimpeded by government interests, to thoroughly monitor and report on labour conditions in exporting garment enterprises, encouraging gradual improvement in respect of labour laws. All these factors have contributed to the flourishing of independent, opposition and ruling party-aligned, unions, and their maturation into confederations that are now beginning to organize other sectors of the Cambodian economy, demand higher wages, and taking to the streets in great numbers in 2013/14.

In other respects, it might be said that UCTA and BFC have been skilfully manipulated by the Hun Sen government to support its neo-patrimonial interests. It has managed to house an internationally renowned transnational mechanism at the same times as avoiding undertaking reforms which would threaten the political economy of neo-patrimonalism. The bilateral trade agreement between the US and Cambodia aimed to encourage Cambodia to enact and apply adequate public labour regulation.[123] Instead of keeping a check on the government this way, BFC operates at an enterprise level. However, many of the gravest labour standard breaches are caused by laws that are weakly implemented. As Ath Thorn said in interview, 'Cambodia has strong laws that are weakly implemented'.[124] By focusing on factory-level monitoring in the export sector of the garment industry, the structural logic of BFC has allowed the government to avoid certain responsibilities and exercise patrimonial power—often with violent force—without suffering formal sanction.

The Hun Sen government and the Cambodian elite have slowly sought to benefit from the garment industry and reassert their patrimonial power in the following notable ways. Firstly, because the industry is almost entirely foreign owned, Cambodia's elite has not had to assume the risks of investment, yet it has found various ways to benefit from the UCTA and the arrangements that were put in place once the agreement ended. We can see this in a number of respects. It has captured the system of export licenses to its advantage. The provision of export licenses gives elites power over an industry that it is otherwise disembedded from. It also provides a means for extraction. Factories make gifts to the officials in charge of doling out discretionary licenses. The withholding of export licences might have been a source of punitive authority over factories—the apex of the regulatory pyramid, were it not for its regulatory capture by the Hun Sen government. Instead, the licences are a source of patrimonial power.

Secondly, the government has also been saved from investing in its own Labour Inspectorate and instead depends on foreign expertise (in much the same way as under the French protectorate)—though BFC is becoming increasingly locally run. BFC acts as a functional rival to the Labour Inspectorate instead of a complementary and capacity building mechanism. As a consequence, the Ministry of Labour continues to operate in much the same way as it has since the Paris Peace Accord of 1991. Labour inspectors are underpaid. In fact, garment workers are paid more than labour inspectors. Labour inspectors are forced to supplement their wages with bribes or second jobs—either way they are ineffectual in enforcing labour standards and do not impede the patron-client relations between factories and high ranking officials.

Thirdly, BFC does not inhibit what is viewed as the most important factor in production for investors in Cambodia—low wages. The minimum wage has been judged

[123] Kolben, 'Trade, Monitoring, and the ILO: Working to Improve Conditions in Cambodia's Garment Factories' 81.

[124] Interview with Ath Thorn.

to be below a living wage by the government's own committee, allowing Cambodia to remain as a remarkably low unit labour cost country. A human resource manager interviewed for this study explained that the reason buyers source from Cambodia is due to 'labour cost, compared with other countries. For example, the labour cost in Thailand is about $300, so the buyers shifted to us. Our minimum wages are about $100, and we have stable politics. That's why some buyers come to us instead of Pakistan, where labour cost is low but politics are not stable'.[125] By providing low wages and political stability, Cambodia's elite upholds its implicit bargain with factory owners who are obliged to pay considerable sums to patrons. The existence of BFC has allowed buyers to benefit from the BFC's goodwill, and to fulfil the buyers' promises of corporate social responsibility by sourcing from an 'ethical location'. This gives Cambodia a competitive advantage in the global garment export market. According to Ken Loo, head of the body that represents factories: 'Buyers want low costs and the ability to hide behind BFC's branding'.[126]

None of this detracts from the achievements of BFC. BFC is in most respects an exemplary monitoring and reporting institution. It has trained and employs a large number of Cambodian professionals who conduct monitoring without any suggestion of corruption. Although the head of BFC is an American, other senior staff are Cambodian. Like the Arbitration Council of Cambodia, it has demonstrated (most importantly to Cambodians) that Cambodians are capable of acting with integrity as regulators.[127] The culture of widespread corruption can be displaced with the right incentives and oversight.

Further, BFC has helped to stamp out child labour and many of the worst human rights breaches that plagued factories in the early years of Cambodia's garment industry. Without BFC, bolstered by the vocal presence of international labour rights groups, it is easy to imagine that the Cambodian garment industry would be more like that of Bangladesh. The combination of UCTA, subsequent trade arrangements and BFC has contributed a great deal to the formalization of the garment industry, with emerging flow on effects for other sectors. In many ways, then, the study of BFC provides a case study of the complexity and slipperiness for transnational mechanisms of achieving regulatory goals in a context of widespread and entrenched corruption due to the dominance of neo-patrimonial interests. In turn, it also provides a case study of the constrained capacity of such initiatives to contribute to the formalization of the entire workforce or to expedite the transformation and long-run sustainability of local regulatory institutions.

[125] Interview with Buth Rithy, Human Resource Manager, API Medical, 25 March 2014.

[126] Interview with Ken Loo, General Secretary, Garment Manufacturers Association, Phnom Pehn, Cambodia, 21 March 2014.

[127] Interview with An Nan.

8

Four Experiments in Reducing Informality

Realizable Models of Institutional Change

8.1 Introduction

This study has examined four regulatory experiments in reducing informality in work and improving labour standards. The purpose of this chapter is to compare these innovations and draw out lessons about the way that institutional change has occurred. Regulatory agents have found novel ways to address the unresponsiveness of the traditional methods of state-based labour regulation identified in Chapter 2. The initiatives have in common that they (a) expand or sidestep the employment relationship so as to encompass broader forms of work (with the exception of the Cambodian initiative) and (b) increase the strength of regulation in order to push against countervailing pressures which lower working conditions. However, each initiative has achieved this in different ways and to different extents. This comparative chapter provides an opportunity to compare these different methods and explore why some levers are stronger than others.

None of the models entail comprehensive reform of the way work is regulated in a nation. Nor do they fundamentally challenge the international institutional arrangements, which have altered and undermined the power of national institutions to regulate work, and which were seen to be at play in each of the case studies. They have instead sought solutions which were politically feasible and improve the conditions of a specific group of workers—homeworkers, headload workers, garment workers. They arose out of particular political moments and institutional trajectories. This is not to downplay in any way the effort that was required by the agents of change in each case. Labour activists died in the struggle for improved labour conditions in more than one of the cases, and the changes were a consequence of years of strategizing, mobilizing, and campaigning. Nonetheless, the reforms attained in the cases were achieved over a period of a decade or so. They may therefore represent realizable models of purposeful institutional change for those hoping to replicate them.

It is the contention of this chapter that the innovations were realizable because they *added to* or *augmented* traditional labour laws. Each is a type of co-regulation, entailing the combining of two or more regulatory systems. The Cambodian experiment involved the combining of an international trade preference and monitoring system, overseen by the International Labour Organisation, with the existing state-based labour law system. The Australian innovation entailed the combining of private monitoring and labelling with the state-based labour law system. The Indian regulatory development created a new state-orchestrated system, which adds to and sits aside from the existing labour law system. The Bulgarian expansion of employment law was the consequence of social dialogue processes through which private industrial relations parties negotiated an outcome before it was enacted into law. The case studies give us an opportunity, then, to explore and compare the dynamics of co-regulation in practice.

The idea of collaborative governance or co-regulation has received a great deal of attention in the regulatory literature in recent years, particularly when it entails the combination of private and state-based regulation—also known as New Governance. It represents an emerging alternative to traditional command-and-control approaches to making, implementing, and enforcing policy.[1] It is seen as a way to overcome a number of the limitations of traditional state-based regulation by bringing in new regulatory techniques and regulatory agents to bolster existing state-based systems.[2]

It often assumed that co-regulation will lead to new synergies and *complementarity* between the two systems, where one system bolsters the strength and efficacy of the operation of another. However, an emerging literature suggests that when regulatory systems are added to each other, they can interact in a range of different ways. The combination can lead to regulatory *expansion* in the sense that a broader range of regulatory targets are reached and/or a broader range of tools are deployed. They can lead to *rivalry*, seen in cases where one system is viewed as an alternative to the other, and the two systems operate in competition.[3] Sometimes, one system *displaces* the other. For example, private governance systems can create network or ensemble regimes with the capacity to substitute government entirely.[4] Indeed, in living, 'actually-existing' experiments in co-regulation, relationships between combined systems are by no means stable. They are prone to changing loyalties and priorities amongst the actors involved. Sometimes, what was intended as a complement acts as a rival to the existing regime. In the Cambodian example studied, for instance, the Better Factories Cambodia project was designed to complement and bolster the local system of labour inspectors, but due to domestic dynamics, might also be seen as a rival. Literature on the relationship of state and private regulation tends to neglect a very common insight in institutional theory—that institutions evolve.[5] The literature tends, instead, to assume static relationships and treat the systems as functionalist wholes. By adopting a historical institutionalist approach, this study has shown that taking time and institutional evolution more seriously can help to better clarify how one form of co-regulation might be transformed from complementarity to rivalry and displacement, and so on.

This chapter hopes to perform two tasks, then. First, it aims to describe and compare different schemes for regulating work. Second, it hopes to contribute to the literature on co-regulation by comparing the evolution and interaction of the combined systems in each case.

[1] Lisa Blomgren Bingham, 'The Next Generation of Administrative Law: Building the Legal Infrastructure for Collaborative Governance' 10 Wisconsin Law Review 297 300.

[2] Virginia Haufler, *A Public Role for the Private Sector: Industry Self-Regulation in a Global Economy* (Carnegie Endowment for International Peace 2001); Peter Utting, *Rethinking Business Regulation: From Self-Regulation to Social Control* (2005); Kevin Kolben, 'Integrative Linkage: Combining Public and Private Regulatory Approaches in the Design of Trade and Labor Regimes' (2007) 48 Harvard International Law Journal 203.

[3] David M. Trubek and Louise G. Trubek, 'New Governance & Legal Regulation: Complementarity, Rivalry and Transformation' 13 Columbia Journal of European Law 539 543.

[4] Tracy M. Roberts, 'Innovations in Governance: A Functional Typology of Private Governance Institutions' 22 Duke Environmental Law & Policy Forum 67 69.

[5] J. Mahoney and K. Thelen, 'How Institutions Evolve: Insights from Comparative-Historical Analysis' in J. Mahoney and D. Rueschemeyer (eds), *Historical Analysis in the Social Sciences* (Cambridge University 2003).; Sabrina Zajak, 'Complementarity as Institutional Co-Evolution and Co-Production: The Case of Working Conditions in Chinese Supply Chains' (Conference presentation, 5th ECPR Regulatory Governance Conference Barcelona June 2014).

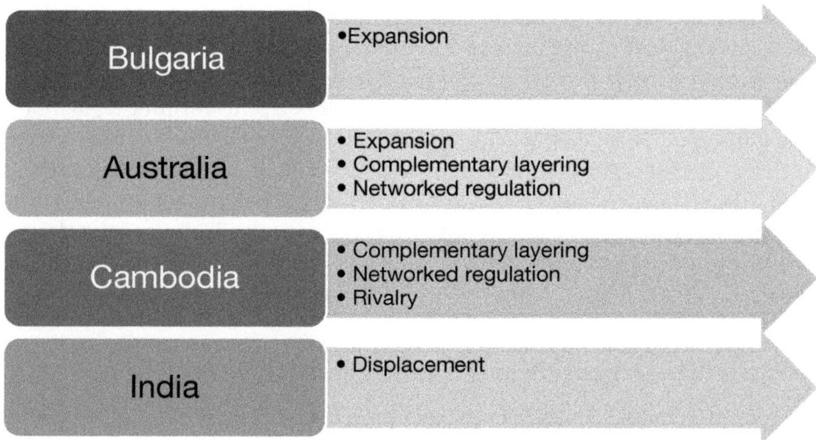

Figure 8.1 Regulatory strategies in each case study country

8.2 Institutional Evolution: Expansion, Complementarity, Rivalry, and Displacement

Each of the cases augmented traditional labour law in different but overlapping ways. The regulatory strategies observed in the case studies can be characterized in the terms shown in Figure 8.1 drawn from the regulatory and institutional literature.

The section adopts surgical metaphors to explain the strategies. The particular form of augmentation or co-regulation is described, and the extent to which it adds levers and regulatory incentives is accessed.

8.2.1 Bulgaria—expansion

In Bulgaria, the sole regulatory strategy observed was the expansion of the employment relationship to include home-based workers. This entails widening the scope of regulation so that a broader group of people are regulated. Adopting a medical metaphor, this strategy can be compared with the widening of arteries as a solution when they are narrow or blocked, known as angioplasty.

When an angioplasty is performed, a stent is inserted into the artery to keep it open and allow blood to flow through freely.[6] The regulatory strategy of expanding the employment relationship is like an angioplasty in the sense that it allows more people to flow through this regulatory channel and enjoy its benefits and protections.

This regulatory strategy reflects a view that the cause of informalization is that the scope of regulation is too narrow. This view has been adopted by the International Labour Organisation and is reflected in Convention No. 177 and Recommendation No.184. Convention No. 177 is an attempt to ensure that homeworkers across the world are treated equally with other workers and have the same rights.

From a regulatory perspective the strategy pursued to tackle informality is quite limited. It does not challenge the basic logic of the employment relationship or bring

[6] See the image here for a pictorial description of the process: http://galleryhip.com/stent-insertion.html.

in more regulatory agents to increase the power of the primary regulator. Just as, in the case of an angioplasty, the surgeon determines that the artery has sufficient integrity, this strategy assumes that the employment relationship is still the right regulatory channel for workers' rights. The locus of responsibility in this form of regulation lies with the employer. Thus, to flow through this regulatory channel, workers need an identifiable primary employer on whom they are dependent or who subjugates them in some way. The strategy excludes those who cannot identify a primary employer or who are not sufficiently dependent on the employer. Because of this, it does not deal with the broader dynamics of the supply chain and global trade by targeting other parties in value chains in even a limited sense.

8.2.2 Australia—expansion and complementary layering

In Australia, the regulatory strategy entails both expansion, similar to that seen in Bulgaria but, in all but one state, limited to clothing workers. It also entails layering of new instruments and regulatory agents which complement and bolster the existing rules. Adopting the medical metaphor, once again, we could say that first an angioplasty was performed, and subsequently a pacemaker was added.[7]

For Mahoney and Thelen, layering occurs when new rules are attached to existing ones, thereby changing the ways in which the original rules structure behaviour.[8] 'Complementary layering' can be thought of as adding a pacemaker to a heart. A pacemaker uses low-energy electrical pulses to overcome faulty electrical signalling in a heart. Likewise, a complementary institution strengthens and/or alters the signalling or incentives in an existing institution where that institution was sending imperfect or contradictory signals. The layered institutions complement formal government at key junctures, creating a networked or ensemble regime.[9]

The regulatory signal is strengthened by adding new actors as well as additional regulatory levers. In this complementary networked regulatory system, the state draws on the power of non-state actors who are allies in increasing compliance, including the relevant Union and Fair Wear, and aims to build consent from industry bodies through incorporating them into processes such as the Ethical Clothing Australia committee which oversees the operation of the Code. By adding actors, traditional regulatory agents in labour market regulation that were struggling to have influence (state labour bodies and the union) become stronger by networking with other weaker actors (FairWear, churches, and community groups).

A particularly strong feature of the Australian innovation is that it addresses supply chain dynamics operating at a national level. This occurs through the involvement of actors who have influence at different stages of the supply chain. The power of actors at the top of the supply chain—consumers and retailers—is enrolled against those lower in the supply chain—manufacturers.[10] A weakness is that it only addresses supply chain dynamics within the bounds of Australia and does not redress more global influences.

[7] See the image here for a pictorial description of a pacemaker's role: http://www.nlm.nih.gov/medlineplus/ency/imagepages/19566.

[8] J. Mahoney and K. Thelen, 'A Theory of Gradual Institutional Change' in J. Mahoney and K. Thelen (eds), *Explaining Institutional Change: Ambiguity, Agency and Power* (Cambridge University Press 2010) 16.

[9] T. M. Roberts, 'Innovations in Governance: A Functional Typology of Private Governance Institutions' 22 Duke Environmental Law & Policy Forum 67.

[10] J. Braithwaite, 'Responsive Regulation and Developing Economies' (2006) 34 World Development 884.

The regulatory signal is also strengthened by adding new regulatory levers to the existing penalties that could be meted out against non-complying employers through traditional labour law techniques. These include transparency, the capacity of the union to trace the entire supply chain, redress against parties higher in the supply chain, and market-based incentives and disincentives. Instead of seeing hard laws and market-based soft laws as alternatives, the strength of this system is that it sees different mechanisms as being best used in combination—as complements to each other.[11]

As explored in Chapter 5, this strategy was pursued in the social context of Australia in the 1990s and 2000s. The layering strategy fitted with the rise of consumer rights and a preference for voluntarism over mandatory regulation. The market-based system that has been layered on the existing labour laws is consistent with a particular form of capitalism that is generally referred to as neo-liberalism, though Australia's variety of capitalism is quite mixed.[12] The size of large apparel retailers and brands, and the amount that they spend on advertising, leaves them particularly vulnerable to naming and shaming strategies. At the same time as labour rights have been declining in strength and as an idea, consumer rights have gained prominence. The labelling system has been argued for on the basis of brand transparency: consumers have a right to know how the products they buy are made and make decisions about what they buy on this basis. Without a labelling system, they cannot make informed choices.

Unions and allied groups used the increasing purchase of consumer rights, as an idea, to legitimize the creation of a new institution which would be layered on the old. This usage of legitimated ideas—'transparency' and 'consumer rights'—allowed the unions and community organizations to experiment without encountering absolute resistance. In the process, they also legitimated their own place as regulatory agents.

8.2.3 Cambodia—complementary layering evolves into rivalry

Like Australia, the strategy pursued in Cambodia has entailed a type of complementary layering. New institutions and regulatory agents, as well as new levers, have been added to the existing labour market regulation institutions, like adding a pacemaker to strengthen the regulatory signal. Here, this has occurred without expanding the scope of regulation. (No arterial widening, or angioplasty, was conducted in this case.) Labour market regulation in Cambodia continues to be based on the employment relationship.

In Cambodia, the layering has entailed the adding of levers and agents. First, the US–Cambodia trade agreement (UCTA) added an important lever which provided a particularly strong incentive for Cambodia to improve labour standards in export apparel industry. Under the UCTA agreement, Cambodia received preferential trade access to the US if it could demonstrate that it was incrementally improving the conditions of garment workers and increasing adherence to the Cambodian labour code. This was a particularly crucial step in a political context of corruption and neo-patrimonialism where the state was more focused on extraction than implementing industrial policy and structural adjustment aimed at upgrading industry and formalizing work. The trade preferences contributed greatly to the growth of the apparel industry. The ILO's Better Factories Cambodia (BFC) project was developed to conduct monitoring. The BFC became an important regulatory agent in the process of formalization

11 G. Gunningham and P. Grabosky, *Smart Regulation* (Clarendon Press 1998) 14.

12 R. Mitchell and others, *Law, Corporate Governance and the Management of Labour: A Study of Australian Regulatory Style and Business Practice* (Ashgate 2011).

of Cambodia's labour force, ensuring that industrialization was accompanied by improvements in labour standards. Buyers were added as regulatory agents, also, as BFC reports were sold to them and became the most legitimate measure of factory labour standards.

Streeck and Thelan anticipate that new layers may gradually empower an unintended group, and thus sow the seeds of radical institutional transformation.[13] The analysis conducted in Chapter 8 shows that this is indeed the case, though currently, this institutional transformation is moving in two contradictory directions. Firstly, although the purpose of UCTA and BFC was to complement and bolster existing labour laws and labour market institutions, the BFC has in some respects acted as a *rival* to the Cambodian Labour Inspectorate in the garment industry. It has greater legitimacy and integrity in the eyes of the international community, and efforts to work with the Labour Inspectorate have largely failed. The Labour Inspectorate continues to monitor garment factories, but its capacity has not been greatly enhanced by the operation of BFC in the country. It continues to operate at a low capacity on a predatory basis, collecting bribes and rarely reporting or penalizing factories for breaches of labour standards.

Secondly, in a contradictory development, the combination of UCTA trade incentives linked to labour conditionalities and BFC have encouraged the development of a dynamic union movement. An active union movement has matured as the garment industry has formalized, resulting in the birth of a strong democratizing force which is now acting as a countervailing influence on the extractive tendencies of the government. In this sense, the operation of UCTA and BFC contributed to the growth of an indigenous democratization movement which has been focused on raising the minimum wage and more fairly distributing the benefits of Cambodia's impressive economic growth.

8.2.4 India—experimental displacement

Unlike the other cases, in Maharashtra, regulation of Mathadi (head- load) work has occurred through creating an alternative institution, rather than building on existing institutions of labour market regulation. It bypasses the employment relationship in favour of a triangular relationship, regulated through Mathadi Boards. This is a form of 'displacement', which, for Mahoney and Thelen occurs when existing rules are replaced by new ones. Often, displacement occurs when there is a revolution or regime change.[14] The Mathadi Boards were developed in the wake of Indian independence and with the threat of communism looming.

'Experimental displacement' is a useful strategy when an existing institution is failing, but there are political economy reasons that mean that full displacement is difficult.[15] These reasons can include investment in the existing, older institution by interest groups, path dependency and so on. In the case of *complementary layering*, the existing institution remains in the long term, but is reinforced by the layering of

[13] Thelen and Streeck, *Beyond Continuity: Institutional Change in Advanced Political Economies* (Oxford University Press 2005).

[14] R. Collier and D. Collier, *Shaping the Political Arena* (Princeton University Press 1991).

[15] The idea of 'experimental displacement' was inspired by Mariana Moto Prado's idea of an 'institutional bypass' which she identifies as a stand-alone institution that is set up to act as an experimental alternative to an existing, deficient institution: Mariana M. Prado, 'Institutional Bypass: An Alternative for Development Reform' (SSRN eLibrary 2011) https://papers.ssrn.com/sol3/papers.cfm?abstract_id=1815442.

additional actors and instruments. In the case of *experimental displacement*, the existing institution stays in the immediate term, but may be replaced as it is demonstrated through the regulatory experiment that alternative, more efficacious means of attaining regulatory goals is possible.

The core institution is displaced by a new institution that provides largely the same functions in a different way. Experimental displacement can be thought of as being similar to a coronary bypass. Prado, from whom this concept is borrowed, refers to it as an 'institutional by-pass':[16]

> Like coronary bypass surgery, in which transplanted blood vessels are used to create a new circulatory pathway around clogged or blocked vessels ... [it] creates new pathways around clogged or blocked institutions. Unlike other procedures that try to unblock clogged arteries, or expand narrow ones, the institutional by-pass simply ignores the existence of the unhealthy artery and creates a new pathway for blood flow. An institutional bypass uses the same strategy: it does not try to modify, change or reform existing institutions. Instead, it tries to create a new pathway in which efficiency and functionality will be the norm.

(To be clear: the organ in this metaphor that is being by-passed is the artery, not the heart.)

Experimental displacements are useful when problems in an existing institution seem intractable, despite attempts at reform. It helps to overcome extreme institutional inertia and path dependency. The idea is that if the experiment is successful, it will demonstrate that it is possible to break with existing detrimental and non-virtuous patterns of behaviour within the existing institution that are hampering its efficient conduct.

In a coronary artery bypass, a new artery is added to bypass a blocked one.[17] In the case of Mathadi workers, the employment relationship as a vessel for protection was blocked to them. It seemed politically implausible to argue for its expansion, so instead, it was bypassed or displaced.

The Mathadi Board system which displaced labour laws for these workers performs all the functions of a normal labour law system, as well additional features, including health and education services, which have made great differences to the human development of Mathadi workers and their families. The Act that creates the Mathadi Boards and these various regulatory functions is neat and succinct. All the rules are in one place. This is a clear benefit of displacement over layering.

A further advantage is that the displacement strategy has allowed regulators to experiment with different tools and levers from those traditionally used in labour law. The Boards gain their power by modifying the operation of the market. Rather than using the usual command and control model of sanctioning non-complying labour users seen in most employment law systems, the Boards ensure that compliance occurs by acting as an intermediary in the hire and payment of workers. The Boards are an effective model of regulation because they have a monopoly on the supply of labour. Normally, labour relations systems impact on labour supply and demand indirectly through regulating occupational training, qualifications, and pay rates. Most labour relations systems do not impinge on the operation of labour markets beyond these means. Controlling the supply of labour is a stronger lever than the tool kit of enforcement mechanisms normally available to regulators. Indeed, it might be considered a

[16] Mariana M. Prado, 'Institutional Bypass: An Alternative for Development Reform' SSRN eLibrary 3.

[17] See the pictorial representation of the process here: http://mycardiacwebsite.com/Coronary%20Artery%20Disease/treatment_for_cad.html.

small scale 'governance' mechanism, like tariffs, as opposed to 'regulatory' mechanism, strictly speaking.[18]

Controlling the supply of labour is a particularly important strategy in a context in which informalization is exacerbated by the over-supply of labour due to the circulation of within-country migrants in India. As we saw in Chapter 7, the circulation of labour has been exacerbated by colonial land laws which expelled certain castes and classes from land tenure or left them with insufficient land to live from. State-based land reform processes which followed independence in India did not generally provide adequate land packages to those who had been dispossessed to allow them to stay on the land, leading to the circulation of millions seeking work in India's cities.

An additional benefit of displacing or bypassing the normal industrial relations system is that a *localized* strategy has been made possible. Boards are organized around the target populations—on the docks, in the markets—and respond to the particular needs of those populations. Hospitals have been created in response to community demand for health services, for instance. Further, because the system is imbued with a sense of experimentation and freed of path dependency, Boards have felt at liberty to try out new strategies to achieve improved health and human development of Mathadi workers. If the system was part of the normal labour relations system, the provision of health services might not be seen to be a role of the institutional complex.

This regulatory strategy reflects the political economy of Maharashtra in the 1960s. The threat of communism and the desire for industrial peace following rioting on behalf of Mathadi workers provided strong incentives for policy makers to develop this system. Mumbai was rivalled only by Kolkata as the centre of trade union based Marxist politics in India in the 1950s and 60s. The riots had caused considerable social and financial losses, and a number of workers had been killed, inciting further rioting. Social reformers such as Annasaheb Patil, in memory of whom a public holiday is held in Maharashtra, were able to broker peace, and stop rioting, by negotiating for the establishment of Mathadi Boards. Although the brokered deal created a labour monopoly system, this was seen to be worthwhile to stop the violent deaths and resume work on the docks. (Though labour users complain about these characteristics of the system today.)[19]

8.3 Conclusion

Some authors have proposed features which make co-regulation or New Governance mechanisms more likely to succeed. Cristie Ford, for example, suggests that such characteristics include broadly framed goals, stakeholder participation, flexibility, revisability, monitoring and peer-review, transparency, a data-based approach, learning-oriented approaches, and multi-level governance.[20] These attributes may describe an ideal type. However, the analysis conducted in this study would warn away from functionalist check lists of this type.

What explains why regulatory innovation occurs? The case studies suggest that innovation tended to occur around labour concerns that were prevalent and politically

[18] J. Braithwaite, C. Coglianese, D. Levi-Faur 'Can Regulation and Governance Make a Difference?' (2007) Regulation & Governance 1, 1–7.

[19] Government of India, *2nd Report of the National Commission on Labour 129*, 1969.

[20] Cristie Ford, 'New Governance in the Teeth of Human Frailty: Lessons from Financial Regulation' (2010) [2010] Wisconsin Law Review 441.

salient in the national or international context. We saw this in the case of India, where Mathadi workers gained political purchase in connection with the anti-Brahmin tendencies of India's independence movement. In the Cambodian example, a number of factors converged at once. The coincidence in timing of Cambodia's emergence from state socialism and Cambodia's desire to gain trade access to the US converged with a new experimental spirit in international labour organizing in the US labour movement and the Clinton administration's openness to influence from peak labour organisations. At the same time, also, the ILO was searching for relevance in a changing international landscape. This led to an experiment that has since been replicated in a number of additional countries—known as the Better Work Program. Without the convergence of these political and institutional dynamics, the original experiment would never have occurred.

Regulatory change in all instances was a consequence of the persistent strategies of certain social and political actors. Understanding the effect of these agents' ideas and the context in which they were acting is essential for explaining the way in which these actors have bought about institutional change, and the form and orientation this change has taken.[21] For the creation of Mathadi Boards, the agents of change were worker associations and anti-poverty campaigners. Here, instead of building on existing labour laws, the protagonists created a new labour market regulation institution. This strategy was made possible by the change sweeping India in the wake of independence. In Australia, by contrast, the push for institutional reform came from the relevant union and a coalition of community organizations. In the Australian case, rather than putting aside the standard labour market institutions, new regulatory agents and instruments were added to it to bolster its impact and widen its scope. This strategy was consistent with the rise of consumer rights and anxieties about ill-managed refugee resettlement policies. In Bulgaria, the innovation entailed expansion of the employment relationship to include home-based workers in keeping with a European Union recommendation, reflecting Bulgaria's desire to demonstrate normative alignment with values seen to be dominant in central Western Europe.

Instead of approaching public-private regulatory complementarities as functional synergies that emerge automatically, or through technical design, this study has found that they are political processes that are closely connected to national institutions and national and international political economy dynamics. In some respects, this points to the futility of designing functional ideal-type co-regulations or New Governance. Actually-existing institutions are always 'second best' outcomes that result from complex dynamics.[22] On the other hand, as the efforts of the next chapter exemplify, it is sometimes the job of regulatory theorists to imagine and design new models. The impetus for such imagining is particularly strong when the problem is as vast and devastating to human well-being as precarious and insecure informal work.

[21] Daniel Béland, 'Ideas and Institutional Change in Social Security: Conversion, Layering, and Policy Drift' 88 Social Science Quarterly 20.

[22] D. Rodrik, 'Second-best Institutions', in American Economic Review: Papers & Proceedings, 2008. Available at http://j.mp/2o5scFj.

9

A Long-Term Vision

Scaling up Experiments and Overcoming Orchestration Deficits to Reduce Informality

9.1 Introduction

It is close to 100 years since the Treaty of Versailles, 1919, was enacted, creating the International Labour Organisation and enshrining the principle of a living wage in international law.[1] A century later, we lack the means to guarantee a living wage to a large proportion of the world's population leaving an estimated 327 million people to live in extreme poverty, and 967 more in moderate and near poverty.[2] A significant reason for this is that they work informally: their work sits outside legal regulation.

This chapter canvasses a long-term vision for improving the lives of those poor and precarious workers who work in informal conditions. The four initiatives described in the case studies, and compared in the previous chapter, provide a clue to techniques for regulating for formalization in the immediate future. This chapter proposes a bolder, transnational, networked initiative that aims to promote a global living wage and regulate supply chains. The chapter puts forward three interrelated regulatory pathways out of informality. First, the promotion of International Living Wages through an international instrument such as an International Labour Organization (ILO) Convention or United Nations treaty, which would also establish an International Living Wage disputes mechanism for enforcement of these minima; second, the setting up of National Supply Chain Tribunals empowered to hear disputes concerning non-payment of living wages due to supply chain dynamics, and to hold parties in the supply chain responsible for non-payment; third, the fostering of local pathways out of informality.

Since its inception, the ILO has established standards (conventions) that establish the conditions under which work ought to be occurring. However, the institutional framework backing these standards is not up to the task of promoting and enforcing those standards. Sabel, O'Rourke, and Fung issued a challenge when they wrote:[3]

> [T]he ILO's "Declaration of the Fundamental Principles and Rights at Work"—express the public's moral convictions about the respect due to labor as a partner in global production, and its determination that these convictions be honored. The open and crucial question, then, is how to construct a regulatory framework that protects vulnerable groups against the abuses identified in core labor standards?

[1] According to the accounts of James T. Shotwell who participated in the Conference as part of the United States Delegation, the idea of a living wage was uncontroversial: James T. Shotwell, *The Origins of the International Labor Organization* (Columbia University Press 1934) Volume 2, 306.

[2] International Labour Office, *World Employment and Social Outlook: Trends 2016* 19.

[3] Sabel, O'Rourke, and Fung.

The proposal canvassed in this chapter answers this most urgent of challenges by addressing the dynamics of informalization described in this book in a number of respects.

First, the proposal establishes an *orchestrating* role for the ILO and/or other international organizations (IOs). A significant gap in the ecosystem of transnational labour governance is the absence of an international authority with the power to steer and coordinate regulation. In 2016 the ILO raised concern about its governance deficit in relation to global supply chains.[4] Abbot and Snidel have argued that a key problem is that the international system lacks a central 'state'.[5] Following Abbot and Snidel's cue, this chapter proposes a new role for IOs as orchestrators of decentralized regulation. The benefit of expanding the role of existing IOs is that they are seen as relatively independent of individual states, and even more so of firms. This allows them to act as 'honest brokers' acceptable to multiple stakeholders. Further, because IOs provide neutral forums with strong legitimacy and expert support, they have significant authority to convene multi-stakeholder groups and reap the benefits of the increased participation—including a range of civil society organizations in transnational governance that soft law initiatives have fostered.[6] This chapter proposes that IOs can act as bridges between local, national, and international regulatory scales.

Because the focus of this study is on labour informality, the proposals herein primarily advocate an expanded role for the ILO. To date, the ILO has largely failed to deal with globalized causes of labour problems: the ILO's standards were designed for national systems of regulation, allowing for national interpretations and selection of standards to ratify or to ignore.[7] Despite going beyond mere inter-governmentalism, thanks to its tripartite dimension (comprising government, employer and worker representatives), the ILO's capacity for setting standards considerably exceeds that for ensuring their implementation and compliance.[8] In the rare cases where a country has been condemned for breaching one of its core labour standards, the ILO itself cannot enforce any sanctions. The schemes canvassed in this chapter thus suggest an expanded and revamped role for the ILO in orchestrating transnational labour governance. This vision is aimed at restoring the ILO's capacity to act as an agency mediating the more negative consequences of globalization.

Second, the proposal is *multi-level* in nature. Approaches to reducing informality and protecting vulnerable workers against abuses of core labour standards tend be *either* international *or* domestic. Many private, soft law initiatives and transnational labour campaigns are international in scope, circumventing the state.[9] In contrast, the ILO has struggled to shift to a more globalized strategy. Its key policy document presenting its solution to informality, 'Transitioning from the Informal to the Formal Economy',[10] for instance, lists a large number of domestic policy approaches, while

[4] In its *Decent Work in Global Supply Chains* report for the 2016 International Labour Conference it recognized that, 'Consideration could therefore be given to the role of the ILO with regard to support, administration, facilitation and/or hosting of public, private and social governance systems': International Labour Office, *Decent Work in Global Supply Chains: Report to the International Labour Conference, 105th Session* (2016) 66.

[5] Abbott and Sindal 553. [6] Ibid. 575.

[7] Guy Standing, 'The ILO: An Agency for Globalization?' 39 Development and Change 355 357.

[8] Guglielmo Meardi and Pail Marginson, 'Global Labour Governance: Potential and Limits of an Emerging Perspective' 28 Work, Employment & Society 651 656.

[9] Kenneth W. Abbott and Duncan Snidal, 'Strengthening Institutional Regulation Through Transnational New Governance: Overcoming the Orchestration Deficit' 42 Vanderbilt Journal of Transnational Law 501 (Trubek and Trubek).

[10] At its 317th Session (March 2013) the Governing Body decided to place a standard-setting item on the agenda of the 103rd Session (June 2014) of the Conference on facilitating transitions from the

completely disregarding transnational supply chains or international institutional factors.[11] It remains to be seen whether the ILO can produce a more globalized strategy in relation to global supply chains.[12] Rejecting the limits of these two approaches, this chapter argues that in light of the multi-level scale of many of the causes of informality, greater orchestration is required at the international level to address transnational pressures on national labour markets, and to coordinate between regulators operating at different levels.

Third, the proposal is for a system that is mutually *re-inforcing* at the national and international levels. The case studies observed a range of factors undermining the capacity of state-based regulation. These included regional and international trade agreements and well as the downwards pressure of supply chains. The weakening of state power has been used as a justification for normative claims about the inadequacies of the state and the need for non-state regulation.[13] Building on insights described in Chapter 8 of this book, the proposal in this chapter builds a model of complementary state and non-state-based regulation, and complementary international and national regulation. The state should be held to account for the rights of its citizens, but it needs help doing so, in light of the strength of countervailing forces.

Fourth, the proposal attempts to apportion *responsibility* where there are a number of players that shape the conditions of workers.[14] Employment law pins all the responsibility on one player: the employer. The scheme proposed herein responds to the diffuse nature of control and influence on informality and precariousness. One of the aims of this book has been to deepen our understanding of the social relations underpinning work and the interaction of relations of production with national institutions and international governance institutions. The case studies attempted to parse the nature of private regulatory power within complex supply chains and other productive relations. The scheme proposed here apportions responsibility based on evidence of influence.

Fifth, the scheme proposes effective *regulatory incentives* and creates a *virtuous cycle of enforcement*. The case studies illustrate that the most powerful methods of changing business behaviour are not necessarily traditional legal sanctions. Regulators must consider what will have the greatest leverage over businesses and bring about long term change in business behaviour. The uneven distribution of risk throughout the supply chain suggests that enforcement tools should be more alive to the structural place of parties in supply chains. It also presents a strong impetus to search for new, more powerful penalties and incentives. The chapter canvasses the staying of export or

informal to the formal economy, under the double discussion procedure, which means that this item was dealt at the 2014 session and the 104th Session of the Conference (2015):ILO, *Transitioning from the Informal to the Formal Economy* (2014).

[11] The document makes reference to 'global production networks, migration, global economic cycles and variations in global commodity and food prices which affect: the level of vulnerability of economic units and workers in the informal economy' but fails to propose any policy strategies to address these dynamics: ibid.

[12] See the 'ILO Roadmap on Decent Work in Global Supply Chains' page for updates on the strategy at http://www.ilo.org/ipec/Action/CSR/clp/news/WCMS_567493/lang--en/index.htm, accessed 14 January 2018. See also: International Labour Office, *Decent Work in Global Supply Chains: Report to the International Labour Conference, 105th Session,* (2016).

[13] Held discusses this tendency in David Held, *Democracy and the Global Order: From the Modern State to Cosmopolitan Governance* (Stanford University Press 1995); David Held and Anthony McGrew (eds), *Governing Globalization: Power, Authority and Global Governance* (Polity Press 2002). Amoore has argued that this is central to neoliberal programmes of the restructuring of labour and working practices: Louise Amoore, 'Risk, Reward and Discipline at Work' 33 Economy and Society 174.

[14] Hyde.

import licences, as well as the suspension of intellectual property rights where appropriate, as a targeted penalty.

The proposals pitched in this chapter for a Global Living Wage instrument, a Global Living Wage Dispute Mechanism and National Supply Chain Tribunals are bold ambitions. Their articulation was made possible by putting questions of political feasibility largely to one side. The hard-headed realist would be rightly sceptical about the probability of the visions sketched in this chapter being realized, in view of the likely barriers to their establishment. Even with support by key countries and concerted campaigning by relevant coalitions, it could easily take decades to bring such a scheme to fruition. Specific concerns regarding the feasibility of the vision are briefly addressed in the course of the outline. A final section of this chapter anticipates and addresses key likely objections.

9.2 First Pathway: Promoting a Global Living Wage

9.2.1 Justification

The Declaration concerning the aims and purposes of the ILO (Declaration of Philadelphia) stresses the 'solemn obligation of the ILO to further among nations programmes that will achieve ... a minimum living wage to all employed and in need of such protection'. The right to a living wage is, in addition, established in several ILO declarations and conventions:

- Constitution of the ILO, 1919: Preamble of the Charter;
- ILO Declaration on Social Justice for a Fair Globalization, 2008;
- Convention 131 and 156 (indirectly) and Recommendations 131 and 135 (indirectly).

Despite this broad rhetorical support, the ILO, together with its tripartite partners, has been unable to deliver living wages to date. And, arguably, the principle has not been given the importance it is due. For example, it was not included in the Core Labour Standards.[15] This section proposes one possible mechanism for fulfilling the obligation to ensure a living wage to all workers.

Historians trace the concept of the living wage evoked in the ILO's Declaration of Aims and Purposes back to the 1870s, and the onset of industrialization in the UK.[16] Many countries now implement a minimum wage of some type.[17] Living wages formed a cornerstone of the New Deal legislation implemented by President Roosevelt in the US between 1933 and 1938.[18] In India, the principle of a Living Wage is enshrined in the constitution and minimum wages have been envisaged as a key method for improving the lives of informal workers in India, where they apply regardless of employment status.[19]

[15] ILO Declaration on Fundamental Principles and Rights at Work, see http://www.ilo.org/declaration/lang--en/index.htm, accessed 15 January 2018.

[16] Mark Brenner, 'Defining and Measuring a Global Living Wage: Theoretical and Conceptual Issues', prepared for the conference, Global Labor Standards and Living Wages, at the University of Massachusetts-Amherst, April 19–20, 2002.

[17] OECD, OECD Employment Outlook 1998 (OECD Publishing 1998) Chapter 2.

[18] Thomas Kochan, 'Wages and the Social Contract' *The American Prospect* (22 April 2007).

[19] Minimum Wage Act, 1948, India. Problems with implementation and enforcement have undermined this aim in many states of India.

Despite their widespread adoption, in many countries, government-set minimum wages fall far short of what many estimate to be a living wage.[20] According to one calculation, half of all countries set a minimum wage at less than the global poverty level.[21] A consequence of this failure to set living wages is that real wages have fallen rather than increased in the past two decades across much of the world. In Mexico, for example, real wages fell by 25–40 per cent in the 1990s, and the minimum wage, when it was paid, fell to forty-five cents an hour.[22] In other countries, it is not just a problem that minimum wages are set too low, they are often not enforced:

> Minimum wage policies, to be useful, need to be well enforced … Unfortunately, in many countries, labour inspection services are understaffed and penalties are too weak. As a result, minimum wages too often remain a 'paper tiger' rather than an effective policy.[23]

Indeed, while much of the focus of debates is about what level minimum wages should be set, little attention has been given to how to promote normative acceptance of the idea of living wages, or how to ensure compliance and promote collective means of enforcement.[24] The proposal herein attempts to overcome these gaps.

Further, few countries have a universal minimum wage system that applies across all industries and occupations. In many countries, various categories of formal workers are exempt.[25] Even fewer countries cover non-standard or informal workers.[26] The proposal herein insists on universal coverage.

One of the factors that differentiates poorer and richer countries is that a living wage is higher than the median wage in poor countries, and lower than the median wage in richer countries. Empirical research conducted within the ILO suggests that living wage rates are around 2–3 times the median wage rate in low income study countries, and around 2/3rds the median wage rate in high income study countries.[27] Figure 9.1 shows the differences in median and living wage rates across the world.

For example, the median wage in Bangladesh in 2005 was between 4.92 and 9.80 Taka (BDT) per hour. However, Anker estimates that in order to earn a living wage, the hourly pay should have been 16.04 Taka.[28] In contrast, the median Swiss employee earned between 29.81 to 34.78 Swiss Francs. Anker calculated that a living wage rate per hour would be around 20.79 Swiss Francs,[29] showing that the median rate is higher than the living wage rate, which is surely desirable. The aim should be to have most—indeed all—people in a society enjoying more than a living wage.

[20] Dain Bolwell, 'To the Lighthouse Towards a Global Minimum Wage: Building on the International Poverty Line' (Adelaide) 42 Australian Bulletin of Labour 1 9 Ethical Trading Initiative, 'Living Wage: Make it a Reality' (ETI Conference 2008 Workshop 5) 1.

[21] Bolwell 9.

[22] Allen D. Engle Sr, Norbert F. Elbert, and Judith W. Spain 'Sell Global, Pay Local—The Ethics of Taller Product Markets, Lower Labor Markets, and Informed Consent in Global Employment Contracts' 22 Business & Professional Ethics Journal 25.

[23] ILO, *Global Wage Report 2008/09* (2008) 52.

[24] Chiara Benassi, *The Implementation of Minimum Wage: Challenges and Creative Solutions* (IDEAS Working Paper Series from RePEc, 2011).

[25] Disabled workers are often excluded or come under separate regulations. Apprentices and trainees are also often excluded. In some countries, public servants are also not covered (France, Greece and Luxembourg). Sub-minimum rates are common for young workers: OECD Chapter 2.

[26] Bolwell 2.

[27] Richard Anker, *A New Methodology for Estimating Internationally Comparable Poverty Lines and Living Wage Rates* (Policy Integration Department Statistical Development and Analysis Group, International Labour Office 2005) xi; Richard Anker and Martha Anker, *Living Wages around the World: Manual for Measurement* (Edward Elgar 2017).

[28] Ibid. 104. [29] Ibid. 104.

- 2 to 3 times the median wage rate in low income countries
- 1.5 to 3.5 times the median wage rate in Transition Economy countries
- 60 per cent to 1.0 times the median wage rate in non-Transition Economy middle-income countries
- 60 to 80 per cent of the median wage rate in high-income countries

Figure 9.1 Differences in median and living wage rates[a]
[a]Anker 103.

It is difficult for single countries to act alone to increase minimum wages. Networks of suppliers and factory owners often put pressure on governments not to raise wages or extend rights to peripheral workers, so as to maintain low labour unit costs through functional flexibility. As described in Chapter 7, fear in Cambodia that work will move to other poor countries resulted in the minimum wage only being raised by small increments in 2013 and 2014, despite broad public support for increases and mass protests. Interview evidence collected for this book from the four countries studied confirmed that factory owners and managers are highly cognisant of the risk of capital flight. Factory owners in Bulgaria stated in interviews that orders from their suppliers had shifted to Asian producers. They had not lost work altogether, but the volumes of orders had decreased as Asian producers became more competitive thanks to lower unit labour costs and changes in trade rules.

At the heart of the informality and poverty problem, then, lies the question of how to induce developing and developed countries alike to raise minimum wages and enforce labour laws. This dilemma is particularly stark in relation to poor countries whose main competitive advantage is perceived to be low unit labour costs. These countries lack the incentive to raise wages, and other nations lack the ability to force them to do so.[30]

To overcome this collective action problem, today, there is growing movement for *international* floor wages. The Asia Floor Wage Alliance, for example, is an alliance led by trade unions in the key garment producing countries in the Asian region.[31] Central to their demands is the call for a living wage to be paid to all garment workers. This has led to the development of the Asia Floor Wage calculation.[32] The group proposes that a Living Wage calculation across the region is key to ensuring workers receive a decent wage, but also that wage differences do not mean companies pull out of one country to move manufacturing to a country with lower costs—thus avoiding the so called race to the bottom.[33] An additional contemporary model for the generation of an international floor wage comes from the ILO's Joint Maritime Commission: the only

[30] This dilemma has a strong analogy in the area of climate change: how to create incentives for the major developing countries to reduce carbon emissions: Michael P. Vandenbergh and Mark A. Cohen, 'Climate Change Governance: Boundaries and Leakage' 18 NYU Environmental Law Journal 221.

[31] Asia Floor Wage Alliance, *Stitching a Decent Wage across Borders: the Asia Floor Wage Proposal* (2009).

[32] Anannya Bhattacharjee, Sarita Gupta, and Stephanie Luce, 'Raising the Floor: The Movement for a Living Wage in Asia' 18 New Labor Forum 71.

[33] Emma Harbour, 'Focus: Raising the Bar in the Struggle for Living Wages' International Centre for Trade Union Rights 21 International Union Rights 19; participant observation: 'Living Wage Benchmarks: Dealing with Regional Variations' Thematic Workshop, Clean Clothes Campaign Global Forum 2014, Hong Kong, 19 November 2014.

statutory international wage-fixing mechanism, it determines international minimum wages for that most international category of workers—seafaring maritime workers.[34]

There is a long history of the application of nation-specific living wage calculation methods.[35] In line with the contemporary focus on international floor wages, more recent work of this type has been directed at calculating internationally comparative living wages. The Clean Clothes Campaign is working on defining and calculating living wages for garment producing regions.[36] Similar efforts have occurred within the ILO's research arm to develop internationally comparable living wage metrics, with major advances in recent years led by the Ankers.[37]

This section canvasses a concrete regulatory mechanism for achieving international living wages. The proposal was originally developed in conversations and email exchanges with John Braithwaite, and is built on in substantial ways here.[38] It also builds on other proposals in the literature.[39] The importance of such a development is not only that it would reduce informality, but also that it would address the problem of growing within-country equality and, eventually, between country inequality.[40] As Chapter 1 of this study showed, inequality and informality are intimately linked, both causally and empirically.

9.2.2 How it could work

One way that the strong disincentive for individual governments to increase minimum wages can be overcome is to put in place regulatory strategies to increase minimum wages across regions and internationally.

This chapter proposes that the logic of the Asian Floor Wage campaign is sound.[41] However, such a movement requires the support of IOs. It is suggested, then, that a key ultimate objective would be an ILO Convention or UN Treaty for signatory nations to increase statutory living and minimum wages (referred to as a Global Living Wage instrument in this section). Though previous ILO Conventions have created obligations

[34] Fabrizio Barcellona, 'A Global Minimum Wage' 21 International Union Rights 17. See also, the Joint Maritime Commission's page at http://www.ilo.org/global/docs/WCMS_162320/lang--en/index.htm, accessed 14 January 2018.

[35] Brenner.

[36] Clean Clothes Campaign, *Tailored Wages: Are the Big Brands Paying the People who Make our Clothes Enough to Live on?* (2014).

[37] It is beyond the scope of this study to compare methods. The method is clearly set out in Richard; Anker, *Estimating a Living Wage: A Methodological Review* ([ILO, 2011); Anker, *A New Methodology for Estimating Internationally Comparable Poverty Lines and Living Wage Rates;* Anker and Anker. In any case, it is assumed that agreement on the method of calculation is to be reached through multiparty negotiation, since it is, at heart, a political decision.

[38] The author is extremely grateful for John Braithwaite's generosity in sharing his idea, being open to various modifications, and his comments on the development of this first pathway out of informality.

[39] Thomas Palley, 'The Economics of Wage-Led Recovery: Analysis and Policy Recommendations' 3 International Journal of Labour Research 219.

[40] United Nations Research Institute for Social Development, *Combating Poverty and Inequality: Structural Change, Social Policy and Politics: Overview* (United Nations Research Institute for Social Development 2010)] Thomas W. Pogge, 'Properties of Global Justice' 32 Metaphilosophy 6.

[41] This is not to suggest that raising minimum wages is the only way of improving the livelihoods of the poor. Raising minimum wages is part of a wage-led strategy. In countries where low wage workers are concentrated in the bottom of the family income distribution, it is more likely that low-income families will benefit from minimum-wage increases. However, where unemployment is the main problem, and families are without labour income, they will not benefit directly from increases in the return to labour and other strategies are required: OECD 49.

to set minimum wages, they have not set aims for incremental increases or provided for a means of enforcement.

It is proposed that implementation could occur in two stages. The first stage would be for all countries to *raise minimum wages to a living wage rate*. The Global Living Wage instrument would set a timeline for all countries to legally mandate a minimum wage which reflected a living wage in keeping with the calculation agreed through a tripartite process.

Here, the Ankers' recent work calculating a living wage based on food and service baskets for each country in the world is particularly important for setting minima.[42] It is vital that the minimum wage apply to all workers regardless of employment status in order for it to be of use in increasing the living standards of non-standard, informal workers. As living minimum wages are the bare 'minimum', it would be up to national industrial relations processes, such as collective bargaining agreements, to increase wage packages to reflect appropriate rates of pay, including additional benefits appropriate to that country system. Countries would also be free to conduct normal sectoral bargaining or set different minimum wages across regions based on the cost of living in different parts of the country. Living minimum wages should also be combined with other effective poverty reduction measures.[43]

The next stage would be to move countries towards *a global average minimum wage*, based on purchasing power parity (PPP), meaning that it is adjusted for local living costs. PPP is employed as a measure to compare income levels across different countries. It is used to determine the adjustments needed to be made in the exchange rates of two currencies to make them at par with the purchasing power of each other.

The aim of this second stage is to ensure that income does not stagnate at a living wage level, but rather that wages continue to increase across nations. A secondary aim of this step is to begin reducing both within-country and between country-inequality. Why should such vast differences exist between countries in income? If a country had a *below* average minimum wage based on PPP it would be required by the instrument to increase the minimum wage by an agreed quantum—say 2 per cent per annum in real terms (adjusted for inflation). This is preferable to Thomas Palley's suggestion for a global minimum wage that is a fixed per cent—he suggests fifty per cent—of the country's median wage.[44] The reason for this is because living wages are higher than the country's median wage in the poorest countries. If the minimum wage in Bangladesh was set at half the median wage, this would make it unacceptably low.

The targets proposed here are merely suggestions, and others have gone into a great deal more detail debating the methods for calculations. The exact figures would be a question for further empirical research, public debate and negotiation.

[42] Anker and Anker. An alternative is Bolwell's suggestion that the global minimum be set at the poverty line as this is the first of the Millennium Development Goals/Sustainable Development Goals and widely accepted and understood, compared with Anker's method which is more complicated and less widely understood and accepted: Bolwell 25.

[43] Successful anti-poverty measures vary from country to country. India's Mahatma Gandhi National Rural Employment Guarantee Scheme, introduced from 2005 under which the state provides a minimum of 100 days of paid manual work per year to rural households, appears to have enjoyed some success in reducing poverty: Rhonda Breitkreuz and others, 'The Mahatma Gandhi National Rural Employment Guarantee Scheme: A Policy Solution to Rural Poverty in India?' 35 Development Policy Review 397. Such a scheme may be inappropriate elsewhere, where tax-related methods are more likely to be successful.

[44] Palley.

9.2.3 Role for the ILO and other International Organizations

Though the idea of a Global Living Wage is not novel, what is lacking from most proposals is a method of orchestration and enforcement. The proposal conceives of a strong role for the ILO, in concert with other IOs. The United Nations would have a particularly important role, as the reduction of poverty is the number one goal of the Sustainable Development Goals. A Global Living Wage instrument would give expression to this most important of goals. Strong cooperation with the World Bank and International Finance Corporation, which already occurs in relation to the Sustainable Development Goals, would be required.

One option would be for a Convention to be generated through the conventional ILO tripartite process, whereby the ILO's technical advisors would draft a recommendation and that recommendation would be debated at the ILO's conference. The tripartite process provides a strong role for government, employer organizations and trade unions in negotiating conventions. A second option would be for the generation of an international treaty by the United Nations.

The ILO and other companion IOs would then have the following responsibilities:

1. Overseeing the process of ratification. It is suggested that that a 'Living Wage list' and 'Poverty Promoting List' could be publicized (see below) to encourage ratification
2. Determining globally comparative living wages and globally comparative minimum wages. As discussed, the ILO has already made considerable progress towards this aim in empirical terms[45]
3. Monitoring compliance with the Global Living Wage instrument
4. Overseeing the establishment and running of the Global Living Wage Dispute Mechanism
5. Setting up domestic tribunals and training national tribunal members (outlined in the following section)
6. Convening forums for information sharing and learning amongst stakeholders regarding enforcement in the Global Living Wage Dispute Mechanism and national tribunals
7. Compiling data on complaints and orders made by national tribunals
8. Coordinating the advancement of enforcement strategies with other IOs and relevant national government bodies.

9.2.4 Incentives for compliance

9.2.4.1 Incentives for states to participate and comply

The political strategy at first would be to build up a 'Living Wage list' of countries that had ratified the Global Living Wage instrument. Governments that signed up for the 'Living Wage list' of early joiners would most likely gain two key benefits: (a) the types of inwards investment seen in Cambodia due to the presence of the Better Factories Project (described in Chapter 7), and (b) enhanced domestic campaign contributions and mobilization of voter support from unions and the domestic social movement

[45] Anker, *Estimating a Living Wage: A Methodological Review*; Anker, *A New Methodology for Estimating Internationally Comparable Poverty Lines and Living Wage Rates*.

in support of living wages and equality. Transnational companies could sign up to a pledge to conduct business preferentially with 'Living Wage list' companies.

Likewise, a 'Poverty Promoting List' of countries which do not ratify the Global Living Wage instrument and with minimum wages below the living wage level would then be compiled. This would allow for greater mobilization to target listed states. Transnational firms that conduct business in 'Poverty Promoting List' countries could also be targeted with strikes, consumer boycotts, adverse publicity, and Fair Trade decertification, in keeping with the campaign currently underway by groups like the Asian Floor Wage Alliance.[46] The global trade union movement and allied NGOs could be energized to build a fund to support those who went on strike for higher wages in 'Poverty Promoting List' countries.[47] The global anti-poverty social movement could experiment with all manner of creative strategies that might bring grief to 'Poverty Promoting List' businesses. A particularly effective example of this strategy was Brazil's National Slave Eradication Pact launched in 2005. More than 400 companies representing almost 30 per cent of Brazil's gross domestic product signed up to the pact, pledging to keep their businesses free of forced labour proactively and cut commercial ties with businesses profiting from slavery. The project compiled a 'dirty list', which publicly named almost 300 companies, from major brands to small enterprises, who were found to be profiting from slave labour.[48]

Countries that ratified the Global Living Wage instrument, but subsequently failed to implement or enforce it, could be relegated to the 'Poverty Promoting List' based on ILO monitoring.

The importance of this element of the strategy—a global campaign—is not just that it encourages participation, it is also that it promotes the *idea* of a living wage. It adds to the normative strength of the concept. This, it is hoped, will promote self-regulation by business and reduce need for punitive strategies.

9.2.4.2 Incentives for unions to take action

The case studies conducted in this study have shown that often trade unions are reluctant to, or lack the knowledge to, represent the poorest and most marginalized workers, including informal workers. This finding was particularly stark in the Bulgarian case study. In Cambodia also, unions are only just beginning to organize peripheral and informal workers. They are clinging to an industrial or Fordist model of capitalism, focused on trying to stop further outsourcing and vertical disintegration. A significant minority of the trade union movement is reimagining itself and becoming more international in its focus. However, even for these innovative trade unions, the focus still tends to be on core industrial workers.

There is a risk that governments could cultivate support from trade unions and social democratic publics by ratifying the Global Living Wage instrument, while assuring their private sector that they would do nothing to enforce its terms. This could certainly lead to the failure of the Global Living Wage proposal. It is therefore of

[46] Bhattacharjee, Gupta, and Luce.

[47] Such strategies are currently being generated by groups such as the Clean Clothes Campaign in relation to garment industry workers Clean Clothes Campaign.

[48] Menaka Mahajan, *The Political and Moral Economy of Combatting Labor Exploitation: A Study of Brazil's Policy Evolution* (ProQuest Dissertations Publishing 2015); Samuel Antero, 'Understanding the Eradication of Slave Labour in Contemporary Brazil—An Implementation Perspective' 34 Policy Studies 89.

crucial importance to note that state enforcement of a living minimum wage cannot be assumed.

For this reason, a strong role for worker and anti-poverty organizations is built into enforcement mechanisms. Worker empowerment is both a preventive strategy and a form of enforcement by a non-state actor. Having a strong counterpart is a deterrent for noncompliant states and business because they must then take into account a possible reaction and consequence of non-compliance.[49]

A model could be the US False Claims Act *qui tam* provisions.[50] Such *qui tam* provisions were primarily designed for whistle-blower enforcement with fraud against the government, but also exist for money laundering, tax evasion, and bribery in the US.[51] Under that system of enforcement, whistle-blowers receive a quantum of the fine or damages awarded against a wrongdoer:

> Qui tam is a unique mechanism in the law that allows citizens with evidence of fraud against government contracts and programs to sue, on behalf of the government, in order to recover the stolen funds. In compensation for the risk and effort of filing a qui tam case, the whistleblower or "relator" may be awarded a portion of the funds recovered, typically between 15 and 25 per cent.[52]

Qui tam provisions have been credited as a highly effective regulatory tool.[53] Braithwaite argues that the networked governance quality of the qui tam enterprise creates a circle of accountability in which whistle-blower, NGO, law firm, relevant state department and judge are each checking abuse of process by one another.[54] It is an expedient way of enlisting knowledgeable insiders to the public interest.[55]

9.2.4.3 Enforcement: Global Living Wage Dispute Mechanism

The enforcement strategies could have an international and national component. One reason it may be preferable for the multilateral instrument to take the form of a treaty is so that it could give rise to an international enforcement mechanism—a Global Living Wage Dispute Mechanism. It is envisaged that this mechanism would allow unions and other interested parties to bring claims, at an international level, against states on behalf of worker-citizens for failing to enforce minimum living wage laws and be awarded a portion of any of the funds recovered. The primary remedy would be the

[49] Benassi 10.

[50] *Qui tam* is a shortened form of *Qui tam pro domino rege, quam pro se ipso in hoc parte sequitur*, which means 'He who brings an action for the King as well as for himself': John Braithwaite, 'Flipping Markets to Virtue with Qui Tam and Restorative Justice' 38 Accounting, Organizations and Society 458.

[51] David Freeman Engstrom, 'Private Enforcement's Pathways: Lessons from Qui Tam Litigation' (2014) [2014] 114 Columbia Law Review 1913.

[52] TAF Education Fund, *False Claims Act Overview* (2015).

[53] See for example Brief Amicus Curiae of AARP in Support of Respondent at 4–6, *Schindler Elevator Corp. v. United States ex rel. Kirk*, 131 S. Ct. 1885 (2011) (No. 10-188), 2011 WL 288888 which sites 'FCA is the single most effective tool in the fight against fraud perpetrated against the government' and crediting qui tam provisions with achieving large recoveries for federal treasury while also combating substandard healthcare. See also Pamela H. Bucy, 'Private Justice', 76 S. Cal. L. Rev. 1, 53 (2002) who describes FCA's *qui tam* regime as 'extraordinarily successful as a regulatory tool'.

[54] John Braithwaite, *Regulatory Capitalism: How it Works, Ideas for Making it Work Better* (Elgar 2008) 69.

[55] P. H. Bucy, 'Private Justice' (2002) [2002] 76 Southern California Law Review 1; P.H. Bucy, 'Game Theory and the Civil False Claims Act: Iterated Games and Close-Knit Groups' (2004) [2004] 35 Loyola University Chicago Law Journal 1021.

recovery of unpaid remuneration. The state would be ordered to pay unpaid entitlements to those workers who had not been paid the living wage.

Higher penalties might be exacted against states where evidence was presented of corruption such as the taking of bribes by labour inspectors, which is common in countries like Cambodia (see Chapter 7).[56] Not only is this justifiable on justice grounds, but also, anti-corruption enforcement might be the domain where it will prove easiest to mobilize transnational political support for qui tam, outside of the labour movement. It is also in keeping with a broader trend towards the global harmonization and transnational reach of corruption laws: a potent set of legal mechanisms now permits legal institutions in one country to regulate and provide redress for corrupt acts involving public officials from other countries backed by the United Nations Convention against Corruption (Doc. A/58/422).[57]

Via the National Supply Chain Tribunal, the state could then recover these funds from the relevant employers or other parties within the supply chain, who are found to have practices that affect the employer's or contractor's ability to provide a living wage, legal remuneration, or related conditions to the worker. This pathway is discussed further in the next section of this chapter. This would create an incentive for states to make claims against employers and other parties in the supply chain through the National Supply Chain Tribunal. It would also trigger action by labour inspectorates to monitor and collect evidence in supply chains. It would further act as an incentive to ensure that the tribunals were active and did not only represent the interests of capital.

When I have presented this proposal for a Global Living Wage Dispute Mechanism, I have found it to be controversial. Some believe that claims should be made directly against responsible businesses in the Global Living Wage Dispute Mechanism, not against states. They want a way to hold business to account at an international level. They believe that a mechanism that allows claims against states will further undermine state power and credibility. It is more likely, in my view, that a claim may be made against the state, and subsequently the state will not bring a claim against business in the National Supply Chain Tribunal, thereby effectively subsidising business underpayment of workers. For this reason it may be preferable to allow joint claims against states and business in the Global Living Wage Dispute Mechanism. The main point is that states should be responsible for monitoring and enforcing living minimum wages and currently there is no way to hold states to account for this duty.

The potential of being awarded a portion of funds recovered through the Global Living Wage Dispute Mechanism would provide an incentive for worker organizations to find and encourage whistle-blowers against states who fail to enforce living minimum wages. The award of a portion of the amount recovered could provide a major source of funding to worker organizations and other concerned groups, underwriting expanded transnational activities. This would boost recruitment of new union members, particularly from sweatshops and home-based workers.

An example of the process is illustrated in Figure 9.2.

There is no reason why trade unions and other labour organizations should not pursue claims against businesses using anti-corruption laws of this type today, where

[56] The exact portion of funds to be recovered by the trade union whistle-blower, and the question of whether it would be paid by the state on top of the quantum for unpaid wages, would be a matter for debate.

[57] Kevin E. Davis, Guillermo Jorge, Maíra Rocha Machado, *Transnational Anti-Corruption Law in Action: Cases from Argentina and Brazil* (Global Administrative Law Series, Institute for International Law and Justice, New York University School of Law, IILJ 2014/1, 2014).

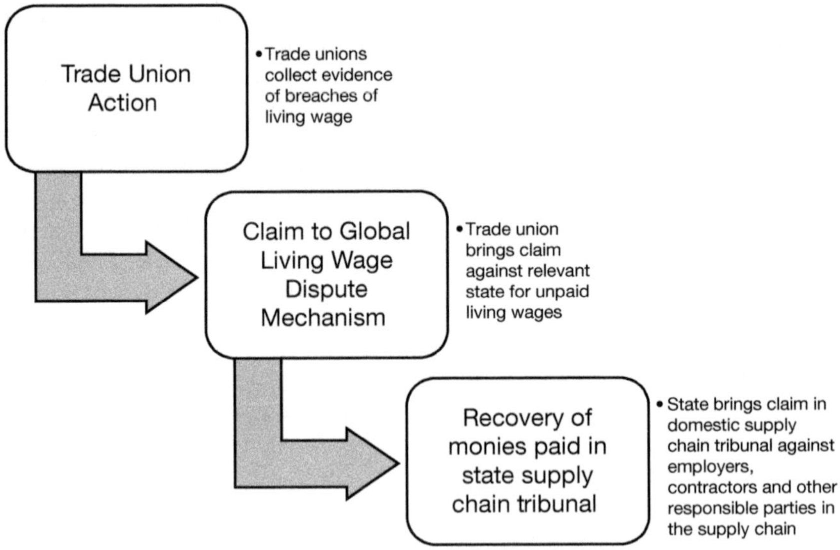

Figure 9.2 Example process in the Global Living Wage Dispute Mechanisms and National Supply Chain Tribunal

there is evidence that a business has paid bribes to avoid the enforcement of labour laws.[58] Such claims could be initiated in the country in which the corruption occurred, or in the home-country of the transnational business. The latter is useful as foreign institutions are likely to be less impeded by local political obstacles. Where qui tam provisions exist, as in the US, such cases would be financially beneficial for the international trade union movement, as well as an innovative method of encouraging the enforcement of labour laws.

9.2.5 Ratcheting up domestic supply chain enforcement strategies

It would be the responsibility of the ILO to compile data regarding complaints and orders made by National Supply Chain Tribunals (whose functions are outlined in the next section of this chapter) regarding the practices of parties in supply chains. Where there was evidence of particularly egregious practices by parties in the supply chain such as child labour and forced labour or widespread exploitation of other types, the ILO and companion IOs would have responsibility for ratcheting up enforcement strategies (see Figure 9.3). Here, there are opportunities for experimentation. The ILO may bring parties together to create Global Framework Agreements or new global industry-wide performance standards.

[58] There is also a shift towards the privatization of transnational corruption law enforcement, in keeping with the proposal here: Kath Hall, 'Strategic Privatisation of Transnational Anti-Corruption Regulation' (2013) 28 Australian Journal of Corporate Law 60.

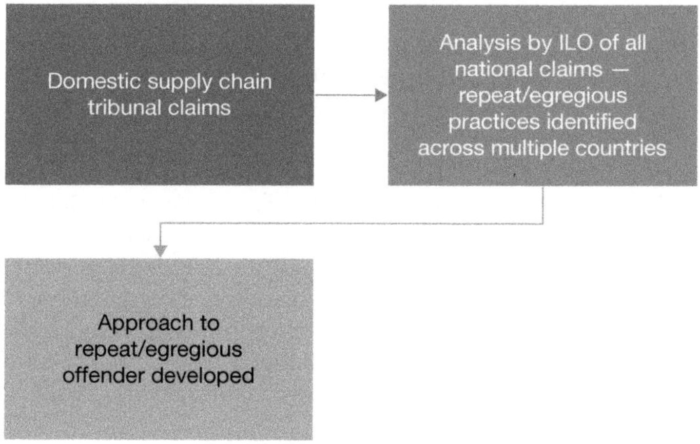

Figure 9.3 Ratcheting up domestic supply chain enforcement strategies

9.3 Second Pathway: National Supply Chain Tribunals

The second pillar of the strategy would create national tribunals which are able to remedy disputes over unpaid living wages (ex post remedies) and create positive obligations for those with power in supply chains, including buyers and financers. This section examines existing initiatives which provide ex post remedies and positive duties, before outlining a proposal for national-level tribunals.

9.3.1 Ex post remedy: joint and vicarious liability of buyers, parent companies and financiers

9.3.1.1 Justification

The capacity to bring claims against buyers and parties high in the supply chain is a vital step in reducing downwards pressure from within value chains and promoting living wages. Chapter 6 illustrated how right of recovery of unpaid remuneration from parties upwards in the supply chain, developed in the Australian initiative, offers the opportunity to address the uneven distribution of risk throughout the supply chain. The right of recovery of unpaid remuneration from parties upwards in the supply chain helps to overcome a significant limitation of traditional employment regulation. While the employment contract makes only those who directly contract with the worker responsible for their rights and conditions, joint and vicarious liability provisions target a wider array of responsible parties. The point is to avoid arguments about employment status which preoccupy labour lawyers by developing a legal jurisprudence of 'responsibility' commended by Alan Hyde.[59]

The method found in the Australian Textile Clothing and Footwear (TCF) regulation described in Chapter 6 is just one technique. Other examples drawn from elsewhere in the world are Law No 20 123 in Chile—which establishes vicarious liability

[59] Hyde 84.

for 'recipient companies' for the obligations of contract workers, and the 'Hot Goods' or 'Hot Cargo' provisions in section 15(a) of the U.S. Fair Labour Standards Act.[60] During the late 1990s and early 2000s, the US Department of Labour creatively leveraged hot goods injunctions to compel apparel buyers to participate in a Department of Labour programme, in which the buyers agreed to monitor (typically through contract monitors) and assure compliance at their contract facilities.[61] The Californian 'brother's keeper' law makes liable for labour code violations anyone who enters 'into a contract or agreement for labor or services ... where the contract agreement does not include sufficient funds to allow the contractor to comply with all applicable local, state and federal laws or regulations governing the labor or services to be provided'.[62] Similarly, the state of New York does so when the manufacturer knew or should have known of the contractor's violations (New York Labor Law, s. 345a(1)).[63] These examples show that vicarious liability can be achieved by various means.

There are also historical precedents for mechanisms of this type. Indeed, de Lagerie argues that improvements to the conditions of outsourced labour have historically occurred when legislatures have recognized the necessity of regulating the entire integrated productive chain, rather than just the direct employer–employee relationship. Changes to articles L. 721-1ff. of the French Labour Code in 1957 extended liability for home-based worker conditions to principal employers in a manner similar to the Australian expansion of the definition of employer.[64]

More broadly, the expansion that has occurred in the area of torts in a number of jurisdictions points to an increasing willingness of courts to recognize a duty of care where a third party wrongfully harms another person, even absent a special relationship.[65] Under the principle of 'enabling torts' an actor who 'sets the stage' for a third party's bad acts with a foreseeable expectation that another person will suffer harm is responsible alongside the primary wrongdoer if that harm in fact occurs.[66]

Additionally, a number of initiatives allow claims to be brought against parties who in some way enable harm including financiers, lead firms in supply chains and so on. The OECD Guidelines for Multinational Corporations allow claims to be brought against banks and investors in National Contact Points, the dispute resolution bodies established under the Guidelines.[67] The Guidelines are recommendations addressed by governments to multinational enterprises operating in or from adhering countries (the

[60] 29 U.S.C. § 215(a)(1) (2012) ('[I]t shall be unlawful for any person to transport, offer for transport, ship, deliver, or sell in commerce, or to ship, deliver, or sell with knowledge that shipment or delivery or sale thereof in commerce is intended any goods in the production of which any employee was employed in violation of section 206 [statutory minimum wage] or 207 [maximum hours]').

[61] David Weil and Carlos Mallo, 'Regulating Labour Standards via Supply Chains: Combining Public/Private Interventions to Improve Workplace Compliance' 45 British Journal of Industrial Relations 791; Mark Anner, Jennifer Bair, and Jeremy Blasi, 'Toward Joint Liability in Global Supply Chains: Addressing the Root Causes of Labor Violations in International Subcontracting Networks' (2013–2014) [2013–2014] 35 Comparative Labor Law & Policy Journal 1 38.

[62] California Labor Code s. 2810(a).

[63] Anner, Bair, and Blasi 41.

[64] Pauline Barraud de Lagerie, 'The Wages of Sweat: A Social History Perspective on the Fight Against Sweatshops' 55, Supplement 1 Sociologie du Travail e1 e8.

[65] For examples from the US, see Kenneth S. Abraham, *The Forms and Functions of Tort Law* (4th edn, Foundation Press 2012); Robert L. Rabin, 'Enabling Torts' 49 DePaul Law Review 435 442–3.

[66] Rabin 442–3.

[67] http://oecdwatch.org/publications-en/Publication_2995.

OECD members plus Argentina, Brazil and Chile). Such claims have been brought against banks[68] and investment funds.[69]

9.3.2 Positive duty of due diligence for buyers, parent companies, and financiers

9.3.2.1 Justification

The duties proposed thus far are ex post options, in the sense that they extend the capacity of claimants to bring claims or recover unpaid wages and conditions against parties who are not the direct employer once losses have *already* occurred. An ideal supply chain regulation regime would strive primarily to *prevent* violations and *promote* a higher standard of behaviour within supply chains, subsidiaries and borrowers through the imposition of *positive duties*.[70] There are two problems with relying on liability regimes alone. Firstly, unless there is strict liability, if candidates for responsibility can successfully show that their action was not voluntary or that they were excusably ignorant, then their responsibility is usually mitigated if not dissolved.[71] Secondly, such regimes fail to address structural or systemic causes of injustice. The justification for the imposition of a positive duty is that parties bear responsibility for structural injustice because they contribute, by their actions, to the processes that produce unjust outcomes. Responsibility derives from belonging together with others in a system of interdependent processes of cooperation and competition, through which parties seek benefits and aim to realize certain goals.[72]

The principle of 'due diligence' developed by Professor John Ruggie, UN Special Representative (UNSR) of the Secretary General on Business and Human Rights, has given a boost to this principle of positive duties.[73] Ruggie and his team developed a 'Protect, Respect and Remedy' Framework, the basic principles of which were presented in the UNSR's 2008 Annual Report.[74] The 'due diligence' framework provides a

[68] For example, specific Instances (claims) have twice been brought against ANZ bank in the Australian national contact point. The most recent claim was *EC and IDI vs. Australia and New Zealand Banking Group*, filed 6 October 2014; Equitable Cambodia and Inclusive Development International, *Specific Instance under the OECD Guidelines for Multinational Enterprises submitted to the Australian National Contact Point (NCP) for the OECD Guidelines: Inclusive Development International (IDI) and Equitable Cambodia (EC) Against Australia New Zealand Banking Group (ANZ), concerning financial services provided to Phnom Penh Sugar Company* (2014).

[69] For example, see the complaint brought against Dutch and Norwegian Pension funds regarding investments in South Korean company, POSCO, Netherlands National Contact Point, *Initial Statement ABP/APG - Lok Shakti Abhiyan, KTNC Watch, Fair Green and Global Alliance, Forum for Environment and Development* (2013).

[70] Farrell 1507.

[71] Iris Marion Young, 'Responsibility and Global Justice' (2006) [2006] 23 Social Philosophy and Policy 102.

[72] Ibid. 119.

[73] UN OHCHR, *Human Rights and Transnational Corporations and Other Business Enterprises* (2005) para 1(a).

[74] John Ruggie, *Promotion and Protection of All Human Rights, Civil, Political, Economic, Social and Cultural Rights, Including the Right to Development: Protect, Respect and Remedy: a Framework for Business and Human Rights. Report of the Special Representative of the Secretary-General on the issue of human rights and transnational corporations and other business enterprises, John Ruggie* (2008).

way for businesses to put in place internal planning and management processes which take into account human rights. This is consistent with 'management-based regulation', as opposed to say, performance-based regulation which is more concerned with outcomes.[75]

The UNSR took a cautious approach to recommending state intervention in the area of imposing a positive duty of due diligence on businesses. However, there is a clear shift away from accepting a voluntary approach, evidenced by the passing of two resolutions in June 2014 at the 26th Session of the UN Human Rights Council in support of the exploration of 'legal and practical measures to improve access to remed[ies], judicial and non-judicial, for victims of business-related abuses, including the benefits and limitations of a legally binding instrument'.[76] A draft treaty was released in July 2018. It is not yet clear if a Business and Human Rights Treaty will gain sufficient support to be passed.

In the meantime, however, support has burgeoned for the imposition of positive duties of due diligence on large business by individual states, with various OECD countries taking significant steps in recent years:

- the duty of vigilance obligation[77] for French parent and subcontracting companies to 'identify risks and prevent serious violations of human rights and fundamental freedoms, the health and safety of both people and the environment' enacted in February 2017 by French Parliament.[78]
- a mandatory human rights due diligence law under consideration in Switzerland,[79] where the necessary signatures have been collected for a referendum.
- the Dutch Child Labour Due Diligence Bill adopted by Dutch Parliament in February 2017.[80] If approved by the Dutch Senate, the law will require companies to identify whether child labour is present in their supply chains and—if this is the case—develop a plan to combat it. It will come into effect January 1, 2020.[81]
- the UK Modern Slavery Act that requires businesses to publish an annual statement if they have an annual turnover above a threshold (£36 million) describing what steps they are taking to eradicate human trafficking and slavery in their supply chains.[82]
- an Australian bill based on the UK's Modern Slavery Act, with a revised Act likely later in 2018.[83]

[75] Ngaire Woods and David Graham, 'Making Corporate Self-Regulation Effective in Developing Countries' 34 World Development; Neil Gunningham, 'Integrating Management Systems and Occupational Health and Safety Regulation' 26 Journal of Law and Society 192; Braithwaite and Drahos, 'Ratcheting Up and Driving Down Global Regulatory Standards'.

[76] See UN Human Rights Council, *Human rights and transnational corporations and other business enterprises A/HRC/26/L.1* (2014); UN Human Rights Council, *Elaboration of an international legally binding instrument on transnational corporations and other business enterprises with respect to human rights A/HRC/26/L.22* (2014).

[77] Cossart, Chaplier, and Lomenie 320; Slater.

[78] Green.

[79] Swiss Coalition for Corporate Justice.

[80] Child Labour Due Diligence (Wet Zorgplicht Kinderarbeid); Oonk.

[81] Netherlands.

[82] Modern Slavery Act 2015 UK, http://www.legislation.gov.uk/ukpga/2015/30/contents/enacted/data.htm.

[83] Commonwealth of Australia, Australian Government Response to the Joint Standing Committee on Foreign Affairs, Defence and Trade Committee report: Trading Lives: Modern Day Human Trafficking (Oct. 27, 2014), http://www.aph.gov.au/parliamentary_business/committees/house_of_representatives_committees?url=jfadt/slavery_people_trafficking/report.htm.

- the California Transparency in Supply Chains Act (SB-657), approved in October 2010 that imposes duties on companies that operate transnationally.[84] The law requires all apparel and footwear retailers as well as manufacturers with global sales of more than USD $100 million a year to make disclosures. The disclosures must specify if an audit was conducted by a third party or through a company's internal department to evaluate and address risks of human trafficking and slavery within the business's local and international supply chains.[85] Training must also be provided employees and management on slavery and human trafficking risks mitigation. The Act also contains an enforcement provision.[86]

Over thirty initiatives of this type have been coded and assessed by the current author, Irene Pietropaoli and Madeline Winterbottom in a publicly available spread sheet.[87] This analysis forms the basis of the proposal made herein.

An older model for sharing responsibility amongst players in the supply chain comes from the United States in the first half of the twentieth century, where triangular collective agreements were formed between unions, the contractors who gave the work to home-based and sweatshop workers, and lead firms in supply chains.[88] In 1923, the union negotiated collective bargaining agreements with both the apparel contractors that directly employed the union's members as well as with the jobbers that, as clients of the contractors, 'indirectly employed' garment workers.[89] The agreements contained a number of provisions that promoted long term, stable relationships between buyers and contractors. The aim was to preclude jobbers from constantly switching between contractors to secure a short-term advantage on price. These agreements had a marked impact on the conditions of employment for unionized garment workers. Time series data presented by Anner et al.[90] indicate that gains on the wages front were indeed significant. During the middle decades of the twentieth century, the earnings of garment workers—a heavily feminized and, at least in New York, largely immigrant workforce—kept pace with general manufacturing wages.[91] Sadly, the jobbers' agreements did not survive the globalization of production in the TCF industry.[92]

The most similar contemporary example is the Framework Agreement between IndustriALL Global Union and Inditex, the apparel giant, which was renewed in 2014.[93] This was the first of its kind to cover an international retail supply

[84] Reese Darragh, 'California's New Supply Chain Transparency Law' (2011) [Wilmington Group PLC Haymarket Media, Inc.] 8 Compliance Week 12.

[85] A key flaw in this model is its reliance on auditing. The fundamental limitations of audits, in a variety of settings, has been well documented, see Steven Kelman, *Regulating America, Regulating Sweden: A Comparative Study of Occupational Safety and Health Policy* (The MIT Press)1981); Marilyn Strathern, *Audit Cultures* (Routledge 2000); Michael Power, *The Audit Society: Rituals of Verification* (Oxford University Press 1997).

[86] Eric Eastham and Mitch Danzig, 'California's New Forced Labor Disclosure Law: Empowering Consumers While Burdening Supply Chain' *SDCExec* (11 January 2012).

[87] See https://shelleymarshall.net/labour-regulation-of-global-supply-chains for a table comparing initiatives that regulate work in supply chains from around the world.

[88] Barraud de Lagerie e8.

[89] Mark Anner, Jennifer Bair, and Jeremy Blasi, 'Toward Joint Liability in Global Supply Chains: Addressing the Root Causes of Labor Violations in International Subcontracting Networks' 35 Comparative Labor Law and Policy Journal 1: 20; ibid.

[90] Ibid.

[91] Ibid. 18.

[92] Ibid. 20.

[93] IndustriALL Participant Observation: 'Jenny Holdcroft, Policy Director, IndustriALL Global Union' presentation, Clean Clothes Campaign Global Forum 2014, Hong Kong, 19 November 2014 (2014).

chain.[94] Under the agreement, both parties undertake to collaborate to ensure the sustainable and long-term observance of all international labour standards across Inditex's operations, including its suppliers.[95] Further useful models which regulate employment security come from the global approach pursued by groups such as the Workers' Rights Consortium[96,97] and the International Union League for Brand Responsibility,[98] such as the agreement between the Central General de Trabajadores Union of Honduras and retailer Fruit of the Loom which provides for employment security.[99]

In addition to establishing an ex post right of recovery, the Australian example explored in this study also established a range of positive duties for apparel businesses at different levels of the supply chains. These include providing 'work records', establishing whether suppliers are contracting to home-based workers, and ensuring that those workers are being provided with their lawful pay and registering to use home-based workers. These duties only apply to domestic supply chains, however.

9.3.3 How it could work

Each country that has ratified the Global Living Wage instrument will be under an obligation to set up a tribunal with powers to (a) adjudicate disputes that arise as a consequence of breaches of worker's rights within supply chains, and (b) create positive duties for parties within the supply chains. Under the international instrument, tribunals would have powers to make orders in relation to parties within supply chains who are domiciled either inside the jurisdiction, or outside the jurisdiction of the tribunal as long as the matter concerns a worker within the national jurisdiction of the tribunal.

Rather than becoming bogged down in arguments about legal doctrine in relation to strict and vicarious liability or the duty of care,[100] the proposal here is to adopt the approach taken by the Australian Road Safety Remuneration Act 2012 (Cth).[101] The Act created a labour tribunal with power to make orders concerning various matters

[94] Frederick Mayer and John Pickles, *Re-embedding the Market: Global Apparel Value Chains, Governance and Decent Work* (Palgrave Macmillian 2014) 27.

[95] Industriall, *Inditex* (11 July 2014 edn).

[96] Participant Observation: Conversation with Scott Nova, Executive Director, Workers Rights Consortium at Clean Clothes Campaign Global Forum 2014, Hong Kong, 20 November 2014; Participant Observation: Conversation with Yannick Etienne, Spokeswoman, ESPM-BATAY OUVRIYE, Haiti, at Clean Clothes Campaign Global Forum 2014, Hong Kong, 20 November 2014.

[97] The Workers' Rights Consortium was developed in 1999 by the United Students Against Sweatshops (USAS) in cooperation with the Union of Needletrades, Industrial and Textile Employees (UNITE); the American Federation of Labor-Congress of Industrial Organizations (AFL-CIO); and a number of human rights, labour, and religious NGOs: Dara O'Rourke, 'Outsourcing Regulation: Analyzing Nongovernmental Systems of Labor Standards and Monitoring' 31 Policy Studies Journal 1.

[98] The International Union League for Brand Responsibility is a global organization of workers who make products for multinational brands, such as clothing, footwear, and textiles. It is running a concerted campaign to encourage multinational brands to take responsibility and guarantee living wages, safe factories, and stable jobs.

[99] Anner, Bair, and Blasi, 34; Participant Observation: 'Winning and Enforcing Brand and Employer Commitments to Higher Wages and Union Rights' Thematic Workshop, Clean Clothes Campaign Global Forum 2014, Hong Kong, 19 November 2014.

[100] See Alan Hyde's detailed proposal for a twenty-first century version of *respondeat superior* for labour rights violations down the supply chain: Hyde.

[101] This Act was repealed by the Road Safety Remuneration Repeal Act 2016 (the Repeal Act). The Tribunal and the Orders that the Tribunal made ceased to operate at 12am on Thursday 21 April 2016. For more information see: https://www.fairwork.gov.au/about-us/legislation/road-safety-remuneration-system, accessed 14 December 2017.

in relation to safety and remuneration within the transport supply chain. The Act employed concepts and terminology that are particularly helpful in addressing the commercial pressures that emanate from parties in supply chains that impact working conditions.[102]

The tribunal would have the power to:

- make living wage orders where matters concern supply chain parties;
- approve and assist with negotiations for supply chain collective agreements;
- deal with certain disputes relating to participants in the supply chain and enforce existing orders;
- conduct research into supply chain dynamics that impact pay, conditions and related matters.

9.3.3.1 Redress

The tribunal would be charged with adjudicating disputes in relation to remuneration and related conditions about practices of one or more participants in the supply chain (including employers, contractors, buyers, agents, financiers, and so on) in relation to a worker if:[103]

(a) the worker contends that the practices affect the employer's or contractor's ability to provide a living wage, legal remuneration, or related conditions to the worker;

(b) the employer or contractor of the worker contends that the practices affect the employer's or contractor's ability to provide a living wage, legal remuneration, or related conditions to the worker;

(c) the labour inspectorate contends that the practices affect the employer's or contractor's ability to provide a living wage, legal remuneration, or related conditions to the worker.

As explained in the First Pathway above, where claims have been made against the state at the Global Living Wage Dispute Mechanism for unpaid remuneration, the National Supply Chain Tribunal would have jurisdiction to hear disputes regarding recovery of such funds from parties in the supply chain. Amounts would then be awarded against different parties in the supply chain based on their contribution to the problem. As Benassi points out, back pay compensation may also constitute a form of punishment if it is more costly to the employer or other responsible party than the compliance with the minimum wage. For instance, arrears in the UK take the rate of inflation into account, and therefore the final settlement amount is higher than the regular payment of the minimum wage.[104]

[102] For an analysis of the operation of the Act before it was repealed see: Richard Johnstone, Igor Nossar, and Michael Rawling, 'Regulating Supply Chains to Protect Road Transport Workers: An Early Assessment of the Road Safety Remuneration Tribunal (Australia)' 43 Federal Law Review 397. The Act was repealed by a Conservative government in order to 'restore freedom for parties to negotiate the most appropriate contractual arrangements': Explanatory Memorandum to the Road Safety Remuneration Repeal Act. 2016 http://parlinfo.aph.gov.au/parlInfo/search/display/display.w3p;query=Id%3A%22legislation%2Fems%2Fr5655_ems_581c6c2e-60bc-4887-87c7-47591032ef6b%22, accessed 14 December 2017.

[103] The language proposed here reflects that of Road Safety Remuneration Act 2012 (Cth) s. 43.

[104] Benassi 17.

9.3.3.2 *Positive duties*

The National Supply Chain Tribunals could also impose positive duties, which could include ways of reducing or removing remuneration-related incentives, pressures, and practices that contribute to payment of remuneration that is less than a living wage, breaches of labour laws, and unsafe work practices. Such orders may impose requirements, in relation to:[105]

(a) an employer or hirer/contractor of a worker to whom the order applies;

(b) a participant in the supply chain in relation to whom the order applies, including financiers, buyers, agents and so on.

9.3.3.3 *Extraterritorial powers*

The tribunal would have the power to make orders against parties in the supply chain domiciled outside of the country in which the work was occurring, as long as sufficient evidence was present concerning the manner in which the practices of the entity impact working practices and conditions, and the complaint concerned one or more workers within the jurisdiction of the tribunal.

9.3.3.4 *Workers not employees*

The powers of the tribunal would not be limited to employees, allowing a wider range of workers to bring claims than under most labour law systems which base labour protections on the employment contract. The provisions will explicitly refer to workers and empower the tribunal to make orders in relation to living and minimum wages in accordance with the Global Living Wage instrument (the first pathway).

9.3.3.5 *Benefits of a specialist tribunal*

It is recommended that the tribunal be created as an adjunct to existing labour relations tribunals or social dialogue institutions, and existing institutions be given the power to refer matters to the specialist tribunal where the matter concerns parties within a supply chain. The reason for this is that it is important that tribunal members have and build specialist knowledge in the field of supply chain dynamics. It is particularly crucial that they develop specialist knowledge of work relations that sit outside the traditional employer–employee relationship. Participant observation of Australian Fair Work Commission (the Australian industrial relations tribunal) hearings concerning the outwork provisions of the relevant clothing collective agreement suggest that tribunal members can be limited in their thinking about supply chain dynamics, as they are accustomed to dealing with employment matters without such attendant dynamics.[106]

The creation of *new* tribunals, and the selection of independent tribunal members with the assistance of the ILO, can help to overcome problems of bias and corruption that mar the delivery of justice in many developing countries. This follows the insights of the previous chapter which discussed the benefits of ‘rivalry’ or ‘displacement’ as a

[105] The language proposed here reflects the Road Safety Remuneration Act 2012 (Cth) s. 27.

[106] Participant Observation: Textile, Clothing and Footwear and Associated Industries Award 2010, Review of all modern awards after first two years (2013), Fair Work Commission (2013).

means of achieving institutional change. The chapter expounds the benefits of 'experimental displacement' as a strategy when an existing institution is failing, but there are political economy reasons that mean that full displacement is difficult or undesirable. An example of experimental displacement or rivalry which is relevant to the development of tribunals is the establishment of the Cambodian Arbitration Council as an industrial relations tribunal. It was set up with the assistance of the ILO and other international bodies, is staffed by local professionals who were selected through a painstaking process which aimed to ensure their independence and has thus far avoided the corruption charges regularly levelled against judges in the Cambodian court system.[107]

There is a great deal of literature expounding the benefits of tribunals as 'deliberative arenas'.[108] Such benefits include: cheapness and ease of accessibility; freedom from technicality—simplified rules of evidence and procedure reduce legal costs, and allow people to represent themselves—expert knowledge by tribunal members of their particular subject. Regardless of these flexibilities, tribunals still offer reasoned judgments which allow for both sides to make amendments, for appeals, and for justice to be seen to be done. They provide a means to achieve enforced self-regulation in which social actors devise their own standards and implementation methods subject to public oversight and, frequently, mandatory criteria. The members of industrial relations tribunals tend to draw equally from labour and employers, with an independent chair.

The tribunals envisaged here would be empowered to make consent orders where the parties have reached settlement before hearings, or through the negotiation process facilitated by the tribunal. Where there is no agreement reached between the parties, the tribunal will reach a decision, publish the reasons for the decision on the internet, and make an order. It will be able to enforce or modify existing orders where a dispute is notified to the tribunal. It is envisaged that such a dispute notification will occur when a representative organization fills in a simple form with a brief outline of the matter in dispute, making the tribunals highly accessible.

9.3.4 Incentives for compliance activities

By giving state labour inspectorates the right to recover unpaid remuneration and entitlements from employers and other parties in the supply chain, the Tribunal creates an incentive for state labour inspectorates to be more active in inspecting, collecting evidence and prosecuting both employers and non-employer principals. Where claims have been made against the state in the Global Living Wage Dispute Mechanism, the incentive will be particularly strong, as the state will desire to recover funds already paid to workers. It is hoped that this will assist in overcoming the barriers against action by state inspectorates seen, for example, in the Cambodian case study, where the inspectorate rarely enters the factory floor.

By granting employers and principals the right to contend that the practices of other parties in the supply chain have affected the employer's or contractor's ability to provide a living wage, legal remuneration or related conditions to the worker, an incentive is created for employers and contractors to effectively 'join' other parties to the claim and provide evidence regarding the practices of these parties. Other parties

[107] Interview with Liv Sovanna; interview with Ing Sothy, Arbitrator, Cabodian Arbitration Council, Phnom Penh, 28 March 2014; interview with Ann Vireak; interview with An Nan.

[108] Eric A. Posner and John C. Yoo, 'Judicial Independence in International Tribunals' 93 California Law Review 1; S. Cooney, J. Howe and J. A. Bogdandy, *International Judicial Lawmaking on Public Authority and Democratic Legitimation in Global Governance.* (Springer 2012).

in the supply chain, including buyers, financiers, agents and so on, will then be in the position of defending their practices, and providing contrary evidence.

The Tribunals will also give workers, employers, contractors, other parties in the supply chain and their representatives significant opportunities for participation in remediation and problem-solving processes in relation to supply chain problems. Importantly, the tribunals will operate as forums through which remediation efforts are incorporated into collective bargaining processes.[109] The approach to enforcement proposed here would meld traditional compliance and commitment approaches.[110] The aim would be to foster stability, mutual respect, trust, and even reciprocity, throughout supply chains.

9.3.4.1 Collective agreements

The Tribunal will have the power to approve and assist with negotiations for supply chain collective agreements between buyers, producers and unions. Such agreements may take a form similar to those of the 'jobbers agreements' in the early twentieth century in the USA, or global framework agreements (both discussed above). The content of these collective agreements would be subject to negotiation, and thus would vary in a way that would respond to the national institutional setting, industry and supply chain dynamics in which the dispute and subsequent negotiations took place.[111]

9.3.4.2 Other orders

The Tribunal will be empowered to make a wide range of orders in relation to disputes bought before it in order to reduce or remove remuneration related incentives, pressures and practices that contribute to payment of remuneration that is less than a living wage, breaches of labour laws and unsafe work practices. Such orders can be requested by the parties to the dispute. The idea is that the international instrument would encourage experimentalism, and the ILO would share learning across countries about the benefits of different orders. Three standard orders that could be made include (a) payment of unpaid remuneration, (b) orders for supply chain parties to provide training, and (c) assistance to their suppliers and orders for the implementation of performance standards or industry codes of conduct. Where non-compliance is particularly stark or repeated, the tribunal could order more stringent penalties, such as (d) suspension of intellectual property rights.

9.3.4.3 Payment of unpaid remuneration and entitlements

The Tribunal will make orders for payments of unpaid remuneration and other entitlements to workers or to the state where the state has paid through the Global Living Wage Dispute Mechanism. Based on the evidence presented to it, and its own

[109] Dara O'Rourke, 'Multi-stakeholder Regulation: Privatizing or Socializing Global Labor Standards' 34 World Development 899 910.

[110] R. Locke, M. Amengual, and A. Mangla, 'Virtue out of Necessity? Compliance, Commitment, and the Improvement of Labor Conditions in Global Supply Chains' 37 Politics & Society 319 344.

[111] For an excellent discussion of new developments in collective bargaining beyond the employment relationship see: Mccrystal Shae, 'Collective Bargaining Beyond the Boundaries of Employment: A Comparative Analysis' 37 Melbourne University Law Review 662.

inquiries, it will determine the share to be paid by different parties in the supply chain. If responsibility for non-payment is found to be shared between different parties, for example, by the direct employer/principal and also the buyer, amounts will be apportioned between the parties.

9.3.4.4 *Training and assistance*

Where the evidence suggests that non-payment of proper remuneration is a consequence of the information asymmetries or low-levels of competence of certain parties in the supply chain, tribunals will be able to make orders for supply chain parties such as buyers and financiers to provide training and assistance to suppliers. This will encourage processes of root-cause analysis, joint problem solving, information sharing, and the diffusion of best practices throughout the supply chain.[112] As Locke et al.[113] document:

> [T]here now exists an extensive body of literature on regulatory effectiveness (or lack thereof) in an array of arenas that indicates that companies comply with laws, regulations, and standards not simply because these 'amoral calculators' have been 'deterred' by the threat of sanctioning but instead because many of them have been assisted and/or educated to comply with regulations and standards.

Without such assistance, the tribunal risks rejection by small and medium-sized entities, as seen in the Australian case study where such businesses feel unfairly targeted and burdened by supply chain regulations.

9.3.4.5 *Performance standards and industry codes of conduct*

The tribunal will be empowered to make orders for the implementation of performance standards and industry codes of conduct. Such orders may be the consequence of the tribunal's research activities or may be ordered at the request of parties to a dispute. Such orders will be made where sufficient evidence has been provided that the performance standard or industry code of conduct has produced, or will produce, improved compliance with labour standards through changed practices throughout the supply chain.

9.3.4.6 *Suspension of intellectual property or import licences*

Where breaches are particularly egregious, or parties refuse to adhere to orders, more powerful incentives may be necessary. There is significant evidence that large businesses are frequently willing to write off fines as a cost of doing business. There are also examples of transnational business ignoring court and regulatory orders made in developing countries.[114] As John Braithwaite argues: 'More punishment translates to less crime only at those points on the deterrence curve where deterrence effects exceed defiance effects'.[115] This points to the need to search for new and creative enforcement methods.

[112] Locke, Amengual, and Mangla 321. [113] Ibid. 327.

[114] One of the most high-profile examples is Shell's failure to pay fines ordered by Nigerian regulators. The National Oil Spill Detection and Response Agency imposed a USD $5 billion fine for environmental damage, which Shell refused to pay. The fine was subsequently reduced to $4 billion by the Nigerian parliament. However, Shell still refused to pay. See: Abraham Terngu, 'Nigeria's Parliament Says Shell Should Pay $4 Billion for 2011 Oil Spill' *Reuters* (Abuja, 26 November 2014) http://www.reuters.com/article/2014/11/26/us-nigeria-oil-shell-idUSKCN0JA23Z20141126.

[115] Braithwaite, 'Flipping Markets to Virtue with Qui Tam and Restorative Justice'.

One option is the use of embargos or the suspension of import and export licences. The US 'Hot Goods' provisions demonstrate the impact of using substantial novel penalties, which interrupt the flow of goods, to change business behaviour.[116] An empirical study of the effectiveness of the provisions by Weil and Mallo shows that the global system of apparel distribution and production of apparel is extremely sensitive to supply chain disruptions.[117] The Cambodian Ministry of Commerce has the power to suspend export licences as part of the Better Factories system studied in Chapter 7 of this book. However, the Cambodian Ministry of Commerce appears never to have invoked this power, pointing to a potential fear by governments of wielding such a strong regulatory lever. There may therefore need to be regional or international levels to the enforcement system, as well, in the form of embargos on the import of offending brands by other signatory nations.[118]

Perhaps the most potent penalty for brands, whose greatest value adding comes from brand recognition, would be the temporary or permanent loss of intellectual property including trademarks, copyright, patents, and so on. This idea builds on the work of Professor Peter Drahos, who suggested this idea in general terms in conversation. If Nike, for example, lost its trademark on the 'swoosh' for a fixed period, this would be a very damaging sanction. It is acknowledged that penalties related to intellectual property would not be effective against parties in the supply chain that do not rely on their brand for the success of their business. The suspension of intellectual property posited here provides only one creative example of the way new sanctions need to more effectively target various parties in supply chains.

Such penalties are currently being imposed in other policy areas, so there is no reason for them not to be applied in the field of labour regulation. States, through the World Trade Organisation's dispute resolution panels, have recognized that cross-retaliation based on intellectual property is legitimate. Cross-retaliation is the suspension of concessions in a sector of trade different than the sector in which the trade injury is suffered. A WTO arbitration report in a dispute between the United States and Brazil over US cotton subsidies, for instance, gave Brazil the right to suspend intellectual property obligations.[119]

Intellectual property jurisprudence recognizes that intellectual property is different from other forms of property, designed to serve public policy objectives—not merely the private interests of rights-holders.[120] The granting of intellectual property rights

[116] 29 USC S.215. A suit must be bought by the federal Department of Labor. There is no private right of action: (29 USC S. 217).

[117] Weil and Mallo 809.

[118] This proposal differs from the proposal by Elliott and Freeman, who propose embargoes on nation states Kimberly Ann Elliott and Richard B. Freeman, *Can Labor Standards Improve Under Globalization?* (Institute for International Economics 2003) 136–7. There is a large body of literature that discusses the use of trade sanctions and debate within international organizations. See, for example, Tsogas, who discusses the death of labour clauses in WTO agreements at the 1996 Singapore Ministerial Meeting of the WTO: George Tsogas, *Labor Regulation in a Global Economy* (M.E. Sharpe 2001) 44.

[119] The arbitration arose from a request by Brazil to take countermeasures against the United States for its failure to comply with the rulings of the WTO Dispute Settlement Body in US—Upland Cotton DS267. See Song Guan, 'WTO Retaliation Rules in Subsidy-Related Cases: What Can We Learn from the US-Upland Cotton Arbitration?' 48 Journal of World Trade 815.

[120] See for example, *British American Tobacco Australasia Limited* v *Commonwealth of Australia* [2012] HCA 43 (5 October 2012) in which British American Tobacco and others argued the case against the Tobacco Plain Packaging Act 2011 (Cth). They argued that in effect, the laws extinguish their ability to benefit from statutory intellectual property rights (such as trademarks and copyright images) as well as established goodwill and reputation. A majority of the High Court (Justice Heydon dissenting) rejected these arguments on the basis that there had been no acquisition of property. The judgements stressed that intellectual property law is designed to serve public policy objectives—not merely the private interests of rights-holders. See also the dispute at the World Trade Organisation on

is a form of state recognition of the value of the intellectual content of a good. This value, arguably, includes its ethical integrity. Where such ethical integrity is shown to be tarnished, through the evidence-based system of the tribunals, the state is justified in suspending those rights. States could amend their intellectual property laws to incorporate a way of suspending intellectual property when breaches of living wage rights occur. This would provide a particularly strong sanction at the top of the regulatory pyramid, which ought to increase compliance with more collaborative or softer orders.

9.3.5 Role for the ILO

Here, again, an orchestration role is envisaged for the ILO, contributing to a virtuous cycle of enforcement.

The ILO would play a role in helping to set up tribunals. It would assist with the selection of tribunal members, in a manner similar to that which occurred in the establishment of the Cambodian Arbitration Council. It would also be charged with providing training to Tribunal members following their appointment.

Once a number of Tribunals were running, the ILO would be responsible for collecting and sharing information about the types of orders that have been developed across the tribunals. It would also run training and information sharing on claim-making within the tribunals, for unions and civil society groups with an interest in representing workers. Additional training would be provided for employers and principals on joining other parties to supply-chain claims and the presentation of evidence about the commercial pressures placed on them from buyers and other parties in the supply chain.

The ILO may also have a role in providing specialist evidence in claims where disputes arise over whether the amount paid by a buyer is adequate to allow a supplier to pay living wages to its workers. Miller proposes a method for calculating a 'standard minute value' that can be used in the labour costing of garments. The method measures the time it takes to sew a garment and calculates the labour cost based on minimum wages.[121]

9.4 Third Pathway: Local Bridges out of Informality

Local bridges out of informality are also required for precarious workers. Not all of the informal workers examined in this study were linked to international supply chains. Own-account informal workers in Bulgaria often produce only for domestic markets, for example. Even for those who were linked to international supply chains in some way, the causes of their informality often had local as well as international dimensions. Another example is drawn from the Mathadi workers in India, who load and unload international goods. The factors that contributed most to the informality of this group of workers, however, seemed to be primarily local.

It is the contention of this study that domestic strategies should follow from the type of analysis conducted in the case study chapters, as opposed to choosing from a 'drop-down menu' of approaches to mitigating informality. Local strategies need to respond to the particular histories and political economy dynamics that produce and entrench

this matter, WTO, *Australia — Certain Measures Concerning Trademarks and Other Plain Packaging Requirements Applicable to Tobacco Products and Packaging: Dispute DS434* (2014).

[121] Doug; Miller, *Regulating the 'Wage Effort Bargain' in Outsourced Apparel Production: Towards a Model* (Palgrave Macmillian 2014) 122.

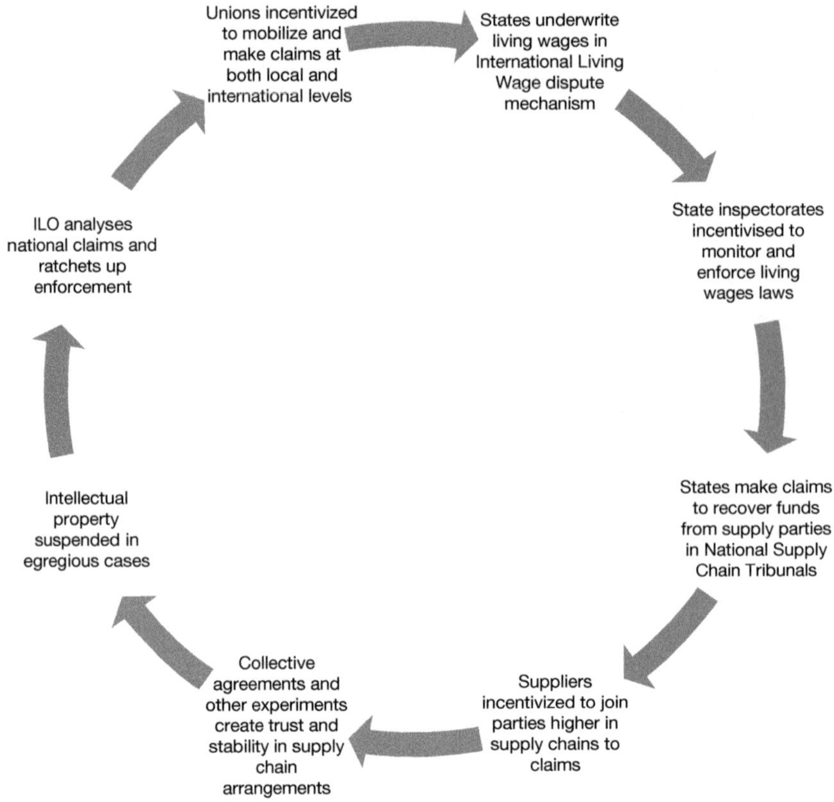

Figure 9.4 Virtuous circles of enforcement and international orchestration

inequality and informality. For example, the trauma identified as a cause of Vietnamese refugees becoming trapped in informal, home-based work in the chapter on Australia can only be identified through population specific studies.

Nonetheless, the range of local bridges out of informality which have been experimented with world-wide provide useful lessons for policy makers searching for new policies and strategies. This section briefly mentions a few important strategies. Local pathways are well developed in policy documents such as the ILO's 'Transitioning from the informal to the formal economy',[122] which articulates domestic strategies, and thus are not the focus of this chapter.

9.4.1 Decoupling labour rights such as social insurance from employment status

The case studies presented here provide useful models for extending definitions of 'employee' or decoupling labour rights from employment status. There are many proposals for the decoupling of labour rights from employment status that are too numerous to discuss in detail here.[123] Instead, the aim has been to observe examples in practice.

[122] ILO, *Transitioning from the informal to the formal economy*.

[123] L. F. Vosko, '"Decent Work": The Shifting Role of the ILO and the Struggle for Global Social Justice' 2 Global Social Policy 19; A. Trebilcock, 'Using Development Approaches to Address the

The provision of social protections, including pensions and social safety nets through welfare boards and means other than as a condition of employment is an important development.[124] There is a growing body of literature that demonstrates the importance of social insurance in reducing informality.[125]

9.4.2 Mobilization

The case studies suggest that a first, vital step is to foster the capacity of local worker organizations to mobilize and organize workers for the improvement of labour standards.[126] Unions cannot rely on the methods developed in Fordist settings. It is hoped that the proposals canvassed here will increase incentives for unions and other worker organizations to monitor and organize informal work.

9.4.3 Control of the supply of labour

Two interrelated causes of informality are the oversupply of labour and the lack of training and support provided to informal workers. Several countries have seen the emergence of workers' cooperatives as a means of supplying labour and providing training.[127] In Colombia, for example, workers join workers' cooperatives to produce goods or perform work or services.[128] The Mathadi boards examined in the chapter on India also show that associations of workers were a prerequisite to the effective functioning of these tripartite boards which act as a monopoly on the supply of this category of labour.[129] The limitation of this strategy is that it only assists a small subset of informal workers.

Challenge of the Informal Economy for Labour Law' in G. Davidov and B. Langille (eds), *Boundaries and Frontiers of Labour Law: Goals and Means in the Regulation of Work* (Hart 2006); H. Arthurs 'What Immortal Hand or Eye? Who Will Redraw the Boundaries of Labour Law?' in G. Davidov and B. Langille (eds), *Boundaries and Frontiers of Labour Law: Goals and Means in the Regulation of Work* (Hart 2006).

[124] Katherine V. W. Stone, 'Legal Protections for Atypical Employees: Employment Law for Workers without Workplaces and Employees without Employers' 27 Berkeley Journal of Employment & Labor Law 251; Participant Observation: 'Homebased Workers Struggle: Formalization for Informal Workers, New Strength to Labour Movement' thematic workshop, Clean Clothes Campaign Global Forum 2014, Hong Kong, 20 November 2014; Naci Gundogan, *Can Denmark's Flexicurity System Be Replicated in Developing Countries? The Case of Turkey* (Anadolu University 2009); Maria Sabrina De Gobbi, *Flexibility and Security in Labour Markets of Developing Countries: In Search of Decent Work for All* (Employment Policy Papers, 2007); Paul Vandenberg, *Is Asia Adopting Flexicurity? A Survey of Employment Policies in Six Countries* (Economic and Labour Market Papers, 2008).

[125] See, in particular, the edited volume that reviews social protection policies in countries with a large informal sector Markus Frölich and others (eds), *Social Insurance, Informality, and Labor Markets: How to Protect Workers While Creating Good Jobs* (Oxford University Press 2014) and the series on gender, social insurance, and informal work which can be found at https://www.odi.org/publications/10407-extending-social-insurance-informal-workers-gender-analysis, accessed 3 August 2016.

[126] Sabel, O'Rourke, and Fung: 31; Ursula Huws, *Action Programmes for the Protection of Homeworkers: Ten Case Studies from Around the World* (International Labour Office 1995); Burchielli and others; Bijal Raval and SEWA Academy Research Team, *Multiple Work Status of Women in the Informal Economy* (SEWA 2001).

[127] Participant Observation: 'Worker Cooperatives in Action' thematic workshop, Clean Clothes Campaign Global Forum 2014, Hong Kong, 19 November 2014 (2014); Clarence G. Pascual Subregional Office for South-East Asia and the Pacific, *Social and Economic Empowerment of Women in the Informal Economy: Impact Case Study of Sikap Buhay* (ILO 2008).

[128] However, the ILO notes that there have been reports that this system has given rise to fraudulent employment relationships, which have attracted penalties. In Colombia, news reports referred to an investigation involving 200 workers cooperatives, which found that 'some temporary work agencies were operating under the guise of cooperatives in order to evade tax and social security contributions': ILO, *The Employment Relationship, Report V(I) 44.*

[129] K. Sankaran, 'Protecting the Worker in the Informal Economy: The Role of Labour Law', in Judy Fudge, Shae McCrystal and Kamala Sankaran (eds), *Challenging the Legal Boundares of Work Regulation* (Hart 2012).

9.4.4 Land reform

The Indian example studied shows the importance of land reform for stopping or reducing the 'circulation of labour' described in the chapters on India and Cambodia—whereby workers leave the country-side and flood cities in search of work, contributing to oversupply and vulnerability.[130]

9.5.5 Insurance and tax incentives

Various temporary incentives can be used to shift enterprises from informality to formality and encourage formal employment. One example is provided by the Shanghai Municipal Government. In 1996, the Shanghai Municipal Government introduced a policy and regulatory regime to facilitate the development of the informal economy as a means of providing employment for unemployed workers.[131] The policy encourages individuals to establish individual ventures or small firms in certain types of activities. The enterprises established under the policy are called 'informal labour organisations'. The Shanghai Labour Bureau encourages these 'informal labour organisations' to develop to a point where they can register with authorities and transfer to the formal economy.

Some of the preferential policies enjoyed by 'informal labour organisations' include:

- Social insurance (employers and employees pay a lower base rate and lower contributions)
- Free training opportunities
- An exemption from local taxes for a period of three years. This exemption continues to apply to enterprise that have converted during the three-year period into registered individual households or small enterprises
- Support for credit
- The subsidy and employment of informal labour organizations that provide public works
- Risk insurance and
- Voluntary provision of advice and assistance by experts.

By September 2001, a survey by the Shanghai Bureau of Labour and Social Security of 500 'informal labour organisations' found that 25 per cent of such entities had entered the formal economy.[132] This points to the importance that incentives are temporary and show clear evidence of transitions from informality to formality.

9.5 A Defence of the Proposal

The author acknowledges that the proposal canvassed here is bold, and is likely to take a number of decades to bring to fruition. Part of the proposal is a practical path to

[130] Peter Peek and others, *State Policies and Migration: Studies in Latin America and the Caribbean* (Croom Helm 1982); J. Breman, Outcast Labor in Asia: Circulation and Informalization of the Workforce at the Bottom of the Economy (Oxford University Press, New Delhi 2010).

[131] Jude Howell, *Good Practice Study in Shanghai on Employment Services for the Informal Economy* (China, 2002).

[132] Ibid. 13.

building social movement momentum towards the gradual construction of reforms. Specific objections to the feasibility of the vision have been briefly addressed in the course of this chapter. The following broad additional defences are made to objections that are likely to be raised in relation to the proposal:

Sceptics might argue that the approach recommended here marks a significant digression from current arrangements. In response, this chapter has shown that the vision is consistent with the direction of the explosion of non-state, co-regulation and state-based initiatives aimed at regulating social harm within supply chains. The proliferation of initiatives of particular types suggests a growing shared understanding of transnational labour standards and to a common discourse around it.[133] The simple growth of the system must be explained by some sort of function, whether the declared ones, tacit ones, or even unintentional ones.[134] It is for this reason that the proposals in this chapter have taken, as their departure point, trends emerging in the experimental field of soft law and New Governance initiatives.

Indeed, there are many components of the network of regulations in place. The ILO is already experimenting with transnational regulation and monitoring through its Better Factories Cambodia and Better Work projects. It has been searching for international relevance, and this would provide it. Transnational deployment amongst unions searching for a way to improve work across nations is growing. Worker organizations with the capacity to organize and mobilize informal workers are developing. A campaign for international living wages is already underway. National industrial relations tribunals exist in many or most countries around the world. The model for the supply chain tribunal is an existing tribunal in Australia with authority to regulate the entire chain of transport—the Road Safety Tribunal and language used by the Road Safety Remuneration Act 2012 (*Cth*)—which enjoys a strong reputation and support across the industry. The crucial thing is to coordinate the network that is already in place and bolster its functioning so as to create a virtuous cycle of incentives and enforcement.

A second objection may be that the proposal, by allowing for claims against states for living wages, is against state interests, and therefore states are unlikely to support the creation of a binding international instrument, such as a treaty. Why would they support a mechanism that allows for claims to be made against them? This realist argument has merit. However, the process outlined offers a means to muffle the strength of this argument by allowing states to recover any funds paid from business in national supply chain tribunals. Thus, while the proposal does require deeper engagement by state parties, the distribution of risk does not fall wholly on the state. Increasing numbers of states are showing an interest in finding new ways to bring transnational business to account for breaches of human rights within their borders. There may be those amongst them, who, under sufficient domestic and international pressure, would take the lead in developing a framework agreement for a treaty of the type envisaged in this chapter. The strongest indication of this is UN Human Rights Council resolution (A/HRC/26/L.22), drafted by Ecuador and South Africa, establishing an open-ended intergovernmental working group on a legally binding instrument on transnational corporations and other business enterprises with respect to human rights. The resolution was supported by China and India, amongst the twenty countries that voted for the resolution. If these powerful BRICS could be convinced that a mechanism of this type was practically feasible, and in their interests, it may have legs. In a conversation

[133] Meardi and Marginson 656. [134] Ibid. 656.

with South African Human Rights Commissioner Janet Love, she suggested that South Africa's willingness to push for a treaty was driven by the fact that its constitution places direct positive duties on corporations to uphold human rights. Current international practices therefore lag behind South Africa's.[135]

An additional defence against this objection is the fact that the Global Living Wage Dispute Mechanism has a parallel in the world of state-investor relations, where claims can be made by investors against states. Over the last decade there has been a massive increase in cases of investor–state dispute settlement under arrangements that provide foreign investors with considerable legal protection and access to international arbitration. As of the end of 2013, the total number of known cases was 568. By then, 98 countries had responded to one or more claim.[136] One example is the dispute that arose after Australia introduced legislation in 2011 that requires that all tobacco products be sold in plain brown packaging. Health warnings would still be included on cigarette packets, but logos would disappear. Several companies unsuccessfully challenged the legislation as an expropriation of their intellectual property in Australia's High Court. Philip Morris International then pursued arbitration under a bilateral trade agreement between Hong Kong and Australia which provided for investor-state arbitration. The company was familiar with these processes, having already launched a dispute against Uruguay for similar tobacco packaging requirements.

From a normative perspective it could be argued that if investors can make claims of this type against states, then why not labour? The fact that investors—who are likely to oppose the development of labour–state dispute settlement mechanisms—already reap the benefit of its own analogue may render objections of this type less legitimate. From a political economy perspective, there is no doubt that the rise of claims by business in investor-state dispute settlement procedures is evidence of the increasing strength of capital vis a vis the state. Nonetheless, these claims do give rise to new potential normative claims by labour for similar procedures.

The primary, overall defence of the proposal is the impetus for its creation. This is primarily a normative and justice-based argument. Inequality is rising and precarious work is growing. This is unacceptable. It is hard, under current conditions, to reduce inequality, informality, and poverty in single countries. It is a hazardous undertaking for states to raise wages in light of the risk that certain kinds of production will move to lower labour unit cost countries. Economies are so interlinked that globally orchestrated solutions to these grave social problems are required.

9.6 Conclusion

This chapter has pitched a novel, multi-level regulatory scheme for tackling inequality and reducing informality. The scheme bridges governance gaps at the national and international levels in relation to breaches of labour-related human rights. This chapter contends that the proliferation of supply chains is not an insurmountable policy challenge. Rather, the case studies show that opportunities already exist to adopt the best aspects of past regulatory frameworks and combine these with chain of responsibility

[135] Participant observation: conversation with South African Human Rights Commissioner, Janet Love, Oxfam Melbourne, 6 February 2015.

[136] UN Conference on Trade and Development, *Recent Developments in Investor-State Dispute Settlement (ISDS)* (2014) 1.

innovations that regulate beyond the traditional employment relationship, in order to provide better outcomes for supply chain labour.[137]

The scheme canvassed here builds on the innovations of the four initiatives studied, as well as the ever-expanding number of soft and New Governance initiatives worldwide, mining the insights they provide into how to produce institutional change. The Global Living Wage Dispute Mechanism provides a way to reduce inequality and promote higher remuneration for the poorest workers, at the same time as minimizing the risk of capital flight as this occurs. Importantly, it provides incentives for national labour inspectorates to become more active in pursuing higher remuneration for poor workers, thereby facilitating institutional reform and the national level. The National Supply Chain Tribunals offer a means to redress downwards pressure within supply chains—something national institutions are currently failing to do. This is a major gap in the current regulatory environment, given the scale and severity of problems caused by supply chain dynamics for working conditions. The Tribunals posited here are designed in such a way as to allow sensitivity to the structural standing of different parties in the supply chain, recognize the separation of control and ownership, be responsive to the nature of influence and control wielded by different parties, and bridge asymmetries in information and trust between parties. They are institutions of enforced self-regulation, based on internationally and nationally agreed minima.

The deployment of new penalties and incentives is crucial to the success of this scheme. The scale of the problem and the extent of social harm caused by informality calls for maximum strength regulatory levers. The imposition of fines has been shown to be a weak disincentive against non-compliance with laws for transnational business. Sometimes, creative enforcement methods are right under our noses. The suspension of intellectual property is proposed as the sanction at the top of the enforcement pyramid. This sanction takes aim at the most vulnerable area for brands. Its strength should increase compliance with other types of orders, contributing to a virtuous cycle of compliance at the heart of the design of this novel regulatory initiative.

It is hoped that by creating a form of networked regulation, drawing in expertise of several kinds, offering concrete operational capacities (including resources) and acting independently from the targets of regulation,[138] these new mechanisms will provide strong pathways out of informality and towards high labour conditions for vulnerable workers. Ultimately, however, their prospect for success depends on the extent of mobilization of workers and their allies in utilizing them, and the beneficence of forward-thinking industry leaders in seeing them as opportunities for reducing governance risks and promoting greater cooperation within supply chains.[139]

[137] Rawling and Kaine 257.
[138] Abbott and Sindal 549.
[139] Anner, Bair, and Blasi 42–3.

10

Conclusions

10.1 Introduction

The realities of work today require a re-conceptualization of labour regulation. Labour law is failing millions of workers around the world. According to the most recent estimates, non-agricultural work in the informal economy represents 82 per cent of total employment in South Asia, 66 per cent in sub-Saharan Africa, 65 per cent in East and South-East Asia (excluding China), 51 per cent in Latin America, and 10 per cent in Eastern Europe and Central Asia.[1] It was a main source of support for many affected by the Global Financial Crisis of 2008.[2]

The case studies outlined in this book have explored the ways that vast economic transformation and globalisation created new conditions that impede the realization of labour standards that evolved throughout the nineteenth and twentieth centuries within the frameworks of nation states.[3] Four case studies of informal work were conducted in this book, using a historical institutionalist approach to studying changes in the context in which labour regulation has occurred over time. Spanning poor, middle income and developed countries, the cases studied load-carrying (Mathadi) workers in India, immigrant industrial clothing outworkers in Australia, garment workers in Cambodia, and workers in Bulgaria who rely on a range of home-based work to survive. The cases were selected for their insights into the causes of informality and because innovative regulations have been developed to improve the conditions of the workers in each country. The book has compared these advances in the regulation of work, asking what can be learned for purposeful institutional change elsewhere in the world.

Since the 1970s international organizations have been grappling with the problem of informal work, recommending different remedies in keeping with policy trends of the time. The focus was mainly on the economic South until the US financial crisis when precarious and unregulated work increased dramatically in the North. Informal work was a major focus for the ILO in 2014 and 2015 with its chief governing body dedicating two sessions (103rd and 104th sessions of the Conference) to the question of how to bring workers under the scope of formal regulations and improve working conditions. Despite bountiful evidence concerning the 'governance gap'[4] and the

[1] International Labour Organization and WIEGO, *ILO: Women and Men in the Informal Economy: A Statistical Picture* (2018).

[2] R. Torres, *World of Work Report 2009: The Global Jobs Crisis and Beyond* (ILO 2009).

[3] Yossi Dahan, Hanna Lerner, and Faina Milman-Sivan, *Global Justice and International Labour Rights* (Cambridge University Press 2016) 4.

[4] G. Davidov and Brian Langille, 'What is International Labour Law For?' 3 Law and Ethics of Human Rights 47; Brian Langille, 'Putting International Labour Law on the (Right) Map' in Adelle Blackette and Christian Levesque (eds), *Social Regionalism in a Global Economy* (Routledge 2011); Adelle Blackette, 'Situated Reflections of International Labour Law, Capabilities, and Decent Work: The Case of Centre Maraicher Eugene Guinois' Revue Quebecoise de Droit International 223; Judy Fudge, 'The New Discourse of Labour Rights: From Social to Fundamental Rights' 29 Comparative Labour Law and Policy Journal 29.

'deterritoralisation of labour law',[5] recommendations made by ILO were primarily national in scope. Yet, the studies conducted in this book have found that many of the causes of informality are transnational in scope. As a consequence, even if the policies recommended are efficiently implemented, they are unlikely to address the growing problem of precarious work. In 2016, at its 105th session, the International Labour Conference again had the opportunity to consider the re-territorialization of labour law when it considered supply chains.[6] On this occasion, the decision was to 'review this issue and convene, as soon as appropriate'.[7] The question of how to regulate work in light of its evolution is likely to continue to weigh on the ILO for many years to come unless it formulates new approaches.

This book has canvassed a new initiative that aims to promote a global living wage and regulate supply chains. The proposal includes the establishment of an international disputes mechanism for enforcement of global wage minima, combined with tribunals that operate at national levels that are empowered to hold parties in the supply chain accountable. The approach suggests novel tools and incentives for unions and state labour departments to become more active in mobilizing and regulating this precarious workforce, and for businesses to change their behaviour. It is hoped that this proposal will inform future debates about the regulation of work that occurs within the ILO and elsewhere.

10.2 Overlapping Dynamics of Informalization

Before suggesting a new way to regulate transnational work, this book sought to understand why informality has persisted despite economic development in many countries. Historical institutionalism was selected as the primary method for the empirical study presented in this book as it pays attention to the ways in which institutions structure and shape political behaviour and outcomes over time. This book employed this approach to studying changes in the *context* in which labour regulations operate, changes to *labour regulation* itself, and changes in the *nature of work* in each case study country. A broad account of the factors that have put pressure on or changed the nature of the labour market in each case was made possible by this approach.

By deploying a historical institutionalist approach, this study has shown that the dynamics that shape the lives of informal workers today are structural consequences of decisions and aggregate local and international economic processes beginning a number of decades ago, and possibly far further back in history. Persons stand in systematically different and unequal social positions due to the way institutions operate together.[8] Rather than being a static condition, the factors that constrain and enable individual possibilities are ongoing processes in which many actors participate.

[5] Guy Mundlak, 'De-Territorializing Labor Law' 3 Law and Ethics of Human Rights 189.

[6] International Labour Office, *Decent Work in Global Supply Chains: Report to the International Labour Conference, 105th Session, 2016.*

[7] International Labor Conference, *Provisional record, Fourth item on the agenda: Decent work in global supply chains, Reports of the Committee on Decent Work in Global Supply Chains: Resolution and conclusions submitted for adoption by the Conference, 105th Session, Geneva, May–June 2016* (2016).

[8] Marion Young 114.

There are a number of causes of informality, which more than one of the case studies have in common. These can be identified in short hand as follows:

1. Mass migration or circulation of labour within countries and between countries
2. Large scale macro-economic and institutional liberalization
3. Integration of previously separate economic systems as socialist and capitalist systems were combined following the fall of the Eastern bloc and the opening to global trade
4. New organization of production resulting in the vertical disintegration of productive units (firms) and the expansion of supply chains
5. The explosion of new, non-employment forms of work
6. Complexity and scale of production outstripping national labour regulation systems
7. Lack of transnational orchestration in labour regulation results in gaps in the scale of labour regulation.

The case studies explored how populations' experience of these dynamics varied based on the mediation of these forces by local institutions and cultures. And yet, similar dynamics were found to be at play across the cases. This chapter explores these common dynamics in further detail.

10.2.1 Mass migration and circulation of labour

The mass upheaval and circulation of workers was a prominent feature of informality in all cases studied. In the Indian and Cambodian cases, internal circulation was, in the earlier periods of the studies, caused by colonial land and taxation laws that expelled populaces from their land. Having little or no land to cultivate, people become redundant in primary production and were converted into a huge reserve army of labour. Subsequent upheaval of the population in Cambodia was caused by civil war. Later, the dynamics of industrialization caused further internal migration in both countries. In the case of Australian outworkers, Vietnamese emigrants were driven by poverty, political oppression under socialist rule, and civil war to leave their home country, arriving as refugees in Australia. The years spent in refugee camps shaped their capacity to take up employment once they finally reached Australia.

These internal and international migrants failed to become absorbed in steady, permanent employment, creating a precariat class.[9] The populations of workers studied became stuck in informal work with low wages, payment by piece rate or job work, insecure work, erratic working hours, no written labour contracts, and an absence of institutional representation.[10] Because of the difficulties of finding steady employment, this migrant labour often remained unsettled. Mathadi workers circulated back to their villages. In the case of India, this circulation is encouraged by labour laws which sought to maintain the links of migrant workers with their villages so as to avoid burdening the social security system. Young, female Cambodian garment workers also return to their villages to marry and raise children. These case studies observed the continual

[9] Standing, *The Precariat: The New Dangerous Class*.

[10] J. Breman, *Outcast Labor in Asia: Circulation and Informalization of the Workforce at the Bottom of the Economy* (OUP 2010) 2.

circulation, rather than the permanent outmigration, of workers from the countryside, to cities, and back to the country-side.

Further, the informal economy has not been shown to have an infinite capacity to absorb surplus workers. Migrant workers often find themselves crowded out of the job markets with which they are familiar, forced to re-circulate and search for work elsewhere. Though circulation may not have caused informality in Bulgaria it was still present as a dynamic. Workers hoped to find new sources of earnings by traveling to other parts of the European Union in search of work. Lack of opportunities for work in Bulgaria today finds more Bulgarians working abroad than in Bulgaria.[11] Conditions of insecurity have left these workers in a state where they are continually in search of new prospects for income generation and in a constant state of vigilance, with little assistance and poor information about opportunities. Migration caused by global warming and extreme weather events is likely to result in higher numbers of informal workers in future years.

10.2.2 Large scale macro-economic and institutional liberalization of economies

A further dynamic driving the informalization of work evident across all of the case studies was the large-scale macro-economic and institutional liberalization of economies which took place across the world in the 1980s and 1990s. There was trend towards the disbanding of collective institutions designed to facilitate price coordination, privatization of state-owned companies, accompanied by broader processes of both price liberalization and trade liberalization. Such changes were facilitated by the design of regional and international level policy regimes and institutions in which global production and trading relations (and associated investment regimes) are constituted. Liberalization of labour regulation also occurred across many countries. Indeed, as Adams and Deakin observe, the trend towards increased non-standard work, particularly as embodied in precarious forms of work, has been exacerbated by 'conscious policy choices that have privileged casualization, wage suppression, and the fiscalization of employment over the promotion of stable work and a living wage'.[12]

The effects of liberalization were most stark in the Bulgarian case, where the transition from state socialism to capitalism catapulted the working population from full employment to entrepreneurism and informality. It exposed its citizens to great market instability seen in hyperinflation and the eventual loss of over 50 per cent of citizen's savings. Though not on the same scale or with the same impact across the entire population, Australia undertook a programme of liberalization over a similar period that included the floating of currency and the reduction of tariffs and non-tariff protections amongst a suite of other measures. Trade protections had not just acted as an element of industrial policy to that point, they had very explicitly been part of the arsenal of labour protections aimed at providing job security and boosting domestic employment. Those most exposed to liberalization experienced the end of this employment security. Workers who were unable for various reasons to take up the opportunities of structural adjustment and employment programmes—such as

[11] Sofia News Agency (anon), 'More Bulgarians Working Abroad Than in Bulgaria' (Sofia 6 November 2015) http://www.novinite.com/articles/171684/More+Bulgarians+Working+Abroad+Than+in+Bulgaria accessed 15 January 2018.

[12] Zoe Adams and Simon Deakin, 'Institutional Solutions to Precariousness and Inequality in Labour Markets' 52 British Journal of Industrial Relations 779, 780.

the new Vietnamese immigrants studied in the case study in this book—were left stranded in this state of insecurity.

10.2.3 Integration of previously separate economic systems

This liberalization of economies, and the fall of the Eastern bloc, resulted in the integration of economic systems on a scale not previously witnessed. Prior to this integration, Eastern bloc countries had primarily traded amongst themselves, for instance. There was some trading with countries external to the bloc, but the rules of the Council for Mutual Economic Assistance guided the countries towards highly specified internal trade. After the transition to capitalism, these countries opened themselves to investment and trade with countries across the world, competing for trade access. The case studies of Bulgaria and Cambodia document the types of trade deals made, and the way that these agreements influenced the economy and the nature of work. Bulgaria's integration was shaped by the multilateral Europe Agreements, amongst others, while Cambodia's was greatly influenced by bilateral agreements such as the US-Cambodia Bilateral Textile Agreement. These agreements created preferential arrangements for the more powerful parties to the agreements, and encouraged further liberalization. Though the US–Cambodia Bilateral Textile Agreement included a labour clause which put in train the creation of Better Factories Cambodia, in return for quotas, Cambodia agreed to reduce tariffs on its apparel and textile imports, and not to exercise non-tariff restrictions, such as import licensing. This restricted the use of industrial policy and techniques for upgrading which might have assisted with the promotion of higher wage employment and increased job quality.

Both countries entered the global economy with the rest of the Eastern bloc and much of Asia, and at a time when the global rules of trade were encouraging the greater integration of economies across the globe. The merger of economic systems that were once largely separate produced a global oversupply of labour without a significant increase in the global stock of capital.[13] Capital-poor transition countries competed for a share of existing global investment, offering favourable terms to attract finance. Not all investment is created equally. While some capital, supported by supportive institutional frameworks, encouraged high value-added production, investment in Cambodia and Bulgaria was concentrated in low value-added areas. For the garment industry, both countries saw their production reduced to the cut, make and trim or outward processing sector of the industries, where competition on the basis of low unit labour costs is highest. This promoted flexibilization and put great pressure on wages, fostering informality.

The availability of this new pool of cheap labour for countries like Australia encouraged the outsourcing of production to cheaper production countries. Australian manufacturers saw their orders drop markedly, with enterprise after enterprise folding or adapting by outsourcing work to informal home-based outworkers.

10.2.4 New organization of production

As a consequence of the large scale macro-economic reform and integration of economies during this period, production of apparel and textiles, toys, footwear, home electronics, and other consumer goods destined primarily for consumer markets in

[13] Polaski.

the industrialized world spread throughout the world, with manufacturing tending to cluster in a range of developing countries.[14] Cambodia, for example, was a major beneficiary of the relocation of garment production.

Businesses in industrialized countries vertically disintegrated: that is, large, multi-function corporations broke up into smaller units. The outsourcing of production, or vertical disintegration, occurred in a significant number of industries, as producers recognized that they could not themselves maintain cutting-edge technology in every field required for the success of their product.[15] Businesses sought the benefits of lowering overheads and cheaper labour by passing risks and costs onto others in the supply chain. Complex and lengthy supply chains emerged, with risk being passed down the chains to workers, further exacerbating informal conditions.

10.2.5 Explosion of new forms of work

As competitive pressures were passed down supply chains, the size of the 'precariat' class swelled.[16] To survive, these workers had to be immensely flexible. The workers studied in Bulgaria were continually on the lookout for new sources of income. They performed a wide range of odd jobs, sometimes self-employed, sometimes engaged in waged labour, sometimes a blurry combination of both. The necessity not to specialize in one occupation, but rather to pursue a range of diverse activities, flows from a shortage of work and from the seasonal fluctuations which are inherent to the informal economy.[17] Industrial outwork in the clothing industry, for example, comes in spurts, associated with fashion seasons. Cessation of production in countries such as Bulgaria and Cambodia is also caused by a shortage in raw materials, cuts in the electricity supply, or lack of availability of transport.

Though self-employment is described, in a large part of the literature, as the backbone of the informal economy,[18] many workers of this type are either conducting camouflaged or open forms of waged labour. There is no reason to describe waged labour as a phenomenon that is bound to the formal sector based on the work observed in the case studies. Waged labour does not always take the form of an unequivocal and direct employer–employee relationship, however. There are different intermediaries—those who provide raw materials and then collect semi-finished or finished products from home-based industrial workers in the Australian study, or the middle people who recruit and supervise Mathadi workers, who function as agents for the eventual labour users.

The workers in all case studies had in common that they carry a high burden of risk in production. They need to remain available for as long as there is a need for their labour, into the evening and night. Overtime pay has been a big issue for Cambodian garment workers since the late 1990s. Australian industrial outworkers frequently work through the night to finish a job, pausing in the morning to feed their children breakfast. These

[14] Richard Appelbaum, 'Giant Retailers and Giant Contractors in China: Emergent Trends in Global Supply Chains' 9–11 March 2006, working paper prepared for Princeton University Conference, Observing Trade: Revealing International Trade Networks; Hugh Collins, 'Independent Contractors and the Challenge of Vertical Disintegration to Employment Protection Laws' 10 Oxford Journal of Legal Studies 353.

[15] Ronald Gilson, Charles Sabel, and Robert Scott, 'Contracting for Innovation: Vertical Disintegration and Interfirm Collaboration' 109 Columbia Law Review.

[16] Standing, *The Precariat: The New Dangerous Class 969*.

[17] Breman 218.

[18] Keith Hart, 'Informal Income Opportunities and Urban Unemployment in Ghana' March Journal of Modern African Studies 66–70.

periods of overemployment are often followed by periods of unemployment for all except the Cambodian workers studied this book. When there is little or no work for hours, days or seasons, the workers studied in Australia, Bulgaria and India receive no continued payment or compensation.

The characteristics of working relations observed in the case studies indicate that it is more accurate to describe the workforce as fragmented rather than dualist. The world of work cannot be divided into formal and informal sections. The research conducted for this book suggests a more graduated and varied model that draws attention to the enormous diversity of work conditions within both the formal and informal economies.

10.2.6 The complexity and scale of production outstrips national labour regulation systems

State capacity has been weakened by the increasing complexity and informality associated with post-Fordist processes of capitalist development.[19] Such increasing complexity and informality operate to make regulation ever more difficult in large part because the organization of production has simply become more complicated. The broad trend towards vertical disintegration has resulted in: (a) a proliferation of corporate forms and relations; and (b) a proliferation of people who would previously have been employed inside a firm being engaged in alternative ways. Workers performing the same tasks might be engaged as casual workers, dependent contractors, independent contractors, and employees or contractors of labour hire agencies.[20] The same work might be conducted in a factory or in a home. Labour relations have become far more convoluted.

The structuring of supply chains in organizationally complex and pluralized ways can make it very difficult for state-based regulators to *identify a clear locus of power and control*, and thus to determine appropriate regulatory subjects and agents. Who should be held responsible for the poor conditions of workers, when so many parties are involved in passing work down the supply chain? Where production occurs in transnational, integrated supply chains, control is wielded in a diffuse, multipolar manner. These changes have created problems for labour law, which has increasing difficulty in defining an 'employer' and an 'employee'; yet these remain the parties between whom the bilateral employment relationship is assumed to have taken place.[21] Without the changes in the scope of regulation of work of the type seen in the regulatory innovations studied in this book, increasing numbers of workers will be left outside the reach of labour regulation and the social protections and welfare benefits which are most often attached to this legal relationship.

In addition, the scale of production across and between countries has outstripped the scale of state-based labour regulation. It is increasingly difficult for national regulations to deal with increased cross-border movement of labour and services and with multinational companies.[22] According to UN Special Representative for Business and Human Rights, John Ruggie:[23]

[19] David Harvey, *The Condition of Post-Modernity: An Enquiry into the Origins of Cultural Change* (Blackwell 1990).

[20] Marshall. [21] ILO, *The Employment Relationship, Report V(I)*.

[22] Meardi and Marginson 655.

[23] Ruggie, *Promotion and Protection of All Human Rights, Civil, Political, Economic, Social and Cultural Rights, Including the Right to Development: Protect, Respect and Remedy: a Framework for Business and Human Rights. Report of the Special Representative of the Secretary-General on the issue of human rights and transnational corporations and other business enterprises, John Ruggie.*

The root cause of the business and human rights predicament today lies in the governance gaps created by globalization - between the scope and impact of economic forces and actors, and the capacity of societies to manage their adverse consequences. These governance gaps provide the permissive environment for wrongful acts by companies of all kinds without adequate sanctioning or reparation.

10.2.7 Lack of transnational orchestration

Though production has globalized, there is an absence of an international authority with the power to steer and coordinate regulation across states. The international system lacks a central 'state'.[24] The ILO plays an important role in setting standards and reporting on the application of these standards in member states. However, the ILO cannot enforce any sanctions against countries that fail to implement and enforce labour standards. Though institutions that orchestrate, enforce, and hear disputes concerning the application of transnational regulation exist in other areas, no such institution exists in the area of the regulation of work.

10.3 The Impetus for a New International Labour Law

The dynamics identified across the cases that have caused and exacerbated informality, summarized in this chapter, provide a strong impetus for the type of initiative proposed in the previous chapter. The strength and scale of these dynamics implies that there is little chance that precarious work will be replaced by decent and dignified work without strong regulatory intervention. There are two main reasons for this. First, the fact that informality remains a stable feature of labour markets across much of the developing world defies the idea that economic transformation in the Economic South is essentially a delayed repetition of the processes of industrialization and urbanization that laid the foundations for the Western welfare state in the early twentieth century. The standard account of economic development—often attributed to Simon Kuznets—has inequality rising during the early stages of industrialization but then falling steadily as incomes converge and over-all living standards rise.[25] No convergence of incomes—or greater equality—is evident across many developing countries where precarious work is prevalent. A convergence is not arising from market dynamics, nor is it being encouraged by the embedding of markets in social regulation which would encourage the redistribution of wealth. Workers in the Economic South have never enjoyed a 'New Deal', and there is no sign of one on its way. Second, the prevalence of informality in the Economic North indicates that the forms used to harness the capitalism of old no long work. The great social pacts of the twentieth century are dead. Why? Because the dynamics of capital accumulation have changed.

What is called for, then, is a new international labour law which responds to these new dynamics and promotes a global living wage. The new system described in the previous chapter has a number of important features:

1. It overcomes important limitations in labour law by establishing enforceable rights to minimum pay regardless of employment status AND providing rights and obligations against non-employer parties in supply chains

[24] Abbott and Sindal 553.

[25] Simon Kuznets, 'Economic Growth and Income Inequality' XLV The American Economic Review 1.

2. It induces developing and developed countries alike to raise minimum wages to living wage levels and enforce labour laws
3. It moves countries towards a global average minimum wage, based on purchasing power parity
4. It fosters a renewed role for the ILO as an orchestrator of this system of regulation
5. It provide incentives for trade unions to mobilize and monitor the conditions of precarious, peripheral workers, facilitating the reinvention of the union movement as a movement for representation of the precariat and a progressive force for all workers
6. It provides incentives for states to monitor and enforce minimum wage laws, and punishes those states that are particularly corrupt in their non-enforcement of minima
7. It proposes new, powerful incentives to encourage compliance and behavioural change amongst businesses.

The cases of labour regulation innovation studied in this book have demonstrated that leaps in regulatory innovation occur under special circumstances: in order to stem the risk of a communist take-over, the Maharashtra state government caved to demands for special protections for head-load workers; under the influence of guilt Bill Clinton's Democratic government included a social clause in its trade agreement with Cambodia. It may require greater social unrest or particular pressures for the international community to take the grand steps necessary to stem current trends.

What will happen if we fail to develop a new international labour law of this type that underpins a global living wage? New patterns of capital accumulation are promoting increased inequality and a growing precariat class. As Picketty writes: the 'forces of divergence can at any point regain the upper hand, as seems to be happening now, at the beginning of the twenty-first century', and if current trends continue, 'the consequences for the long-term dynamics of the wealth distribution are potentially terrifying'.[26] The great social pacts of the twentieth century were adopted to promote industrial peace. Standing calls the precariat the 'dangerous class'. The years in the aftermath of the global financial crisis were particularly turbulent. The expression of dissatisfaction with the economic and social situation had started to decline in many regions, but as the economic situation began to deteriorate once more, most notably in developing economies, social unrest became more apparent.[27] 'The biggest dangers', declares Standing, 'are social illnesses and the risk that populist politicians will play on their fears and insecurities to lure them onto the rocks of neo-fascism, blaming 'big government' and 'strangers' for their plight'.[28] Many countries around the world have teetered on a brink of a far right election victory in recent years because of the power of this blaming. Since Trump was elected in 2016 the list of ills and insiders that have not been blamed for the US's waning economic and political power is rapidly diminishing. Beyond electoral risks, it is clear that the churning of labour and the growth of the working poor in absolute numbers is producing collateral damage in society.[29] This churning will only increase as the number of climate refugees rises. Under such circumstances, a new vision of a global scale for the decommodification of work is urgently required.

[26] Piketty. [27] International Labor Office 22.

[28] Guy Standing, 'The Precariat—The New Dangerous Class' Policy Network Essay http://eprints.soas.ac.uk/15711/1/Policy%20Network%20article,%2024.5.11.pdf accessed 4 March 2015.

[29] Munck 757.

Bibliography

Labour Statisticians, Seventeenth International Conference of (2003)

Abbott A, Time Matters: On Theory and Method (University of Chicago Press 2001)

Abbott K and Snidal D, Regulatory Standards for Global Production: The Evolving Role of the State—and Its Shadow (2006)

Abbott KW and Snidal D, 'Strengthening Institutional Regulation Through Transnational New Governance: Overcoming the Orchestration Deficit' 42 Vanderbilt Journal of Transnational Law 501

Abercrombie N, Hill S, and Turner BS, Penguin Dictionary of Sociology, vol 4 (Penguin 2000)

Abraham KS, The Forms and Functions of Tort Law (4th edn, Foundation Press 2012)

Adams Z and Deakin S, 'Institutional Solutions to Precariousness and Inequality in Labour Markets' 52 British Journal of Industrial Relations 779

Adler D, 'Informalizing the Formal: Labour Relations in Cambodia' 1 Justice for the Poor

AFW Alliance, *Stitching a Decent Wage Across Borders: The Asia Floor Wage Proposal* (Asia Floor Wage Alliance 2009)

Agarwala R, 'An Economic Sociology of Informal Work: The Case of India' in Bandelj N, Economic Sociology of Work, vol 18 (Emerald Group Publishing Limited 2009)

Agreement Relating to Trade in Cotton, Wool, Man-Made Fiber, Non-Cotton Vegetable Fiber and Silk Blend Textiles and Textile Products Between the Government of the United States of America and the Royal Government of Cambodia (1999)

Alavi H, 'India: Transition from Feudalism to Colonial Capitalism' 10 Journal of Contemporary Asia 359

Amanpour C, 'Bulgaria Suffers Winter of Economic Pain: Socialists Agree to Discuss Early Elections' CNN Interactive (Sofia, 13 January 1997) http://edition.cnn.com/WORLD/9701/13/bulgaria/index.html?eref=sitesearch accessed 20 October 2014

Amoore L, Globalization Contested: An International Political Economy of Work (Manchester University Press 2002)

Amoore L, 'Risk, Reward and Discipline at Work' 33 Economy and Society 174

Anker R, A New Methodology for Estimating Internationally Comparable Poverty Lines and Living Wage Rates (Group International Labour Office 2005)

Anker R, Estimating a Living Wage: A Methodological Review (ILO 2011)

Anker R and Anker M, Living Wages Around the World: Manual for Measurement (Edward Elgar 2017)

Anner M, Bair J, and Blasi J, 'Toward Joint Liability in Global Supply Chains: Addressing the Root Causes of Labor Violations in International Subcontracting Networks' 35 Comparative Labor Law & Policy Journal 1

Antero S, 'Understanding the Eradication of Slave Labour in Contemporary Brazil—An Implementation Perspective' 34 Policy Studies 89

Appelbaum R, 'Giant Retailers and Giant Contractors in China: Emergent Trends in Global Supply Chains' 9-11 March, 2006 working paper prepared for Princeton University Conference, Observing Trade: Revealing International Trade Networks

Arbex M and O'Dea D, 'Informal Work Networks' 44 Canadian Journal of Economics 247

Arnold D and Han Shih T, 'A Fair Model of Globalisation? Labour and Global Production in Cambodia' 40 Journal of Contemporary Asia 401

Arthurs H, 'What Immortal Hand or Eye? Who Will Redraw the Boundaries of Labour Law?' in Davidov G and Langille B (eds), Boundaries and Frontiers of Labour Law: Goals and Means in the Regulation of Work (Hart 2006)

Asuyama Y and others, 'Firm Dynamics in the Cambodian Garment Industry: Firm Turnover, Productivity Growth and Wage Profile under Trade Liberalization' 18 Journal of the Asia Pacific Economy 51

Athreva B, Labor Conditions in Cambodia's Garment Industry (International Labor Rights Forum 1996)

Australian Bureau of Statistics, 4102.0—Australian Social Trends, 1994 (Canberra, Australia, 1994)

Awchat A, 'Hamals of Poona-III: Rudiments of Organisation' 11 Economic and Political Weekly 942

Ayres I and Braithwaite J, Responsive Regulation: Transcending the Deregulation Debate (Oxford University Press 1992)

Bacchetta M, Ernst E and Bustamante J, Globalisation and Informal Jobs in Developing Countries (ILO and WTO 2009)

Baldwin R and Black J, 'Really Responsive Regulation' 71 Modern Law Review 59

Bank AD, Cambodia's Garment Industry: Meeting the Challenge of the Post-Quota Environment (Asian Development Bank, Manilla, 2004)

Barcellona F, 'A Global Minimum Wage' 21 International Union Rights 17

Barraud de Lagerie P, 'The Wages of Sweat: A Social History Perspective on the Fight Against Sweatshops' 55, Supplement 1 Sociologie du Travail e1

Bartlett W and Rangelova R, 'Small Firms and Economic Transformation in Bulgaria' 9 Small Business Economics 319

Beck U, 'Politics of Risk Society' in Franklin J (ed.), The Politics of Risk Society (Polity Press 1998)

Becker E, When the War Was Over: Cambodia and the Khmer Rouge Revolution (PublicAffairs 1998)

Begg B, Pickles, J, Smith, A, 'Cutting it: European Integration, Trade Regimes, and the Reconfiguration of East-Central European Apparel Production" 35 Environment and Planning A 2191

Béland D, 'Ideas and Institutional Change in Social Security: Conversion, Layering, and Policy Drift' 88 Social Science Quarterly 20

Benassi C, The Implementation of Minimum Wage: Challenges and Creative Solutions (IDEAS Working Paper Series from RePEc, 2011)

Beresford M, 'The Cambodian Clothing Industry in the Post-MFA Environment: A Review of Developments' 14 Journal of the Asia Pacific Economy 366

Berlemann M, Nenovsky N, and Anker R, Lending of First Versus Lending of Last Resort: The Bulgarian Financial Crisis of 1996/1997 (Dresden discussion paper in economics, No 11/03, 2003)

Better Factories Cambodia, Thirty First Synthesis Report on Working Conditions in Cambodia's Garment Sector (2013–2014)

Better Factories Cambodia, 'Better Work' (2014) http://betterfactories.org/?page_id=312 accessed 4 October 2014

Better Factories Cambodia, Statement of the Project Advisory Committee of Better Factors Cambodia (2014)

Bhattacharjee A, Gupta S, and Luce S, 'Raising the Floor: The Movement for a Living Wage in Asia' 18 New Labor Forum 71

Biagi M, 'Labour Law in Small and Medium-Sized Enterprises: Flexibility or Adjustment?' 16 Comparative Labor Law Journal 439

Bitzenis A, 'What Was Behind the Delay in the Bulgarian Privatization Process? Determining Incentives and Barriers of Privatization as a Way of Foreign Entry' 39 Emerging Markets Finance & Trade 58

Black J, 'Critical Reflections on Regulation' 27 Australian Journal of Legal Philosophy 1

Blackette A, 'Situated Reflections of International Labour Law, Capabilities, and Decent Work: The Case of Centre Maraicher Eugene Guinois' (2007) Revue Quebecoise de Droit International 223

Blomgren Bingham L, 'The Next Generation of Adminstrative Law: Building the Legal Infrastructure for Collaborative Governance' 10 Wisconsin Law Review 297

Bogdandy A, International Judicial Lawmaking on Public Authority and Democratic Legitimation in Global Governance. (Springer 2012)

Bolwell D, 'To the Lighthouse Towards a Global Minimum Wage: Building on the International Poverty Line' 42 Australian Bulletin of Labour 1

Boyd DE and others, 'Corporate Social Responsibility in Global Supply Chains: A Procedural Justice Perspective' 40 Long Range Planning 341

Braithwaite J, 'Responsive Regulation and Developing Economies' 34 World Development 884

Braithwaite J, Regulatory Capitalism: How it Works, Ideas for Making it Work Better (Elgar 2008)

Braithwaite J, 'Flipping Markets to Virtue with Qui Tam and Restorative Justice' 38 Accounting, Organizations and Society 458

Braithwaite J, Coglianese C, and Levi-Faur D, 'Can Regulation and Governance Make a Difference?' 1 Regulation and Governance 1

Braithwaite J and Drahos P, 'Ratcheting Up and Driving Down Global Regulatory Standards' 42 Development 109

Braithwaite J and Drahos P, Global Business Regulation (Cambridge University Press 2000)

Braithwaite V, 'The Hope Process and Social Inclusion' 592 Annals of the American Academy of Political and Social Science 128

Breitkreuz R and others, 'The Mahatma Gandhi National Rural Employment Guarantee Scheme: A Policy Solution to Rural Poverty in India?' 35 Development Policy Review 397

Breman J, Outcast Labor in Asia: Circulation and Informalization of the Workforce at the Bottom of the Economy (Oxford University Press, New Delhi 2010)

Brenner M, 'Defining and Measuring a Global Living Wage: Theoretical and Conceptual Issues' Prepared for the conference, Global Labor Standards and Living Wages, at the University of Massachusetts-Amherst, April 19–20, 2002

Bucy PH, 'Private Justice' 76 Southern California Law Review 1

Bucy PH, 'Game Theory and the Civil False Claims Act: Iterated Games and Close-Knit Groups' 35 Loyola University Chicago Law Journal 1021

Buechler SM, Women's Movements in the United States: Woman Suffrage, Equal Rights, and Beyond (Rutgers 1990)

Bulgarian Foreign Investment Agency, Reasons for Investing in Bulgaria (Government of Bulgaria 2002)

Bulgarian Gender Research Foundation, Social Environment and Standards at the Workplace in the Garment Industry (results from preliminary research carried out within a Clean Clothes Campaign international project, Sofia 2001)

Burchielli R and others, 'The FairWear Campaign: An Ethical Network in the Australian Garment Industry' 90 Journal of Business Ethics 575

Carson E, Social Networks and Job Acquisition in Ethnic Communities in South Australia (Canberra: Australian Govt. Pub. Service 1995)

Chang D-O, 'Informalising Labour in Asia's Global Factory' 39 Journal of Contemporary Asia 161

Charrad MM, 'Central and Local Patrimonialism: State-Building in Kin-Based Societies' 636 The Annals of the American Academy of Political and Social Science 49

Charrad MM and Adams J, 'Introduction: Patrimonialism, Past and Present' 636 The Annals of the American Academy of Political and Social Science 6

Chen M, 'Women and Informality: A Global Picture, the Global Movement' 21 SAIS Review 71

Chong A and Gradstein M, Inequality and Institutions (Inter-American Development Bank 2004)

Clean Clothes Campaign, Tailored Wages: Are the Big Brands Paying the People who Make our Clothes Enough to Live on? (2014)

Coase R, The Firm, the Market and the Law (University of Chicago Press 1988)
Coase RH, 'The Problem of Social Cost' 3 Journal of Law and Economics 1
Cock AR, 'External Actors and the Relative Autonomy of the Ruling Elite in Post-UNTAC Cambodia' 41 Journal of Southeast Asian Studies 241
Colins H, 'Independent Contractors and the Challenge of Vertical Disintegration to Employment Protection Laws' 10 Oxford Journal of Legal Studies 353
Collier R and Collier D, Shaping the Political Arena (Princeton University Press 1991)
Collins H, 'Ascriptions of Legal Responsibility to Groups in Complex Patterns of Economic Integration' 53 Modern Law Review 731
Collins H, 'Independent Contractors and the Challenge of Vertical Disintegration to Employment Protection Laws' 10 Oxford Journal of Legal Studies 353
Comaroff J and Comaroff JL, 'Millennial Capitalism: First Thoughts on a Second Coming' 12 Public Culture 291
Committee on Petitions FLS, Ministry of Labour and Employment, Nineteenth Report (Government of India 2006)
Compa L and Vogt JS, 'Labor Rights in the Generalised System of Preferences: A 20 Year Review' 22 Comparative Labor Law & Policy Journal 199
Cooney S, Howe J, and Murray J, 'Time and Money under Workchoices: Understanding the New Workplace Relations Act as a Scheme of Regulation' 29 University of New South Wales Law Journal 215
Cossart S, Chaplier J, and Lomenie TBd, 'The French Law on Duty of Care: A Historic Step Towards Making Globalization Work for All' 2 Business and Human Rights Journal 317
Countouris N, 'Book Review of 'Boundaries and Frontiers of Labour Law' 36 Industrial Law Journal 250
Cregan C, Home Sweat Home (Melbourne: The Department of Management, University of Melbourne 2002)
Cregan C, 'Vietnamese Outworkers in the Australian Garment Industry: Sweated Labour and the Social Wage' Melbourne: The Department of Management, University of Melbourne 2002)
Creighton B and Stewart A, Labour Law (5th edn, Federation Press, Sydney 2010)
Dahan Y, Lerner H, and Milman-Sivan F, Global Justice and International Labour Rights (Cambridge University Press)
Daniel EV and Knudsen JC (eds), Mistrusting Refugees (University of California Press 1995)
Darragh R, 'California's New Supply Chain Transparency Law' 8 Compliance Week 12
Datta RC, 'Public Action, Social Security and Unorganised Sector' 33 Economic and Political Weekly L2
Davidov G, 'Enforcement Problems in "Informal" Labor Markets: A View from Israel' 27 Comparative Labor Law & Policy Journal 3
Davidov G and Langille B (eds), Boundaries and Frontiers of Labour Law: Goals and Means in the Regulation of Work (Oxford/Hart 2006)
Davies ACL, Perspectives on Labour Law (Cambridge University Press 2004)
Davies P and Freedland M, 'The Disintegration of the Employing Enterprise and its Significance for the Personal Scope of Employment Law' (Conference, The Scope of Employment Law: Re-drawing the Boundaries of Protection Conference 2005)
De Gobbi MS, Flexibility and Security in Labour Markets of Developing Countries: In Search of Decent Work for All (Employment Policy Papers, ILO 2007)
de Soto H, 'Dead Capital and the Poor' 21 SAIS Review 13
Deakin S and Wilkinson F, The Law of the Labour Market: Industrialization, Employment and Legal Evolution (Oxford University Press 2005)
Department of Education EaWR, Employment Outlook for Manufacturing (SkillsInfo Report A10-0081, Canberra: Australian Government, 2011)

Department of Industry Tourism and Resources, Review of the Textile, Clothing and Footwear Strategic Investment Program Scheme—Report (Australia 2002)
Derks A, Khmer Women on the Move: Exploring Work and Life in Urban Cambodia (University of Hawaii Press: Honalulu 2008)
Deshpande P, 'Caste as Maratha: Social Categories, Colonial Policy and Identity in Early Twentieth-Century Maharashtra' 41 Indian Economic & Social History Review 7
Deshpande R, 'Organising the Unorganised: Case of Hamal Panchayat' 34 Economic and Political Weekly 19
DiCaprio A, 'The Demand Side of Social Protection: Lessons from Cambodia's Labor Rights Experience' 48 World Development 108
Diviney E and Lillywhite S, Ethical Threads: Corporate Social Responsibility in the Australian Garment Industry (Brotherhood of St Laurence, 2007)
Donella C, 'Globalization and Labour: A Case Study of EPZ Workers in Malaysia' 19 Economic and Industrial Democracy 253
Dube SC, Indian Village (Cornell University Press 1955)
Eastham E and Danzig M, 'California's New Forced Labor Disclosure Law: Empowering Consumers While Burdening Supply Chain' (SDCExec 11 January 2012)
Economic Commission for Europe, Outward Processing Trade Between the European Union and the Associated Countries of Eastern Europe: The Case of Textiles and Clothing (Economic Bulletin for Europe, Vol 47, UNECE: Geneva 1995)
Edgell S, Gottfried H, and Granter E, The Sage Handbook of Sociology of Work and Employment (SAGE Publications 2016)
Editorial, 'Scuttling Land Reform' 10 Economic and Political Weekly 656
Editorial, 'Bulgaria: Parliament Approves Principle Pension System Reform' (Balkans.com 2010) https://www.reuters.com/article/bulgaria-pension/bulgarian-parliament-approves-pension-reforms-idUSL5N1084LV20150728 accessed 21 October
Editorial, 'Panel to Discuss Removal of Organised Labourers from Mathadi Act' The Indian Express (Pune, 19 February 2010) Express News Service
Eichengreen B and Kohl R, The External Sector, the State and Development in Eastern Europe (BRIE Working Paper 1998)
Eisenhardt K, 'Building Theories from Case Study Research' in Huberman AM and Miles MB (eds), The Qualitative Researcher's Companion (Sage 2002)
Ellem B, In Women's Hands? A History of Clothing Trades Unionism in Australia (New South Wales University Press 1989)
Elliott KA and Freeman RB, Can Labor Standards Improve Under Globalization? (Institute for International Economics 2003)
Engels C, 'Subordinate Employees or Self-Employed Workers?' in Blanpain R (ed), Comparative Labour Law and Industrial Relations in Industrialised Market Economies (10th edn, Wolters Kluwer, Alphen aan den Rijn 2010)
Engle Sr AD, Elbert NF, and Spain JW, 'Sell Global, Pay Local—The Ethics of Taller Product Markets, Lower Labor Markets, and Informed Consent in Global Employment Contracts' 22 Business & Professional Ethics Journal 25
Engstrom DF, 'Private Enforcement's Pathways: Lessons from Qui Tam Litigation' 114 Columbia Law Review 1913
Equitable Cambodia and Inclusive Development International, Specific Instance under the OECD Guidelines for Multinational Enterprises submitted to the Australian National Contact Point (NCP) Against Australia New Zealand Banking Group (ANZ), concerning financial services provided to Phnom Penh Sugar Company (2014)
Ethical Trading Initiative, 'Living Wage: Make it a Reality' (ETI Conference 2008 Workshop 5)
Euroactiv, 'Bulgaria: Poor not Just by EU standards' (2010) http://www.euractiv.com/en/en-largement/bulgaria-poor-not-only-eu-standards-news-493653 accessed 11 November

Eurofund, 'Bulgaria; Self-Employed Workers' (2009) <http://www.eurofound.europa.eu/comparative/tn0801018s/bg0801019q.htm>

European Commission, Modernising Labour Law to Meet the Challenges of the 21st Century (2006)

European Commission, Mental Health, Part 1: Report, Fieldwork: February–March 2010 (Special Eurobarometer 345, European Commission, October 2010)

European Foundation for the Improvement of Living and Working Conditions, 'Capacity Building for Social Dialogue in Bulgaria' (2006)

European Industrial Relations Observatory On-Line, 'Social Partners Agree Regulation of Home-Based Work' (2010) http://www.eurofound.europa.eu/eiro/2010/07/articles/bg1007011i.htm accessed 14 October

Eurostat, 'Euro Area Unemployment Rate at 10.1%' (STAT/11/5, 7 January 2011) file:///C:/Users/Pc/Downloads/STAT-11-5_EN.pdf accessed October 20

Farrell N, 'Accountability for Outsourced Torts: Expanding Brands' Duty of Care for Workplace Harms Committed Abroad' 44 Georgetown Journal of International Law 1491

Fenwick C and others, Labour and Labour Related Laws in Small and Micro Enterprises: Innovative Regulatory Responses (ILO 2008)

Fioretos O, 'Historical Institutionalism in International Relations' 65 International Organization 367

Ford C, 'New Governance in the Teeth of Human Frailty: Lessons from Financial Regulation' [2010] Wisconsin Law Review 441

Freedland M, 'Burying Caeser: What was the Standard Employment Contract?' in Stone KVW (ed.), Rethinking Workplace Regulation: Beyond the Standard Contract of Employment (Russell Sage Foundation 2013)

Fudge J, 'The New Discourse of Labour Rights: From Social to Fundamental Rights' 29 Comparative Labour Law and Policy Journal 29

Fudge J, 'Blurring Legal Boundaries: Regulating for Decent Work' in Fudge J, McCrystal S and Sankaran K (eds), Challenging the Legal Boundares of Work Regulation (Hart 2012)

Fukuyama F, Trust: The Social Virtues and the Creation of Prosperity (Free Press 1995)

Gainsborough M, 'Elites Vs. Reform in Laos, Cambodia, and Vietnam', 23 Journal of Democracy 34

Garibaldi P, Makovec M, and Stoyanova G, From Transition to EU Accession The Bulgarian Labor Market During the 1990s (World Bank Technical Paper No 494, WTP494, May 2001)

Genov N (ed.), Unemployment: Risks and Reactions (UNESCO–MOST, Paris; Friedrich Ebert Stiftung, Bonn and Sofia 1999)

Gereffi G, 'Global Commodity Chains: New Forms of Coordination and Control Among Nations and Firms in International Industries' 1 Competition and Change

Gereffi G, Humphrey J, and Sturgeon TJ, Developing a Theory of Global Value Chains: A Framework Document (2002)

Gershon Nimbalker CCaHW, Behind the Bar Code: The Fashion Report (Baptist World Aid Australia and Not For Sale Australia, 19 August 2013)

Gilson R, Sabel C, and Scott R, 'Contracting for Innovation: Vertical Disintegration and Interfirm Collaboration' 109 Columbia Law Review

Gottesman E, Cambodia after the Khmer Rouge: Inside the Politics of Nation Building (Yale University Press 2003)

Government of India, National Commission on Labour (1967)

Government of India, National Commission on Rural Labour (Archives of Indian Labour, Delhi, 1991)

Government of India, Report of the National Commission on Rural Labour, Volume 1: Main Report (New Delhi, Ministry of Labour, 1991)

Government of India, 2nd Report of the National Commission on Labour (2002)

Government of India, Second National Commission on Labour Report (2002)

Government of India, Annual Report to the People on Employment (2010)

Granovetter M, 'Economic Action and Social Structure: The Problem of Embeddedness' 91 The American Journal of Sociology

Davis Paul and Green Michael, 'France Adopts a New Law Requiring Companies to Diligence their Supply Chains in Relation to Human Rights, Environmental, and Health and Safety Issues' Latham & Watkins (blog) (April 21, 2017) https://www.lexology.com/library/detail.aspx?g=488454ab-fcba-4b0f-b5cd-d6f9e783e60d

Guan S, 'WTO Retaliation Rules in Subsidy-Related Cases: What Can We Learn from the US-Upland Cotton Arbitration?' 48 Journal of World Trade 815

Gundogan N, Can Denmark's Flexicurity System Be Replicated in Developing Countries? The Case of Turkey (Anadolu University 2009)

Gunningham G and Grabosky P, Smart Regulation (Clarendon Press 1998)

Gunningham N, 'Integrating Management Systems and Occupational Health and Safety Regulation' 26 Journal of Law and Society 192

Hall JA, 'Human Rights and the Garment Industry in Contemporary Cambodia' 36 Stanford Journal of International Law 119

Hall JA, 'The ILO's Better Factories Cambodia Program: A Viable Blueprint for Promoting International Labor Rights?' 21 Stanford Law & Policy Review 427

Hall K, 'Strategic Privatisation of Transnational Anti-Corruption Regulation' 28 Australian Journal of Corporate Law 60

Hall PA and Thelen K, 'Institutional Change in Varieties of Capitalism' 70(1) Socioeconomic Review

Hamm P, King LP, and Stuckler D, 'Mass Privatization, State Capacity, and Economic Growth in Post-Communist Countries' 77 American Sociological Review 295

Harbour E, 'Focus: Raising the Bar in the Struggle for Living Wages' 21 International Union Rights 19

Hardt M and Negri A, Commonwealth (Harvard University Press, Cambridge, MA 2011)

Harriss J, Institutions, Politics and Culture: A Case for 'Old' Institutionalism and the Study of Historical Change (Working Paper Series, Development Studies Institute LSE 2002)

Hart K, 'Informal Income Opportunities and Urban Unemployment in Ghana' 11 March Journal of Modern African Studies

Harvey D, The Condition of Post-Modernity: An Enquiry into the Origins of Cultural Change (Blackwell 1990)

Harvey D, 'The Right to the City' 27 International Journal of Urban and Regional Research 939

Harvey D, The Spaces of Global Capitalism (Verso 2006)

Haufler V, A Public Role for the Private Sector: Industry Self-Regulation in a Global Economy (Carnegie Endowment for International Peace 2001)

Hecker M, 'Lesson from the East: International Labor Rights and the U.S.–Cambodia Trade Agreement of 1999' 26 Buffalo Public Interest Law Journal 39

Held D, Democracy and the Global Order: From the Modern State to Cosmopolitan Governance (Stanford University Press 1995)

Held D and McGrew A (eds), Governing Globalization: Power, Authority and Global Governance (Polity Press 2002)

Holcroft J, 'Export Processing Zones—Globalisation's Great Deceit' (2003) http://www.industriall-union.org/archive/imf/export-processing-zones-globalisations-great-deceit accessed 12 December 2017

Howe J, '"Deregulation" of Labour Relations in Australia: Towards a More "Centered" Command and Control Model" in Arup Cea (ed.), Labour Law and Labour Market Regulation: Essays in the Construction, Constitution, and Regulation of Labour Markets and Work Relationships (Federation Press 2006)

Howell J, Good Practice Study in Shanghai on Employment Services for the Informal Economy (China 2002)
Hughes C, 'Transnational Networks, International Organizations and Political Participation in Cambodia: Human Rights, Labour Rights and Common Rights' 14 Democratization 834
Hurley J, Garment Industry: Subcontracting and Workers Rights, Report of Women Working Worldwide. Action Research in Asia and Europe (Working Women Worldwide, Manchester Metropolitan University, Manchester 2003)
Huws U, Action Programmes for the Protection of Homeworkers: Ten Case Studies from Around the World (International Labour Office 1995)
Hyde A, 'Legal Responsibility for Labour Conditions Down the Production Chain' in Fudge J, McCrystal S, and Sankaran K (eds), Challenging the Legal Boundaries of Work Regulation (Hart Publishing 2012)
Iankova EA, 'Multi-Level Bargaining during Bulgaria's Return to Captialism' 54 Industrial and Labor Relations Review 115
Iliopoulou D, 'The Uncertainty of Private Property: Indigenous versus Colonial Law in the Restructuring of Social Relations in British India' 26 Dialectical Anthropology 65
ILO, The Employment Relationship, Report V(I) (95th Sesssion, 2005)
ILO, Global Wage Report 2008/09 (2008)
ILO, Transitioning from the Informal to the Formal Economy (2014)
Immigration Museum Victoria, History of Immigration from Vietnam (Victoria, Australia, 2013)
India Go, Report on Definitional and Statistical Issues Relating to Informal Economy (2008)
Industriall, Inditex (11 July 2014 edn)
Industry Commission, The Textile, Clothing and Footwear Industries (1997)
International Human Rights and Conflict Resolution Clinic SLS and Worker Rights Consortium, Monitoring in the Dark: An Evaluation of the International Labour Organization's Better Factories Cambodia Monitoring and Reporting Program (2013)
International Labor Conference, provisional record, fourth item on the agenda: 'Decent Work In Global Supply Chains', Reports of the Committee on Decent Work in Global Supply Chains: resolution and conclusions submitted for adoption by the Conference, 105th Session, Geneva, May–June 2016
International Labor Office, World Employment Social Outlook: Trends 2016 (2016)
International Labour Office, A Global Alliance against Forced Labour: Global Report under the Follow-up to the ILO Declaration on Fundamental Principles and Rights at Work 2005 (INTERNATIONAL LABOUR CONFERENCE, 93rd Session 2005, Report I (B), 2005)
International Labour Office, Global Employment Trends 2012 (Geneva, International Labour Office, 2012)
International Labour Office, World Employment Social Outlook: The Changing Nature of Jobs (2015)
International Labour Office, Decent Work in Global Supply Chains: Report to the International Labour Conference, 105th Session, 2016, (2016)
International Labour Office, World Employment and Social Outlook: Trends 2016 (World of Work 2016)
International Labour Organization, The Scope of the Employment Relationship (ILO 2003)
International Labour Organization, The Employment Relationship (2005)
International Labour Organization and WEIGO, ILO: Women and Men in the Informal Economy: A Statistical Picture (2002)
International Labour Organization and WEIGO, ILO: Women and Men in the Informal Economy: A Statistical Picture (2012)
Interview with Aleksandar Zagorov, Confederate Secretary Podkrepa, Sofia, Bulgaria, 21 September 2010

Interview with An Nan, Arbitration Council, Phnom Penh, Cambodia, March 26 2014
Interview with Ann Vireak, Arbitration Council, Phnom Penh, Cambodia, 28 March 2014
Interview with Arun S. Ranjane Jt. General Secretary, Akhil Bharatiya Mathadi Transport & General Kamgar Union, March 2011
Interview with Ath Thorn, President of Cambodian Labor Confederation and President of Coalition of Cambodia Apparel Workers Democratic Union, Phnom Penh, Cambodia, March 19, 2014
Interview with Baburao Ramisthe, General Secretary, Akhil Bharatiya Mathadi Transport & General Kamgar Union, March 2011
Interview with Basirun Nabi Khan, Office Operations Manager Cambodia and Vietnam, H&M, Phnom Penh, Cambodia 27 Mar 2014
Interview with Buth Rithy, Human Resource Manager, API Medical, 25 March 2014
Interview with Chea Sophal, Senior Program Officer and Team Leader, Monitoring, Better Factories Program, Phnom Penh, Cambodia, 19 March 2014
Interview with Coen Kompier, International Labour Organization, Workshop at India International Centre, Delhi, December 2013
Interview with David Welsh, Cambodia Program Director, AFL-CIO Solidarity Center, Phom Penh, Cambodia, 20 March 2014
Interview with Ing Sothy, Ing Sothy, Arbitrator, Cabodian Arbitration Council, Phnom Penh, 28 March 2014
Interview with Ken Loo, General Secretary, Garment Manufacturers Association, Phnom Pehn, Cambodia, 21 March 2014
Interview with Liv Sovanna, Arbitrator, Cambodian Arbitration Council, Phomn Pehn, Cambodia, 26 March 2014
Interview with Manohar Gajare, Former Jt. Commissioner of Labour, Government of Maharashtra, March 2011
Interview with Morm Nhim, President, National Independent Federation Textile Union of Cambodia, Phnom Penh, Cambodia, 20 March 2014
Interview with RS Dhumal, Secretary, Transport & Dock Workers Union, Mumbai, March 2011
Interview with Sheila Balla, Workshop at India International Centre, Delhi, December 2013
Interview with Mr. Sony at Cambodia Federation of Labor Service, Phom Penh, Cambodia, 21 March 2014
Interview with Tola Moun, Community Legal Education Center, Cambodia, 27 March 2014
Interview with Tor Bon Thorn, Tor Bon Thorn, Deputy Director, Labour Inspectorate, Ministry of Labour, Phnom Penh, Cambodia, 2014
Jessop B, The Social Embeddedness of the Economy and its Implications for Economic Governance (http://www2.cddc.vt.edu/digitalfordism/fordism_materials/jessop2.htm 2001)
Jhabvala R, 'Unorganised Workers Bill: In Aid of the Informal Worker' 40 Economic and Political Weekly 2227
Johnstone R, Mayhew C, and Quinlan M, 'Outsourcing Risk? The Regulation of Occupational Health and Safety Where Subcontractors Are Employed' 22 Comparative Labor Law & Policy Journal 351
Johnstone R, Nossar I, and Rawling M, 'Regulating Supply Chains to Protect Road Transport Workers: An Early Assessment of the Road Safety Remuneration Tribunal(Australia)' 43 Federal Law Review 397
Joshi A and Moore M, 'Enabling Environments: Do Anti-Poverty Programmes Mobilise the Poor?' 37 The Journal of Development Studies 25
Jütting JP and de Laiglesia JR, Is Informal Normal? Towards More and Better Jobs in Developing Countries (OECD 2009)

Kahn-Freund O, 'Servants and Independent Contractors' 14 The Modern Law Review 504

Kalleberg A, 'Precarious, Informalizing, and Flexible Work' 57 American Behavioral Scientist 289

Kaplinsky R, 'Globalisation and Unequalisation: What Can Be Learned from Value Chain Analysis?' 37 Journal of Development Studies 117

Kapur S and Kim S, British Colonial Institutions and Economic Development in India (No 12613, NBER Working Papers from National Bureau of Economic Research, Cambridge, USA 2006)

Kelman S, Regulating America, Regulating Sweden: A Comparative Study of Occupational Safety and Health Policy (The MIT Press 1981)

Kessin K, 'Social and Psychological Consequences of Intergenerational Occupational Mobility' 77 The American Journal of Sociology 1

Knudsen J, 'The Growth of Private Regulation of Labor Standards in Global Supply Chains: Mission Impossible for Western Small- and Medium-Sized Firms?' 117 Journal of Business Ethics 387

Kochan T, 'Wages and the Social Contract' The American Prospect (April 22 2007)

Kohler Reissman C, 'Narrative Interviewing' in Jupp V (ed.), The Sage Dictionary of Social Research Methods (Sage 2006)

Kolben K, 'Trade, Monitoring, and the ILO: Working to Improve Conditions in Cambodia's Garment Factories' 7 Yale Human Rights and Development Law Journal 79

Kolben K, 'Integrative Linkage: Combining Public and Private Regulatory Approaches in the Design of Trade and Labor Regimes' 48 Harvard International Law Journal 203

Krasner S, 'Sovereignty: An Institutional Perspective' 21 Comparative Political Studies 66

Krippner G and others, 'Polanyi Symposium: A Conversation on Embeddedness' 2 Socio-Economic Review

Kristal T and Cohen Y, 'The Causes of Rising Wage Inequality: The Race Between Institutions and Technology' 15 Socio-Economic Review 187

Kucera D and Xenogiani T, 'Persisting Informal Employment: What Explains It?' in Jütting JP and de Laiglesia JR (eds), Is Informal Normal? Towards More and Better Jobs in Developing Countries (OECD 2009)

Kunthear M and Teehan S, 'Workers "Locked Inside" During Overtime Strike' The Phnom Penh Post (4 March 2014) https://www.phnompenhpost.com/national/workers-'locked-inside'-during-overtime-strike

Kuznets S, 'Economic Growth and Income Inequality' XLV The American Economic Review 1

Labriadis L, 'Subcontracting in the Greek Garment Industry and the Opening of the Balkan Markets' 9 Cyprus Journal of Economics

Lal D, 'Agricultural Development in Maharashtra: Some Aspects' 4 Economic and Political Weekly A207

Lall S, 'The Employment Impact of Globalization in Developing Countries' in Lee E and Vivarelli M (eds), Understanding Globalization, Employment and Poverty Reduction (Palgrave Macmillan 2004)

Lamm F and Walters D, 'Regulating Occupational Health and Safety in Small Businesses' in Bluff E, Gunningham N, and Johnstone R (eds), OHS Regulation for a Changing World of Work (General 2004)

Langille B, 'What is International Labour Law For?' 3 Law and Ethics of Human Rights 47

Langille B, 'Putting International Labour Law on the (Right) Map' in Blackette A and Levesque C (eds), Social Regionalism in a Global Economy (Routledge 2011)

Lewis WA, The Theory of Economic Growth (Allen and Unwin 1955)

Litner B, 'One Big Happy Family in Cambodia' Asia Times (20 March 2007) http://www.atimes.com/atimes/Southeast_Asia/IC20Ae03.html accessed 14 July 2014

Lo N, 'The Chinese/Khmer Divide in Factories' The Phnom Penh Post (16 June 2006) http://www.phnompenhpost.com/national/chinesekhmer-divide-factories accessed 14 July 2014

Locke R, Amengual M, and Mangla A, 'Virtue Out of Necessity? Compliance, Commitment, and the Improvement of Labor Conditions in Global Supply Chains' 37 Politics & Society 319

Lofland J, 'Analytic Ethnography: Features, Failings, and Futures' in Huberman AM and Miles MB (eds), The Qualitative Research Companion (Sage 2002)

Macdonald K and Marshall S, 'Transnational Business and the Politics of Social Risk: Re-Embedding Transnational Supply Chains Through Private Governance' in Lange B, Haines F, and Thomas D (eds), Regulatory Transformations: Rethinking Economy-Society Interactions (Hart Publishing 2015)

Macdonald K and Marshall S (eds), Fair Trade, Corporate Accountability and Beyond: Experiments in Globalising Justice (Ashgate 2010)

Machado KEDGJMR, Transnational Anti-Corruption Law in Action: Cases from Argentina and Brazil (Global Administrative Law Series, Institute for International Law and Justice, New York University School of Law, IILJ 2014/1)

Mahajan M, The Political and Moral Economy of Combatting Labor Exploitation: A Study of Brazil's Policy Evolution (ProQuest Dissertations Publishing 2015)

Mahey P and others, The Plural Regulation of Work: A Pilot Study of Restaurant Workers in Yogyakarta, Indonesia (Centre For Employment and Labour Relations, Law Centre For Indonesian Law, Islam and Society, Asian Law Centre 2017)

Mahoney J and Thelen K, 'A Theory of Gradual Institutional Change' in Mahoney J and Thelen K (eds), Explaining Institutional Change: Ambiguity, Agency and Power (Cambridge University Press 2010)

Maiti D, 'Precarious Work in India: Trends and Emerging Issues' 57 American Behavioral Scientist 507

Maloney W, 'Informality Revisited' 32 World Development 1159

Marion Young I, 'Responsibility and Global Justice' 23 Social Philosophy and Policy 102

Markus Frölich and others (eds), Social Insurance, Informality, and Labor Markets: How to Protect Workers While Creating Good Jobs (Oxford University Press 2014)

Marrese M, 'CMEA: Effective but Cumbersome Political Economy' 40 International Organization 287

Marshall S, 'An Exploration of Control in the Context of Vertical Disintegration, and Regulatory Responses' in Arup C and others (eds), Labour Law and Labour Market Regulation: Essays in the Construction, Constitution, and Regulation of Labour Markets and Work Relationships (Federation Press 2006)

Marshall S, Taylor K, and Balaton-Chrimes S, Rajasthan Stone Quarries: Promoting Human Rights Due Diligence and Access to Redress in Complex Supply Chains (2016)

Mayer F and Pickles J, Re-embedding the Market: Global Apparel Value Chains, Governance and Decent Work (Palgrave Macmillian 2014)

Mayhew C and Quinlan M, Outsourcing and Occupational Health and Safety: A Comparative Study of Factory-based and Outworkers in the Australian TCF Industry (International Journal of Health Services 1999; 29(1):83–107)

McAdam D, Tarrow S, and Tilly C, Dynamics of Contention (Cambridge University Press 2001)

McAllister I, 'Occupational Mobility among Immigrants: The Impact of Migration on Economic Success in Australia' 29 International Migration Review 441

McIntyre K, 'Geography as Destiny: Cities, Villages and Khmer Rouge Orientalism' 38 Comparative Studies in Society and History 730

McMillan M and Rodrik D, Globalization, Structural Change, and Productivity Growth (Harvard University 2011)

Meardi G and Marginson P, 'Global Labour Governance: Potential and Limits of an Emerging Perspective' 28 Work, Employment & Society 651

Medvedev K, 'Picking up the Threads: Model Approach Helps Cambodia Design a New Fashion Image' 41 Women's Studies Quarterly 131

Mehmet O, 'Development in a Wartorn Society: What Next in Cambodia?' 18 Third World Quarterly 673

Miller D, Regulating the 'Wage Effort Bargain' in Outsourced Apparel Production: Towards a Model (Palgrave Macmillian 2014)

Mitchell R and others, Law, Corporate Governance and the Management of Labour: A Study of Australian Regulatory Style and Business Practice (Ashgate 2011)

Mohapatra PP, 'Regulated Informality:Legal Constructions of Labour Relations in Colonial India 1814–1926' in Lucassen J and Bhattacharya S (eds), Workers in the Informal Sector: Studies in Labour History 1800–2000 (Macmillan, New Delhi 2005)

Muasher M, 'World Bank Confronts Cambodia Corruption' The Wall Street Journal (18 October 2007) http://online.wsj.com/news/articles/SB119266729725862803 accessed 14 July 2014

Munck R, 'The Precariat: A View from the South' 34 Third World Quarterly 747

Mundlak G, 'De-Territorializing Labor Law' 3 Law and Ethics of Human Rights 189

National Statistical Office of Thailand, The Informal Employment Survey (2016)

Navaretti G, Galeotti, M, and Mattozzi, A, 'Moving Skills from Hands to Heads: Does Importing Technology Affect Export Performance in Textiles' 33 Research Policy 879

Netherlands ICot, Child Labour Due Diligence Law for Companies Adopted by Dutch Parliament (2017)

Netherlands National Contact Point, Final Statement ABP/APG - Lok Shakti Abhiyan, KTNC Watch, Fair Green and Global Alliance, Forum for Environment and Development (2013)

Nicholson P and Low S, 'Local Accounts of Rule of Law Aid: Implications for Donors' 5 Hague Journal on the Rule of Law 1

Noronha E, 'Bombay Dock Labour Board 1948-1994: From Insecurity to Security to Insecurity?' 36 Economic and Political Weekly 4851

North DC, 'The New Institutional Economics and Third World Development' in Harriss J, Hunter J, and Lewis CM (eds), The New Institutional Economics and Third World Development (Routledge 1995)

Nossar I, Johnstone R, and Quinlan M, 'Regulating Supply-Chains to Address the Occupational Health and Safety Problems Associated with Precarious Employment: The Case of Home-Based Clothing Workers in Australia' 17 Australian Journal of Labour Law 137

Nuon V and Serrano M, Building Unions in Cambodia: History, Challenges, Strategies (Friedrich-Ebert-Stiftung Office for Regional Cooperation in Asia 2010)

O'Riain S, 'States and Markets in an Era of Globalization' 26 Annual Review of Sociology 187

O'Rourke D, 'Outsourcing Regulation: Analyzing Nongovernmental Systems of Labor Standards and Monitoring' 31 Policy Studies Journal 1

O'Rourke D, 'Multi-Stakeholder Regulation: Privatizing or Socializing Global Labor Standards' 34 World Development 899

OECD, OECD Employment Outlook 1998 (Paris: OECD Publishing 1998)

Olsen J, 'Institutional Design in Democratic Contexts' 5 The Journal of Political Philosophy 203

Omvedt G, 'Non-Brahmans and Communists in Bombay' 8 Economic and Political Weekly 749

Oonk G, Child Labour Due Diligence Law for Companies Adopted by Dutch Parliament (India Committee of the Netherlands 2017)

Organisation for Economic Co-operation and Development, OECD Economic Surveys: Bulgaria 1997 (OECD Publishing, Paris, 1997)

Organisation for Economic Co-operation and Development, OECD, Divided We Stand: Why Inequality Keeps Rising (Organisation for Economic Co-Operation and Development, Paris 2011)

Organisation for Economic Co-operation and Development, OECD, In It Together: Why Less Inequality Benefits All (Organisation for Economic Co-operation and Development, Paris 2015)

Organisation IL, Employment Relationship Recommendation (2006)
Ornati OA (ed.), Jobs and Workers in India (Cornell University Press 1955)
Palley T, 'The Economics of Wage-Led Recovery: Analysis and Policy Recommendations' 3 International Journal of Labour Research 219
Parella K, 'Outsourcing Corporate Accountability' 89 Washington Law Review 747
Participant observation: Conversation with Janet Love, South African Human Rights Commissioner, Oxfam Melbourne, 6 February 2015
Participant observation: Conversation with Scott Nova, Executive Director, Workers Rights Consortium at Clean Clothes Campaign Global Forum 2014, Hong Kong, 20 November 2014
Participant observation: Conversation with Yannick Etienne, Spokeswoman, ESPM-BATAY OUVRIYE, Haiti, at Clean Clothes Campaign Global Forum 2014, Hong Kong, 20 November 2014
Participant observation: Fair Work Commission, Participant observation of hearing for Textile, Clothing and Footwear and Associated Industries Award 2010, Review of all modern awards after first two years (2013) Fair Work Commission 2013
Participant observation: 'Homebased Workers Struggle: Formalization for Informal Workers, New Strength To Labour Movement' thematic workshop, Clean Clothes Campaign Global Forum, Hong Kong, 20 November 2014
Participant observation: Jenny Holdcroft, Policy Director, IndustriALL Global Union presentation, Clean Clothes Campaign Global Forum, Hong Kong, 19 November 2014
Participant observation: 'Living Wage Benchmarks: Dealing with Regional Variations' thematic workshop, Clean Clothes Campaign Global Forum, Hong Kong, 19 November 2014
Participant observation: Senate Hearing inquiry into the Fair Work Amendment Bill, Senate Hearing inquiry by the Education, Emloyment and Workplace Relations Legislation Committee into the Fair Work Amendment (Textile, Clothing and Footwear Industry) Bill 2011
Participant observation: 'Winning and Enforcing Brand and Employer Commitments to Higher Wages and Union Rights' thematic workshop, Clean Clothes Campaign Global Forum, Hong Kong, 19 November 2014
Participant observation: 'Worker Cooperatives in Action' thematic workshop, Clean Clothes Campagn Global Forum, Hong Kong, 19 November 2014
Pascual CG and International Labour Organization. Subregional Office for South-East Asia and the Pacific, Social and Economic Empowerment of Women in the Informal Economy: Impact Case Study of Sikap Buhay (ILO, Subregional Office for South-East Asia and the Pacific 2008)
Peck J, 'Outwork and Restructuring Processes in the Australian Clothing Industry' 3 Labour and Industry
Peck J, Work-Place: The Social Regulation of Labor Markets (Guilford Press 1996)
Peek P and others, State Policies and Migration: Studies in Latin America and the Caribbean (Croom Helm 1982)
Peerenboom R, Petersen CJ, and Chen AHY, Human Rights in Asia: A Comparative Legal Study of Twelve Asian Jurisdictions, France and the USA (Routledge 2006)
Pellissery S, 'Social Embeddedness of Informal Labour Markets: How Effective Are Public Works Programmes for Social Security in India?' ('Social security and the labour market: A mismatch?' The role of social security in relation to the labour market and employment policies, 5th International Research Conference on Social Security)
Petkov K, Informal Economy: Re-Conceptualisation and Policy Approaches (CEE/NIS 2006)
Petkov P, Statistical Research of Working at Home in Bulgaria (Unpublished doctoral dissertation, Tsenov Academy of Economics, 2006)
Piketty T, Capital in the Twenty-First Century (Goldhammer A tr., The Belknap Press of Harvard University Press 2014)

Podolny JM, 'A Status-Based Model of Market Competition' 98 American Journal of Sociology 829
Pogge TW, 'Properties of Global Justice' 32 Metaphilosophy 6
Polanyi K, The Great Transformation: The Political and Economic Origins of Our Time (Beacon Press 1944)
Polanyi K, The Great Transformation (Beacon Press 1957)
Polaski S, 'Combining Global and Local Forces: The Case of Labor Rights in Cambodia' 34 World Development 919
Polaski S, Harnessing Global Forces to Create Decent Work in Cambodia (Research Series, 119, International Labour Organization, International Institute for Labour Studies, 2009)
Portes A, Castells M, and Benton LA, The Informal Economy: Studies in Advanced and Less Developed Countries (Johns Hopkins University Press 1989)
Posner EA and Yoo JC, 'Judicial Independence in International Tribunals' 93 California Law Review 1
Power M, The Audit Society: Rituals of Verification (Oxford University Press 1997)
Prado MM, 'Institutional Bypass: An Alternative for Development Reform' SSRN eLibrary
Productivity Commission, Modelling Economy-Wide Effects of Future TCF Assistance (Productivity Commission Research Report, Australian Government, June 2008)
Quinlan M, Mayhew C, and Bohle P, 'The Global Expansion of Precarious Employment, Work Disorganization, and Consequences for Occupational Health: Placing The Debate in a Comparative Historical Context' 31 Int J Health Serv 507
Rabin RL, 'Enabling Torts' 49 DePaul Law Review 435
Ramirez-Machado JM, Domestic Work, Conditions of Work and Employment: A Legal Perspective (ILO 2003)
Rani U, Impact of Changing Work Patterns on Income Inequality (Discussion Paper Series, International Institute for Labour Studies 2008)
Raval B and Team SAR, Multiple Work Status of Women in the Informal Economy (2001)
Rawling M and Kaine S, 'Regulating Supply Chains to Provide a Safe Rate for Road Transport Workers' 25 Australian Journal of Labour Law 237
Reichman N, 'Moving Backstage: Uncovering the Role of Compliance Practices in Shaping Regulatory Policies' in Baldwin R, Scott C, and Hood C (eds), A Reader on Regulation (Oxford University Press 1998)
Rennie S and others, 'Orchestration from Below? Trade Unions in the Global South, Transnational Business and Efforts to Orchestrate Continuous Improvement in Non-State Regulatory Initiatives' 40 University of New South Wales Law Journal 1275
Reynaud E, The International Labour Organization and the Living Wage: A Historical Perspective (ILO 2017)
Roberts TM, 'Innovations in Governance: A Functional Typology of Private Governance Institutions' 22 Duke Environmental Law & Policy Forum 67
Rodrik D, 'Second-Best Institutions' (2008 American Economic Review, American Economic Association, vol. 98
Ruggie J, 'International Regimes, Transactions and Change: Embedded Liberalism in the Postwar Economic Order' 36 International Organization
Ruggie J, Promotion and Protection of All Human Rights, Civil, Political, Economic, Social and Cultural Rights, Including the Right to Development: Protect, Respect and Remedy: a Framework for Business and Human Rights. Report of the Special Representative of the Secretary-General on the issue of human rights and transnational corporations and other business enterprises, John Ruggie. (2008)
Sabel C, O'Rourke D, and Fung A, Ratcheting Labor Standards: Regulation for Continuous Improvement in the Global Workplace (Columbia Law School of Public Law & Legal Theory Research 2000)

Samuelson M, 'The Australian Case for Protection Re-examined' 54 Quarterly Journal of Economics 143
Sassen S, 'The Informal Economy: Between New Developments and Old Regulations' 103 Symposium: The Informal Economy 2289
Scott A, 'Occupational Health and Safety in SMEs' 9 Small Enterprise Development 14
Scott C, Cafaggi F, and Senden L (eds), The Challenge of Transnational Private Regulation: Conceptual and Constitutional Debates (Wiley-Blackwell 2011)
Scott JC, 'Patron-Client Politics and Political Change in Southeast Asia' 66 The American Political Science Review 91
Secretary General UN, Situation of Human Rights in Cambodia, Report of the Secretary General, Fifty-third session, General Assembly, Agenda Item 110 (b), Human Rights Questions: Human rights questions, including alternative approaches to improving the effective enjoyment of human rights and fundamental freedoms (United Nations, A/53/400 1998)
SEED, Decent Employment through Small Enterprises: A Progress Report on SEED Activities (ILO 2003)
Selznick P, The Moral Commonwealth: Social Theory and the Promise of Community (University of California Press 1994)
Sen A, Inequality Reexamined (Harvard University Press 1992)
Sen A, Development as Freedom (Oxford University Press 1999)
Senate Economics Reference Committee, Outworkers in the Garment Industry (1996)
Shae M, 'Collective Bargaining Beyond the Boundaries of Employment: A Comparative Analysis' 37 Melbourne University Law Review 662
Shah P, 'An Overview of Cambodian Women Working in the Garment Industry' 28 Asia Pacific Research Journal 1
Shankaran K, 'Protecting the Worker in the Informal Economy: The Role of Labour Law' (Scope of Labour Law: Re-drawing the Boundaries of Protection 2005)
Sharma RN, 'Mega Transformation of Mumbai: Deepening Enclave Urbanism' 59 Sociological Bulletin 69
Shotwell JT, The Origins of the International Labor Organization (Columbia University Press 1934)
Singh MK, 'Industrial Relations in Maharashtra' 18 Indian Journal of Industrial Relations 549
Slater C, 'How the French Are Tackling Modern Slavery' Human Rights First (blog) (24 March 2017) https://www.humanrightsfirst.org/blog/how-french-are-tackling-modern-slavery accessed 7 January 2018
Snider L, 'Accommodating Power: The 'Common Sense' of Regulators' 18 Social Legal Studies 179
Sofia News Agency, 'More Bulgarians Working Abroad than in Bulgaria' (Sofia) http://www.novinite.com/articles/171684/More+Bulgarians+Working+Abroad+Than+in+Bulgaria accessed 15 January 2018
Sotharith C, 'Industrial Readjustment in Cambodia' in Ueki Y and Bhongmakkapat T (eds), Industrial Readjustment in the Mekong River Basin Countries: Toward the AEC, (BRC Research Report No 7, Bangkok Research Centre, IDE-JETRO, Bangkok, Thailand, 2012)
Spenner KI and Jones DC, 'Social Economic Transformation in Bulgaria: An Empirical Assessment of the Merchant Capitalism Thesis' 76 Social Forces 937
Spooner D, 'Organising Home-Based Workers in Bulgaria' (Global Labour Institute, 2013) http://www.globallabour.info/en/2013/08/space_and_patience_organising.html accessed 22 October 2014
Stake RE, 'Qualitative Case Studies' in Denzin NK and Lincoln YS (eds), The Sage Handbook of Qualitative Research (3rd edn, Sage 2005)
Standing G, The Precariat: The New Dangerous Class (Bloomsbury Academic 2011)

Standing G, 'The ILO: An Agency for Globalization?' 39 Development and Change 355

Steel Z and others, 'Long-Term Effect of Psychological Trauma on the Mental Health of Vietnamese Refugees Resettled in Australia: A Population-Based Study' 360 The Lancet 1056

Steinmo S, 'What is Historical Institutionalism' in Della Porta D and Keating M (eds), Approaches to the Social Sciences (Cambridge University Press 2008)

Stone KVW, 'Legal Protections for Atypical Employees: Employment Law for Workers without Workplaces and Employees without Employers' 27 Berkeley Journal of Employment & Labor Law 251

Stone KVW and Arthurs HW (eds), Rethinking Workplace Regulation: Beyond the Standard Contract of Employment (Russell Sage Foundation 2013)

Strathern M, Audit Cultures (Routledge 2000)

Streeck W and Thelen K, 'Introduction: Institutional Change in Advanced Political Economies' in Streeck W and Thelen K (eds), Beyond Continuity: Institutional Change in Advanced Political Economies (Oxford University Press 2005)

Supiot A, Meadows P and European Commission, Beyond Employment: Changes in Work and the Future of Labour Law in Europe (Oxford University Press 2001)

Tache I and Neesham C, 'The Performance of Welfare Systems in Post-Communist Europe: The Cases of Romania and Bulgaria' 2 International Journal of Economic Research 90

TAF Education Fund, False Claims Act Overview (2015)

Tait N, 'Bulgaria: Europe's Quick Response Solution?' (Bulgarian Association of Apparel and Textile Producers and Exporters, 2007) http://www.bgtextiles.org/?cid=78&NewsId=421 accessed 20 October

Tekle T (ed.), Labour Law and Worker Protection in Developing Countries (International Labour Office 2010)

Terngu A, 'Nigeria's Parliament Says Shell Should Pay $4 Billion for 2011 Oil Spill' Reuters (Abuja, 26 November 2014) http://www.reuters.com/article/2014/11/26/us-nigeria-oil-shell-idUSKCN0JA23Z20141126

Textile Clothing and Footwear Union of Australia, The Hidden Cost of Fashion: Report on the National Outwork Information Campaign (Textile Clothing and Footwear Union of Australia 1995)

Thelen K, 'Historical Institutionalism in Comparative Politics' 2 Annual Review of Political Science 369

Thelen K, 'Timing and Temporality in the Analysis of Institutional Evolution and Change' 14 Studies in American Political Development 102

Thelen K, 'How Institutions Evolve: Insights from Comparative-Historical Analysis' in Mahoney J and Rueschemeyer D (eds), Historical Analysis in the Social Sciences (Cambridge University 2003)

Thelen K, 'Institutions and Social Change' in Shapiro I and Skowronek S (eds), Crafting and Operating Institutions (New York University Press 2006)

Thelen K and Streeck W (eds), Beyond Continuity: Institutional Change in Advanced Political Economies (Oxford University Press 2005)

Tipples R, 'The Human Capability Framework—An Important and Useful Framework for Understanding the Labour Market' 29 New Zealand Journal of Employment Relations 3

Torres R, World of Work Report 2009: The Global Jobs Crisis and Beyond (ILO 2009)

Toscana N, 'Federal Funding Cuts Hits Ethical Clothing Australia's Fight Against Fashion Sweatshops' The Age (Melbourne, 11 June 2014) m.theage.com.au/federal-politics/political-news/federal-funding-cut-hits-ethical-clothing-australias-fight-against-sweatshops-20140611-zs4ay.html accessed 15 June 2014

Trebilcock A, 'Using Development Approaches to Address The Challenge of the Informal Economy for Labour Law' in Davidov G and Langille B (eds), Boundaries and Frontiers of Labour Law: Goals and Means in the Regulation of Work (Hart 2006)

Trubek DM and Trubek LG, 'New Governance & Legal Regulation: Complementarity, Rivalry and Transformation' 13 Columbia Journal of European Law 539
Tsogas G, Labor Regulation in a Global Economy (M.E. Sharpe 2001)
Tyner JA, The Killing of Cambodia: Geography, Genocide and the Unmaking Of Space (Ashgate 2008)
Tyson LDA, 'The Debt Crisis and Adjustment Responses in Eastern Europe: A Comparative Perspective' 40 International Organization 239
UN Conference on Trade and Development, Recent Developments in Investor-State Dispute Settlement (ISDS) (2014)
UN Human Rights Council, Elaboration of an international legally binding instrument on transnational corporations and other business enterprises with respect to human rights A/HRC/26/L.22 (2014)
UN Human Rights Council, Human rights and transnational corporations and other business enterprises A/HRC/26/L.1 (2014)
Un K, 'Cambodia in 2011: A Thin Veneer of Change' 52 Asian Survey 202
Un K, 'Cambodia in 2012: Towards Developmental Authoritarianism?' Southeast Asian Affairs 71
UN OHCHR, Human Rights and Transnational Corporations and other Business Enterprises (2005)
United Nations Development Programme, Humanity Divided: Confronting Inequality in Developing Countries (United Nations Development Programme, Bureau for Development Policy, New York 2013)
United Nations Research Institute for Social Development, Combating Poverty and Inequality: Structural Change, Social Policy and Politics: Overview (United Nations Research Institute for Social Development 2010)
Utting P, Rethinking Business Regulation: From Self-Regulation to Social Control (United Nations Research Institute for Social Development 2005)
Uzzi B, 'Social Structure and Competition in Interfirm Networks: The Paradox of Embeddedness' 42 Administrative Science Quarterly 35
Vandenberg P, Is Asia Adopting Flexicurity? A Survey of Employment Policies in Six Countries (Economic and Labour Market Papers, ILO 2008)
Vandenbergh MP and Cohen MA, 'Climate Change Governance: Boundaries and Leakage' 18 NYU Environmental Law Journal 221
Vannarith Chheang and Shintaro Hamanaka, Impediments to Growth of the Garment and Food Industries in Cambodia: Exploring Potential Benefits of the ASEAN-PRC FTA (Asian Development Bank Working Paper Series on Regional Economic Integration No 86, September 2011)
Vickery M, Kampuchea: Politics, Economics, and Society (F. Pinter, L. Rienner Publishers 1986)
Vosko LF, '"Decent Work": The Shifting Role of the ILO and the Struggle for Global Social Justice' 2 Global Social Policy 19
Vosko LF, Managing the Margins: Gender, Citizenship, and the International Regulation of Precarious Employment (2009)
Wade R, 'Financial Regime Change?' 53 New Left Review
Wade R, 'The Invisible Hand of the American Empire' in Rosenthal JH, Rosenthal JH, and Barry C (eds), Ethics & International Affairs: A Reader (3rd edn, Georgetown University Press 2009)
Wallace C and Latcheva R, 'Economic Transformation outside the Law: Corruption, Trust in Public Institutions and the Informal Economy in Transition Countries of Central and Eastern Europe' 58 Europe-Asia Studies 81
Walque Dd, 'The Socio-Demographic Legacy of the Khmer Rouge Period in Cambodia' 60 Population Studies 223
Washbrook DA, 'Law, State and Agrarian Society in Colonial India' 15 Modern Asian Studies 649

Weber M, Economy and Society; An Outline of Interpretive Sociology (Bedminster Press 1968)
Weber M, General Economic History (Transaction Books 1981)
Weber M and Whimster S, The Essential Weber: A Reader (Routledge 2004)
Weil D and Mallo C, 'Regulating Labour Standards via Supply Chains: Combining Public/ Private Interventions to Improve Workplace Compliance' 45 British Journal of Industrial Relations 791
Weller S, Retailing, Clothing and Textiles Production in Australia (Working Paper No 29, Centre for Strategic Economic Studies, Victoria University, October 2007)
Wells D, '"Best Practice" in the Regulation of International Labor Standards: Lessons of the U.S.–Cambodia Textile Agreement' 27 Comparative Labor Law & Policy Journal 357
White S, Creating an Enabling Environment for Micro and Small Enterprise Development in Thailand (ILO Working Papers 1999)
Williams C and Windebank J, Informal Employment in the Advanced Economies: Implications for Work and Welfare (Routledge 1998)
Willis JW, Foundations of Qualitative Research: Interpretive and Critical Approaches (Sage 2007)
Women Working Worldwide, Jennifer Hurley (ed.), Garment Industry: Subcontracting and Workers Rights (Manchester Metropolitan University, Manchester 2003)
Woods N and Graham D, 'Making Corporate Self-Regulation Effective in Developing Countries' 34 World Development
Woolcock M and Narayan D, 'Social Capital: Implications for Development Theory, Research, and Policy' 15 The World Bank Research Observer 225
World Bank, Growth, Poverty and Inequality: Eastern Europe and the Former Soviet Union (Washington, DC: World Bank, 2005)
WTO, Australia—Certain Measures Concerning Trademarks and Other Plain Packaging Requirements Applicable to Tobacco Products and Packaging: Dispute DS434 (2014)
Zabludovsky G, 'The Reception and Utility of Max Weber's Concept of Patrimonialism in Latin America' 4 International Sociology 51
Zajak S, 'Complementarity as Institutional Co-Evolution and Co-Production: The Case of Working Conditions in Chinese Supply Chains' (ECPR Regulatory Governance Conference 2014)
Zlateva V, 'Employment Conditions of Homeworkers' (European Working Conditions Observatory 2010) http://www.eurofound.europa.eu/ewco/2011/01/BG1101021I.htm accessed 15 October
Zlateva V, 'National Agreements for Home-Based Workers and Telework' (Eironline, European Industrial Relations Observatory On-Line 2011) https://www.eurofound.europa.eu/sr/publications/article/2011/national-agreements-for-home-based-workers-and-telework, accessed 22 October

Index